Ethics & International Affairs

Joel H. Rosenthal
Christian Barry
Editors

Ethics & International Affairs
A Reader

Third Edition

Published in Cooperation with Carnegie Council
for Ethics in International Affairs

Georgetown University Press ⟿ Washington, D.C.

Georgetown University Press, Washington, D.C.
www.press.georgetown.edu

Library of Congress Cataloging-in-Publication Data

Ethics & international affairs : a reader / Joel H.
Rosenthal and Christian Barry, editors.—3rd ed.
        p. cm.
    "(c) Carnegie Council for Ethics in International
Affairs."
    Includes bibliographical references and index.
    ISBN 978-1-58901-272-1 (paperback : alk. paper)
    1. International relations—Moral and ethical
aspects.   I. Rosenthal, Joel H., 1960–   II. Barry,
Christian.   III. Carnegie Council for Ethics in
International Affairs.   IV. Title: Ethics and
international affairs.
JZ1306.E87   2009
172'.4—dc22
                                            2008042359

♾ This book is printed on acid-free paper meeting the
requirements of the American National Standard for
Permanence in Paper for Printed Library Materials.

15 14 13 12 11   9 8 7 6 5 4 3
First printing

Printed in the United States of America

Contents

Preface

Ethics & International Affairs—the quarterly journal of the Carnegie Council—is now in its third decade. The inaugural issue appeared in 1987, when the idea of a world without the Soviet Union was not yet seriously considered, and ethics and public policy at the international level were debated within the confines of controlling ideas, such as "containment" and "moral equivalence." More than twenty years later we still find value in realist frameworks, yet we also welcome the growth of a new, less encumbered literature addressing issues of global scope and concern.

Contributors to *Ethics & International Affairs* draw on applied ethics and international normative theory to address moral problems in world politics. Whether the problem be well known or overlooked, long-standing or immediate, local or truly international, our authors apply moral reasoning—informed by facts and shaped by the structures of philosophical and social scientific inquiry—to deepen understanding and push toward some resolution. In this way, our approach is *normative*; that is, it prescribes and explains expected and required behavior in accordance with ethical systems and intuitions. Yet it is also *empirical* in that it places policy choices within historical and political contexts. Over the years we have witnessed an increase in the number and range of authors writing about world politics who combine normative and empirical work.[1] However, to the extent that this increase has been a consequence of new global dilemmas and worrisome trends, we may view it less as an occasion to indulge in celebration, and rather as cause for a redoubling of rigor and creativity in the field of international ethics.

But what is this "field" of international ethics? Who, in particular, are we referring to? With its methods and problems intersecting with a range of other fields and disciplines, as well as implicating several levels of analysis—from individuals to global society—international ethics is not a field that can be clearly delimited, or even identified with a single university department (as if it were confined to universities at all). At its theoretical core, international ethics can be said to overlap with that aspect of the international relations field that engages realism and its critics, as well as with discussions of cosmopolitanism and *its* critics arising among moral and political philosophers.

Of course, this is a mold that will be quickly broken, even by the chapters in this volume, which have been penned also by economists and historians.[2] However, even focusing only on the international ethical debates within and between the fields of international relations and philosophy, it is safe to say that, with their growing technical maturity, the range of included perspectives, their responsiveness to real-world developments, and the willingness on the part of political scientists and philosophers to borrow from, talk to, and collaborate with one another, the field has made definite strides forward in recent years.[3]

International ethicists have also displayed a steady tendency toward specialization, endeavoring to add value and gain traction on an issue-by-issue basis. Today, the field takes in debates about atmospheric justice, sovereign debt, human rights trials, and, among others, the topics broached in these pages: war and postwar reconciliation, intervention and its prospects, the boundless question of how communities can best determine just principles of authority and inclusion, and the ethics and politics of global inequality. Whereas the previous editions of this book were structured in an open-ended manner, with sections on "theory," "culture," and "issues," the contents of this volume are instead ordered by topic, recognizing and reflecting the increased maturity and self-consciousness of the field. Needless to say, the contributions to theory and awareness of culture are no less salient in the present edition than in the past, but the context for them is now given as "topics in international ethics" rather than, say, questions of whether there is even a role for ethics in international affairs.

In making the selections of which conversations and contributions to include in this new edition, the aim has certainly not been to generate the greatest "hits" of international ethics, nor the greatest "misses" of global public policy, as if there had not been innumerable worthwhile contributions elsewhere in the literature, or as if the chosen topics are those we regard as most pressing or most deserving of wide discussion. Even though in the case of every contribution included here the discussion is ongoing rather than closed, the conversations should be taken as invitations to normative, empirical discussions and studies of whichever international issues are uppermost in readers' minds. The aim in making the current selections was to serve the contemporary international ethics classroom as efficiently as possible, as well as to invite and inform other new readers in the field. We have thus compiled resources that we suspect will be of special value in engaging and instructing a new generation of international ethicists and informed members of world society.

We hope we have balanced these desires—to supply a volume fit for the ethics classroom, and to reflect the growing maturity of the field—without misrepresenting or overdetermining the shape of the discussions from which the selections presented here are drawn. Helpful here may be the fact that each of the four sections offers a slightly different experience of the debate it confronts. The section on war gives a sense of how its interlocutors have stepped in to confront the normative dimensions of new security challenges, such as the demands of justice in "transitions," particularly in the aftermath of war, and the shake-up of the normative order suggested by the concept of "prevention"—with the discussion underwritten in no small part by the seminal contributions of Michael Walzer, critiqued from a realist perspective in the first of our chapters. The intervention section takes a slightly different tack, exploring the theory, history, politics, and prospects of normative evolution with regard to sovereignty and its exceptions. The section on governance, meanwhile, provides the material for a sophisticated consideration of how discussions of justice and legitimacy differ, and how they are interrelated, as we begin to think across borders—in this case, of nation and gender—and up and down levels of international life. Finally, the section on global economic justice rolls out a number of discrete approaches to framing and analyzing the predicaments of economic inequality and underdevelopment. The volume as a whole thus provides a sampling of the many ways in which one can encounter the literature on moral problems in international affairs, and, as mentioned, it invites readers to fill the gaps, whether through further reading or through developing their own contributions.

There are a number of other more general remarks to make about the essays in this reader: these relate less to issues of structure and how the essays reflect the field than to how a reading of these texts can deepen our understanding of important themes in international ethics and provide material out of which to construct some guidance for the literature moving forward. We have, after all, some obligation to redirect as well as to reflect. The first point to make is that, even while their work increases in specialization and sophistication, international ethicists will find it valuable to remain alive to the basic questions and limits of ethical reasoning: How should one live? By what values and standards? And how can the trade-offs inherent in political choice be managed? As representative of the best work in our field, the essays in this volume take it as a given that politics is an arena of imperfection: to engage in ethical reflection is simply to ask, Can we do better? At the very least, with clear thinking, good ideas, and the mustering of international political will, the worst policies can be avoided.

Second, one should note that the debate in this reader takes place in an interconnected world, with globalization unleashing and empowering new actors and possibilities. In the past, international relations scholars focused rather narrowly on the behavior of states. Today we see world-changing concentrations of power in multinational corporations, nongovernmental organizations (NGOs), and international institutions. Indeed, the world's largest corporations, such as Wal-Mart and Microsoft, are themselves some of the world's largest economies. NGOs, such as Human Rights Watch and Médecins Sans Frontières, demand the attention of superpowers, middle powers, and failing states alike. And international organizations, such as the United Nations and the World Bank, assert themselves in decisive ways on a variety of functional issues, ranging from environmental regulation to humanitarian relief and poverty alleviation. The project of updating our normative and empirical tool kit and vocabulary to respond to this changing global picture remains far from complete. International ethicists must, and surely will, continue the process of engaging the ethics of global business, global civil society, and global governance alongside, but not independent of, considerations of just war and other such topics that predate and still pervade the global village. Part of the mission of international ethics moving forward will be to better grasp how the "international" and the "global" are related.

Third, we should endorse the notion that monism—a single-minded, all-or-nothing approach to ethics and international affairs—is simply inadequate. Human judgment is known to be faulty and limited. New information often changes our views: while "truth" may be our ultimate goal and guide, our understanding of it may change over time. The first of Hans Morgenthau's "Nine Rules of Diplomacy" has especially lasting value in light of the current political climate in the United States. It reads simply: "Diplomacy must be divested of the crusading spirit."[4] Humility is required even in the face of conviction; international ethicists, for instance, must not be driven by the combative spirit often inherent in scholarly debates to let their professional convictions override what we should all agree on: that perhaps we are wrong.

Another unifying theme in these essays is an abandonment of ideology in favor of an enlightened realism that emphasizes pluralism. According to "enlightened realists," conflict is neither fated nor random. Interests are neither fixed nor self-defined. Decisions can be made according to reason, always requiring the weighing of claims in light of evidence. Some of our authors might prefer the label "realistic utopians."[5] They would see their work as describing the gap between what we ought to be doing and what we are doing. If we can sketch out what is morally desirable, we then have an end or a goal by which we can set the direction of our policies and gauge our results. To the extent that a meeting of enlightened realists and realistic utopians offers a fair portrayal of contemporary international ethics, it is an encouraging portrayal—certainly more so than the earlier image of realists confronting idealists.

Finally, a discernible "weak universalism" threads through the work in this volume. By "universalism" we mean a shared commitment to universal human dignity and social justice. The modifier "weak" acknowledges the pluralistic notion that shared principles of humanity will take different forms in different circumstances. The essays that follow seek neither perfection nor homogenization; rather, they pursue mutual understandings based on what is common in human experience. Paradoxically, the most common aspect of human experience is difference itself. How we live with difference—especially in light of common problems—will continue to be one among the many pressing questions faced by international ethicists.

It is in the spirit of mutual learning that we offer these essays for your consideration. The inquiry is open and unfinished, as it should be. We urge you to carry that inquiry on.

NOTES

1.   For a discussion of the relationship between empirical and normative research on world politics, see Christian Reus-Smit and Duncan Snidal, "Reuniting Ethics and Social Science," *Ethics & International Affairs* 22, no. 3 (2008): 261–71.

2.   Over the years *Ethics & International Affairs* has also welcomed contributions from psychologists, sociologists, lawyers, theologians, regional specialists, activists, policymakers, and policy professionals, among others.

3.   See, for instance, the essay by the ethicist Allen Buchanan and the political scientist Robert O. Keohane in this volume, as well as their "The Preventive Use of Force: A Cosmopolitan Institutional Proposal," *Ethics & International Affairs* 18, no. 1 (2004): 1–22. For an example of a philosopher and an economist collaborating on a pressing topic of global scope and concern, see Christian Barry and Sanjay G. Reddy, *International Trade and Labor Standards: A Proposal for Linkage* (New York: Columbia University Press, 2008).

4.   Hans J. Morgenthau, *Politics Among Nations: The Struggle for Power and Peace*, seventh edition (New York: McGraw Hill, 2006), 559.

5.   The term *realistic utopia* appears in John Rawls's *Law of Peoples* (Cambridge, MA: Harvard University Press, 1999). Rawls's vision of international ethical principles takes human nature as we find it.

Acknowledgments

Ethics & International Affairs is a collaborative enterprise. The journal has always been the work of many hands, all of them distinguished and committed to the highest principles of scholarship and professionalism.

We would like to thank the editorial teams, past and present, who brought to life the work in this volume. Included in these teams is our Editorial Advisory Board. Its members have been a consistent source of ideas and inspiration, and we thank all who have served since 1987.

Special thanks are due to recent members of our editorial staff: Deborah Washburn, Paige Arthur, Lydia Tomitova, Catherine Lu, and Matt Peterson; as well as to our current team: John Tessitore, Zornitsa Stoyanova-Yerburgh, Adam Freeman, and copy editor Bill Harris. The talent represented in this group is extraordinary.

For help in preparing the book manuscript, warm thanks to Dennis Doyle, Sulakshana Komerath, Naomi Kennedy, Eva Hausteiner, and Christopher DeVito. And for all their energy and creativity in ensuring wide circulation and promotion of the journal, thanks also to Deborah Carroll, Madeleine Lynn, Melissa Semeniuk, and Terri Teleen.

We have been most fortunate to interact with colleagues at Georgetown University Press, who have been wonderfully encouraging and a pleasure to work with. We thank especially press director Richard Brown and acquisitions editor Don Jacobs, in addition to the entire staff. Their enthusiasm and support are deeply appreciated.

Finally, *Ethics & International Affairs* is made possible by the support of the Carnegie Council for Ethics in International Affairs. Eva Becker, vice president for finance and administration, has been the journal's business manager since its inception. She is a true champion for its work.

Leadership begins at the top, and *Ethics & International Affairs* has earned the stalwart support of the Council's Board of Trustees, represented by its current executive committee—Alexander H. Platt, Charles W. Kegley Jr., and Jonathan E. Colby—and program committee—Michael Joseph Smith, Barbara Crossette, William Felice, John Langan, SJ, and Elisabeth Sifton. We are grateful to these leaders for giving their time, talent, energy, and resources to the Council's mission of being the "voice for ethics" in international affairs. Thanks to them, these voices are being heard by you and by our readers all around the world.

PART ONE

~

Conflict and Reconciliation

Is war always wrong? Or can the use of large-scale, organized violence some-times be justified? Does it even make sense to apply moral principles to war? What have theorists and philosophers had to say about the problem, and how has the discussion developed in the course of history and in response to events? What is a so-called just war? What does it mean to have a just cause? How likely and imminent does an attack have to be to justify preemptive war? Does a responsible government act to deter its enemies, or strike first to neutralize potential threats? What justifies prevention? Is war a realm of necessity, or of ethics? What is a just peace?

In Defense of Realism

A Commentary on *Just and Unjust Wars*

David C. Hendrickson

JUST AND UNJUST WARS made its appearance in the wake of an unpopular and unsuccessful war. It condemned that war, both the reasons for entering it and the methods of waging it. *Just and Unjust Wars* also appeared at a time when the principal military disposition governing America's relations with its then-great adversary seemed destined to persist indefinitely. While lamenting the "necessity" imposed by deterrence, Michael Walzer reluctantly approved of that arrangement despite the fact that it rested on the threat to destroy millions of noncombatants. "We threaten to do evil in order not to do it and the doing of it would be so terrible that the threat seems in comparison to be morally defensible."[1] The moral condemnation of the unthinkable—nuclear war—was thus balanced by the acceptance of the arrangement that constituted at the time the limiting condition of all our lives.

Walzer's work is directed against "realism," against the view that presumably denies the "moral reality" of war and its conduct. Realism, Walzer argues, considers war to be "a world apart . . . where self-interest and necessity prevail."[2] In this world, right and wrong, justice and injustice, have no place. If war belongs to the realm of necessity, it makes no more sense to pass moral judgment on it than it would to pass moral judgment on catastrophes occurring in nature. These catastrophes—a flood or an earthquake—may have awful consequences, but they cannot pose moral dilemmas. They are neither just nor unjust. Realism is considered to say the same of war.

Just and Unjust Wars proceeds from the assumption, and conviction, that neither the resort to war nor the conduct of war may escape moral judgment. "I am going to assume throughout," Walzer declares at the outset of his study, "that we really do act within a moral world; that particular decisions really are difficult, problematic, agonizing, and that this has to do with the structure of that world; that language reflects the moral world and gives us access to it; and finally that our understanding of the moral vocabulary is sufficiently common and stable so that shared judgments are possible."[3] The just war Walzer intends to "recapture" for political and moral theory is to displace a view of war identified, in the main, with realism.

The assumption that political realism can be reduced not simply to "moral skepticism" but to a kind of moral atheism is often adopted by contemporary writers on the ethics of statecraft. Curiously, self-proclaimed realists rarely say this; it is the critics of "realism" who insist that the central core of the doctrine—deserving the most elaborate refutation—is that morality must be banished from the realm of international affairs. Walzer is not alone in taking this version of realism as his point of departure, but there is a certain irony in his decision to do so. For there are important respects in which *Just and Unjust Wars* begins by rejecting realism and ends by accepting it—rejecting, that is, the more extreme (or vulgar) claims that are often identified with realism while accepting some classic realist precepts.

Such a thesis can only be advanced with reticence, for the central claims of political realism are frequently subjected to wildly divergent interpretations. Realism may be best characterized, we think, as indicative of a general disposition toward politics. It emphasizes the egocentricity of human beings, particularly when they act in groups. It sees conflict as a never-ending feature of the human condition, which can be mitigated in particular settings but never overcome. It sees moral exhortation as something that is easily swept aside or distorted when it is in the interest of political communities to do so. It insists that politics neither follows nor reflects a simple rational scheme; that statecraft must always proceed from a given situation which may gradually be altered but which cannot suddenly be transformed either by an act of will or by an appeal to reason; that attempts to transform society—particularly international society—underrate the forces resistant to change and consequently the repressive measures necessary to overcome resistance; and that whatever the professions of those who wield power, the political actor seldom if ever acts for reasons as disinterested as are invariably alleged. These are all empirical observations, and though they certainly bear on the ethical questions raised by the conduct of statecraft they do not constitute an ethical doctrine. Their chief implication is a counsel against the adoption of ethical systems that demand too much abnegation or sacrifice—systems that, as Montesquieu said, "convince everybody, but change nobody."

The realist, then, is skeptical both of men and of the possibilities of political action.[4] His emphasis is on the limitations attending the conduct of statecraft. As such, he is resistant to schemes of universal order and security. Instead, his outlook tends toward particularism; he takes his bearings from existing diplomatic constellations. He tends to value order over justice, or at least to see order as a fundamental condition of justice. His is an inherently conservative view of politics in which prudence is given a central place.

Although these are the general characteristics of realism, it does not follow that those who share them—realists—will entertain the same views about policy. There is no straight line leading from these characteristic features of realism to "good policy." This is so even if we define good policy, as realists do, as policy calculated to preserve the independence and well-being of the political community. To be sure, realism prescribes prudence; it insists that the political actor concern himself with the probable consequences of action. But prudence cannot in itself provide the purposes for which political action is undertaken; it cannot provide even the basis of a political ethic. Prudence places no restraints on political action other than caution and circumspection; it sets no limits to self-interest other than those limits imposed by the situation in which policy must be conducted; it is compatible with any and all purposes holding out the prospect of success. Before the statesman can be prudent, there must be something for him to be prudent about. Realism holds that he must be prudent about the security and independence of the state.

The essential claim of realism may be better understood if we look at two well-known formulations of the rights and duties of states, and ask whether realism, properly understood, is incompatible with either. In his *Spirit of the Laws*, Montesquieu held that "le droit des gens"—variously translated as the right or law of nations—"is by nature founded on the principle that the various nations should do to one another in times of peace the most good possible, and in times of war the least ill possible, without harming their true interests." Alexander Hamilton's formulation, at first glance, was similar. He did not advocate "a policy absolutely selfish or interested in nations," but insisted rather that "a policy regulated by their own interest, as far as justice and good faith permit, is, and ought to be, their prevailing policy." Both these formulations recognize the priority of what Vattel called "the duties to oneself" over "the duties to others," but qualify or limit the pursuit of such duties (or "national interests") in different ways. Montesquieu is not normally considered a realist, but the utilitarian character of his formulation, together with the primacy it allows for the pursuit of national self-interest, closely resembles the way in which most realists reason about ethics and statecraft.[5]

Hamilton's formulation, ironically, is more restrictive than Montesquieu's; the counsel of this great American realist is, if taken literally, inconsistent with "realism." States, he says, are to pursue their interests within the limits imposed by justice and good faith. Realists, by contrast, have normally said that states may break faith and employ unjust means when their survival and independence are threatened. Publicists of the law of nations denied this exemption. Though the right of self-preservation, according to Vattel, carried with it "the right to whatever is necessary for that purpose . . . , these means must not be unjust in themselves, or such as the natural law absolutely prohibits." Those who took the other side of this argument based the exemption on the old

Roman doctrine of public safety—*salus populi suprema lex est*. Though the doctrine of necessity or of "public safety" is rightly identified with realism, it is sometimes affirmed by personages not normally thought of as realists. Jefferson, for instance, held that "[a] strict observance of the written laws is doubtless one of the high duties of a good citizen, but it is not the highest. The laws of necessity, of self-preservation, of saving our country when in danger, are of higher obligation." Such is what all realists have believed; such is their distinctive claim.[6]

If realism does not and cannot provide the answer to what constitutes "good policy," it does hold out an answer to one, and perhaps the most profound, moral dilemma of statecraft: that of the means states may employ when their security and independence are threatened. While realism recognizes the "moral reality" of war, and thus the imperative that war's conduct ought to be subject to moral and legal constraints, it also recognizes that where the state's independence and continuity are in jeopardy, the statesman may—indeed, should—take whatever measures are required to preserve such independence and continuity. The ancient doctrine of "necessity" in statecraft is at once very old and very contemporary. We have only recently escaped its oppressive grip, having lived almost constantly with it from World War II until the end of the age of deterrence, circa 1990. In this period, necessity not only formed the limiting conditions of our lives but, in nuclear deterrence, seemed to express a near permanent state of things.

The argument of necessity in statecraft is not to be taken literally. Clearly, at the root of this view is not simply an explanation but a choice. The necessity that is presumably imposed on the statesman is in the end a "moral necessity" enjoining him to do that which is necessary to preserve the state's independence and survival. What appears as a necessity does so because a moral choice has already been made. The appeal to necessity is compatible with restraint on state action as long as those restraints do not appear to jeopardize the independence and survival of the political collective. The concept of necessity only constitutes a permission to override moral and legal restraints in "extreme" situations ("when the safety of the state is in question"); by evident implication, this very limitation constitutes a recognition that such restraints are obligatory in "normal" circumstances. But whether restraints can be observed will depend upon the immediate circumstances in which the statesman must act and not upon abstract considerations (or upon a retrospective wisdom and detachment the actor cannot have).

There is no difficulty in cataloguing the many abuses to which the appeal to necessity, the heart of the doctrine of reason of state, has led in practice. These abuses, moreover, are not accidental; they are built into the very character of the doctrine and may be traced to the uncertainty that attends the concept of the collective "self" as well as the nature of the society in which states must define the self and its necessities. For that society renders tenuous the distinction between security and survival. In collapsing this distinction, as states are prone to do, the door is opened to all kinds of abuses. Still, it does not follow that it is meaningless to speak of the self-preservation or survival of states. The condition of necessity may, and does, arise. Reason of state declares that when it does, all other considerations should be subordinated to the safety of the state.

Walzer does not reject the argument of necessity. What he terms "supreme emergency" serves, in principle, the same purpose as does the doctrine that has always been closely identified with realism. It is the case that Walzer accepts necessity only with great reluctance and unease. "I want to set radical limits to the notion of necessity," he insists on more than one occasion. More than this, he makes an impressive and commendable effort to do so. Even so, in the end he comes back to the conclusion others, mainly realists, have come back to. The demands of necessity are not denied. "Can soldiers and statesmen override the rights of innocent people for the sake of their own political community?" he asks, and replies: "I am inclined to answer this question affirmatively, though not without hesitation and worry."[7]

Nor does Walzer differ substantially from realism in the defense he gives on behalf of supreme emergency or necessity. "The survival and freedom of political communities—whose members share a way of life, developed by their ancestors, to be passed on to their children—are the highest values of international society."[8] This is said in reference to the threat posed by Nazism, but Walzer acknowledges that lesser challenges, if they threaten the survival and freedom of a political community, have similar moral consequences. At the same time, he says that he is not sure that he can "account" for the "different and larger prerogatives" of political communities since he does not believe "in ascribing to communal life a kind of transcendence."[9] But whether the political community is invested with intrinsic worth and transcendent value or is seen instead as being not the source but the indispensable condition of value (as liberal democracies have done), the practical result is the same. As the indispensable condition of value, certainly of those values identified with individual freedom, the state is endowed with "a kind of transcendence," to use Walzer's expression, that serves to justify the extreme measures which may be taken to preserve it.

Walzer, then, has a close affinity to realism with respect to both the value he places on the political community and his willingness to justify the sacrifice of innocents in the name of "supreme emergency." Short of these extreme situations, however, he insists that the duty to avoid harm to the innocent in war is of overriding importance and cannot be abridged by utilitarian calculation. The realist need not differ in this, but he may do so, and, considering his regard for the consequences of action, will likely do so. For most realists, measures in violation of the war convention may be justified if they shorten the war and substantially decrease the total amount of human suffering. To state the argument in this form is not to show that utilitarian calculation is justified in every particular instance, or even in most instances; the consequentialist may certainly require a strong burden of proof—as we would do—to override the otherwise obligatory rule. Still, the argument over the legitimacy of utilitarian calculation in war displays the contrast between realism and a deontological ethic in an acute form, as do the recent debates provoked by the fiftieth anniversary of the destruction of Hiroshima and Nagasaki. All those who, in the recent debates, justified the bombing did so not on the basis that anything is permitted in war—nobody but a barbarian can deny that the destruction of a city is, on its face, a moral enormity—but by claiming that the use of atomic weaponry saved hundreds of thousands of American and Japanese lives. Even if one accepts Walzer's judgment that such utilitarian calculations are "fantastic, godlike, frightening, and horrendous"[10]—for they surely are—it is difficult to avoid the conclusion that the refusal to have considered the consequences of not dropping the bomb would have been, in the circumstances, equally "fantastic, godlike, frightening, and horrendous." It is difficult, moreover, to resist the conclusion that dropping the first bomb at least did save many more lives than would have been lost had this decision been refused. It did put an end, as Churchill said, to "the vast, indefinite butchery." Walzer argues that the alternatives ought not to have been what they were, because unconditional surrender was a war aim that ought not to have been entertained. Even if this argument is in principle granted, in the summer of 1945 the larger parameters of the policy of unconditional surrender would have been exceedingly difficult to change (though assuredly the U.S. government was in the wrong in not making explicit before Hiroshima its subsequent acceptance of the emperor's role in the reconstruction of Japanese life, just as it was grossly in the wrong in not allowing sufficient time for Japanese reconsideration after the first bomb was dropped). If the realist, by virtue of his consequentialist calculations, may fairly be charged with a greater willingness to justify Hiroshima-like acts, the moralist remaining faithful to absolute injunction (save when the heavens are *really* about to fall) is stuck on the horns of a dilemma equally profound. Neither alternative, in truth, is satisfactory or can be accepted without the gravest misgivings.

THE LEGALIST PARADIGM

In part two of *Just and Unjust Wars*, Walzer presents a theory of aggression that seeks to articulate the common moral perceptions governing the resort to force. At the core of this theory is a "legalist paradigm" that he calls "our baseline, our model, the fundamental structure for the moral comprehension of war." The paradigm posits "an international society of independent states" whose dominant values are "the survival and independence of the separate political communities." To intervene in the internal affairs of these states violates their rights; such intervention is proscribed by the legalist paradigm. But the core of the legalist paradigm is the proscription of the extreme form of intervention: aggression. "Any use of force or imminent threat of force by one state against the political sovereignty or territorial integrity of another constitutes aggression and is a criminal act." When aggression occurs, states are justified in making "two kinds of violent response: a war of self-defense by the victim and a war of law enforcement by the victim and any other member of international society."[11] The law enforcers may not only repulse, they may also punish, and indeed the need for punishment is greater than it is in domestic society because aggression constitutes a more serious matter for international society than crime does for domestic society. International society, he writes, "is unlike domestic society in that every conflict threatens the structure as a whole with collapse. Aggression challenges it directly and is much more dangerous than domestic crime, because there are no policemen. But that only means that the 'citizens' of international society must rely on themselves and on one another." Unless the rights of the member states are vindicated, "international society collapses ['at least sometimes'] into a state of war or is transformed into a universal tyranny."[12]

Though the legalist paradigm is fundamentally important in the moral comprehension of war, when standing alone it is nevertheless deemed inadequate by Walzer. There is a set of hard cases which makes the paradigm seem excessively dangerous, rigid, inhumane, or unjust. Walzer therefore undertakes a set of revisions to the paradigm, in which he allows for the first use of force in certain circumstances. When states face "a manifest intent to injure, a degree of active preparation that makes that intent a positive danger, and a general situation in which waiting, or doing anything other than fighting, greatly magnifies the risk," they have a right to use force first.[13] They may override the norm against intervention in the internal affairs of other states in order to assist national liberation movements (but not to put an end to domestic tyranny); to balance the interventions of other powers (a counterintervention whose aims must be limited to leveling the playing field among domestic disputants for power); and to put an end to acts—genocide, massacre, enslavement—that shock the moral conscience of mankind. Finally, he elaborates the war aims that states may legitimately embrace once at war, allowing for punishment and "reasonable prevention" but stopping well short of "unconditional surrender."

All of the issues raised in Walzer's examination of the legalist paradigm have been raised anew in the twenty years since the publication of the book, particularly with the end of the Cold War. The Iraqi invasion of Kuwait presented a classic case of aggression; the U.S.-led response drew attention to the prospect of organizing the international community on the basis of a shared commitment to collective security, and raised as well the problem of legitimate aims in a war whose justification was defensive but whose motives were in an important sense preventive. The internal catastrophes that have befallen various states—

mostly in Africa, but elsewhere as well—have raised anew the question of humanitarian intervention, though in a way that has reversed the traditional ideological faultlines: the Right is skeptical of assuming responsibility, the Left now wishes to take up the white man's burden. Walzer's rethinking of this issue is itself symbolic of this broader transformation. Whereas previously he had sought to justify a right of humanitarian intervention, he now speaks of an imperative duty—"Whenever the filthy work can be stopped, it should be stopped." And whereas previously he had conceived of humanitarian intervention as a kind of one-night stand, he now contemplates a far more permanent relationship, whether in the form of "trusteeship" or "protectorate." In the mid-1970s, humanitarian intervention by the Western powers was difficult to separate from neocolonialism, and Walzer seemed uncomfortable with any enterprise suggestive of a revival of it. Now he acknowledges that, while humanitarian interventions undertaken by local powers remain desirable, they will "most often . . . depend on global powers like the United States and (we can hope) the European Community." "Old and well-earned suspicions of American power must give way now to a wary recognition of its necessity."[14]

The end of the Cold War made these humanitarian interventions much more feasible for a time; the international restraints on them diminished and are still remarkably low in comparison with the Cold War years. Domestic restraints have, in the meantime, grown substantially as Western publics have shown themselves distinctly unhappy about interventions that threaten to be protracted or costly (in lives or money). For a time, it seemed as if the end of the Cold War would also relieve the nuclear anxieties that grew up in the 1980s— and it did do that so far as conflicts among the great powers were concerned— but anxiety over the nuclear problem has not, more broadly, been eased. It is now focused on the proliferation of weapons of mass destruction by "rogue states." That prospect, in turn, has raised the issue of the legitimacy of preventive war, which Walzer considered extensively in *Just and Unjust Wars*, though not in relation to the nuclear problem.

It is a characteristic feature of many of the post–Cold War crises that they have raised simultaneously many issues that Walzer considered separately; Bosnia is the paradigmatic instance. Has this been a civil war, or a war of aggression? In considering our response, are we to look at it as posing the problem of counterintervention, secession, or humanitarian intervention? Or are all these questions hopelessly mixed up together, as were once the peoples of Bosnia? These complications make difficult a proper reading of *Just and Unjust Wars*, for the justification and scope of outside intervention, if permissible at all, is crucially dependent on how the issue is framed. Yet despite all the changes that the end of the Cold War has brought in the understanding of these issues, *Just and Unjust Wars* remains a remarkably fresh treatment of them—a not inconsiderable achievement after a lapse of twenty years, which happened to coincide with a revolution in world politics.

There are certain respects in which the legalist paradigm does correspond closely to realist assumptions. For realists, as Robert Gilpin has put it, "the building blocks and ultimate units of social and political life are not the individuals of liberal thought nor the classes of Marxism [but] . . . tribes, city-states, kingdoms, empires, and nation-states."[15] While Walzer insists that the rights of states rest ultimately on the rights of individuals, it is the right to enjoy a community of their own that is seen as fundamental. His bow to liberal premises does not alter the conclusion that there are sharp moral restrictions on the right of outsiders to interfere with or otherwise shape the domestic struggles to define the character of these communities. As liberal critics have frequently complained, Walzer's approach is remarkably state-centric. It is true that, for Walzer, the fundamental value is the nation or community rather than the state, and this distinction has important implications for his treatment of "national liberation" and secession. Even so, the moral significance accorded the nation or community must normally result in practice in giving virtually equal significance to the autonomy of the institution—the state—indispensable to the protection of the nation or community. Then, too, Walzer's insistence on the right of the collective to live its own life in its own way, even if this entails autocracy or other sorts of domestic practices incompatible with liberal democracy, makes for a strong presumption against outside interference. In this respect, at least, Walzer seems closer to a realist perspective than to cosmopolitanism or to Marxism or to "reform intervention."

AGGRESSION AND NEUTRALITY

If in his defense of the nonintervention norm, Walzer arrives at a destination close to that of realism, his theory of aggression is distinct from realism in several respects. This is above all true with regard to his commitment to "moralizing" all of the issues raised by aggression—a proclivity that, to the realist, is suggestive of certain dangers (to which we shall return). It is not easy, however, to get a clear fix on precisely what is enjoined on us by a commitment to Walzer's moral framework. Though most of the assumptions underlying Walzer's theory of aggression also form part of the theory of collective security, Walzer stops short of embracing that theory. He appears to have little faith in the idea that the determination of aggression ought to be made by any centralized organs of international society (a suspicion of multilateralism that extends as well to other issues regarding the use of force, such as humanitarian intervention or preventive war). Nor does he normally speak in *Just and Unjust Wars* in terms of a duty to come to the aid of states threatened by aggression, only a right to do so. A right to come to the aid of threatened states, however, would also appear to encompass a right not to do so, and indeed later in the book Walzer defends the right of states to remain neutral. Whereas "it is the tendency of the theory [of aggression] to undermine the right of neutrality and to require

widespread participation in the business of law enforcement"[16]—an attribution
that emphasizes the similarity of the legalist paradigm to collective security—it
is the obligation of leaders of a neutral state confronted by aggression elsewhere
to consult primarily the rights of their own citizens. "[T]he leaders of such a
state are not required to calculate as if every human life carried the same moral
weight for every decisionmaker at every moment in time. Their people's lives
are not international resources to be distributed in war so as to balance the risks
or reduce the losses of other people." Likening the situation of the neutral to
that of the citizen confronted with a domestic crime against a neighbor, Walzer
insists that "the same solidarity that makes noninvolvement at home morally
questionable may well make it obligatory in the international arena: this group
of men and women must save one another's lives first."[17] In both affirming the
centrality of the legalist paradigm and insisting that states retain a right of neutrality in the face of this morally coercive structure, Walzer seems almost to
stand in two different intellectual worlds—the world of the nineteenth-century
nationalist who considered neutrality as a valuable institution for the limitation
of armed conflict and who thought that his principal duty was to attend to the
needs of his own society, and the world of the twentieth-century internationalist, who thinks, with Harry Truman, that "aggression anywhere in the world is
a threat to peace everywhere in the world" and, with George H. W. Bush, that
"every act of aggression unpunished . . . strengthens the forces of chaos and
lawlessness that, ultimately, threaten us all."

Despite this ambivalence, Walzer is clearly uncomfortable with the right of
neutrality. States have a moral right to it, he says at one point, but it is a right
that would often be "ignoble" to exercise. He would "often be inclined" to
argue with those who embrace its self-regarding (or unilateral) perspective.[18]
His qualifications of the right of neutrality in fact go further than a broad
sense of unease over its exercise. His presentation of these qualifications is not
systematic, and one must tease them out of the text. But they are there. First, if
a neutral state has "incurred obligations" toward other peoples—"for the sake,
perhaps, of collective security—then, of course, [it] cannot allow them to die."[19]
Second, "if one imagines a particular aggressor moving on from one triumph
to another, or if one imagines a radical increase in the incidence of aggression
as a result of this particular triumph, then it has to be said that peace and
freedom are in general danger. And then continued neutrality is not morally
feasible; for while a neutral state has or may have a right to let others die in
quarrels of their own, it cannot let them die on its behalf."[20] Third, neutral
states have an obligation to impose economic sanctions "against an aggressor,
even if the costs to itself are considerable," unless such sanctions seem "likely
to involve it in the fighting."[21]

Each of these qualifications raises puzzling issues. If one keeps in mind the
larger framework of *Just and Unjust Wars*, with its emphatic defense of the war
convention, the duty to impose economic sanctions in the face of aggression

must, at a minimum, be seriously qualified. This is so because thoroughgoing sanctions, if they are severe enough to hold out even the promise of effectiveness, will inevitably constitute a direct attack on the lives and well-being of innocent civilians. There are, of course, various forms of economic sanctions, ranging from the mild to the severe; but the more severe they are—the more they approximate the naval blockade—the more destructive their impact on the lives of the sick, the young, and the aged. One might even go so far as to say that the moral framework of *Just and Unjust Wars* effectively proscribes those measures short of war in which liberal opinion once invested so much hope as a means of overcoming the dilemmas of war. The idea that "peaceable coercion" might be a satisfactory substitute for war is an old one, particularly among Americans. Insofar as such measures go beyond symbolic measures of disapproval, however, they would seem to be proscribed by the war convention. Writing of the British blockade of Germany during World War I, Walzer notes that "if the success of the British strategy did not depend upon civilian deaths, it nevertheless required that nothing at all be done to avoid those deaths. Civilians had to be hit before soldiers could be hit, and this kind of attack is morally unacceptable."[22] Hitting civilians before soldiers is, of course, precisely what economic sanctions do. In this qualification of the right to neutrality, Walzer clearly had in mind an image of war in which involvement in the fighting meant the serious risk of substantial casualties to the forces of the outside state considering intervention. Experience has subsequently called that once inescapable association into question, for there are some methods of military attack—the unmanned cruise missile, for instance—that, although expensive, pose no direct risk of casualties to the intervening forces. Even more traditional forms of aerial attack, under circumstances of technological dominance, impose but a modest risk of such casualties. If one attends to the values that Walzer wished to conserve in drawing this qualification as he did, one might readily conclude that the ostensible duty (to impose economic sanctions) is not really a duty, because sanctions beyond the symbolic are disallowed by the war convention, whereas military intervention is a duty if the risks to the intervening forces can be minimized or eliminated. Whether the balance of these duties might be altered by considerations of equity (or "burden-sharing") raises further questions that are not, however, addressed in Walzer's discussion.[23]

The obligation to keep promises also raises interesting issues, especially for the citizens of a power that has made a habit of extending promissory notes in the name of collective security. If the obligation is taken at face value, it would seem to apply even to promises which, on reconsideration, ought not to have been made. It may be recalled that the principal justification for continuing America's war in Vietnam was that the United States had committed itself to the South Vietnamese government and people. It is true that the nonmoral goods of "prestige" and "credibility" were invoked by American leaders to justify the continuation of the commitment, but they also said that the United

States had a moral commitment to the Vietnamese from which it could not walk away. Is there an escape clause for keeping promises? Are they to be kept only when convenient to do so, broken only when some overriding state necessity seems to dictate, or kept regardless of the consequences? The issue raised here shows that political action will frequently require a choice among conflicting moral duties. On this issue, at least, Walzer provides no criteria by which to make the choice. More generally, the issue shows that political action is very difficult to circumscribe within moral restraint. The moralist, as it were, is left agonized by conflicting duties, while the cynic nearly always has available to him a moral duty (keep promises; save your own first) that he can invoke to relieve him of some other moral duty.

Sometimes, indeed, Walzer frames the conflict of moral duties in a way virtually indistinguishable from the more conventional calculations of statecraft. Consider his second qualification of the right to neutrality, in which he locates the circumstances under which we cannot allow others to die on our behalf. The distinction he makes between a kind of garden-variety aggression and aggressions that threaten further augmentations of power or a radical increase in the general incidence of aggression carries the same implications, and involves the same calculations, as the old doctrine of the balance of power, now dressed up in a fetching new garb. In the case of small-scale aggression the victims do not die on our behalf, and we have no duty to intervene. In the case of large-scale aggression, they do die on our behalf, and hence we do have a duty to intervene. In either case, it is the answer to the prudential question—"Will the aggression touch us?"—that would appear to be decisive. This is also the question, interestingly enough, that is decisive for the realist. For the realist, it is because the aggression may, or may not, affect our interests; for the moralist, it is because the aggression may, or may not, alter the relative balance of our duties (to ourselves and to foreigners). But the duty to ourselves (or the sense of solidarity we feel with our fellow citizens) with which the moralist identifies is in fact indistinguishable from the regard the realist expresses for the interest, security, and well-being of his political community. If the former is a moral value, so is the latter. The decision, in either case, is one that will turn on questions of fact—or prudential anticipation—and not on the distinct values of the realist and the moralist.

If these considerations do not resolve with absolute clarity the balance to be struck between the conflicting claims of intervention and isolation, of getting involved and staying out, of law enforcement in response to aggression and the duties to oneself preserved by the institution of neutrality, Walzer's subsequent essay on humanitarian intervention would seem to do so. The rule, it will be recalled, is that "whenever the filthy work can be stopped, it should be stopped." Yet wars of any kind are almost always associated with acts "that shock the moral conscience of mankind."[24] The sack of Kuwait City, the assassination of village officials in South Vietnam, the "ethnic cleansing" and war crimes that have occurred in Bosnia—the list, alas, might be extended almost indefinitely. Whether humanitarian outrages occur as a consequence of wars of aggression or of civil conflicts would appear to be irrelevant in determining the duty to respond. If the rule in regard to humanitarian intervention is as stated, this rule would apply just as much, and probably more, to the victims of aggression as to the victims of civil conflicts, for the reason that the victims of aggression lose not only individual rights but also collective rights. Within Walzer's moral framework, they have much more to claim—not only their rights as human beings, but their rights as members of international society. If all these qualifications of the right of neutrality do not quite obliterate it, they do show that something well beyond a right to respond to aggression and closely approximating a duty to do so is readily deducible from Walzer's discussion.

Walzer's presentation of these issues is made in a way that emphasizes the rights and obligations of all states, but they are, of course, intensely relevant to Americans. Since World War II, the United States has taken the legalist paradigm and its norm against aggression to be of central importance in its understanding of American purposes in the world. The three major wars the United States has fought in the postwar period—in Korea, Vietnam, and the Persian Gulf—were all justified as a vindication of this norm, the defense of which was considered to be of overriding importance if the society of states were to be preserved. That is suggestive of a certain irony, for while *Just and Unjust Wars* was provoked by protest against the war in Vietnam, American intervention in Vietnam was provoked—certainly it was justified throughout—by the very legalist paradigm that Walzer defends. Walzer, of course, is at pains to show that the legalist paradigm did not apply to the conflict in Vietnam, that the war was and remained primarily a civil conflict. The fact remains that the legalist paradigm, if placed at the center of our moral comprehension of war, is highly supportive of the commanding role in international society that the United States has assumed since World War II. If that paradigm is to be enforced, and if crimes against the society of states are to be punished, the American role is going to be crucial, for no other state has the requisite military means to make this claim effective. Walzer's subsequent rhetorical question regarding the duty of humanitarian intervention—if not us, then who?—may also be raised with respect to the defense against aggression. The answer, in either case, seems clear.

It is from the perspective of a global hegemonic power whose interests lie in the preservation of the status quo that the legalist paradigm might perhaps best be considered. From this perspective, the paradigm imposes certain restrictions on the use of force that are, by and large, quite easy to live with. The paradigm's prohibition against "preventive wars, commercial wars, wars of expansion and conquest, religious crusades, revolutionary wars, [and] military interventions"[25]—especially if certain exceptions are allowed—by and large coincide with the interests of such a state. They might be defended, as Walzer does, on the grounds of moral principle, but they are just as easily defensible on considerations of self-interest. If the realist proclivity is to emphasize the latter, that is because he believes that self-interested motives are likely to be the controlling ones; but he may, and we do, recognize that moral considerations are relevant to the discussion. Realism does not entail, as it were, a principled opposition to principle. It does require the recognition, however, that principle is unlikely to be a controlling motivation of human conduct unless it is mixed with the stronger alloy of self-interest. And it entails the recognition that the political interest that now dictates a conservative regard for legality and the existing right of possession formerly dictated expansion and conquest.[26]

If the legalist paradigm broadly corresponds with the interests of the status quo power, it might be thought that the realist inhabiting the territory of such a power might be ill-disposed to raise any objections against it. Yet American realists have been in fact highly uncomfortable with the approach to the world the legalist paradigm encourages us to take. They have distinguished sharply between the attempt to articulate moral and prudential restraints on *our own conduct* and the attempt to enforce, through war, the same restraints on the conduct of other states. These are very different enterprises, and just as one may aspire to virtuous conduct in personal morals while also, and without contradiction, thinking it highly pernicious for the state to attempt to stamp out private vice, so one may recognize the obligatory character of certain restraints embodied in the legalist paradigm while also recognizing the dangers of enforcing this code on the states of international society. With that latter enterprise in mind, the realist believes that the insistence that aggression is a crime and aggressors are criminals, together with the thoroughgoing moralization of conflicts, will lead to certain bad consequences in practice. What are those consequences?

In the first place, the paradigm discourages the compromises that are the lifeblood of politics; its watchword is the principled resistance to aggression, not the adjustment to power. Conflicting interests may often prove amenable to diplomatic adjustment and compromise, but to negotiate with evildoers is simply to reward the crime of aggression. President George H. W. Bush's formula for dealing with Iraq—"no negotiations, no compromises, no attempts at face saving and no rewards for aggression"—is a succinct expression of the attitude the paradigm engenders. This is not an abuse of the legalist paradigm so much as it is simply the use of it. It is the attitude that logically follows from making it the centerpiece of our understanding of the origin of conflicts. It may be admitted that this propensity is appropriate in some circumstances (Hitler *was* an evil man), or that realism may as easily slide into cynicism as moralism into fanaticism. We should—all of us—hope that there is a better choice in political ethics than that between the degenerate realist who is immune to the most elementary moral appeal and the degenerate moralist who is lost to the last insanities of unforgiving passion. The question is one of degree. Nevertheless, we think there is much merit in the traditional realist argument that conflicts often arise, in Herbert Butterfield's phrase, between parties that are a little too willful on one side and a little too proud on the other; that, considered dispassionately, the moral, historical, and strategic claims that the parties to conflicts make with utter conviction are often pretty sound *on both sides*, if we grant to either that regard for the security and well-being of their community which are thought perfectly unobjectionable when applied to our own; that the settlement of political disputes and the maintenance of international order will frequently require acknowledging the utility of certain well-known devices in international relations, like the recognition of spheres of influence, that are incompatible with the legalist paradigm but are indispensable if war is to be avoided; that political settlement will often mean waiving the considerations of justice to which each of the parties to a conflict feels morally entitled because doing so is the only way to avoid a further descent into small-scale violence or large-scale war. Considerations of justice are certainly not irrelevant to the maintenance of peace; a settlement perceived to be profoundly unjust will clearly be less stable than one anchored in mutual perceptions of equity. But to accept the argument from justice is also, in many circumstances, to accept the logic of war, with all of the uncontrollable and demonic features that wars characteristically display.[27]

There is also the danger that the acceptance of the legalist paradigm may, as a practical matter, relax the constraints on the conduct of war which Walzer identifies with the "war convention." He clearly wishes to maintain those constraints within the limits imposed by "supreme emergency." Nevertheless, the importance that is placed on the defeat of aggression, and the rhetoric imputing criminality that attends the response to aggression, easily lends itself to a progressive relaxation of the restrictions on means. Walzer, of course, recognizes this dilemma and urges that our desire to repress criminality not degenerate into an acceptance of criminal measures in the prosecution of war. He is right, moreover, to observe that the desire to win will be in tension with the restraints imposed by the war convention even in the absence of the moral fervor that the legalist paradigm encourages. The point remains that this tension will be (and has been) exacerbated by the moral fervor with which war is conducted in a democratic age.

There is, finally, a broader tension that seems particularly relevant to the American position as the global hegemonic enforcer of the legalist paradigm. The central injunction of the war convention is that belligerents have no right to imperil civilian lives. They must not only not aim at the evil effect but also seek to minimize it, accepting risks to their own soldiers. The central injunction of contemporary American strategy, and one which must necessarily be accepted as a condition of public support for an activist American role, is that every measure be taken to minimize the risk of American casualties. It is the latter injunction, not the former, that is going to be controlling in the wars that America fights. That attitude may not be morally appropriate; that it is very powerful seems incontestable. The collision of these rival injunctions, it may be admitted, does not inescapably lead to a relaxation of the war convention, for technological advances allowing for more discriminate targeting (and a world public opinion sensitive to civilian suffering) work in the other direction. Still, one must be impressed by the degree to which the frontiers of "military necessity" may be enlarged by the need to satisfy domestic public opinion that every measure has been taken to minimize the risk to American combatants. An overwhelming disproportion between U.S. and enemy casualties, and a readiness to accept collateral civilian suffering in the name of minimizing the casualties of U.S. forces, seems an inescapable corollary—a condition even—of the assumption by the United States of the role of enforcer of the legalist paradigm.

ANTICIPATIONS

The legalist paradigm rests upon, or derives from, the intuitive or common sense notion that one has a right to defend what is one's own and no right to take through force what is not. A sense of the moral rightness of this claim is so basic to elementary notions of justice that it is difficult to see how any ethical system would be concerned with denying it (though it might be, and has been, thought legitimate to override it in certain circumstances). Despite the intuitive appeal of the aggression/self-defense dichotomy, it has proven to be very difficult to arrive at a legal definition of aggression acceptable to all the parties to international society. The emphatic declaration of the legalist paradigm—"Any use of force or imminent threat of force by one state against the political sovereignty or territorial integrity of another constitutes aggression and is a criminal act"[28]—is intended to chain up the dogs of war, but it does so in the manner of a straitjacket. It is too restrictive. It is too easy to imagine circumstances in which acts short of war constitute a threat to the security or independence of another state. If states—even states whose interests lie in the preservation of the status quo—were to adhere rigidly to the legalist paradigm and to its general prohibition against the first use of force, they might, in some circumstances, risk their security or survival. Hence the formula must be revised. Walzer's revision, previously cited, is one that falls somewhere in the middle of a continuum stretching from preemption against imminent attack to preventive war against "distant danger." The Israeli decision to launch the 1967 war is then justified by Walzer as a reasonable anticipation, not because the Arab forces were on the point of imminent attack, but because their mobilization created a strain on Israel (dependent as it was on reserve mobilization) sufficiently onerous and threatening as to justify the first use of force. The eighteenth-century preventive wars to preserve the balance of power, on the other hand, are condemned.

The issue that has raised, for our generation, the problem of preventive war is that of the proliferation of weapons of mass destruction. On the face of it, it would seem that the criteria laid down in *Just and Unjust Wars* would forbid such wars. "The mere augmentation of power," Walzer writes, "cannot be a warrant for war or even the beginning of warrant."[29] This is so, in the language of Vattel, even when a state that is "on the point of receiving a formidable augmentation of power . . . has given signs of injustice, rapacity, pride, ambition, or of an imperious thirst of rule."[30] Vattel's criteria, Walzer insists, are too permissive: "Instead of previous signs of rapacity and ambition, current and particular signs are required; instead of an 'augmentation of power,' actual preparation for war; instead of the refusal of future securities, the intensification of present dangers."[31] The relevance of these criteria to the nuclear problem is not, it must be said, altogether clear. For all the advantages offered by Walzer's casuistical method, here is an instance where obscurity—rather than, as normally, illumination—seems to result from it. How are we to read the decision by a "rogue state"—a North Korea, an Iraq, an Iran—to acquire such weapons, in circumstances where their enemies are in possession of them? Does that decision constitute merely an augmentation of power stemming from defensive motives or an actual preparation for war? Does it indicate a refusal of future securities or an intensification of present dangers? Is it, in and of itself, a current and particular sign of rapacity, or are we alarmed primarily because the regimes in question have given previous signs of evil conduct? Here, as elsewhere, it is the prudential reading of dangers, for both the realist and the moralist, that is determinative of our attitude; the prudential question—what is the reasonable anticipation?—swamps the attempt to enclose war within a set of moral restraints. Unless the absolute ban on the first use of force is accepted—and Walzer, with the realists, insists that it should not be—we are left with inherently vague criteria to which the facts, as it were, can always be adjusted.

It is a curious feature of the contemporary discussion of preventive war to stop proliferation that self-described realists have taken a far less alarmist view of the dangers of proliferation than have others. They have not been among the proponents of preventive war. Walzer, however, is willing to entertain the possibility. In a symposium at the Carnegie Council in 1996 (at which this essay was first presented), in response to a query from the floor, Walzer indicated that he was not disposed to raise a moral objection to preventive war for this purpose, a view that is probably much closer to the prevailing consensus than is the stance generally adopted by realists (though their emphasis, of course, would be on the prudential dangers raised by this project).[32] This is a curious inversion because realism is most often associated with the doctrine that the security of states would be imperiled by rigid adherence to the legalist paradigm, while moralists want to circumscribe that discretion more fully within a set of moral prohibitions. The reasons for this inversion do not arise primarily, it would seem, from varying ethical perceptions—no one is looking to increase the danger of nuclear war—but from differing readings of the motives that lead states to acquire such weapons and a greater degree of confidence (on the part of realists) in the workability of nuclear deterrence if nuclear proliferation

occurs. It is possible that the unwillingness of many moralists to accept deterrence, which requires for its effectiveness the making of immoral threats, may
lead them to look with greater favor on ways of escaping this condition, even if
it requires war to do so. In that sense, varying ethical perceptions may help
explain the "curious inversion." Whether this has influenced Walzer's willingness to look favorably on preventive war we do not presume to say—his defense
of nuclear deterrence in *Just and Unjust Wars* would indicate a contrary conclusion—but a profound sense of moral unease over the making of immoral
threats was often a starting point of the projects to escape deterrence proposed
over the past generation: strategic defenses, world government, unilateral disarmament. The advocates of "Star Wars," Catholic just war theorists, and peace
demonstrators with grim masks of death and destruction were as one in their
moral condemnation of deterrence and in their doubts over its continued efficacy; their strange alliance on these two vital points in the 1980s has undoubtedly helped reinforce the contemporary case for preventive war to stop
proliferation. The reasons for the inversion, finally, are also attributable to the
resistance of realists to "criminalizing" the enemy, and hence also to their
greater willingness to recognize that the putatively insane leaders of such states
share the same fears that make the possession of weapons of mass destruction
seem imperative for our own safety.[33]

Ethical perceptions, therefore, are not exactly irrelevant to the debate over
what to do about proliferation. In the larger sense, however, prudence remains
determinative, and the attempt to resolve the problem through articulating a
set of moral restraints is like building a dike in the middle of the ocean. The
water, being rather ingenious, manages to find its way around. Once one decides
that an absolute prohibition against the first use of force is too restrictive, it is
extremely difficult to state the exceptions in such a way that they will not prove
highly elastic in practice, and the standing temptation will be to claim the exceptions for ourselves and to deny them to others—a strange inversion of the moral
theorist's claim to impartiality. If this conclusion is thought excessive with
regard to the problem of war more generally, it must, at least, be accepted with
regard to the question of proliferation. The position of the nuclear powers is
that they get to keep their weapons, and no one else (save a few of their allies)
has the right to acquire them. One of those powers—the United States—claims,
or is seriously tempted to claim, a right to prohibit further proliferation through
force. If this position can be justified, it can only be justified by invoking the
imperious demands of necessity or the overarching requirements of world
order. To get at it through the legalist paradigm—with its assumption of the
equality of states and its prohibition of the first use of force—is a testament
to man's ingenuity rather than to his willingness to submit himself to moral
restraint.

INTERVENTIONS

One of the most striking—and to us, persuasive—themes in *Just and Unjust Wars* is its defense of the nonintervention principle. The date of the book's publication, 1977, ironically marked the beginning of an American attempt to vigorously promote human rights and democracy in the world. In this respect, at least, the argument of *Just and Unjust Wars* has stood athwart the general tendency of the times, which have witnessed increasing agreement, among both philosophers and politicos, on the proposition that intervention is morally justified for such purposes. Even adherents of the nonintervention norm have argued that Walzer's criteria are too restrictive in principle or cannot in any case be reached on the basis of his starting point, which recognizes the priority of the rights of individuals. These critics would open the door in principle to intervention for human rights or democracy, while recognizing the merit of the prudential considerations (it will be ineffective; it will be destructive of international order; it will increase the danger of war; it will lead to the sacrifice of the rights or interests of your own citizens) that ought to restrain its exercise. Other critics have been far more hostile to Walzer's defense of nonintervention, and have insisted that intervention, far from being proscribed, is an imperative duty for foreign states.

Walzer's reply is that the objection to intervention is in fact a principled one; that the circumstances that justify revolution do not, at the same time, justify foreign intervention; that when "invasions are launched by foreign armies, even armies with revolutionary intentions, and even when revolution is justified, it is entirely plausible to say that the rights of subjects and citizens have been violated. Their 'slowness' has been artificially speeded up, their 'aversion' has been repudiated, their loyalties have been ignored, their prudential calculations have been rejected—all in favor of someone else's conceptions of political justice and political prudence."[34] The ground that Walzer takes here (as well as the exceptions that he later makes to the nonintervention norm) are broadly rooted in John Stuart Mill's essay on nonintervention. "The members of a political community must seek their own freedom, just as the individual must cultivate his own virtue," as Walzer summarizes Mill's position. "They cannot be set free, as he cannot be made virtuous, by any external force."[35]

One can reach the nonintervention principle through various routes, and we do not propose to investigate further here the various grounds on which it might be defended. In general, we sympathize with the pluralist conception of international society underlying Walzer's defense of it, think the prudential reasons against its violation to be normally cogent, and believe that a certain respect ought to be accorded any rule of long-standing authority in the law of nations, as the rule against intervention certainly is. So, too, we agree that, though the norm be central and the values protected by it of vital significance to the society of states, there are certain cases where "revisions" to it seem appropriate. Walzer's revisions, however, are in need of revising. In the support that Walzer's interpretation countenances for outside aid to secessionist movements, it is far too permissive. In its devaluation of the importance of pacification in its treatment of counterintervention and legitimate war aims, it is too restrictive. The revision regarding humanitarian intervention, finally, is not as helpful to the problem as it may at first sight appear.

Let us take the last point first. One must certainly acknowledge that a rule forbidding intervention in any circumstances is too rigid. When a state has failed and it is a mockery of words to speak of a state protecting collective autonomy, surely it is reasonable to grant to outside states a qualified right of intervention. Indeed, one must agree that there is in certain circumstances a duty to take action. Though "state failure" is difficult to define precisely, the anarchical circumstances that prevailed in Somalia before the American intervention surely constituted a case where a duty existed to do something to relieve the suffering, if it could be done at acceptable cost. Whether the duty is trumped by some other duty—and how those "duties" and "acceptable costs" are defined—are the questions, not whether the duty as such exists. Walzer treated the right/duty question in a somewhat ambiguous manner in *Just and Unjust Wars*, insisting that there was no moral reason to await international authorization before acting, and that "any state capable of stopping the slaughter has a right, at least, to do so." In his more recent work, he has, as we have seen, recognized the existence of a duty far more emphatically.

There are, however, several problems raised by his treatment of the subject. In the first place, the criterion he employs in *Just and Unjust Wars* is not "state failure" but acts—genocide, massacre, enslavement—that shock the moral conscience of mankind. He also says, however, that outside states have no right to intervene in civil wars. The criteria, standing alone, have intuitive appeal. They do not stand well together, however, because civil wars are invariably associated with acts that shock any conscience capable of shock—more so, indeed, than wars generally. Fully persuasive is the classic wisdom, memorably conveyed by Thucydides, that civil wars are the worst, that they sink man to a level of moral depravity far beyond that which he falls into as a consequence of interstate war. Far from being unusual, acts that are shocking—unbelievable cruelties, gratuitous desecrations, vicious lies—are entirely typical. Thucycides' description of this descent, and of the inversion of human personality that occurs in civil war, is classic not simply because it is powerfully expressed, but because it can stand, with little alteration, as an accurate summation of what has happened to human character in a hundred subsequent conflicts.

There are certainly acts that, in their scale, are beyond shocking in the sheer magnitude of the evil entailed, and which make the impartial spectator ashamed to belong to the human race. The destruction of European Jewry and of other peoples by the Nazis; Stalin's war against the kulaks, among half a dozen other enormities; the Turkish genocide against the Armenians; what the Khmer Rouge did in Cambodia—all these can be placed in this infamous category, though the list is certainly not exhaustive. The circumstances in which they occurred, however, cast doubt on whether a duty to intervene can withstand the force of objections on the other side. Two of these occurred in the midst of great wars. In the Armenian case, it is difficult to see what outside powers might have done. The British were incapable of forcing the Straits; how might they have intervened in Turkey, save at a price that might have lost them the war in the West? In World War II, there was certainly moral culpability in not bombing the extermination camps. Was there also moral culpability, on the part of Roosevelt and Churchill, in not allowing contact with, or giving any support to, the Germans who sought to kill Hitler? A very substantial portion of the Jewish victims of the Holocaust—probably most—were killed after the failure of the plot against Hitler's life in June 1944, and four to five million Germans perished between that date and the end of the war. Why was nothing more done? The principal reason is that both men feared that Stalin, if word of such transactions got back to him, would beat the Allied leaders to the punch and make (again) a separate peace with Hitler. The consequence of not doing more was odious, but it was also reasonable to fear the odious consequences of doing more. Evil consequences were stamped on the face of either alterative. In the case of Cambodia, other states may have had a duty to intervene, but American intervention fell in the realm of the impossible. We had been saving Southeast Asia from itself for more than ten years and had revolted against the consequences of that enterprise; to go back in, after so short a time, was out of the question, even though in this case America had an indirect responsibility for consequences that, though neither intended nor foreseeable, could plausibly be traced in part to its acts. Equally out of the question was a war against Stalinist Russia in 1933, or indeed at any time, on the grounds that the Communists had committed atrocious acts. The extreme cases, in short, are those where there usually—perhaps invariably—exist imperative considerations on the other side that make the duty of humanitarian intervention either impossible or fraught with enormous risk.

There is a third difficulty with defining the rule for humanitarian intervention in terms of acts that shock the moral conscience of mankind. It is that mankind's capacity for shock seems not simply unrelated, but in many circumstances inversely related, to considerations of quantity. The televised atrocity is worth ten thousand casualties. The war between Armenia and Azerbaijan entailed ethnic cleansing on a scale approaching that of Bosnia; the civil war in Angola entailed horrors that surpassed the Bosnian experience. For the man in the street, however, the former events have an epistemological status comparable to Bishop Berkeley's tree that fell in the forest without anyone present to hear. Did it make a noise? The issue raised here goes beyond the selective reporting of Western media. It concerns the profound disjunction between the morally significant and the psychologically "real," between the abstract statistics that ought to move us and the concrete event or image that does. Even if the other difficulties with this criterion are put to one side, Walzer might have better made his appeal to acts that ought to shock the moral conscience of mankind, but by no means invariably do. To have put it this way would have attested to several unpleasant facts about human beings: that we are most shocked when such acts are infrequent, and most inured to shock when they become typical. (What was shocking to the American mind in 1937 was vastly different from what was capable of shocking it in 1945.) So, too, what is shocking, and what is deemed par for the course, is invariably tainted with the partialities, enmities, and interests of outside governments and publics, just as the knowledge of it frequently comes filtered through the distortions and magnifications of the partisans themselves.

However an objective criterion is stated, there are undoubtedly a substantial number of cases that would potentially fall within it. Walzer is surely right to insist that an inability to do everything does not constitute a good reason for doing nothing, and that the existence of interested motives (which are always present in political action) does not, in and of itself, demonstrate the absence of the good intentions and consequences by which the act must be justified. These psychological considerations, however, are quite relevant to the ability of outside powers to conduct humanitarian interventions that bear a meaningful relationship to the goals ostensibly pursued. The reason is the instability of human compassion—the way, for instance, that the image of the starving or mangled child comes to be counterbalanced by the image of the soldier being dragged through the streets of Mogadishu. The fear that domestic public opinion will revolt against any costly or protracted involvement, in turn, imposes a caution on intervening powers that inevitably produces unintended consequences and may produce pernicious ones.[36] It probably rules out, as a practical matter, the kind of long-term arrangements—the imposition of a "protectorate" or "trusteeship"—that Walzer, quite plausibly, has concluded will be necessary if a lasting good is to be promoted through humanitarian intervention. Instead, the objectives of humanitarian intervention come to be limited to feeding the hungry—sometimes with the odious consequence, as in Rwanda, of feeding the perpetrators of genocide and aiding them in the reconstitution of their forces. When the purposes of the intervention are restricted to humanitarian objectives and do not address the political causes that invariably underlie such disasters, such consequences seem almost a foregone conclusion.

These considerations do not, of themselves, fatally weaken the case for humanitarian intervention. Recent experience has been various, with each case having very different characteristics. There is a good argument to be made that the Somalia intervention did save a large number of lives and historic communities, and was justifiable on that ground alone. The humiliations it entailed, it is true, imposed real costs on the American government, and those count heavily against the prospect of any future intervention that promises to end with a comparable embarrassment. A vital interest—the reputation for constancy—can be impaired by an intervention even if a vital interest does not prompt it in the first place. But it may be argued that the humiliations stemmed primarily from the foreign policy of crime and punishment— particularly the hare-brained scheme to put a price on Farah Aideed's head (which was then followed by the spectacle, about equal parts absurd and ridiculous, of the U.S. government casting blame for the failure on everyone and everything but itself, though it enjoyed near total control of the operation). The Bosnian intervention, in its various phases, has been very different in motivation and purpose from that of Somalia, since a vital interest—that which the United States and its allies have in the maintenance of European order—is engaged there, as it was not in Somalia. Given the primacy of political motive in leading the United States to broker a settlement, it is questionable whether that intervention—certainly the phase of it since Dayton—should be seen as a case of humanitarian intervention. The earlier phase of UN intervention has of course been subjected to strong criticism, but the failure there was not in feeding the hungry—a further humanitarian disaster was averted by the United Nations Protection Force (UNPROFOR)—but in not devising a coherent political strategy that would bring the war to an end. It is in Rwanda where the unintended consequences seem most pernicious, and where the desire to be seen as doing good, as opposed to actually doing it, seems the leading motivation of outside governments. The predominance of this motive would count more against the actions of outside governments if anyone knew how a lasting good might be feasibly promoted through intervention. Unfortunately, no one does.

These considerations attest to the difficulty of formulating any general rule regarding humanitarian intervention; but they are also perfectly compatible with the recognition that there is both a right and a duty to do it under certain conditions. The question is how to draw those conditions. There is, one should think, no duty if the intervention entails a serious injury to the intervening state. (Morally speaking, the prospect of modest casualties to the intervening forces cannot be said to fall within the meaning of "serious injury," though politically speaking it does, and it is probably useless to state any rule that, if acted upon, would lead an intervening government through a cycle of embarrassing actions that, while injuring itself, provided no great or lasting benefit to those ostensibly aided.) Nor, under these circumstances, would there be a right, since the existence of a serious injury would mean that statesmen had ignored their primary obligation, which is to their own people.

Secondly, there is the question of whether such interventions may be undertaken unilaterally or require authorization from multilateral organizations. It is useful to recall that the skepticism traditionally reserved by publicists for humanitarian intervention went beyond the fact that states, and not individuals, were the subjects of international law. That skepticism was also based on the reasonable supposition that selfish motives would inevitably predominate, whence arose the strong doubt that it ought to be authorized. Multilateral authorization goes a long way toward meeting this objection, even if much arm twisting is employed in getting it. Walzer placed little importance on this criterion in *Just and Unjust Wars*, and it is certainly possible to imagine cases where unilateral action would be justified. By the same token, however, one must insist that, in today's generally permissive circumstances, the requirement of multilateral authorization is of much greater weight. Its absence would, at the least, constitute a strong presumption against the existence of either a right or duty to conduct such interventions, though not perhaps a conclusive argument on either score.

Finally, there must be a plausible design to promote a result in which the good consequences clearly outweigh the bad. That criterion may seem hopeless because it requires weighing incommensurables—lives, reputations, interests, responsibilities, endurance. But it must be taken seriously. If in the past the presence of selfish motives led publicists to doubt a right of humanitarian intervention, an equal if not greater cause for worry today is that the sentiments of compassion that prompt intervention will lead, as a consequence of their fleeting and unstable character, to unintended and even pernicious consequences.

SELF-DETERMINATIONS

Walzer's "second revision" to the legalist paradigm holds that "states can be invaded and wars justly begun to assist secessionist movements (once they have demonstrated their representative character)."[37] It is unclear whether Walzer would require that the secessionist community already be "engaged in a large-scale military struggle for independence"[38] or merely that "a community actually exists whose members are committed to independence and ready and able to determine the conditions of their own existence."[39] If the latter, the desire for independence and the possibility of external aid may operate together in a way that is potentially quite destructive of international order. Secession has an unenviable track record of being closely associated with civil war; as a general remedy for the problems of nationalism and ethnicity, it seems highly toxic in its effects and utterly frightening if carried to its logical conclusion: "an infinity of little, jealous, clashing, tumultuous commonwealths, the wretched nurseries of unceasing discord and the miserable objects of universal pity or contempt."[40] No people can be denied a right of revolution, if the oppression be unbearable and every other mode of resistance is unavailing. To encourage such claims before their achievement, however, would serve to encourage a fracturing of territorial integrity that would menace political stability over most of the world. One shudders at the consequences that would ensue from the application of this principle in Africa or the Caucasus or the Indian subcontinent. Walzer would presumably wish to separate the emergence of a movement for national self-determination from the encouragement that outside powers may give it, authorizing a right of external support when it has achieved a self-sustaining character, but not of initial encouragement. In practice, those two things will be very difficult to separate.

The conditions under which aid may be legitimately extended to secessionist movements is not, we should add, entirely clear to us from Walzer's account. The relevant principle seems to be "always act so as to recognize and uphold communal autonomy"[41]—communal autonomy being identified not with the state but the nation. But if communal autonomy is the central value which Walzer seeks to uphold, there would seem to be no reason to require "large-scale belligerency" to show that a community exists that wishes to be self-determining. Its inability to mount an insurrection, more often than not, will reflect its weakness, and there is no reason to assume that, because it is weak, it is also inauthentic or unrepresentative. If the extension of aid to such groups is not authorized, the basic reason seems to be "because the morally exact principle is also very dangerous."[42]

Its dangers are well illustrated by the Yugoslav crisis. The willingness of the Western powers to recognize Bosnian independence played an important role in giving the Bosnian government the courage to proceed with its secession from Yugoslavia. This recognition proceeded in defiance of the traditional law of recognition, which requires that a government demonstrate that it enjoys the effective control of its territory, among other criteria, before recognition is accorded. The Bosnian government believed that Western recognition reflected a willingness by outside powers, particularly the United States, to help it secure an independence which the balance of forces then existing gave it no grounds for believing it could secure on its own. In this expectation, it proved to be mistaken. The Bosnian catastrophe sharply highlights the dangers that are associated with outside intervention to support secession, and it casts strong doubt on the proposition that foreigners ought to be granted a right (even a right circumscribed by considerations of prudence) to do it. The older rule, which permitted outside powers to recognize the outcome of local struggles, but not to help precipitate them, would seem to be far more preferable.

The "morally exact" criterion—"always act so as to recognize and uphold communal autonomy"—is not, however, irrelevant to the diplomatic tasks of the West in Bosnia. The peculiar feature of this diplomacy is that, once having violated the principle of nonintervention by prematurely granting recognition to the constituent republics of the Yugoslav state, it then insisted that the territorial integrity of the new states was something sacred and inviolable. The secession of Bosnia from Yugoslavia was encouraged, on the now scarcely credible grounds that this was the best chance of averting war; the secession of Serbs and Croats from Bosnia, however, was forbidden, on the grounds that this would constitute a reward for aggression. Yet there would seem to be no reason why the principle of self-determination is not as valid for the Serbs and Croats as it is for the Muslims. It has been said countless times that the partition of Bosnia would be unjust, but it is difficult to see why this should be the case. It seems to us to be more just—certainly on the Wilsonian criteria that Walzer defends—than any other practical arrangement. If the construction of a Switzerland in the Balkans is under existing circumstances impossible, and it clearly is, we ought to follow its bitter logic to the end. Respect for communal autonomy demands no less.

In an essay subsequent to the publication of *Just and Unjust Wars*, Walzer pursued the theme of national self-determination further.[43] The state system, he argued, could only be transformed if it were first completed; the Wilsonian principle—"for every nation its own state"—pointed the way toward an international settlement. Walzer acknowledged the potential dangers of this enterprise: "The way itself is bloody enough, and there probably are cases where people from different nations are so radically entangled on the same piece of territory that a 'good border' is virtually inconceivable." Still, he thought, "the completion of the state system is a reform worth pursuing." As a general prescription for what ails multiethnic or multinational states, this "reform" is a prescription for much bloodshed. It needs to be recalled that Western and Central Europe, a region of "satisfied" states now capable, on Walzer's account, of transcending the system, only achieved this happy condition as a result of two world wars and the extermination and/or forced expulsion of huge numbers of people.

It is certainly cogent to argue that, *once the breakdown has occurred*, the logic of "separation, secession, partition, liberation" does point to the only real settlement then imaginable. In these circumstances, the prudential claim for security that communities make is going to seem compelling to them and ought to be recognized; the imagined speech that Walzer provides in justification of this is exactly on point: "We and our fellows, members of a people or historical nation, can only guarantee our physical survival, our long-term existence as individuals or as a coherent group, through the medium of sovereign power. We can be sure of no one's protection but our own." In the case of Israel and Palestine, that claim has not unreasonably been seen to justify a partition—and a partition whose logic entails not only separation but also the waiving of the right of return for Palestinians who fled or were expelled from Israel when the state was founded.[44] In the Bosnian case, the application of this principle would seem to require respecting the wishes of Bosnian Serbs and Croats for a reunion with Serbia and Croatia, and the concomitant (though compensated) denial of the right of return to the territory from which the Muslims fled or were expelled. The outside role would be directed not toward denying Serbs, Croats, or Muslims their right of self-determination but toward protecting the Muslims from the unfavorable strategic and economic position to which the mutual recognition of that right would subject them.

We cannot depart this discussion of the second revision without noting how far-reaching is the principle that is claimed. It extends not simply to the support that may be given to secessionist movements; there is no reason why it would not support irredentist claims as well (as long as the community that wishes for self-determination understands that aspiration to mean union—or reunion—with the neighboring community or nation that takes up arms on its behalf). The revision, it may be recalled, is open not only to the United States and its friends but to all states. The support that Germany gave to Sudetenland Germans; that Serbia gave to Bosnian Serbs; that Albania might give to Albanians seeking secession from Macedonia or Serbia; that Russia might give to the "famous twenty-nine millions" in the near abroad; that the Tutsi of Rwanda might give the Tutsi of Burundi or the Hutu of Burundi might give the Hutu of Rwanda—the list of potential cases in which this exception might be claimed with complete plausibility could fill up a page; it covers a fair portion of the world's potential wars. The principle also reaches cases in which no irredentist claim is put forward, such as the support that the Soviet Union and China gave to national liberation movements during the Cold War or that Arab states have given and might yet give to Palestinian aspirations. So numerous are the cases affected by this principle that it represents not simply a "revision" of the legalist paradigm but its near-complete evisceration. It can hardly be deemed surprising that the temptation will be, as it has been, to claim the exception for ourselves and to deny it to others—that strange inversion again.

But the oddities of Walzer's discussion of this principle do not end there. The fact that secessionist or irredentist claims almost invariably affect the communal rights of other peoples—hardly a novel problem, even in 1977—is simply "set aside" by Walzer, on the grounds that it did not "enter into the moral reflections of liberal observers like Mill." To which one can only say that it enters into ours, and has done so since the experience of redrawing borders in Europe after World War I showed that there was scarcely a frontier in Europe that could be drawn in a manner that the peoples on both sides of it—hopelessly entangled as always—would regard as just. It might be argued that Walzer's subsequent qualification of the right to aid nationalist movements—that a state contemplating intervention must "*for moral reasons* . . . weigh the dangers its action will impose on the people it is designed to benefit and on all other people who may be affected"[45]—covers this difficulty (even if he clearly had in mind, as his discussion of 1849 and 1956 would indicate, not the rights of competing nationalities but the dangers of a general conflagration). If so, however, the criteria to be employed in conducting this "weighing" remain thoroughly obscure. The fact that peoples are invariably entangled means that an intervention will invariably subject some "third parties to terrible risks," and whether the subjection cancels the justice, or the justice cancels the subjection, must presumably remain a matter for the determination of the interested parties.

WAR AIMS

Having criticized Walzer for the excessive permissiveness of his framework, it may seem perverse to hold that other elements of his outlook are insufficiently permissive. Nevertheless, questions may certainly be raised about the wisdom of his third and fifth revisions. The third revision of the legalist paradigm permits counterintervention but only for the purpose of leveling the playing field; its goal is not winning the war but "holding the circle, preserving the balance, restoring some degree of integrity to the local struggle."[46] The fifth revision permits states conducting a just war to seek "resistance, restoration [and] reasonable prevention"[47] in the settlements they impose upon defeated states, but holds that to go beyond these limited aims and to opt for a "war of conquest and reconstruction"[48] is generally impermissible. Both formulations have the virtue of seeking to restrain the aims that states may adopt in war, and in theory seem quite sensible. In practice, however, they allow for the distinct possibility that the use of force may simply contribute to prolonging the war, producing not "a better state of peace"[49] but rather an interminable conflict. In either case, this would seem clearly to be a repellent consequence: the use of force must be judged harshly if, at the end of the day, it leads simply to further chaos. War is an act that finds the parties to it in a state of nature; its purpose must be to get them out of that state, rather than to keep them there. Whether that purpose is compatible with limited aims, such as leveling the killing field or refusing occupation and reconstruction, depends on circumstances and is not subject to a priori determination.

The experience of the Gulf War is instructive in this regard. It was our argument in *The Imperial Temptation* that the United States ought not to have gone to war but that, having used force on the scale that it did, and having contributed mightily to the civil war and epidemics that occurred in Iraq, the United States ought to have marched to Baghdad, deposed Saddam Hussein, and imposed a new regime.[50] The policy the United States did pursue at the time, and has pursued subsequently, has imposed an extraordinary collective punishment on the Iraqi people, the sheer scale of which ought to make the moralist cringe. What makes the example particularly disturbing is that the policies that produced this result conformed in vital respects to Walzer's version of the just war. An aggression took place against internationally recognized borders. Authority to repel the aggression was received from the United Nations (not necessary under his criteria, but still a bonus). Military operations, though characterized by the lavish use of force, did not aim directly at civilians. War aims were limited to the restoration of Kuwaiti sovereignty, the attempted destruction of Iraqi armed forces, and the guarantee that Iraq would give up its pursuit of weapons of mass destruction ("reasonable prevention"). When civil war broke out, the initial policy of nonintervention and the subsequent humanitarian intervention on behalf of the Kurds closely followed a Walzerian logic. (We stayed out of the civil war, while intervening—belatedly—to prevent massacre.) Yet the sum total, in human suffering, of all this justice is appalling. To insist that further intervention, under these circumstances, would have deprived the Iraqi people of their right to self-determination seems distinctly unpersuasive. In any case, it is clear that the reason for America's reluctance to impose a new order derived not from legal or moral conviction but from a profound aversion to what was deemed to be a protracted and risky commitment. Having accepted an imperial role, the United States was unwilling to accept the responsibilities of imperial rule. That this course of action conformed so closely to the theory of aggression presented in *Just and Unjust Wars* suggests to us that something is wrong with the theory.

CONCLUSION

The tradition of reflection on the just war that Walzer revived in his book is an honorable one, and Walzer performed a valuable service in investigating it in a way that has made it accessible and interesting to a generation of students. We have sought to show that the work treats the tradition of political realism in a misleading way and that, paradoxically, Walzer is himself close to certain realist themes (though not, of course, to others). If the central claims of realism are fairly considered, Walzer's stance in relation to those claims may not unfairly be seen in the same way that Frederick the Great characterized Maria Theresa's reaction to the partition of Poland: "She wept, but she took."

A legion of critics, following Walzer, has insisted that realist thought is reducible to the doctrine of Thrasymachus in the first book of the *Republic*, that "justice is the advantage of the stronger." To hear them tell of it, realism is nothing better than Thrasymachus on stilts, and they have busied themselves with the task of sawing off the legs of this pernicious doctrine. We do not recognize these caricatures, and would suggest that the critique of realism needs to get beyond the refutation of positions that nobody, save a few college students, actually holds. Realism is concerned not with the refutation of the just war tradition but rather with showing that the use (and not simply the abuse) of some of its categories may lead to pernicious results in practice. Walzer's reconstruction of the tradition is particularly vulnerable to the charge that it encourages a striking permissiveness in the resort to force (both in the latitude given to wars of law enforcement and in some of his revisions to the legalist paradigm); that it underrates the value of pacification in its treatment of counterintervention and legitimate war aims; that it minimizes the dangers of understanding conflicts as contests between good and evil; and that it encourages the false comfort that combatants will in practice respect the limitations of the war convention that he eloquently urges upon us. In making these criticisms, we are not refusing a conversation on the terms by which a more just world can be achieved, but asking that this enterprise give due account to the weaknesses, egocentricities, and delusions of the unhappy species whose improvement is sought.

NOTES

This essay was originally prepared in collaboration with Robert W. Tucker for a symposium held at the Carnegie Council on May 16, 1996. After that symposium, a critique of the paper was provided by symposium chair Terry Nardin to which my coauthor was not inclined to respond, he being otherwise occupied, but which roused me to further effort. The result was an essay over three times as long as the original. At the end of the day, Dr. Tucker insisted that his name be withdrawn from the piece, since it no longer reflected the equality of effort and contribution characteristic of our previous collaborations. I acceded to his determination, though with mixed feelings, for we had developed the critique together and he carefully reviewed all subsequent drafts, correcting various extravagances. He authorizes me to say that he agrees with the argument of the piece, though our inflections differ in a few particulars; readers familiar with his previous work will note places in the essay that bear his imprint. Even where this imprint may not be apparent to others, it is certainly apparent to me, since my thinking on the issues considered in the essay has been deeply affected by his writings and our conversations (and arguments) over the years. In light of this curious history, I have retained the "we" in the essay that follows; and readers are certainly invited to attribute whatever errors remain to his influence. This essay was first published in *Ethics & International Affairs* 11 (1997): 19–53 as part of the special section, "Twenty Years of Michael Walzer's *Just and Unjust Wars*," alongside other critiques by Michael J. Smith, Theodore J. Koontz, and Joseph Boyle, and a response essay by Michael Walzer. The full set of contributions can be accessed online at www.cceia.org/resources/journal/11/special_section/index.html.

1.   Michael Walzer, *Just and Unjust Wars: A Moral Argument with Historical Illustrations*, fourth edition (New York: Basic Books, [1977] 2006), 274.

2.   Ibid., 3.

3.   Ibid., 20.

4.   Realists, of course, are skeptical of women, too; but one must regard as an open question whether the generalizations that classic writers have made regarding the conduct of men in politics and war apply equally to the conduct of women in that realm of action. This is an empirical question, the answer to which is not obvious, and that ought not to be resolved by stylistic convention. The ethical injunctions on either statesmen or stateswomen, however, are certainly the same. When, therefore, the context of our discussion is an ethical requirement rather than an empirical observation, the reader may substitute or add a "she" for a "he," if she or he wishes, for all the "he's" (and their equivalents) that follow.

5.   Montesquieu, *The Spirit of the Laws*, ed. Anne M. Cohler, Basia C. Miller, and Harold S. Stone (Cambridge: Cambridge University Press, [1748] 1989), bk. 1, ch. 3: 7. Raymond Aron, normally considered a realist, made this the epigraph of *Peace and War*, and it may be presumed that he did not do so ironically. Hamilton's Pacificus No. 4 (1793), in which this passage appears, is excerpted in Norman Graebner, ed., *Ideas and Diplomacy: Readings in the Intellectual Tradition of American Foreign Policy* (New York: Oxford University Press, 1964), 61. The context of Hamilton's remarks may be recalled: he was disputing the importance that Jefferson had placed on gratitude in the affairs of states. While recognizing that "faith and justice between nations are virtues of a nature the most necessary and sacred," he was also

intent on showing that the United States had no obligation—stemming either from the precise injunctions of the French alliance or from considerations of gratitude—to join with France in the European war.

6. Emmerich de Vattel, *The Law of Nations or the Principles of Natural Law Applied to the Conduct and to the Affairs of Nations and of Sovereigns* (Washington, DC: Carnegie Institution of Washington, [1758] 1916), 14. A similar qualification appears in Henry Wheaton. Wheaton acknowledged Machiavelli's "patriotic anxiety" but condemned the "atrocious means" and "violent remedies" he counseled. Policy, Wheaton insisted, "can never be separated from justice with impunity. Sound policy can never authorize a resort to such measures as are prohibited by the law of nations, founded on the principles of eternal justice; and, on the other hand, the law of nations ought not to prohibit that which sound policy dictates as necessary to the security of any State" (Henry Wheaton, *Elements of International Law*, ed. George Grafton Wilson [Oxford: Clarendon Press, (1866) 1936], xv.

A doctrine in contrast with the opinion of Vattel and Wheaton was often affirmed in the republican—and Machiavellian—tradition whose passage through time and space was examined in J. G. A. Pocock, *The Machiavellian Moment: Florentine Political Thought and the Atlantic Republican Tradition* (Princeton, NJ: Princeton University Press, 1975). Bolingbroke, for example, held that "there is a law in behalf of the public, more sacred and more ancient too, for it is as ancient as political society . . . the law I mean is that which nature and reason dictate, and which declares the preservation of the commonwealth to be superior to all other laws." Jefferson's affirmation of this traditional view, in the passage cited above, was not without ambiguity. He was responding to his correspondent's query, which was "whether circumstances do not sometimes occur, which make it a duty in officers of high trust, to assume authorities beyond the law"—a question which Jefferson found "easy of solution in principle, but sometimes embarrassing in practice." The "solution" was relevant, in Jefferson's eyes, not only to the practice of constitutional government—and here his concession to reason of state is remarkable given his inveterate insistence on the need for constitutions to bind down those entrusted with power—but also to the conduct of war. When General Washington besieged Yorktown, Jefferson noted, "he leveled the suburbs, feeling that the laws of property must be postponed to the safety of the nation" (Thomas Jefferson to John B. Colvin, September 20, 1810, *Thomas Jefferson: Writings*, ed. Merrill Peterson [New York: Library of America, 1984], 1231). Jefferson's willingness, a few years later, to justify hiring incendiaries to put London to the torch, in retaliation for the burning of Washington DC, gives an idea of how far he was willing to proceed in this vein. His opinion then was that this would be a "justifiable" retaliation for an act that cast the British in their true light (and which made a revealing contrast with Bonaparte, who had not, for all his wickedness, destroyed any public treasures in the European capitals he had occupied). But though "we should now be justifiable in the conflagration of St. James and St. Paul's," in retaliation for "acts of barbarism which do not belong to a civilized age," the United States did not "carry it into execution . . . because we think it more moral and more honorable to set a good example, than follow a bad one" (TJ to Thomas Cooper, September 10, 1814; TJ to Samuel H. Smith, September 21, 1814, *The Writings of Thomas Jefferson*, ed. Andrew Lipscomb and Albert Bergh [Washington DC, 1904–1905], xiv, 186–187, 190).

7. Walzer, *Just and Unjust Wars*, 254.
8. Ibid.
9. Ibid.
10. Ibid., 262.
11. Ibid., 61–62.

12.   Ibid., 59.

13.   Ibid., 81.

14.   See Walzer, "The Politics of Rescue," *Dissent* (Winter 1995): 35–41; also available in his *Arguing About War* (New Haven, CT: Yale University Press, 2004).

15.   Robert G. Gilpin, "The Richness of the Tradition of Political Realism," in *Neorealism and Its Critics*, ed. Robert O. Keohane (New York: Columbia University Press, 1986), 305.

16.   Walzer, *Just and Unjust Wars*, 62.

17.   Ibid., 237.

18.   Ibid., 237–38.

19.   Ibid., 237.

20.   Ibid., 238.

21.   Ibid., 237n.

22.   Ibid., 174.

23.   Whether the risks to intervening forces can be minimized is an issue closely related to the likely conduct of the war, and the experience of the Gulf War raises a further issue in this regard. In his treatment of *jus in bello*, Walzer gives an account of why it is illegitimate to kill enemy civilians, and why legitimate to kill enemy soldiers. However persuasive his discussion is in the abstract, the experience of the war raises questions about its ethical relevance in circumstances where there exists a gross disproportion between the casualties suffered by the combatants. The battle deaths suffered by Iraqi forces have been revised sharply downward since the immediate aftermath of the war, from around 100,000 at the time to somewhere in the vicinity of 25,000. (Some observers put the figure even lower, at around 10,000, attributing the Pentagon's reluctance to move to a lower figure to its embarrassment at grossly overestimating the size of Iraqi divisions in Kuwait at the time of the U.S.–led ground offensive.) Whatever the precise figure, there can be no doubt that at the core of the American war plan was the intention to inflict enormous casualties, and to press the disparity between enemy deaths and our own to an extent virtually unprecedented in war. (The sorts of disparities that occurred in various colonial wars, where one side had got the maxim gun, and the other side had not, constitute something of a precedent for this, but on a lesser scale). Walzer draws attention to this disparity in his preface to the second edition of *Just and Unjust Wars* in his discussion of the aerial attacks on Iraqi columns heading out of Kuwait ("the road of death"), likening it to a "turkey shoot." The importance of that scene in leading American leaders to draw back from pressing the closing of the gate, through which Republican Guard forces escaped, testifies to the importance in war of limitations that spring from a natural revolt against radical disproportion or excess once "the culminating point of victory" has been reached. But there is also the question of whether the demands of *jus in bello*, or at least restraints imposed by the simple humanitarian consideration that those killed are fathers, husbands, and sons, arise before that point of natural revolt, and require among those possessing technological dominance that due care be exercised to avoid such radical disproportion. Hostile critics will understand this requirement as a wish for greater American casualties. It is nothing of the kind. It is simply to affirm that elementary considerations of proportionality remain of crucial relevance in the determination of what constitutes legitimate means in war.

24.   Walzer, *Just and Unjust Wars*, 107.

25.   Ibid., 72.

26.   Though Walzer assigns a "certain presumptive value" to existing boundaries, he acknowledges that "the boundaries that exist at any moment in time are likely to be arbitrary, poorly drawn, the products of ancient wars. The mapmakers are likely to have been ignorant,

drunken, or corrupt" (*Just and Unjust Wars*, 57). It is a peculiar feature of the legalist paradigm that it accords a near-absolute legitimacy to territorial possessions that were acquired illegitimately—a point to which the revisionist powers in the early twentieth century often drew attention. When Japan withdrew from the League of Nations after the league's condemnation of Japanese aggression in Manchuria, the Japanese delegate famously wondered when it was that the Western powers, having acquired their territories in a high-stakes poker game, had decided that the only legitimate game in international politics was contract bridge.

27.   Whether "the right is more precious than peace," or peace is more precious than right, is a hard question to which Walzer, appropriately, gives no dogmatic answer. It is a hard question, particularly for outsiders, because the debate over it always concerns not simply the immediate crisis but the lessons that future combatants will draw from the way it is resolved. Those who have claimed that the right is more precious than peace have also normally claimed that the failure to defend right will simply lead to wider war and will increase the general incidence of aggression in international society. "Pay now, or pay later (a much heavier price)" is their motto. Those who have claimed that peace is more precious than right doubt the deterrent effects of resisting aggression and think that wars more normally arise from local causes that are morally ambiguous than from the "demonstration effects" of crises half-way round the globe. They suspect that to act on the hypothesis of tumbling dominoes will mean unending war for the outsiders who reason in this fashion. The former group likens aggressive war to a prairie fire that will spread rapidly unless immediate action is taken; the latter group likens war to a forest fire that must burn itself out. (For these metaphors, see Frank Ninkovich, *Morality and Power: A History of the Domino Theory in the Twentieth Century* [Chicago: University of Chicago Press, 1994]). The former group tends to analogize war, even civil war, to large-scale aggressive war; the latter group tends to analogize war, even large-scale aggressive war, to civil war. The critique in the above paragraph rests partly upon the persuasiveness of the latter group's reasoning, but the issue, clearly, is a matter of informed speculation rather than scientific proof. "Experience," undoubtedly, "must be our only guide." But Clio's expression is enigmatic.

28.   Walzer, *Just and Unjust Wars*, 62.

29.   Ibid., 79.

30.   Ibid., 78.

31.   Ibid., 81.

32.   Walzer's discussion of this point at the symposium was restricted to one case— Libya—which does not involve nuclear weapons. We have no desire to impute to him a position he does not hold, but think the issue sufficiently important to justify an airing.

33.   This is a feature of realism that is insufficiently appreciated in the critical characterizations of it, but which is particularly marked among diplomatic historians with an affinity for realist premises. It may be objected that such a disposition makes realists insensitive to the moral drama of history; but that failing, if it is one, has the advantage, at least, of allowing a more sympathetic consideration of the motives of historical actors. Realists are suspicious of making everything a matter of moral judgment for the same reason that historians have often shied away from making grand moral judgments of the historical scene and actors they seek to illuminate. Both suspect that this procedure will erect a barrier to understanding. And they think that the road to folly is paved with misunderstood intentions.

34.   Walzer, "The Moral Standing of States: A Response to Four Critics," *Philosophy & Public Affairs* 9, no. 3, (1980): 215.

35.   Walzer, *Just and Unjust Wars*, 87.

36.   For an instructive account of what may be termed the "natural history" of humanitarian intervention, see Clifford Orwin, "Distant Compassion," *National Interest* 43 (Spring 1996): 42–49.

37.   Walzer, *Just and Unjust Wars*, 108.

38.   Ibid., 90.

39.   Ibid., 93.

40.   Federalist No. 9 (Hamilton), *The Federalist Papers*, ed. Clinton Rossiter (New York: New American Library, 1961), 73.

41.   Ibid., 90.

42.   Ibid.

43.   Walzer, "The Reform of the International System," in *Studies of War and Peace*, ed. Øyvind Østerud (Oslo: Norwegian University Press, 1986).

44.   On the circumstances that led to the Palestinian diaspora and the recognition by Israeli leaders that the coherence and viability of Israel depended on a Jewish majority, see Benny Morris, *The Birth of the Palestinian Refugee Problem, 1947–1949* (Cambridge: Cambridge University Press, 1989).

45.   Walzer, *Just and Unjust Wars*, 95.

46.   Ibid., 97.

47.   Ibid., 121.

48.   Ibid., 120.

49.   Ibid., 121.

50.   Robert W. Tucker and David C. Hendrickson, *The Imperial Temptation: The New World Order and America's Purpose* (New York: Council on Foreign Relations, 1992).

Chapter 2

The Slippery Slope to Preventive War

Neta C. Crawford

THE BUSH ADMINISTRATION'S ARGUMENTS in favor of a preemptive doctrine rest on the view that warfare has been transformed. As Colin Powell argues, "It's a different world . . . it's a new kind of threat."[1] And in several important respects, war has changed along the lines the administration suggests, although that transformation has been underway for at least the last ten to fifteen years. Unconventional adversaries prepared to wage unconventional war can conceal their movements, weapons, and immediate intentions and conduct devastating surprise attacks.[2] Nuclear, chemical, and biological weapons, though not widely dispersed, are more readily available than they were in the recent past. And the everyday infrastructure of the United States can be turned against it as were the planes the terrorists hijacked on September 11, 2001. Further, the administration argues that we face enemies who "reject basic human values and hate the United States and everything for which it stands."[3] Although vulnerability could certainly be reduced in many ways, it is impossible to achieve complete invulnerability.

Such vulnerability and fear, the argument goes, mean the United States must take the offensive. Indeed, soon after the September 11, 2001, attacks, members of the Bush administration began equating self-defense with preemption:

> There is no question but that the United States of America has every right, as every country does, of self-defense, and the problem with terrorism is that there is no way to defend against the terrorists at every place and every time against every conceivable technique. Therefore, the only way to deal with the terrorist network is to take the battle to them. That is in fact what we're doing. That is in effect self-defense of a preemptive nature.[4]

The character of potential threats becomes extremely important in evaluating the legitimacy of the new preemption doctrine, and thus the assertion that the United States faces rogue enemies who oppose everything about the United States must be carefully evaluated. There is certainly robust evidence to believe that al-Qaeda members desire to harm the United States and American citizens. The 2002 National Security Strategy makes a questionable leap, however, when it assumes that "rogue states" also desire to harm the United States and pose an imminent military threat. Further, the administration blurs the distinction between "rogue states" and terrorists, essentially erasing the difference between terrorists and those states in which they reside: "We make no distinction between terrorists and those who knowingly harbor or provide aid to them."[5] But these distinctions do indeed make a difference.

Legitimate preemption could occur if four necessary conditions were met. First, the party contemplating preemption would have a narrow conception of the "self" to be defended in circumstances of self-defense. Preemption is not justified to protect imperial interests or assets taken in a war of aggression. Second, there would have to be strong evidence that war was inevitable and likely in the immediate future. Immediate threats are those which can be made manifest within days or weeks unless action is taken to thwart them. This requires clear intelligence showing that a potential aggressor has both the capability and the intention to do harm in the near future. Capability alone is not a justification. Third, preemption should be likely to succeed in reducing the threat. Specifically, there should be a high likelihood that the source of the military threat can be found and the damage that it was about to do can be greatly reduced or eliminated by a preemptive attack. If preemption is likely to fail, it should not be undertaken. Fourth, military force must be necessary; no other measures can have time to work or be likely to work.

A DEFENSIBLE SELF

On the face of it, the self-defense criteria seem clear. When our lives are threatened, we must be able to defend ourselves using force if necessary. But self-defense may have another meaning, that in which our "self" is expressed not only by mere existence, but also by a free and prosperous life. For example, even if a tyrant would allow us to live, but not under institutions of our own choosing, we may justly fight to free ourselves from political oppression. But how far do the rights of the self extend? If someone threatens our access to food, or fuel, or shelter, can we legitimately use force? Or if they allow us access to the material goods necessary for our existence, but charge such a high price that we must make a terrible choice between food and health care, or between mere existence and growth, are we justified in using force to secure access to a good that would enhance the self? When economic interests and vulnerabilities are understood to be global, and when the moral and political community of democracy and human rights are defined more broadly than ever before, the self-conception of great powers tends to enlarge. But a broad conception of self is not necessarily legitimate and neither are the values to be defended completely obvious.

For example, the U.S. definition of the self to be defended has become very broad. The administration, in its 2001 Quadrennial Defense Review, defines "enduring national interests" as including "contributing to economic well-being," which entails maintaining "vitality and productivity of the global economy" and "access to key markets and strategic resources." Further, the goal of U.S. strategy, according to this document, is to maintain "preeminence."[6] The National Security Strategy also fuses ambitious political and economic goals with security: "The U.S. national security strategy will be based on a distinctly American internationalism that reflects the fusion of our values and our national interests. The aim of this strategy is to help make the world not just safer but better." And "today the distinction between domestic and foreign affairs is diminishing."[7]

If the self is defined so broadly and threats to this greater "self" are met with military force, at what point does self-defense begin to look like aggression? As Richard Betts has argued, "When security is defined in terms broader than protecting the near-term integrity of national sovereignty and borders, the distinction between offense and defense blurs hopelessly. . . . Security can be as insatiable an appetite as acquisitiveness—there may never be enough buffers."[8] The large self-conception of the United States could lead to a tendency to intervene everywhere that this greater self might conceivably be at risk of, for example, losing access to markets. Thus, a conception of the self that justifies legitimate preemption in self-defense must be narrowly confined to immediate risks to life and health within borders or to the life and health of citizens abroad.

THRESHOLD AND CONDUCT OF JUSTIFIED PREEMPTION

The Bush administration is correct to emphasize the United States' vulnerability to terrorist attack. The administration also argues that the United States cannot wait for a smoking gun if it comes in the form of a mushroom cloud. There may be little or no evidence in advance of a terrorist attack using nuclear, chemical, or biological weapons. Yet, under this view, the requirement for evidence is reduced to a fear that the other has, or might someday acquire, the means for an assault. But the bar for preemption seems to be set too low in the Bush administration's National Security Strategy. How much and what kind of evidence is necessary to justify preemption? What is a credible fear that justifies preemption?

As Michael Walzer has argued persuasively in *Just and Unjust Wars*, simple fear cannot be the only criterion. Fear is omnipresent in the context of a terrorist campaign. And if fear was once clearly justified, when and how will we know that a threat has been significantly reduced or eliminated? The nature of fear may be that once a group has suffered a terrible surprise attack, a government and people will, justifiably, be vigilant. Indeed they may, out of fear, be aware of threats to the point of hypervigilance—seeing small threats as large, and squashing all potential threats with enormous brutality.

The threshold for credible fear is necessarily lower in the context of contemporary counterterrorism war, but the consequences of lowering the threshold may be increased instability and the premature use of force. If this is the case, if fear justifies assault, then the occasions for attack will potentially be limitless since, according to the Bush administration's own arguments, we cannot always know with certainty what the other side has, where it might be located, or when it might be used. If one attacks on the basis of fear, or suspicion that a potential adversary may someday have the intention and capacity to harm you, then the line between preemptive and preventive war has been crossed. Again, the problem is knowing the capabilities and intentions of potential adversaries.

There is thus a fine balance to be struck. The threshold of evidence and warning cannot be too low, where simple apprehension that a potential adversary might be out there somewhere and may be acquiring the means to do the United States harm triggers the offensive use of force. This is not preemption, but paranoid aggression. We must, as stressful as this is psychologically, accept some vulnerability and uncertainty. We must also avoid the tendency to exaggerate the threat and inadvertently to heighten our own fear. For example, although nuclear weapons are more widely available than in the past, as are delivery vehicles of medium and long range, these forces are not yet in the hands of dozens of terrorists. A policy that assumes such a dangerous world is, at this historical juncture, paranoid. We must, rather than assume this is the present case or will be in the future, work to make this outcome less likely.

On the other hand, the threshold of evidence and warning for justified fear cannot be so high that those who might be about to do harm get so advanced in their preparations that they cannot be stopped or the damage limited. What is required, assuming a substantial investment in intelligence gathering, assessment, and understanding of potential advisories, is a policy that both maximizes our understanding of the capabilities and intentions of potential adversaries and minimizes our physical vulnerability. While uncertainty about intentions, capabilities, and risk can never be eliminated, it can be reduced.

Fear of possible future attack is not enough to justify preemption. Rather, aggressive intent, coupled with a capacity and plans to do immediate harm, is the threshold that may trigger justified preemptive attacks. We may judge aggressive intent if the answer to these two questions is yes: First, have potential aggressors said they want to harm us in the near future or have they harmed us in the recent past? Second, are potential adversaries moving their forces into a position to do significant harm?

While it might be tempting to assume that secrecy on the part of a potential adversary is a sure sign of aggressive intentions, secrecy may simply be a desire to prepare a deterrent force. After all, potential adversaries may feel the need to look after their own defense against their neighbors or even the United States.

We cannot assume that all forces in the world are aimed offensively at the United States and that all want to broadcast their defensive preparations— especially if that means they might become the target of a preventive offensive strike by the United States.

The conduct of preemptive actions must be limited in purpose to reducing or eliminating the immediate threat. Preemptive strikes that go beyond this purpose will, reasonably, be considered aggression by the targets of such strikes. Those conducting preemptive strikes should also obey the *jus in bello* limits of just war theory, specifically avoiding injury to noncombatants and avoiding disproportionate damage. For example, in the case of the plans for the September 11, 2001, attacks, on these criteria—and assuming intelligence warning of preparations and clear evidence of aggressive intent—a justifiable preemptive action would have been the arrest of the hijackers of the four aircraft that were to be used as weapons. But, prior to the attacks, taking the war to Afghanistan to attack al-Qaeda camps or the Taliban could not have been justified preemption.

THE RISKS OF PREVENTIVE WAR

Foreign policies must not only be judged on grounds of legality and morality, but also on grounds of prudence. Preemption is only prudent if it is limited to clear and immediate dangers and if there are limits to its conduct— proportionality, discrimination, and limited aims. If preemption becomes a regular practice or if it becomes the cover for a preventive offensive war doctrine, the strategy then may become self-defeating as it increases instability and insecurity.

Specifically, a legitimate preemptive war requires that states identify that potential aggressors have both the capability and the intention of doing great harm to you in the immediate future. However, while capability may not be in dispute, the motives and intentions of a potential adversary may be misinterpreted. States may mobilize in what appear to be aggressive ways because they are fearful or because they are aggressive. A preemptive doctrine which has, because of great fear and a desire to control the international environment, become a preventive war doctrine of eliminating potential threats that may materialize at some point in the future is likely to create more of both fearful and aggressive states. Some states may defensively arm because they are afraid of the preemptive-preventive state; others may arm offensively because they resent the preventive war aggressor who may have killed many innocents in its quest for total security.

In either case, whether states and groups armed because they were afraid or because they have aggressive intentions, instability is likely to grow as a preventive war doctrine creates the mutual fear of surprise attack. In the case of the U.S. preemptive-preventive war doctrine, instability is likely to increase because the doctrine is coupled with the U.S. goal of maintaining global preeminence and a military force "beyond challenge."[9]

Further, a preventive offensive war doctrine undermines international law and diplomacy, both of which can be useful, even to hegemonic powers. Preventive war short-circuits nonmilitary means of solving problems. If all states reacted to potential adversaries as if they faced a clear and present danger of imminent attack, security would be destabilized as tensions escalated along already tense borders and regions. Article 51 of the UN Charter would lose much of its force. In sum, a preemptive-preventive doctrine moves us closer to a state of nature than a state of international law. Moreover, while preventive war doctrines assume that today's potential rival will become tomorrow's adversary, diplomacy or some other factor could work to change the relationship from antagonism to accommodation. As Otto von Bismarck said to Wilhelm I in 1875, "I would . . . never advise Your Majesty to declare war forthwith, simply because it appeared that our opponent would begin hostilities in the near future. One can never anticipate the ways of divine providence securely enough for that."[10]

One can understand why any administration would favor preemption and why some would be attracted to preventive wars if they think a preventive war could guarantee security from future attack. But the psychological reassurance promised by a preventive offensive war doctrine is at best illusory, and at worst, preventive war is a recipe for conflict. Preventive wars are imprudent because they bring wars that might not happen and increase resentment. They are also unjust because they assume perfect knowledge of an adversary's ill intentions when such a presumption of guilt may be premature or unwarranted. Preemption can be justified, on the other hand, if it is undertaken due to an immediate threat, where there is no time for diplomacy to be attempted, and where the action is limited to reducing that threat. There is a great temptation, however, to step over the line from preemptive to preventive war, because that line is vague and because the stress of living under the threat of war is great. But that temptation should be avoided, and the stress of living in fear should be assuaged by true prevention—arms control, disarmament, negotiations, confidence-building measures, and the development of international law.

NOTES

This essay first appeared in *Ethics & International Affairs* 17, no. 1 (2003): 30–36 as part of the roundtable, "Evaluating the Preemptive Use of Force," edited and introduced by Anthony F. Lang Jr. Also contributing to the roundtable were Chris Brown, Michael Byers, Richard K. Betts, and Thomas M. Nichols. The full set of roundtable essays can be accessed at www.cceia.org/resources/journal/17_1/index.html.

1.   Quoted in James Dao, "Powell Defends a First Strike as Iraq Option," *New York Times*, September 8, 2002.

2.   For more on the nature of this transformation, see Neta C. Crawford, "Just War Theory and the U.S. Counterterror War," *Perspectives on Politics* 1, no. 1 (2003): 5–25.

3.   George W. Bush, "National Security Strategy of the United States of America," September 17, 2002, 14, www.whitehouse.gov/nsc/nss.pdf.

4.   Donald H. Rumsfeld, "Remarks at Stakeout Outside ABC TV," October 28, 2001, www.defenselink.mil/transcripts/transcript.aspx?transcriptid = 2225.

5.   Bush, "National Security Strategy," 5.

6.   U.S. Department of Defense, "Quadrennial Defense Review" (Washington, DC: U.S. Government Printing Office, September 30, 2001), 2, 30, 62.

7.   Bush, "National Security Strategy," 1, 31.

8.   Richard K. Betts, *Surprise Attack: Lessons for Defense Planning* (Washington, DC: Brookings Institution Press, 1982), 14–43.

9.   U.S. Department of Defense, "Quadrennial Defense Review," 30, 62; and George W. Bush, "Graduatlon Speech at West Point," June 1, 2002, www.whitehouse.gov/news/releases/2002/06/20020601–3.html.

10.   Quoted in Gordon A. Craig, *The Politics of the Prussian Army, 1640–1945* (New York: Oxford University Press, 1955), 255.

Chapter 3

Reckoning with Past Wrongs

A Normative Framework

David A. Crocker

MANY NATIONS and some international bodies today are deciding what, if anything, they should do about past violations of internationally recognized human rights. These abuses—which include war crimes, crimes against humanity, genocide, rape, and torture—may have been committed by a government against its own citizens (or those of other countries), by its opponents, or by combatants in a civil or international armed conflict.[1] Some of these societies are making a transition to democracy and some are not.

The challenge of "transitional justice," a term increasingly used, is how an incomplete and fledgling democracy, such as South Africa, Guatemala, South Korea, the Philippines, Argentina, Chile, or El Salvador, should respond (or should have responded) to past evils without undermining its new democratic regime or jeopardizing its prospects for equitable and long-term development. This focus on new democracies has much to recommend it, for it is important that new democratic institutions, where they exist, be protected and consolidated, and that reckoning with an evil past not imperil them.

However, nations other than new democracies also have occasion to decide what they "should do about a difficult past,"[2] and their choices are of intrinsic moral significance as well as relevant for new democracies. These countries, none of which are (now) making a transition to democracy, can be roughly divided into three types: post-conflict societies, such as Bosnia, Cambodia, and Rwanda, that aspire to make a democratic transition but are at present taken up with ongoing security issues following ethnic strife and massacres; authoritarian and conflict-ridden societies, such as Yugoslavia, Indonesia, and Peru, in which both an end to civil conflict and the beginning of democratization may depend on negotiated agreements between the government and its opposition with respect to treatment of human rights violators; and mature democracies, such as the United States, Germany, Japan, France, and Switzerland, that are reckoning with past evils, for example, slavery, war crimes, collaboration with the Nazi extermination efforts, or failures to prevent human rights abuses in their own or other countries.[3] The fashionable focus on new democracies tends to limit what such societies may learn from other attempts to reckon with past rights abuses and to diminish the moral challenge facing nondemocratic and mature democracies as *they* reckon with an unsavory past.

Even in the context of societies making a democratic transition, the term *transitional justice* may be misleading. This is because, like the term *accountability*, transitional justice singles out one morally urgent feature from a complex that has many pressing goals or obligations.

MEANS AND ENDS

Societies and international bodies have employed many means in reckoning with human rights abuses that a prior regime or its opponents have committed. Many discussions assume that there are only two possible responses: trials and punishment, or forgetting the past. For example, upon coming out of hiding and surrendering to the Cambodian government in late December 1998, Khieu Samphan, a former top leader of the Khmer Rouge, urged Cambodians to "let bygones be bygones." During its control of Cambodia from 1975 to 1979, the Khmer Rouge is estimated to have killed between 1.5 and 1.7 million people, including most of the educated class, and to have destroyed much of Cambodian culture. Although he was to backtrack a few days later, Cambodian Prime Minister Hun Sen initially agreed with Khieu Samphan and remarked that Khieu Samphan and another high-placed defector, Nuon Chea, should be welcomed back "with bouquets of flowers, not with prisons and handcuffs" and that "we should dig a hole and bury the past and look ahead to the 21st century with a clean slate."[4]

When trials are judged as impractical and forgetting as undesirable, truth commissions have been advocated (and in some twenty countries employed) as a third way. However, in addition to these three tools there are a variety of other measures, such as international (ad hoc or permanent) criminal tribunals; social shaming and banning of perpetrators from public office ("lustration"[5]); public access to police records; public apology or memorials to victims; reburial of victims; compensation to victims or their families; literary and historical writing; and blanket or individualized amnesty (legal immunity from prosecution).

To decide among the diverse tools, as well as to fashion, combine, and sequence them, a society, sometimes in cooperation with international institutions, ideally should (1) consider what lessons it might learn from other societies, (2) examine its own capabilities and limitations, and (3) set clear objectives for its efforts. The first task is best accomplished by those who will be key actors in their nation's attempts to reckon with an evil past. The second responsibility most obviously falls on historians, social scientists, and legal scholars who are adept at identifying a society's distinctive historical legacies, institutional strengths and weaknesses, and political constraints. The last task, that of identifying goals and standards of evaluation, must be taken up by philosophers and applied ethicists, but not by these alone; citizens, political leaders, policy analysts, and social scientists also have a responsibility to make moral judgments, engage in ethical analysis, and set forth ethically based recommendations.

Although philosophers and other ethicists have not entirely ignored the topic of reckoning with past wrongs, it is legal scholars, social scientists, policy analysts, and activists who have made the most helpful contributions. It is understandable that much of the work on transitional justice has been of an empirical and strategic nature. Fledgling democracies need effective institutions and strategies for addressing prior human rights violations; establishing such arrangements and policies requires a grasp of what works and why. Legal and human rights scholars have focused on what national and international law permits and requires with respect to prosecuting gross human rights violations.[6] They have also reported and assessed the progress of the Bosnian and Rwandan international criminal tribunals, crafted the terms of an agreement on a permanent international criminal tribunal, and argued for the implementation of that agreement.[7] Investigative reporters have described what particular countries and the international community have done and failed to do in their efforts to reckon with past human rights abuses.[8] Principal actors or advisers have written about their experiences and assessed their achievements.[9] Historians and social scientists have addressed the issue of why certain countries decided on particular approaches and the motivations for and consequences of those choices.[10]

However, there are also large and pressing ethical questions. How should "success" with respect to reckoning with past wrongs be conceived? Are the ends that societies seek to achieve and the means they adopt to achieve them consistent and morally justified? Questions such as these should not be overlooked or swamped by legal or strategic considerations.

To be sure, moral concerns are often *implicit* in the existing work on transitional justice, and moral norms of various kinds underlie the institutions and policies that societies already have established to reckon with an evil past. Indeed, one task of ethical analysis with respect to past human rights abuses is to identify and clarify those operative values for which reasonable justification can be given. Michael Walzer's attempt to fashion a new moral theory (with historical illustrations) concerning just and unjust wars between nations can be adapted to the forging of a normative framework to assess what should be done when a society reckons with human rights violations.[11]

When political actors or scholars do explicitly pose ethical questions with respect to addressing past wrongs, they usually do so in relation to only one goal, such as penal justice, truth, or reconciliation, or one tool, such as trials, truth commissions, or amnesties.[12] However, the full range of conceptual and moral issues underlying the many ends and means of transitional justice has not received the sustained analysis it deserves.[13]

CROSS-CULTURAL GOALS

To fashion and evaluate any particular tool to reckon with past evil in a particular society and to combine it with other tools requires not only knowledge of that society's historical legacies and current capabilities but also a grasp of morally important goals and standards of assessment. What goals and norms should be used, where should they come from, and how might they be promoted? In recent writings,[14] I have formulated eight goals that have emerged from worldwide moral deliberation on transitional justice and may serve as a useful framework when particular societies deliberate about what they are trying to achieve and how they should go about doing so.

In the present essay I employ these eight goals to identify and clarify the variety of ethical *issues* that emerge in reckoning with past wrongs, widespread *agreements* about resolving each issue, leading *options* for more robust solutions of each issue, and ways to weigh or *trade-off* the norms when they conflict. My aim is both to show that there are crucial moral aspects in reckoning with the past and to clarify, criticize, revise, apply, and diffuse eight moral norms. The goals that I propose are not a recipe or "one-size-fits-all" blueprint but rather a framework for exploration by which societies confronting past atrocities can decide—through cross-cultural and critical dialogue—their most important goals with respect to the past and the morally best ways to achieve them.

Before setting forth morally urgent ends, two opposing (but dialectically related) goals should be ruled out: vengeance, and disregarding the past in favor of the future. I will not repeat my arguments set forth elsewhere that countries should reject these goals.[15] Two remarks about both goals and a new example about implementing them, however, are in order. First, various tools may be employed to realize each of these morally undesirable ends. Vengeance can be carried out privately (by individuals or groups) or officially (in reprisals and kangaroo courts). A nation can overcome an evil past and attempt to move to a better future by forgiving and forgetting (letting bygones be bygones), outright denial (for instance, that the Holocaust occurred), or rationalization of the past as a necessary evil. Second, attempts to realize each of these goals often lead—either precipitously or eventually—to efforts to achieve the other: the side that has wreaked revenge often attempts to protect itself from counter-revenge by calling for "forgive and forget"; silence about the past may incite revenge for both the original act and its burial.

Both tendencies are illustrated by the case of the thousands of atrocities committed by Croat Nazis (Ustashi) against Serbs, Jews, and Gypsies during World War II, especially in the Jasenovac concentration camp. There is good reason to believe that the breakup of Yugoslavia and the Serb violation of Croat rights during the war between Croatia and Serbia in 1991–92 can be partially explained (not justified) by the genocidal practices of the Croats during World War II and by the failure of postwar Croats and the Tito government to hold either investigations or trials. Serbian philosopher Svetozar Stojanovic observes:

> The communist victor [Tito] in Yugoslavia never seriously looked into Ustashi genocide as an issue or a problem. Instead of carrying out denazification through education . . . he limited himself to the liquidation of captured Ustashis. It is true that Pavelic and the other main criminals had, however, fled abroad, and the new authorities did not endeavor to organize their trial (at least in absentia) like the one in Nürnberg, although they more than deserved it. The karst pits into which Serbs were thrown alive by Ustashis in Herzegovina remained concreted over, and their relatives were not allowed to remove the bodies and bury them. These "concreted pits" have become a metaphor for the communist illusion that enforced silence is the best way to deal with terrible crimes among nations. Perhaps that was why, not only due to his personal nonchalance, Tito never visited Jasenovac.[16]

Truth

To meet the challenge of reckoning with past atrocities, a society should investigate, establish, and publicly disseminate the truth about them. South Africa's Truth and Reconciliation Commission distinguished forensic from emotional and interpretative truth.[17] Forensic truth is information about whose moral and legal rights were violated, by whom, how, when, and where. Given the moral significance of individual accountability, the identity of individual perpetrators, on the one hand, and of moral heroes who sacrificed personal safety to prevent violations, on the other, should be brought to light.

There is also what has been called "emotional truth"—knowledge concerning the psychological and physical impact on victims and their loved ones from rights abuses and the threat of such abuses. The constant threat of such abuses, especially in contexts of physical deprivation, can itself cause overwhelming fear and, thereby, constitute a rights violation. David Rohde makes this point clearly in his agonizing account of the aftermath of the takeover of Muslim Srebrenica by General Ratko Mladic and his Bosnian Serb forces:

> During the trek [the "Marathon of Death" in which thousands of male Bosnian noncombatants and a few soldiers fled Srebrenica], it quickly became clear that the threat to the column was as much psychological as it was physical. Shells abruptly whizzed overhead. Gunfire erupted with no warning. Corpses littered their route. A Serb mortar had landed ahead of them at 1 pm and killed five men. A human stomach and intestines lay across the green grass just below the intact head and torso of a man in his twenties. Mevludin [Oric, a Bosnian Muslim soldier] had seen such things

before; the others hadn't. The image would slowly eat at their minds. Some men were already saying it was hopeless. It was better to kill your-self, they said, than be captured by the Serbs.[18]

Fear also had devastating consequences for the Muslim women and children, herded together in Srebrenica, whose husbands and fathers were taken away and tortured during the night of July 12, 1995:

> She [Srebrenica resident Camila Omanovic] could see what was happen-ing around her, but it was the sounds that haunted her. Screams suddenly filled the night. At one point, she heard bloodcurdling cries coming from the hills near the base. She later decided the Serbs must be playing record-ings to terrorize them. Women gave birth or cried as their husbands were taken away. Men wailed and called out women's names. . . . Panic would grip the crowd. People would suddenly rise up and rush off in one direc-tion. Then there would be silence until the cycle of screams and panic started all over again. Nearly hallucinating, Camila could not sleep. . . . But it was the fear that didn't let her sleep. A fear more intense than anything she had ever felt. A fear that changed her forever.[19]

Finally, there is less individualized and more general truth, such as plausible interpretations of what caused neighbors to brutalize neighbors, governments (and their opponents) to incite, execute, or permit atrocities, and other coun-tries or international bodies to fail to act in time or in the right way.[20]

Knowledge about the past is important in itself. One way to make this point is to say that victims and their descendants have a moral right to know the truth about human rights abuses. Moreover, without reasonably complete truth, none of the other goals of transitional justice (to be discussed presently) are likely to be realized. Appropriate sanctions are impossible without reasonable certainty about the identity of perpetrators and the nature of their involvement. Public acknowledgment must refer to specific occurrences, while reparations presup-pose the accurate identification of victims and the kinds of harm they suffered. If reconciliation in any of its several senses is to take place, there must be some agreement about what happened and why. Former enemies are unlikely to be reconciled if what count as lies for one side are verities for the other.

Yet truth, while important, sometimes must be traded off against other goods. Since the truth can harm people as well as benefit them, sometimes it is better that some facts about the past remain unknown. By deepening ethnic hostility, too much or the wrong kind of truth might impede democratization and reconciliation. Disclosures that satisfy a victim's need to know may incite violence when publicly revealed. The most effective methods for obtaining the truth might violate the rule of law, personal privacy, or the right not to incrimi-nate oneself. Or such methods might be too costly in relation to other goals.

Some truths about the past would be irrelevant to reckoning with past injustices. The general point is that apparently justified efforts in limiting the pursuit or the disclosure of truth imply the need to balance truth against other goals.

Even given that truth is one important good that can be traded off in relation to other goods, many issues remain to be resolved. First, can one plausibly argue that there is one truth about the past and, if so, how should we understand this ideal in relation to the frequently diverse views about the content of this truth? How should a truth commission address diverse interpretations of the past when they emerge in the commission's work or in public reaction to it? My own view is that disagreements should be reduced as much as possible and those that remain should be clearly identified as topics for further public deliberation.[21] Second, to whom and at what cost should the truth be made known? Third, how should we assess truth commissions and other investigative bodies, investigative reporting and historical writing, national trials, international criminal tribunals, and the granting of public access to police files? Given their different standards of evidence and proof, how much and what sort of truth can be reasonably expected from each of these approaches? What are the merits of each method both in reducing disagreement and accommodating or respecting remaining differences? To what extent, if any, might a truth commission impede rather than promote international and domestic judicial determination of individual guilt and innocence? What ethical issues emerge from the various methods of collecting and interpreting information about past abuses?[22]

My general belief, which I cannot develop or defend here, is that there are many different but complementary ways of obtaining reasonable knowledge about the past and that no one means should be overemphasized. Trials, for example, owing to subpoena power and adversarial cross-examination, are usually superior to truth commissions in establishing truths relevant to the guilt or innocence of particular individuals; truth commissions tend to be better than trials in describing the larger institutional patterns contributing to rights violations; historical investigations—often with the advantage of fuller documentation, more ample opportunities to check sources, and greater hindsight than is possible in either trials or truth commissions—are best at sifting evidence and evaluating explanatory hypotheses. Not only can these tools complement each other, but each one can make use of others. Truth commissions often make recommendations to legal proceedings. Historians provide expert testimony in trials and sometimes are members of truth commissions. Investigative reporters and forensic experts have been enormously important in uncovering atrocities and dispelling rumors and false propaganda.[23]

Public Platform for Victims

In any society attempting to reckon with an evil past, victims or their families should be provided with a platform to tell their stories and have their testimony publicly acknowledged. When victims are able to give their accounts and when they receive sympathy for their suffering, they are respected as persons with dignity rather than—as before—treated with contempt. This respect enables those once humiliated as victims to become empowered as citizens. Those once reduced to screams or paralyzing fear now may share a personal narrative. The public character of the platform is essential, for secrecy about human rights abuses, enforced through violence and intimidation, was one of the conditions that made possible extensive campaigns of terror.

Among the unresolved questions that remain is the weight to be given to this goal when the public character of testimony would put former victims, perpetrators, or reporters at substantial risk. After disclosing to the press that the Argentine military did indeed kill some suspected "subversives" and their children by pushing them from airplanes into the sea, a military officer was brutally attacked and his face carved with the initials of the reporters to whom he revealed the truth. Another problem surfaces when a victim's public testimony is not followed up by efforts to heal wounds and compensate for harms.[24] Finally, unless there is independent investigation or cross-examination of accusers, alleged perpetrators may be treated unfairly and due process compromised.

Accountability and Punishment

Ethically defensible treatment of past wrongs requires that those individuals and groups responsible for past crimes be held accountable and receive appropriate sanctions or punishment. Punishment may range from the death penalty, imprisonment, fines, international travel restrictions, and the payment of compensation to economic sanctions on an entire society and public shaming of individuals and prohibitions on their holding public office.

Many questions about responsibility and punishment remain to be answered. How, for example, can accountability be explained and fairly assigned? How should we understand the degrees and kinds of responsibility with respect to the authorization, planning, "middle management," execution, provision of material support for, and concealment of atrocities? Consider also journalist Bill Berkeley's observation about a Hutu *bourgmestre* found guilty (by the International Tribunal for Rwanda) of "nine counts of genocide, crimes against humanity, and war crimes, including rape":

> Jean-Paul Akayesu was neither a psychopath nor a simpleton. He was not a top figure like the former defense minister, Theonoste Bagasora, Rwanda's Himmler, who is now in custody [of the International Tribunal for Rwanda] in Arusha, nor a lowly, illiterate, machete-wielding peasant. He was, instead, the link between the two: an archetype of the indispensable middle management of genocide. He personified a rigidly hierarchical society and culture of obedience, without which killing on such a scale would not have been possible.[25]

Should those who actually commit (minor) abuses be ignored or pardoned in favor of holding their superiors accountable, or should the moral guilt and cumulative impact of those who "merely" followed orders also be recognized? What is needed is a theory—relevant to judging past rights abusers—that identifies those conditions that make an agent more or less blameworthy (and praiseworthy). Recent work suggests that a perpetrator's moral guilt is proportional to what he knew (or could reasonably know) and when he knew it; how much freedom (from coercion) or power (in a chain of command) he had to commit or prevent evil; and what personal risks he ran in performing or forgoing a rights violation.

For which crimes should people be held accountable when a country or the international community is reckoning with past evil?[26] Is it morally justifiable to hold people accountable either for an act that was not illegal at the time it was committed or for one that a government subsequently pardons?[27] Further, an ethics of reckoning with past wrongs would address violations such as war crimes, crimes against humanity, genocide, torture, and rape. This list implies both that Chile erred in restricting its official truth commission to investigating only killings and disappearances and that the International Criminal Tribunal for the Former Yugoslavia achieved moral progress when it convicted persons of rape in the wars in Croatia and Bosnia.

Should the list of human rights violations be extended further than "physical security rights"? Should it include civil and political rights, such as the right of free speech and the rights not to be discriminated against on the basis of race, ethnicity, religion, or gender, and economic rights, such as the right not to be hungry or the right to employment? I return to this issue when I address what long-term economic and political development should aim for so as to protect against a recurrence of past atrocities.

Two additional questions with respect to accountability must be addressed. How should "sins of commission" be morally compared to "sins of omission"? How does the United Nations' failure to bomb the Serbs attacking Srebrenica in July 1995 compare with the atrocities committed by the Serbian forces? To what extent are *groups*—particular police units, political parties, religious bodies, professional associations (e.g., of doctors or lawyers), independence movements (e.g., the Kosovo Liberation Army), governments, and alliances (e.g., the UN, NATO)—and not solely individuals responsible for rights violations?[28] Without a suitably nuanced and graded view of accountability or responsibility, a society falls into the morally objectionable options of, on the one hand, whitewash or social amnesia[29] or, on the other hand, the demonization of all members of an accused group.

Similar questions may be asked with respect to sanctions, whether criminal (punishment), civil, or nonlegal (social shaming, individual lustration, or economic sanctions on an entire society). What types of sanctions are appropriate for what violations, and on what bases? Can justice be achieved through social shaming and moral censure rather than imprisonment? If trials and legal punishments are to be pursued, what purposes can or should they serve? Should a theory of criminal punishment include a retributive element and, if so, how should it be understood, and can retribution be distinguished from revenge?

Legal philosophers and scholars who have addressed reckoning with past political wrongs, such as Carlos Nino and Jaime Malamud-Goti, have tended to reject retributivism in favor of a deterrence or rehabilitation approach.[30] Retributivism, however, is having something of a revival, and I believe that it captures some important intuitions about penal justice. One task facing ethicists is to consider which retributive theory is best in itself and in reckoning with past atrocities. This inquiry would also consider whether the most reasonable approach to punishment would be a "mixed theory" in which a retributive principle, however understood, is coupled with other justifications or functions of punishment, such as protection, deterrence, rehabilitation, and moral education.[31]

Rule of Law

As they reckon with past wrongs, democracies—whether new or mature— should comply with the rule of law, and societies (or their democratic oppositions) that aspire to become democratic should lay the groundwork now for eventual rule of law. The rule of law is a critical part of Nuremberg's complex legacy and is important for any society dealing with an evil past. I here follow David Luban's analysis of rule of law, which itself draws on Lon Fuller.[32]

The rule of law includes respect for due process, in the sense of procedural fairness, publicity, and impartiality. Like cases must be treated alike, and private revenge must be prohibited. Rule of law is especially important in a new and fragile democracy bent on distinguishing itself from prior authoritarianism, institutionalized bias, or the "rule of the gun."

Again, however, there is an ongoing debate on what rule of law should mean and how it should be valued in relation to other goals. Can "victor's justice" be avoided and legal standards applied impartially to both sides in a former conflict? If so, at what cost? Can those suspected of rights abuses justifiably be convicted when their acts—even though prohibited by international law—were permitted by local law, covered by amnesty laws, or performed in obedience to higher orders? In what way, if any, does the ideal of procedural fairness apply to truth commissions, when alleged perpetrators have no right to cross-examine their accusers? (In South Africa, for example, an investigative arm of the TRC determined the reliability of all testimony—whether by victims, alleged perpetrators, or those seeking amnesty.) What if violations of due process result in fuller disclosures or more accurate assignment of responsibility?

Some advocates of due process, skeptical that victor's justice can be avoided, contend that the only ethically justified way to reckon with past political wrongs is to bury the past and move on to a better future.[33] But rule of law, like other ideals, is capable of more or less institutional embodiment. Safeguards fairly protecting both defendants and victims have been developed in local and national jurisdictions and in jurisdictional decisions. Upon learning that one British Law Lord had failed to disclose a relationship to the human rights group Amnesty International, the British Law Lords set aside their initial decision to permit Pinochet's extradition to Spain to stand trial on charges of genocide and other rights abuses. The Pinochet case also shows the lack of both international and Chilean consensus on the issue of when, if ever, a court in one country has the moral or legal right to prosecute alleged human rights violators who are citizens or (former) leaders of other countries. Apart from the question of its impact on Chile's development achievements, international and Chilean opinion is divided about whether Chile's sovereignty would be violated if Pinochet were brought to justice in a foreign country.[34] This question cannot be answered merely by appealing to international law and therefore requires moral reflection, for international law points in different directions and is itself evolving in relation to the Pinochet case.

The International Criminal Tribunals for both Rwanda and the former Yugoslavia have slowly developed and improved the fairness of their procedures. An enormous challenge in implementing the plan for a permanent international criminal court will be to devise fair procedures, including procedures for determining whether international or national courts have jurisdiction.

Compensation to Victims

Compensation, restitution, or reparation, in the form of income, property, medical services, or educational and other opportunities, should be paid to individuals and groups whose rights have been violated. One way of reckoning with past wrongs is by "righting" them—by restoring victims to something approaching their status quo ante.

But if compensation is pursued, pressing questions abound. Who should provide the compensation? Is it fair to use general taxes, when arguably many citizens were not responsible for violations? Or does mere citizenship in a nation that violated rights imply liability? Do German (and U.S.) corporations that used slave labor during World War II owe compensation to the victims or their survivors? What moral obligations, if any, do foreign governments and international civil society have in making reparations to victims of rights abuses? Might requiring guilty perpetrators to provide reparations to their victims be a means for punishing perpetrators or promoting reconciliation between violator and victim?

What form should reparation take and how should compensatory amounts be decided? Is compensation more justified in the form of cash, giving the victim the freedom to decide on its use, or as goods and services related to basic needs? Should compensation be the same for all, even though victims suffered in different degrees and ways, have different numbers of dependents, and have differential access to services depending on where they live? Given the other goals of reckoning with past wrongs, what portion of public resources should be devoted to compensatory justice? What should be done about those victims (or their descendants) the nature or extent of whose injuries—whether physical or psychological—does not become apparent until years after their rights have been violated?

Should groups—for instance, specific Mayan villages in Guatemala or Muslim villages in Bosnia's Drina Valley—as well as individuals be recipients? Is South Africa justified in considering public memorials, such as museums and monuments or days of remembrance, "symbolic compensation" for damage done to the entire South African society?[35]

Recent events suggest that nations and the international community are beginning to answer these questions. Following Chile's example, South Africa is implementing a nuanced "reparation and rehabilitation policy" that defends reparation on both moral ("restoration of dignity") and legal grounds and provides several types of both individual and communal reparation. Individuals are compensated both through monetary packages that take into account severity of harm, number of dependents, and access to social services and through services such as reburials and providing of headstones.

There is widespread approval of recent agreements to compensate Holocaust victims and those who worked as slave laborers for German companies during World War II. Early in January 1999, two Swiss banks—but not the Swiss government—signed an agreement for $1.25 billion in payments to resolve all class action suits and individual claims against the banks. (To be sure, some Swiss claim that they are being unfairly singled out.) The fund will compensate Holocaust victims for a variety of harms, including the loss of bank deposits and insurance policies and the looting of assets by the Nazis.[36] Similarly, the German government has agreed to set up a "compensation fund" (the Remembrance, Responsibility and the Future fund) of $1.7 billion, to be financed by German banks and other corporations (and perhaps by the government), to compensate Holocaust survivors for the companies' role in stealing assets, financing the building of the Auschwitz concentration camp, or making use of slave labor.[37] While these agreements are also prudent ways for the banks and companies to terminate the legal claims against them, the basic principle of the agreements reflects considered judgments about compensatory justice. As German Chancellor Gerhard Schröder remarked, the fund is to fulfill "the moral responsibility of German firms with regard to such issues as forced laborers, Aryanization and other injustice during the Nazi regime." These cases illustrate "the quest," as journalist Roger Cohen puts it, "to find a balance between remembrance and forward-looking themes."[38]

Institutional Reform and Long-Term Development
An emerging democracy fails to make a sustainable transition unless it identifies the causes of past abuses and takes steps to reform the law and basic institutions—government, economic life, and civil society—in order to reduce the

possibility that such violations will be repeated. More generally, reckoning with past political wrongs requires that societies be oriented to the future as well as to the past and present; they must take steps to remedy what caused human rights violations and protect against their recurrence. Basic institutions include the judiciary, police, military, land tenure system, tax system, and the structure of economic opportunities. One temptation in postconflict or postauthoritarian societies is to permit euphoria—which comes with the cessation of hostilities and the launching of a new democracy—to preempt the hard work needed to remove the fundamental causes of injustice and guard against their repetition.

In both Guatemala and South Africa, for example, among the fundamental causes of repression and human rights abuses were racism and deep disparities in economic and political power. A society, whether it already is or whether it aspires to be democratic, must try to remove such fundamental causes of human rights abuses, and to do so in a way that will consolidate its democracy and promote equitable development in the future.

Questions remain, however, with respect to how democratic consolidation and economic development should be conceived. Are free and fair elections sufficient (or necessary) for the former?[39] Are increasing rates of per capita GNP necessary or sufficient for the latter? What should be the fundamental goals of economic and social development?[40] How might past injustices be addressed such that democratic and just development may be promoted and protected? What role, for example, might compensatory transfers to victims play in increasing social equity? When reckoning with *past* injustices does not coincide with or contribute to ameliorating present ones, how much should be spent on the former at the expense of the latter? Development ethicists should join scholars of transitional justice to explore the links between addressing past wrongs and advancing future rights.

Reconciliation

A society (or an international community) seeking to surmount its conflictual or repressive past should aim to reconcile former enemies. There are, however, at least three meanings of reconciliation, ranging from "thinner" to "thicker" conceptions. In the most minimal account, which almost everyone agrees is at least part of what should be meant by the term, reconciliation is nothing more than "simple coexistence,"[41] in the sense that former enemies comply with the law instead of killing each other. Although this modus vivendi is certainly better than violent conflict, transitional societies can and arguably should aim for more: while former enemies may continue to disagree and even to be adversaries, they must not only live together nonviolently but also respect each other as fellow citizens. Mark J. Osiel calls this kind of reconciliation "liberal social solidarity,"[42] while Amy Gutmann and Dennis Thompson term it "democratic reciprocity."[43] Among other things, this implies a willingness to hear each other out, to enter into a give-and-take about matters of public policy, to build on areas of common concern, and to forge principled compromises with which all can live. The process of reconciliation, so conceived, may help prevent a society from lapsing back into violence as a way to resolve conflict.

More robust conceptions of reconciliation have sometimes been attributed to the truth commissions of Chile and South Africa—reconciliation as forgiveness, mercy (rather than justice), a shared comprehensive vision, mutual healing, or harmony.[44] (Both of these commissions include the word "reconciliation" in their name.) Given the depth of hostility between past opponents and objections to coercing mutuality or contrition, these thicker conceptions of reconciliation are more difficult to defend than the thinner notions. An essential task of the ethics of transitional justice is to consider the advantages and disadvantages of going beyond the first or second conceptions of reconciliation to some version of the third notion.[45]

Public Deliberation

Any society reckoning with past atrocities should aim, I believe, to include public spaces, debate, and deliberation in its goals, institutions, and strategies. It is unlikely that in any given society there will be full agreement about the aims and means for dealing with past abuses. And, even if there were agreement, trade-offs would have to be made. All good things do not always go together; sometimes achieving or even approximating one end will come at the expense of (fully) achieving another. Legal sanctions against former human rights violators can imperil a potential or fragile democracy in which the military responsible for the earlier abuses still wields social and political power. In order to protect witnesses or secure testimony from alleged perpetrators, a truth commission's interrogation of witnesses or alleged perpetrators sometimes may have to take place behind closed doors. Testimony by victims and confessions by perpetrators may worsen relations among former enemies, at least in the short run.[46] What is spent on a truth commission or on high-profile trials and punishments will not be available to eradicate infrastructural causes (and effects) of rights violations. A truth commission's exchange of truth for amnesty may preclude achieving penal justice.

What can be aspired to, especially but not exclusively in a new democracy, is that disagreements about ends, trade-offs, and means will be reduced if not eliminated through public deliberation—both national and international—that permits a fair hearing for all and promotes both morally acceptable compromises and tolerance of remaining differences.[47] This public dialogue may be one of the ingredients in or conditions for social reform that replaces a culture of impunity with a culture of human rights. In nondemocratic Cambodia, for example, many citizens are disclosing what they suffered under Khmer Rouge tyranny, debating what should be done, and agreeing that Khmer leaders should be tried:

Countless unburdenings . . . are taking place among Cambodians today as the country seems to be embarking, spontaneously, on a long-delayed national conversation about its traumatic past. . . . The comments also suggest an emerging political assertiveness among people better informed and more aware of their rights. . . . The seemingly near-unanimous view is that Khmer Rouge leaders should be put on trial, if only to determine who is really to blame for the country's suffering—and even if any convictions are followed by an amnesty. . . . With popular emotions stirring, he [Kao Kim Hourn of the Cambodian Institute for Cooperation and Peace] said, "internal pressure on the government has begun to build up." He added: "National Reconciliation at all costs? Bury the past? Forgive and forget? No. I don't think that is the case now." . . . Despite the violent power politics that has persistently stunted the establishment of democracy and human rights, a fledgling civil society has begun to emerge, addressing everything from education to flood control.[48]

CONTEXTUALIZING GOALS AND TOOLS

Although each of the eight goals specified above has prescriptive content, each also allows considerable latitude in devising policies sensitive to specific historical and local facts. Different means may be justified for achieving particular ends, and the selection of means—constrained by local institutional capacities—will have consequences for the priority ranking that any given society assigns to the goals overall. In particular circumstances, the achievement of one or more of the goals would itself be a means (whether one that is helpful, necessary, or the best) to the realization of one or more of the others. For instance, truth may contribute to just punishment, fair compensation, and even reconciliation. When perpetrators are judicially directed to compensate their former victims, steps may be taken toward both retribution and reconciliation.

In summary, I have employed the eight goals to identify the moral aspects of reckoning with past wrongs, the areas of emerging international agreement, and the topics for further cross-cultural reflection and deliberation. Moreover, I propose that the eight goals be employed—and in turn evaluated—as criteria for evaluating the general "success" of various kinds of tools, such as truth commissions,[49] and designing and assessing a package of tools for attaining transitional justice in particular countries.

I recognize that different local conditions have a crucial bearing on the best that can be done in particular contexts. For example, it matters what a given transition is *from* and what it is *to*. Were prior violations perpetrated or permitted by a dictatorship, or did they occur in the context of a civil war, ethnic conflict, or attempted secession? If one of the latter, has the previous conflict been brought to a negotiated end, or was one side unilaterally victorious? How long was the period of violations, and how many people were perpetrators and victims (or both)? Does the particular society have a history of democratic institutions, or was it a long-standing dictatorship? Does the emerging society perpetuate, albeit in a new form, the ruling party, judicial system, and military apparatus of the old regime? What are the strength and potential of democratic governance, the market, and civil society? What is the general level of well-being among citizens, and are there continuing ethnic conflicts or radical economic disparities between segments of society? Each of these factors highlights the dangers of supposing that there is a recipe or single set of policies for reckoning with past wrongs that will be ethically defensible and practically feasible. These factors also indicate that sometimes the best that can be done is to approximate one or more of the eight goals initially or postpone attempts to realize them until conditions are improved. And sometimes excruciatingly difficult trade-offs will have to be made.

CONCLUDING REMARKS

It might be claimed that—regardless of its structure and content—it is neither possible nor desirable to formulate a general, cross-cultural normative framework and that the best that a society can do is to generate various tactics of its own for reckoning with past evil. However, policies and strategies that are designed and implemented solely under pressure of immediate circumstances and without proper attention to the relevant ethical questions are likely to be ad hoc, ineffective, inconsistent, and unstable. Moral questions have a habit of not going away. They may be trumped in the short term by certain strategic and prudential imperatives, and some measure of peace can be established without paying close attention to them. Long-term peace, however, cannot be realized if resentment, bitterness, and moral doubts about the just treatment of perpetrators and victims of human rights abuses linger in the minds of citizens. A general framework inspired and shaped by lessons learned from a variety of contexts can encourage each society reckoning with an atrocious past to realize in its own way as many as possible of the goals that international dialogue agrees are morally urgent.

It might also be argued that much more is needed than a normative framework or "vision." This is correct. But, while far from sufficient, it is essential to get clear on morally based objectives as we reckon with a society's past wrongs. The eminent Costa Rican philosopher Manuel Formosa nicely puts the general point: "It is clear that the new society will not come about just by thinking about it. But there is no doubt that one must begin by setting forth what is important; because, if we do not, we will never achieve it."[50]

NOTES

This essay appeared in *Ethics & International Affairs* 13 (1999): 43–64. It was revised in 2008. I am grateful to David P. Crocker, Stacy Kotzin, Mauricio Olavarria, and colleagues at the

Institute for Philosophy and Public Policy and the School of Public Affairs at the University of Maryland—especially Susan Dwyer, Arthur Evenchik, Peter Levine, Xiaorong Li, Judith Lichtenberg, and other participants in the Transitional Justice Project—for helpful comments on earlier versions of this essay.

1.   The best multidisciplinary collections on transitional justice are Neil J. Kritz, ed., *Transitional Justice: How Emerging Democracies Reckon with Former Regimes*, 3 vols. (Washington, DC: United States Institute of Peace, 1995); Naomi Roht-Arriaza, ed., *Impunity and Human Rights in International Law and Practice* (New York: Oxford University Press, 1995); and A. James McAdams, ed., *Transitional Justice and the Rule of Law in New Democracies* (Notre Dame, IN: University of Notre Dame Press, 1997).

2.   Timothy Garton Ash, "The Truth About Dictatorship," *New York Review of Books* 45 (February 19, 1998).

3.   For these broader issues, see Ash, "The Truth About Dictatorship," and Juan E. Méndez, "Accountability for Past Abuses," *Human Rights Quarterly* 19 (1997): 256–258, and "In Defense of Transitional Justice," in *Transitional Justice and the Rule of Law*, ed. McAdams, 22–23, n. 4.

4.   Seth Mydans, "Under Prodding, 2 Apologize for Cambodian Anguish," *New York Times*, December 30, 1998, and "Cambodian Leader Resists Punishing Top Khmer Rouge," *New York Times*, December 29, 1998.

5.   See Jens Meierhenrich, "The Ethics of Lustration," *Ethics & International Affairs* 20, no. 1 (2006): 99–120.

6.   See Steven R. Ratner and Jason S. Abrams, *Accountability for Human Rights and Atrocities in International Law: Beyond the Nuremberg Legacy* (Oxford: Clarendon Press, 1997); Aryeh Neier, *War Crimes: Brutality, Genocide, Terror and the Struggle for Justice* (New York: Times Books, 1998).

7.   Ruth Wedgwood, "Fiddling in Rome: America and the International Criminal Court," *Foreign Affairs* 77 (November/December 1998): 20–24.

8.   Lawrence Weschler, *A Miracle, A Universe: Settling Accounts with Torturers* (New York: Pantheon, 1990); Roy Gutman, *A Witness to Genocide* (New York: Macmillan, 1993); Tina Rosenberg, *The Haunted Land: Facing Europe's Ghosts After Communism* (New York: Random House, 1995), and "Defending the Indefensible," *New York Times Magazine*, April 19, 1998; David Rohde, *Endgame: The Betrayal and Fall of Srebrenica, Europe's Worst Massacre Since World War II* (Boulder, CO: Westview Press, 1997); Marguerite Feitlowitz, *A Lexicon of Terror: Argentina and the Legacies of Torture* (New York: Oxford University Press, 1998); Roger Cohen, *Hearts Grown Brutal: Sagas of Sarajevo* (New York: Random House, 1997); Chuck Sudetic, *Blood and Vengeance: One Family's Story of the War in Bosnia* (New York: W. W. Norton, 1998); Bill Berkeley, "The Pursuit of Justice and the Future of Africa," *Washington Post Magazine*, October 11, 1998; Philip Gourevitch, *We Wish to Inform You That Tomorrow We Will Be Killed with Our Families: Stories from Rwanda* (New York: Farrar, Straus & Giroux, 1998).

9.   See, for example, the essays by the following authors, in *Transitional Justice*, ed. Kritz, vol. 1, who took part respectively in attempts to reckon with past wrongs in El Salvador, Argentina, and Chile: Thomas Buergenthal, Carlos Nino, and José Zalaguett.

10.   See *Transitional Justice and the Rule of Law*, ed. McAdams; and Mark J. Osiel, *Mass Atrocity, Collective Memory, and the Law* (New Brunswick, NJ: Transaction Books, 1997).

11.   See Michael Walzer, *Just and Unjust Wars: A Moral Argument with Historical Illustrations*, fourth edition (New York: Basic Books, [1977] 2006), xxvii.

12.   See, for example, Donald Shriver, *An Ethic for Enemies: Forgiveness in Politics* (New York: Oxford University Press, 1995); Pablo de Greiff, "Trial and Punishment, Pardon and Oblivion: On Two Inadequate Policies for the Treatment of Former Human Rights Abusers," *Philosophy & Social Criticism* 12 (1996): 93–111; "International Criminal Courts and Transitions to Democracy," *Public Affairs Quarterly* 12 (1998): 79–99; and Lyn S. Graybill, "South Africa's Truth and Reconciliation Commission: Ethical and Theological Perspectives," *Ethics & International Affairs* 12 (1998): 43–62.

13.   One exception to this judgment is Ash, "The Truth About Dictatorship." Although he neither clarifies nor defends his ethical assumptions and although his particular assessments can be disputed, Ash insightfully considers four general measures—forgetting, trials, purges, and historical writing—with lots of variations and examples, especially from East and Central European countries.

14.   David A. Crocker, "Transitional Justice and International Civil Society: Toward a Normative Framework," *Constellations* 5 (1998): 492–517; "Civil Society and Transitional Justice," in *Civil Society, Democracy, and Civic Renewal*, ed. Robert Fullinwider (Lanham, MD: Rowman & Littlefield, 1999); and "Truth Commissions, Transitional Justice, and Civil Society" in *Truth v. Justice: The Morality of Truth Commissions*, ed. Robert I. Rotberg and Dennis Thompson (Princeton, NJ: Princeton University Press, 2000). My list of objectives has benefited from the work of Méndez and Zalaquett as well as from that of Margaret Popkin and Naomi Roht-Arriaza, who formulate and employ four criteria in "Truth as Justice: Investigatory Commissions in Latin America," *Law & Social Inquiry* 20 (1995): 79–116, especially 93–106.

15.   Crocker, "Transitional Justice and International Civil Society," 495–96.

16.   Svetozar Stojanovic, *The Fall of Yugoslavia: Why Communism Failed* (Amherst, NY: Prometheus Books, 1997), 77–78; see also 89–92.

17.   Alex Braine, "The Societal and Conflictual Conditions That Are Necessary or Conducive to Truth Commissions" (paper presented at the South African Truth and Reconciliation Commission Conference, World Peace Foundation, Somerset West, South Africa, May 28–30, 1998).

18.   Rohde, *Endgame*, 226.

19.   Ibid., 230–31.

20.   For investigations of what the United States and other Western powers could and should have done to prevent the Holocaust, see Richard Breitman, *Official Secrets: What the Nazis Planned, What the British and Americans Knew* (New York: Hill and Wang, 1999); and Istvan Deak, "Horror and Hindsight," a review of *Official Secrets* by Richard Breitman, *New Republic*, February 15, 1999. For consideration of the same issues with respect to the failure of the United States, the UN, and the EU to intervene militarily in Croatia and Bosnia in 1991–1995, see Mark Danner, "The US and the Yugoslav Catastrophe," *New York Review of Books* 44 (November 20, 1997).

21.   See my "Truth Commissions, Transitional Justice, and Civil Society."

22.   See, for example, Patrick Ball, *Who Did What to Whom? Planning and Implementing a Large Scale Human Rights Data Project* (Washington, DC: American Association for the Advancement of Science, 1996).

23.   See Mark Danner, "Bosnia: The Turning Point," *New York Review of Books* 45 (February 5, 1998), for a compelling argument that rejects Serb claims that it was Muslims themselves who were responsible for the mortar attack that killed 68 Muslims in a Sarajevan market on February 5, 1994.

24.   Suzanne Daley, "In Apartheid Inquiry, Agony Is Relived but Not Put to Rest," *New York Times*, July 17, 1997.

25.   Bill Berkeley, "Genocide, the Pursuit of Justice, and the Future of Africa," *Washington Post Magazine*, October 11, 1998.

26.   See Michael Walzer, *Just and Unjust Wars*, 304–327; Neier, *War Crimes*, 229–45; Mark J. Osiel, "Obeying Orders: Atrocity, Military Discipline, and the Law of War," *California Law Review* 86 (October 1998): 943–1129.

27.   Peter Quint, *The Imperfect Union: Constitutional Structures of German Unification* (Princeton, NJ: Princeton University Press, 1997), 194–215. Cf. Anne Sa'adah, *Germany's Second Chance: Trust, Justice, and Reconciliation* (Cambridge, MA: Harvard University Press, 1998).

28.   Larry May and Stacey Hoffman, eds., *Collective Responsibility: Five Decades of Debate in Theoretical and Applied Ethics* (Lanham, MD.: Rowman & Littlefield, 1991).

29.   See Carlos Santiago Nino, *Radical Evil on Trial* (New Haven, CT: Yale University Press, 1996), 210–28; Neier, *War Crimes*, 210–28; Peter A. French, ed., *The Spectrum of Responsibility* (New York: St. Martin's Press, 1991).

30.   Nino, *Radical Evil on Trial*, and "A Consensual Theory of Punishment," in *Punishment: A Philosophy & Public Affairs Reader*, ed. A. John Simmons et al. (Princeton, NJ: Princeton University Press, 1995); and Jaime Malamud-Goti, "Transitional Governments in the Breach: Why Punish State Criminals?" in *Transitional Justice*, ed. Kritz, vol. 1.

31.   See, for example, *Punishment*, ed. Simmons et al.; Lawrence Crocker, "The Upper Limit of Punishment," *Emory Law Journal* 41 (1992): 1059–1110; Michael Moore, *Placing Blame: A General Theory of the Criminal Law* (Oxford: Clarendon Press, 1997); and David A. Crocker, "Punishment, Reconciliation, and Democratic Deliberation," *Buffalo Criminal Law Journal* 5 (2002): 509–46.

32.   David Luban, "The Legacies of Nuremberg," in *Legal Modernism: Law, Meaning, and Violence* (Ann Arbor: University of Michigan Press, 1994). Cf. Lon L. Fuller, *The Morality of Law*, revised edition (New Haven, CT: Yale University Press, 1977), 33–39.

33.   See, for example, Stephen Holmes, "The End of Decommunization," and Jon Elster, "On Doing What One Can: An Argument Against Post-Communist Restitution and Retribution," in *Transitional Justice*, ed. Kritz, vol. 1.

34.   Warren Hoge, "Law Lords in London Open Rehearing of Pinochet Case," *New York Times*, January 19, 1999.

35.   *Truth and Reconciliation Commission of South Africa Report*, vol. 5, chap. 5, paras. 27–28 and 85–93.

36.   David A. Sanger, "Gold Dispute with the Swiss Declared to Be at an End," *New York Times*, January 31, 1999.

37.   Roger Cohen, "German Companies Adopt Fund for Slave Laborers Under Nazis," *New York Times*, February 17, 1999. Cohen observes that "since World War Two the German government has paid out about $80 billion in aid, most of it to Jews who survived concentration camps or fled."

38.   Ibid.

39.   See Robert A. Dahl, *Democracy and Its Critics* (New Haven, CT: Yale University Press, 1989), especially chaps. 8, 17, and 18; and Larry A. Diamond, "Democracy in Latin America: Degrees, Illusions, Directions for Consolidation," in *Beyond Sovereignty: Collectively Defending Democracy in the Americas*, ed. Tom Farer (Baltimore: Johns Hopkins University Press, 1996).

40.   See David A. Crocker, *Ethics of Global Development: Agency, Capability, and Deliberative Democracy* (Cambridge: Cambridge University Press, 2008).

41.   Charles Villa-Vicencio, "A Different Kind of Justice: The South African Truth and Reconciliation Commission," *Contemporary Justice Review* 1 (1998): 407–28.

42.   Osiel, *Mass Atrocity*, 17, n. 22; see also 47–51; 204, n. 136; 263–65.

43.   Amy Gutmann and Dennis Thompson, "The Moral Foundations of Truth Commissions" in *Truth v. Justice*, ed. Rotberg and Thompson.

44.   See David Little, "A Different Kind of Justice: Dealing with Human Rights Violations in Transitional Societies," *Ethics & International Affairs* 13 (1999): 65–80.

45.   See Susan Dwyer, "Reconciliation for Realists," *Ethics & International Affairs* 13 (1999): 81–98.

46.   See Gilbert A. Lewthwaite, "In South Africa, Much Truth Yields Little Reconciliation," *Baltimore Sun*, July 30, 1998; and Phylicia Oppelt, "Irreconcilable: The Healing Work of My Country's Truth Commission Has Opened New Wounds for Me," *Washington Post*, September 13, 1998.

47.   See James Bohman, *Public Deliberation: Pluralism, Complexity, and Democracy* (Cambridge, MA: MIT Press, 1996); and Amy Gutmann and Dennis Thompson, *Democracy and Disagreement* (Cambridge, MA: Harvard University Press, 1996).

48.   Seth Mydans, "20 Years On, Anger Ignites Against Khmer Rouge," *New York Times*, January 10, 1999.

49.   See, for example, Priscilla B. Hayner, "Past Truths, Present Dangers: The Role of Official Truth Seeking in Conflict Resolution and Prevention," in *International Conflict Resolution After the Cold War*, ed. National Research Council (Washington, DC: National Academy Press, 2000).

50.   Manuel Formosa, "La Alternativa: Repensar la Revolución," Seminario Universidad, Universidad de Costa Rica, October 23, 1987.

PART TWO

~

Grounds for Intervention

What are the limits of sovereignty and the international legal principle of nonintervention? To what extent is humanitarian intervention now a legitimate practice in international society? How can just and unjust interventions be distinguished? What kinds and degrees of threats to a population justify an international response? Must interventions be authorized by an international body, such as the UN Security Council? When might unauthorized or unilateral interventions be appropriate? Do states have to be democratic and respect human rights in order to earn the right against intervention? Does international society have a moral duty to end the genocide in Darfur? What other kinds of concerns should trigger an interventionist response? Does taking environmentalism seriously require us to further rethink the assumptions of the state system?

Chapter 4

Humanitarian Intervention
An Overview of the Ethical Issues

Michael J. Smith

THE CAPACITY TO FOCUS on the issue of humanitarian intervention represents what Joel Rosenthal has noted as the maturation of the field of ethics and international affairs.[1] If nothing else, the debate surrounding this vexed issue has demonstrated that we have left behind the so-called oxymoron problem: there is no reason now to be defensive about bracketing the terms *ethics* and *international relations*. One can hardly talk about Bosnia, Rwanda, Haiti, Somalia, or any cases of possible outside intervention, without recognizing from the very beginning that ethical dilemmas abound in the way we define our goals, our interests, and the means we use to pursue them. Even Samuel Huntington, not usually known to be a moralist, has asserted that "it is morally unjustifiable and politically indefensible that members of the [U.S.] armed forces should be killed to prevent Somalis from killing one another."[2] Whether or not one agrees with that assertion (I do not), one may note that Professor Huntington speaks in terms of moral justification and regards his view of morality to be, in effect, self-evidently true. Thus even arch-realists invoke morality in urging their preferred policies.

The discussion in this essay proceeds in three unequal stages. First, I present a brief and over-simple sketch of the objective and subjective changes in the broader milieu of international relations as they relate to humanitarian intervention. Second, and more substantially, I survey and analyze the arguments justifying or opposing the notion of humanitarian intervention from realist and liberal perspectives. Finally, I offer the beginnings of my own argument and consider the enormous difficulties of undertaking humanitarian intervention with any degree of effectiveness and consistency.

THE MILIEU

A New International Setting

What are some of the salient changes in the contemporary international system? Perhaps symptomatic of our current confusion is the absence of consensus even on what to call this new system. Is it unipolar? Balance-of-power? A globalized economic system and regional security system? The new world order? We agree only on the term *post–Cold War* and on the idea that we have no exact model for the kind of international system in which we find ourselves. The notion of unipolarity is not terribly helpful: the apparent single "pole," the United States, though quite powerful militarily, has shown that it cannot dominate the system; and functionally and economically the international system can hardly be described as unipolar. So, while apparently appealing, unipolarity doesn't work.

Realist analysts may struggle to find some sort of balance-of-power analogue, but this too is not terribly useful. Power is not fungible in the way that many realists following E. H. Carr have treated it, and much of contemporary international relations involves the intersection of the traditional realm of security and the modern arena of economic interdependence. But even theorists who emphasize the elusiveness of power or who have reclassified kinds of power have not as yet articulated a crystallized conception of the contemporary system.[3] In general, we continue to look for ways in which the contemporary system may or may not be like the balance-of-power system of the nineteenth century, to identify what features of the Cold War system it still has, and to seek other historical models; but it is clear that we are in a system with many aspects we have never before encountered. Although nuclear weapons have not gone away, they no longer structure the international competition. We now have contending successor states within the former Soviet empire in the midst of profound political and economic transformations—transformations as yet incomplete and poorly understood. At the same time, a truly global economy now means that events in the stock markets of Seoul, Bangkok, or Hong Kong reverberate distortedly on Wall Street. In short, the model of billiard ball states combining and colliding in ways beloved of diplomatic history textbooks (and some realists) has given way to a kaleidoscope of factors including nationalism, ethnicity, and religion, as well as security and economics.

Perhaps our understanding of the international system was always oversimplified: states were never billiard balls impermeable to transnational norms, influences, and activities. But the simplifications were defensible as a way to abstract the underlying logic of a system based on discrete sovereign states. Now, with the operational sovereignty of states systemically eroded, we know that no simple model encapsulates the complex reality of contemporary international relations.

If we shift our focus to the level of state actors, we may note some broad trends that at the same time undermine and affirm the idea of national sovereignty as the constituent principle of international society. Consider first the widely noted phenomenon of so-called failed or failing states, which are breaking down as a result of their inability to establish legitimacy with any degree of certainty. In addition, there are states, like Rwanda and Burundi, or Algeria, in which conflicts appear to be endemic or imminent or both. Such conflicts seem now to have greater salience.[4]

Finally, there is the phenomenon of so-called dangerous states: states that may, like Libya or North Korea, challenge the basic tenets of the society of states; states that for various reasons seek to bring attention to themselves through outrageous actions. Such states, because of the danger they pose for other states, may indeed make intervention necessary. For example, it is certainly an open question as to whether we should tolerate the overt acquisition of nuclear weapons by North Korea. When it invaded Kuwait, Iraq provided an occasion for a traditional collective security intervention of the sort envisaged by the framers of the League of Nations Covenant and the UN Charter. As I write this essay, Saddam Hussein's refusal to allow UN inspectors unfettered access to potential weapons sites in Iraq has triggered an international crisis. By the time it appears, we may well have seen another U.S.-led military action against Iraq.

Then there are still cases of old-fashioned aggression, and it is not inconceivable that a state might simply attack another state or help itself to another bit of territory. How dangerous are such renegade states, and what ought we do about them? The overt acquisition of territory or goods by dangerous states will continue to provide a worry for those trying to enforce some version of international order. Together, all these factors at the state level seem to guarantee that we shall have no shortage of occasions for intervention.

A New Climate of Opinion in the 1990s

Thus the objective setting of the international system is not settled, and it is perhaps emblematic of this that we still refer to it as the post–Cold War system. And subjectively, on the issue of humanitarian intervention, we have seen a change even in the brief post–Cold War period in the prevalent attitude toward this issue. For a brief time, from about 1991 to 1993, there existed a sort of Dudley Do-Right euphoria, a sense that we could solve many problems throughout the world just by the use of goodwill and the dispatch of peacekeepers wherever they might be necessary. Thomas Franck characterized the time as an "exciting moment" in which we could begin to intervene on behalf of democratic legitimacy—to create democratically legitimate states everywhere.[5] There was indeed a large increase in the number of humanitarian operations.[6] Since 1993, and the perceived American debacle in Somalia, the attitude toward humanitarian intervention, especially in the United States, has become decidedly more cautious. The most immediate effect of this caution, of course, was the inaction (and worse) of the international community in the face of the conflict between the Hutus and Tutsis in Rwanda. Since then the brutal war in Bosnia, the absence of any international action in the conflict in Chechnya, and a kind of collective sense of shame at the failure of the international community to prevent or arrest the slaughter of tens of thousands of innocent civilians in

Rwanda have all created a new climate of wariness about the whole issue of humanitarian intervention. The puzzled and ineffectual international response to the recurring massacres of villagers in Algeria reflects this same uncertainty.

Moreover, there was always a debate about whether humanitarian intervention is legal under international law. In an incisive review of the issue, Tom Farer concludes: "States will still have to choose between compliance with formal prohibitions [against intervention] and response to urgent moral appeals." Because international law is both "thinly institutionalized" and constantly evolving in ways that reflect emerging normative ideas, an appeal to the law itself cannot solve the underlying moral issues raised by humanitarian intervention.[7]

But such normative consensus is yet to emerge. Even sociologically, the events that may lead to humanitarian intervention are far from clear. Morally, substantively, the issues are deeply controversial. Is humanitarian intervention a rescue operation, a quick in and quick out, leaving the basic norms of sovereignty intact, or is it, rather, an attempt to address the underlying causes of the conflict and even to create the conditions for democracy? If the latter, then the model of going in and getting out quickly is obviously not appropriate. Even Michael Walzer, often criticized for the "statist" character of his theory in *Just and Unjust Wars,* has recently amended his rules for intervention. He now argues that there is an obligation to make sure the conditions that require the intervention in the first place do not simply resume once you leave.[8]

In terms of the subjective environment, there is some question as to whether or not international intervention for humanitarian causes is even moral. Both in the literature and in the pronouncements of leaders and actions of states, there is still a great deal of doubt and suspicion of unauthorized, unilateral intervention. This obviously reflects traditional international law and the traditional rules of a society of states. Recently, the United States has sought to gain multilateral authorization even for its unilateral actions, as was the case in Haiti and, to some extent, even in the Persian Gulf War. As Walzer suggests, there may still be situations in which autonomous unilateral intervention for humanitarian purposes is ethically justified, and certainly from the military point of view the formidable problems of command and control may be simplified when intervention is autonomous and unilateral.[9] But in general it seems that the old norms of sovereignty and nonintervention are still persuasive for states—at least in their official and quasiofficial pronouncements.

What about collective intervention? Traditional international law has been hostile not only to unilateral intervention in domestic affairs but also to collective, coercive action, except in cases of threats to peace, breaches of peace, and overt aggression. The founding fathers of international law have always treated the concept as suspect. The most striking recent development has been some "creative exegesis" (Farer's phrase) on the part of international lawyers as exemplified in the willingness in the Security Council to broaden the traditional definition of threats to peace as a justification for intervention.[10] Was the intervention for the Kurds the application of a new principle of humanitarian intervention on behalf of oppressed minorities? Or was it a simple extension of a classical collective security operation against Iraq? Would it even have occurred if Iraq had not invaded Kuwait? The question is not entirely rhetorical, but almost. The relief action certainly did not recognize a right of Kurdish self-determination, as the UN has proclaimed its respect for Iraqi territorial integrity.

Many of the recent collective interventions in weak states have occurred at the formal request of the state concerned or of all parties involved. In its attempt to restore democracy in Haiti (and of course acting mainly by approving U.S. intervention), the Organization of American States (OAS) moved into new territory by justifying collective intervention. Other UN interventions have mainly concerned emergency relief for violations of minority rights, the monitoring of elections, or more traditional-style peacekeeping missions. When the UN monitored elections in Nicaragua, the operation was explicitly connected to the Central American peace process rather than to concern for democracy per se or human rights. Whether Somalia and Cambodia will be exceptions or the first in a series of temporary takeovers of failed states will depend on the lessons being drawn from those two operations. So far the UN has resisted endorsing a general doctrine, proceeding, as is its wont, case by case. This means that the normative scene is still rather cloudy, and the extent to which we have moved beyond traditional norms is dubious. Even the definition of what constitutes threats to peace is ambiguous. Must an egregious violation of human rights that constitutes a "threat to peace" have an inescapable impact on interstate relations? Or are some violations in themselves, and virtually by definition, threats to peace? The "creative interpretation of its constitutional obligation to maintain peace and security" undertaken by the Security Council cannot by itself solve these ambiguities.[11] If all violations are defined as threats to peace, then the Security Council, in principle, could intervene in the affairs of any state; but if only violations that threaten interstate peace count, then many egregious violations (as, say, in Tibet or East Timor) could go unaddressed.

To summarize the relevance of the changes in the international milieu for humanitarian intervention: First, there is a lack of leadership and clear direction at the top of the system, either among the major states or in the institutions themselves. Former UN secretary-general Boutros Boutros-Ghali was probably out a little too far in front of the member states in his "Agenda for Peace"; his successor now labors to keep the organization financially afloat, especially in the face of U.S. recalcitrance about its debt. The activist phase of interventions, at least in official pronouncements, has receded. Second, there will continue to be occasions for humanitarian interventions, and we will continue to be faced with dilemmas of rescue, peacekeeping, and peace making, to list the problems in ascending order of difficulty. Third, there is no real consensus on when or how to intervene in these conflicts or on who should do so. And fourth, it is also fair to say that such enthusiasm as may have existed for these types of operations from 1991 to 1993 seems by now to have evaporated.

A remark by David Rieff in a recent essay that Western states seek and favor humanitarian intervention seems now to be singularly inapposite.[12] The two most recent instances of American intervention, in Haiti and Bosnia, were undertaken with evident reluctance. The title of the rather dyspeptic monograph written in 1978 by Ernst Haas, "Global Evangelism Rides Again," in 1998 seemed almost quaint; in 2008 perhaps less so.[13] Throughout the 1990s, global evangelism limped along, led by a motley if erudite array of philosophers and human-rights advocates. (Bellicose neoconservatives would not embrace the idea of robust intervention until the second Bush Administration; and even then their justifications were military and ideological, not humanitarian.)[14] More typical is the remark of the freshman Republican member of Congress who, responding to President Clinton's belated speech justifying the Bosnian intervention, said she did not see any reason why we should be sending "our boys" to a country about which we know nothing to stop the fighting there.[15] It is doubtful that she knew how closely she was echoing Neville Chamberlain.

So what does this say? It tells us that we are unlikely to find guidance from leaders, either of major states or of institutions.[16] International lawyers will continue to debate whether or not interventions are legal, and the prescriptions from the political scientists will remain murky. Where does this leave us? These are serious ethical problems that cannot be ignored, and ethicists must be willing to tread where lawyers and politicians fear to go. Thus, on to the arguments about humanitarian intervention itself.

HUMANITARIAN INTERVENTION

A provocative challenge to the very terms of the debate comes from Rieff, who says that in effect humanitarian intervention is just a sop to the Western conscience and that the rich nations are using it as a way to avoid dealing with the chronic and serious issues of poverty and misgovernment in Third World states.[17] This is a legitimate point, but I take it to be a kind of cri de coeur of a committed journalist who has seen some of the worst humanitarian disasters of the decade. The insight, or warning, should act only as the beginning, and not the end, of an argument. Extraordinary and excruciating dilemmas are raised by some of the situations we observe across the world, but throwing up one's hands at the horror of it all or raining down curses on all the world does not help us to address them.

There are various ways to characterize and categorize the positions in the debate, but I have no wish to impose a complicated taxonomy here. Stanley Hoffmann—and more recently Michael Doyle—divides the theoretical approaches to the issue into realist, Marxist, and liberal varieties.[18] One might also divide the theorists into statists, or people who look at states as the source of values, and cosmopolitans. This is the old distinction made famous some time ago by Hedley Bull in *The Anarchical Society*, where he discussed statist and universalist cosmopolitan conceptions of justice.[19] Today, however, the real debate is taking place mainly between realists and liberals.

Realist Arguments

As I have outlined elsewhere, realists, whether they reside in academia or in the military, are traditionally hostile to any intervention that is justified for allegedly ethical reasons.[20] They claim, in general, that there is a self-delusory quality to all ethical justifications regarding state actions. That is a larger argument, which I have tried to address elsewhere.[21] But how does this argument play out when it comes to humanitarian intervention? Realists say two things that are partly incompatible. One is that states only act when it is in their interest to do so and that therefore when they engage in a humanitarian intervention they are really pursuing some other agenda. They may just be worried about prestige or image on the "soft" end of the interest calculus. Or they may have some actual "hard" interests involved, interests that are convenient to subsume under the category of "humanitarian." In any case, say realists, when states intervene for allegedly humanitarian reasons they do not seek disinterestedly to do the right thing; they have "real" interests at stake. However, there is also a kind of political assertion that is slightly incompatible with this one. It says that interventions work and are supported politically only when they are closely connected to real interests. But if the first assertion were true, then the second would not apply: states would act *only* when their interests were really engaged. Apparently states sometimes really do act in spite of the fact that their so-called national interests are not engaged to the degree that realists think they ought to be.

In addition to these not-quite-compatible empirical assertions about why states act, realists also make what amounts to an ethical argument that states are necessarily self-interested creatures and are, by definition, unable to act in other than self-interested ways. To expect them to do so—to support genuinely humanitarian action—is to engage in self-delusion, error, and hypocrisy. Thus the best, indeed most ethical, thing to do is to hold on to a more concrete definition of interests and leave humanitarian interventions to *Médicins sans Frontières*. Humanitarian intervention, therefore, is in a sense a chimera, or, as in Rieff s account, a sop to our collective conscience. Moreover, humanitarian crusades dilute the national purpose, say realists: Only when we recognize the inevitably self-interested character of all our policies can we think clearly about our interests. Realists developed this argument most fully in their opposition to the U.S. intervention in Vietnam. People tend to forget that some of the earliest opponents of that intervention, which was by no means humanitarian, were realists like Hans Morgenthau, George Kennan, and Reinhold Niebuhr, all of whom thought that Vietnam was not a core American interest and that we were vainly seeking to project our anticommunism in ways quite inappropriate to the local conditions.

There is, nevertheless, a quasi-realist case for humanitarian intervention that some have made, and that is to define interests in terms of what Arnold Wolfers called "milieu goals."[22] That is, there is a realist case for structuring a more orderly international system and paying attention to the requirements of leadership by a great power. Realist arguments on behalf of intervention may even invoke credibility ("No one will take us seriously as a great power if we allow this to occur"). If the United States is to be believed about anything it is to do, the argument goes, it cannot allow a group of thugs in Haiti to thumb its nose at everything it says. This is an interesting redeployment of an argument originally made in a very different context. We heard it during the intervention in Vietnam, and we hear it recurringly in debates about how many nuclear weapons we need for what. The argument rests on a broad definition of national interest.

In addressing national interest, one can perhaps distinguish between imperatives and preferences, but even defining what is imperative to a state involves deploying ethical preferences.[23] The classical arguments, again, are made by Wolfers: even "survival" must be defined according to moral values. Consider the different choices made by Czechoslovakia in 1938 and Poland in 1939, when faced with Hitler's demands. The Czech and Polish leaders, like Marshal Pétain and General de Gaulle in the France of 1940, defined "survival of the state" quite differently. Even the apparently starkest imperatives are not straightforward or objective. In the middle of the Vietnam War, Bruce Russett wrote *No Clear and Present Danger,* which for many was an annoying little book. It was annoying because it challenged settled beliefs about World War II, but it was also useful in that Russett showed that it is possible to make the case that there was no clear and present danger to the United States in 1941 and that we did not really need to fight the war the way we did. He argues that we could very well have survived without fighting the Germans or the Japanese. The point here is not to agree with that position but rather to note that values are built into the very notion of what constitutes an imperative. Russett showed that imperatives, even the apparently most obvious ones like resisting Nazi Germany and Tojo's Japan, are not self-evident. They are, in the prevailing jargon, "constructed." And therefore, when one is talking about humanitarian intervention, it is not necessarily helpful to distinguish between imperatives and preferences.

The key questions are, what constitutes an integrated definition of national interest, and what value should be placed on having an international system that acts to prevent the sort of brutal behavior we have been observing in the 1990s? These questions of course lead into order as a justification for intervention. There is a component of morality to order, after all, as well as a quasi-moral notion that imputes to great powers a responsibility to ensure a relatively orderly international system. The realist route to humanitarian intervention thus involves a conception of international society that requires us to define what constitutes acceptable behavior within it. Although this is founded on classical, "statist" values, it still provides a means of justifying humanitarian intervention. Thus one need not be a dewy-eyed idealist to think that there are times when humanitarian intervention can be justified on grounds that are fairly traditional and well connected to definitions of interest.

Liberal Arguments

Whereas liberals have traditionally valued self-determination, community, and shared history, as seen in Walzer's work, there is also within liberalism a more universalist conception of human rights in which sovereignty is a subsidiary and conditional value. Self-determination, after all, has been among the most abused of liberal values. Indeed Amir Pasic has shown in an essay on Bosnia how the liberal value of self-determination can and is used to create what he calls a "negative normative reality" that leads to acts of genocide and ethnic cleansing.[24] A deep fault line of liberal theory runs along the question of how a given community defines itself, what means it can use, what legitimate goals it can pursue to establish its conception of freedom and autonomy, and to what extent outsiders are legitimately a party to these conflicts when they get nasty. Most famously perhaps, and most familiarly, J. S. Mill and Walzer following him have asserted both the virtue and the necessity of Mill's argument of the "arduous struggle of self-help" as the way for a community to achieve freedom and autonomy. This sets the bar rather high, even for humanitarian intervention.

At the noninterventionist end of the liberal spectrum, we find again two sorts of claims—one ethical and one prudential. The ethical claim of the noninterventionists places high value on community in itself, on a notion of shared history—what Walzer calls the "thick" values in his 1995 book *Thick and Thin*.[25] These values are to be respected almost prima facie by outsiders. There is also an ethical component to the historical/empirical claim that unless freedom is "earned" by a people, it will not survive and endure. But what if "earning" communal autonomy and freedom means ethnic cleansing? And, if so, what does that imply for the rest of the international community in terms of its rights and/or obligations to intervene?

Related to the claim about community is a claim about the legitimating function of domestic political processes—apparently almost any domestic political process. In a perhaps unguarded passage in *The Anarchical Society*, Bull wrote that to the extent that the words of a despot are authenticated by a political process, one ought to weigh them more heavily than the pronouncements of, say, Bertrand Russell, Buckminster Fuller, or Norman Cousins (in perhaps descending order of profundity), none of whose pronouncements has been authenticated by any sort of process at all. The political claim is that, unlike individuals, at least spokesmen for states, even authoritarian states, have passed through some political process.

At the same time there may be an unconscious arrogance in assuming that the most extreme leader in a community is necessarily the "right" spokesperson for that community's aspirations. This is a point made well by the late political theorist Judith Shklar in her powerful essay "The Liberalism of Fear."[26] By what right is Radovan Karadzic accepted as the authoritative spokesperson of the Bosnian Serbs? It is not clear who has consulted the ordinary people there. Does Pat Robertson speak for all white, evangelical Christians? Or Louis Farrakhan for African Americans as a group? There is a tendency in an argument that privileges states and domestic political processes, however rudimentary, to over-value the most extreme leader and to reward the people least supportive of peaceful accommodation. The so-called Parliament of Bosnian Serbs came into being solely at the behest of Karadzic and his supporters; its actions in the midst of the diplomacy to end the war in Bosnia conferred no conceivable legitimacy.

These ethical and practical arguments for nonintervention slide almost imperceptibly into prudential claims about order. A prudential concern for order tells us that we cannot license intervention everywhere to everyone who is of a mind to intervene. It would be a recipe for disaster in the international milieu. Not every violation can justify intervention. Pierre Laberge cites a play by Molière in which a wife is suffering a beating at the hands of her husband. To the surprise of a well-meaning stranger who tries to intervene, the wife rudely rejects the offer of help. She tells him to mind his own business, that she and her husband will work out their problems.[27] Noninterventionist liberals make a similar claim: people should be left alone to work out their own governance.

What about the interventionist end of the liberal spectrum? Franck has written that in the light of recent orgies of genocide, Mill's position on the arduous struggle of self-help is a posture of insufferable insouciance.[28] Indeed, if one looks at what occurred even in a success story, South Africa, it is clear that success was the product of more than self-help. A combination of external sanctions and sustained action on the part of the international community sought to convince white South Africans that apartheid was deeply unacceptable, that South Africa would have to abandon it and grant full citizenship rights to the black majority if it were ever to join the international community of states as a fully acceptable member. This external pressure aided the undoubtedly more potent internal developments that ultimately led to the remarkably peaceful transformation. Intervention, after all, can involve more (or less) than sending troops. In the case of South Africa, it involved sustained sanctions at almost every level of international interaction. And many of these sanctions were the product of grassroots activism in the democratic states that were also trading partners, or sporting competitors, of the South African state.

In his deservedly standard treatment of the issue in *Just and Unjust Wars,* Walzer sought to avoid the extreme non- or interventionist positions. Since the book's publication in 1977, people on both sides of the debate have tried to claim him as an ally because his legalist paradigm rests on a tension between the statist and cosmopolitan positions. The book recognizes the pull of one side of an argument even when it lands on the other side. In effect, Walzer tries to ground the legalist paradigm of the rights of states in the rights of individuals— because the rights of states rest on the rights of individuals. But at the same time, states as members of international society are by definition entitled to presumptive legitimacy. The first reading of the rule is that we as outsiders must assume that another state is legitimate unless it has proved otherwise by actions that we cannot ignore. Walzer revises the absolute rule of nonintervention only when the absence of "fit" between people and regime is radically apparent. He cites interventions in civil wars involving secessionist movements; interventions to balance prior interventions; and—here is our focus—interventions to rescue peoples threatened by massacre, enslavement, and (in "The Politics of Rescue") by large-scale expulsion.

Walzer conceives of humanitarian intervention as a kind of international analogue to domestic law enforcement. Governments that engage in acts that allow us to intervene for humanitarian purposes are in effect criminal governments. Those who initiate massacres lose their right to participate in the normal, and even normally violent, processes of domestic self-determination. Governments and armies engaged in wholesale massacres of individuals are readily identifiable as criminal. Hence, humanitarian intervention comes closer than any other kind of intervention to what we commonly regard in domestic society as police work. But can one intervene unilaterally to stop an outlaw? Walzer prefers a collective action, but it seems that he does not insist on it. His discussion conceives of international humanitarian intervention as a rescue operation in which the intervenor goes in and then comes out. In "The Politics of Rescue," Walzer expresses willingness to allow members of the international community to stay a little longer, to move from what Hoffmann calls rescue to the restoration of peace.[29] He does not directly treat the murderous conflicts in failed states or the systematic terrorization of a population by another seeking its own version of self-determination, as in Bosnia. The model is still one of states acting as states to punish a particularly egregious member of the society of states. So the values of community, shared history, and culture—in general, the "thick" values—trump the universalist values of human rights, at least in Walzer's account.

A LIBERALISM OF HUMAN RIGHTS

I would like to sketch very briefly a version of liberalism that, at least ethically, makes the value of sovereignty subordinate to human rights claims.[30] This version rests on a view of liberalism that seeks to value both the universal and the communitarian aspects of the political doctrine. Most communitarian critiques of liberalism fail to recognize the extent to which liberals value community and how liberalism itself embodies a conception of the good. Such critiques take aim at the priority given to rights and try to show how this comes at the expense of the common good. But, in fact, liberalism does work to establish conditions in which individuals will be able to fulfill themselves and their projects, their vision of the good, while respecting the personality and personhood of the projects of others. This means that there are liberal virtues—tolerance is an important one—and also that there are limits to so-called liberal neutrality. At bottom, liberalism seeks to establish a form of social life free of moral coercion even in circumstances of deep social disagreement. A liberal polity is therefore fully entitled to place limits on projects that would impose moral coercion and hamper the ability of individuals to define and pursue their own idea of the good. The goal of a liberal political society is individual autonomy in a community of tolerance. Political society can be regarded as a combined product of history, with its vast share of accidents, upheavals, and manipulations, and of human choice. Thus it is both willed and historical. And very often, as we know from many studies, it is the sort of shared history that is sometimes invented, or re-created, by poets, philosophers, and the like.

Whatever its origins, the moral standing of a society rests on its ability to respect and to protect the rights of its members and on their consent, explicit or implicit, to its rules and institutions. Both the nation, which we define as a group that provides individuals with a sense of social identity and transcends other secular and often religious cleavages, and the state, which we define as a set of institutions that aims at providing individuals in a certain territory with order and a variety of resources, derive their moral standing and their rights from the will and the rights of the individuals that compose the nation and over whom the state rules. Political life is, as a whole, a ceaseless process of accommodation among the rights and duties of individuals within a nation, those of a national group, and those of the state. But here we would join forces with the broader liberal worldview. Neither the group nor the nation nor the state can be seen as possessing inherent rights. The rights they claim derive from individuals. When they define their rights and duties in a way that tramples the basic rights of individuals they forfeit their legitimacy. This version of liberalism recognizes that persons are social beings and that society, therefore, cannot be seen only as protector of private lives and activities from anarchy. Individuals often want to come together to achieve common purposes, to carry on grand designs, to build a common civil culture—sounding all the usual communitarian hymns. Political society is not simply a market for free private enterprise. From a moral point of view we look at social groupings formed by persons as derivative and constructed and as drawing their legitimacy from the will and consent of these persons. Thus in international relations we treat the notion of the morality of states with suspicion. At the same time, we recognize that cosmopolitanism, however desirable it may be as a political goal, does not yet correspond to the choice of the great majority of states or individuals. But we would still insist that community is not a value that trumps all others.

In this conception of liberalism, then, the justification for state sovereignty cannot rest on its own presumptive legitimacy. Instead it must be derived from the individuals whose rights are to be protected from foreign oppression or intrusion and from their right to a safe, "sovereign" framework in which they can enforce their autonomy and pursue their interests. It follows, then, that a state that is oppressive and violates the autonomy and integrity of its subjects forfeits its moral claim to full sovereignty. Thus, a liberal ethics of world order subordinates the principle of state sovereignty to the recognition and respect of human rights. And when an illiberal state is attacked by another one, the defense and integrity of its independence against aggression must be accompanied by an international effort to improve its own human rights record. Steps have been taken for the international protection of human rights that move slowly and haltingly toward this goal. Here, obviously, we have in mind Kuwait. The principle of an individual's right to moral autonomy, or to put it differently, to the human rights enshrined in the Universal Declaration on Human Rights, should be recognized as the highest principle of world order, ethically speaking, with state sovereignty as a circumscribed and conditional norm.

What does this mean for humanitarian intervention? The answer is complex. We have still to maintain and even raise barriers to illegitimate intervention, define the areas, conditions, and procedures for legitimate ones, pay particular attention to both sets of cases and the special problems raised by coercion, particularly military coercion, and proceed as much as possible on a broad basis of consent. What does this mean in practice? I think we must maintain our suspicion of unilateral intervention, because it always contains a component of self-interest, and unilateral intervention risks almost by definition violating the autonomy of the target. Unilateral intervention should thus be presumptively illegitimate, but the presumption can be overridden. Would it have been wrong for the United States to act in Haiti even if it did not have OAS sanction? The point is arguable, but I believe that humanitarian intervention would nevertheless have been justifiable. A blanket requirement for multilateral approval or participation in a case of potential humanitarian intervention may have the unfortunate effect of ensuring that nothing is done. One could certainly argue that Rwanda was a case of "Well, I'll do it if you do it," with nobody willing to take the first step. Meanwhile, tens, even hundreds, of thousands of people were killed in a brutal, low-tech, and rather time-consuming way, largely by machetes. It is quite clear to most people who have studied this case that a modest deployment of international troops placed early and decisively could have prevented a large number of deaths. Because of cases like this, it does not seem reasonable to rule out unilateral action. At the same time, a collective process serves as a check on an individual state's tendency to intervene for self-interested purposes.

When could one intervene collectively? I think that we could build on the emerging consensus on threats to peace, breaches of peace, and acts of aggression—the traditional causes that allow us to intervene in interstate conflict. In domestic affairs the equivalent causes would be domestic policies and practices capable of leading to serious threats to peace, and in cases of egregious violations of human rights—even if those violations occurred entirely within the borders of a given state. A genocide is no less "a common threat to humanity"—the characterization of former UN secretary-general Boutros-Ghali—if it occurs within borders than if it crosses them. The basic principle that should guide international intervention is this: Individual state sovereignty can be overridden whenever the behavior of the state even within its own territory threatens the existence of elementary human rights abroad and whenever the protection of the basic human rights of its citizens can be assured only from the outside.

State sovereignty, in short, is a contingent value: its observance depends upon the actions of the state that invokes it. Members of the international community are not obliged to "respect the sovereignty" of a state that egregiously violates human rights. Why "egregiously"? The sad answer is that the world presents a far too rich array of human rights violations that might justify outside intervention. We must choose among the evils we seek to end. For much of the world, for example, capital punishment violates human rights. Yet few disinterested observers would urge or welcome the forcible landing of an international military force to prevent Virginia's next execution. However one regards capital punishment after due process of law, it cannot compare with the scale of violations that occurred in Rwanda or in the Cambodia of Pol Pot. As one analyst has observed, we currently possess "neither the capabilities nor the willingness to right all wrongs, even the relatively small number of wrongs that are deemed to warrant international action."[31] But as President Clinton put it in his speech justifying the NATO action in Bosnia: "We cannot stop all war for all time. But we can stop some wars. . . . There are times and places where our leadership can mean the difference between peace and war."[32] Some judgment about the scale of evil, and about the capacity we have to end it, must be made.

This process of judgment should, in my view, be multinational. For all the flaws of the UN, it does provide a forum for international debate and for the emergence of consensus. And, as I have suggested, if taken as a general but not rigid rule of thumb, an insistence upon collective, multilateral intervention or, as in Haiti, collectively approved unilateral action can correct for self-interested interventions that are draped in a thin cloak of humanitarianism. At the same time, it may be necessary for a state to declare its intention to act on its own; if the cause is truly just, this very declaration may make collective action more possible. And the intervention may still be just even if its motives are mixed:

the examples of India's intervention in the former East Pakistan and of Tanzania's in the Uganda of Idi Amin are often cited as unilateral interventions that nevertheless ended humanitarian disasters.[33]

What about the problem of consistency? Does the fact that we can do little, if anything, about human rights violations in Tibet have implications for what can be done about human rights violations in Haiti or East Timor? Alas, it seems obvious that there simply won't be consistency, but what does that mean ethically? Is it more ethical to say that since I cannot do everything everywhere consistently I should do nothing? My own view is that the fact that one cannot do everything everywhere does not mean that one should not try to do anything anywhere.

A first stab at setting priorities for action might be to suggest humanitarian interventions where the threats to peace for neighboring states are indeed the greatest. One could also come up with a list that sets the potential costs of the intervention against what might actually be achieved. In short, we could seek to adapt the traditional criteria of the just war tradition to cases of humanitarian intervention.[34] But this does require that we develop the means and capacities for acting in these ways.

I am not sympathetic to those who think that we must reserve our military for a single purpose lest it lose, so to speak, its "purity of essence," to quote a famous (movie) general.[35] It is not inconceivable to me that we can have dual-purpose military organizations. People can be trained to do more than one thing. We do have to address more seriously collective capacities. We have stopped talking about the UN standing force, and the Clinton administration has stopped trying to build up the collective capacities of the UN, apparently because the issue is regarded as a political loser. Nevertheless, there seems to me to be a clear ethical imperative to begin to develop means that are capable of addressing some of the problems that we have been seeing.

But as always in ethical arguments, ought implies can. It is clear that weighing in on the human rights side implies a willingness to intervene far more extensively than we are currently willing to do; and there are significant costs and dangers attached to this willingness. On the other hand, weighing in heavily on the side of traditional sovereignty and nonintervention entails a willingness to turn a blind eye to many outrages in the world. We could say, "Well, it is a pity that people are killing each other and it's true that there is something that we could do about it relatively easily, but it is actually occurring within a state so it's not our business." Surely one of the lessons of the Holocaust is that we should not allow this to occur again. And one of the benefits of the end of the Cold War is that we can now begin to address questions of endemic injustice and human suffering in ways that were not possible when the United States and the Soviet Union were worried about blowing each other up.

There remain formidable worries about the consistency and effectiveness of humanitarian intervention. But one has to begin working those out by deciding how much one is willing to overlook for the sake of sovereign independence. To claim that sovereignty is subsidiary to human rights is not to say that sovereignty is negligible or automatically weaker. Rather, claims to sovereignty are subsidiary in that they do not automatically trump other compelling claims. There may be times when prudence suggests doing something less, but I regard it still as a moral imperative to prevent or mitigate evil when one has the capacity to do so. Thus as an ethical imperative, the issue of humanitarian intervention demands our deepest attention and response.

NOTES

This essay appeared in *Ethics & International Affairs* 12 (1998): 63–79. It is adapted from opening presentations given to the Carnegie Council's Faculty Institutes in 1996 and 1997. I have tried to retain the informal flavor of the discussion and have made only minor changes for this reprint. The essay should be read as reflecting the state of discussion in the mid-1990s.

1.   Joel H. Rosenthal, "Ethics through the Cold War and After," in *Ethics & International Affairs: A Reader*, ed. Joel H. Rosenthal, second edition (Washington, DC: Georgetown University Press, 1999).

2.   Samuel P. Huntington, "New Contingencies, Old Roles," *Joint Forces Quarterly* 2 (Autumn 1992): 338.

3.   See Joseph S. Nye Jr., *Bound to Lead: The Changing Nature of American Power* (New York: Basic Books, 1990), or, much earlier, Stanley Hoffmann, "Notes on the Elusiveness of Modern Power," *International Journal* 30 (Spring 1975): 183–206.

4.   An exhaustive analysis of such conflicts can be found in Ted Robert Gurr, *Minorities at Risk: A Global View of Ethnopolitical Conflicts* (Washington, DC: United States Institute of Peace, 1993).

5.   Thomas M. Franck, "The Emerging Right to Democratic Governance," *American Journal of International Law* 86, no. 1 (1992): 46–91.

6.   For an excellent summary of these operations, see the appendix prepared by Robert C. Johansen and Kurt Mills in Stanley Hoffmann, *The Ethics and Politics of Humanitarian Intervention* (Notre Dame, IN: University of Notre Dame Press, 1996).

7.   Tom J. Farer, "A Paradigm of Legitimate Intervention," in *Enforcing Restraint: Collective Intervention in Internal Conflicts*, ed. Lori Fisler Damrosch (New York: Council on Foreign Relations, 1993), 341.

8.   Michael Walzer, "The Politics of Rescue," in *Dissent* (Winter 1995): 41; also available in his *Arguing About War* (New Haven, CT: Yale University Press, 2004).

9.   Michael Walzer, *Just and Unjust Wars: A Moral Argument with Historical Illustrations*, fourth edition (New York: Basic Books, [1977] 2006), ch. 6.

10.   Farer, "Paradigm of Legitimate Intervention," 320, 330. On the "founding fathers," see J. L. Brierly, *The Law of Nations: An Introduction to the International Law of Peace*, sixth edition (New York: Oxford University Press, 1978), 403 ff., and Richard B. Lillich, ed., *Humanitarian Intervention and the United Nations* (Charlottesville: University of Virginia Press, 1973).

11.   Farer, "Paradigm of Legitimate Intervention," 330.

12.   David Rieff, "The Lessons of Bosnia: Morality and Power," *World Policy Journal* (Spring 1995): 76–88.

13.   Ernst B. Haas, "Global Evangelism Rides Again: How to Protect Human Rights without Really Trying," University of California Policy Paper 5, Institute of International Studies, Berkeley, 1978.

14.   See, for example, Robert Kagan and William Kristol, eds. *Present Dangers: Crisis and Opportunity in American Foreign and Defense Policy* (New York: Encounter, 2000).

15.   Quoted in the *New York Times*, November 18, 1995, A15.

16.   An obvious, and welcome, exception to this came with the publication in late 2001 of the report by the International Commission on Intervention and State Sovereignty (*The Responsibility to Protect* [Ottawa: International Development Research Centre, 2001]). This document (and the accompanying research volume to which I contributed a background paper) does carefully lay out a set of principles to guide consideration of when the "international community" should act in cases of humanitarian emergency. Its conclusions were affirmed at the 2005 World Summit marking the 60th anniversary of the UN.

17.   Rieff, "Lessons of Bosnia."

18.   Hoffmann, "Notes on the Elusiveness of Modern Power," and Michael W. Doyle, *Ways of War and Peace: Realism, Liberalism, and Socialism* (New York: W. W. Norton, 1997).

19.   Hedley Bull, *The Anarchical Society: A Study of Order in World Politics*, third edition (Basingstoke, UK: Palgrave Macmillan, 2002).

20.   Michael J. Smith, "Ethics and Intervention," *Ethics & International Affairs* 3 (1989).

21.   Michael J. Smith, *Realist Thought from Weber to Kissinger* (Baton Rouge: Louisiana State University Press, 1987).

22.   See Arnold Wolfers, "Statesmanship and Moral Choice," in his *Discord and Collaboration: Essays on International Politics* (Baltimore: Johns Hopkins University Press, 1962).

23.   Stanley Hoffmann, "Politics and Ethics of Military Intervention," *Survival* 37 (Winter 1995–1996): 29–51; Wolfers, "Statesmanship and Moral Choice."

24.   Amir Pasic, "Ethics and Reality: The Hard Case of Bosnia," paper presented at the International Studies Association Annual Meeting, San Diego, CA, April 1996.

25.   Michael Walzer, *Thick and Thin: Moral Argument at Home and Abroad* (Notre Dame, IN: University of Notre Dame Press, 1995).

26.   Judith D. Shklar, "The Liberalism of Fear," in *Liberalism and the Moral Life*, ed. Nancy L. Rosenblum (Cambridge, MA: Harvard University Press, 1989).

27.   Pierre Laberge, "Humanitarian Intervention: Three Ethical Positions," *Ethics & International Affairs* 9 (1995).

28.   Franck, "The Emerging Right to Democratic Self-Governance."

29.   Hoffmann, "Politics and Ethics of Military Intervention," 34–46.

30.   The following passage draws on a manuscript in progress written with Stanley Hoffmann; hence the change to the first person plural pronoun.

31.   Franck, "The Emerging Right to Democratic Self-Governance."

32.   Quoted in the *New York Times*, November 28, 1995, A12.

33.   See Walzer, *Just and Unjust Wars*, 102–110.

34.   This seems to me to be the reasoning that underlies the *Responsibility to Protect*, cited above (note 16).

35.   I refer of course to the character in Stanley Kubrick's *Dr. Strangelove*, General Jack D. Ripper.

Chapter 5

The Moral Basis of Humanitarian Intervention

Terry Nardin

If one person is able to save another and does not save him, he transgresses the commandment, Neither shalt thou stand idly by the blood of thy neighbor.
—Maimonides, *Mishneh Torah*, XI

To those for whom the greatest threat to the future of international order is the use of force in the absence of a Security Council mandate, one might say: leave Kosovo aside for a moment, and think about Rwanda. Imagine for one moment that, in those dark days and hours leading up to the genocide, there had been a coalition of states ready and willing to act in defense of the Tutsi population, but the Council had refused or delayed giving the green light. Should such a coalition then have stood idly by while the horror unfolded?
—UN secretary-general Kofi Annan,
Annual Report to the General Assembly, September 20, 1999

HUMANITARIAN INTERVENTION is usually discussed as an exception to the nonintervention principle. According to this principle, states are forbidden to exercise their authority, and certainly to use force, within the jurisdiction of other states. The principle finds firm support in the UN Charter, which permits a state to defend itself from attack but forbids the use of armed force against the territorial integrity or political independence of other states. Taken literally, these provisions prohibit armed intervention, including intervention to protect human rights. And in general, humanitarian intervention finds scant support in modern international law.

There is, however, a much older tradition in which the use of force is justified not only in self-defense but also to punish wrongs and protect the innocent. This tradition is in some tension with modern international law and especially with the UN Charter. It holds that armed intervention is permissible to enforce standards of civilized conduct when rulers violate those standards, and it finds expression today in the widely held opinion that states, acting unilaterally or collectively, are justified in enforcing respect for human rights. It is this enduring tradition, not current international law, that best explains the moral basis for humanitarian intervention.

My strategy in this essay is to relocate discussion of humanitarian intervention, moving it out of the familiar discourse of sovereignty and self-defense and into the discourse of rectifying wrongs and protecting the innocent. I do this in two ways. First, I examine arguments made in early modern Europe for using armed force to uphold natural law. I want to understand how what we now call humanitarian intervention was conceived by moralists, theologians, and philosophers writing about international relations before the emergence of modern international law. My aim is not to read current concerns back into a period that might not have shared them but rather to see whether earlier ideas about the use of force to protect people from injuries inflicted or tolerated by their own governors might illuminate current debates.

Second, I consider how humanitarian intervention is justified within a powerful reformulation of natural law worked out by philosophers influenced by Immanuel Kant. This post-Kantian version of natural law, which I follow Alan Donagan in calling "common morality," suggests why humanitarian intervention remains morally defensible despite modern efforts to make it illegal.[1]

HUMANITARIAN INTERVENTION IN EARLY MODERN NATURAL LAW

In twentieth-century international law, a just war is above all a war of self-defense. But sixteenth- and seventeenth-century European moralists justified war as a way to uphold law and protect rights, of which self-defense was only one. Rulers, these moralists argued, have a right and sometimes a duty to enforce certain laws beyond their realms. Some of these belong to the "law of nations" (*ius gentium*), understood not as international law but as general principles of law recognized in many different communities. This law of nations is an inductively established body of norms common to all or most peoples.

But the most important class of universally enforceable laws is "natural law," understood as comprising precepts that can be known by reason and are binding on all rational beings. What the law of nations and natural law have in common is that each identifies principles more general than the often idiosyncratic norms of particular communities. And in many respects, their principles are similar, though there are glaring exceptions. Slavery, for example, was long regarded as permitted by the law of nations, simply because it was widely practiced. But slavery cannot be defended as permissible under natural law, though many have, mistakenly, so defended it. The right to enforce these laws was understood to justify rulers in punishing moral wrongdoing and defending the innocent, wherever such action was needed.

The medieval literature on just war, like that of modern times, is concerned with wrongs done by one community to another. When Aquinas suggests that a "just cause" is required for resorting to war, he is thinking of situations in which one community acts to punish another. "Those who are attacked," he says, "should be attacked because they deserve it on account of some fault."[2] And he goes on to quote Augustine, for whom a just war is one that "avenges wrongs"—for example, when a state "has to be punished for refusing to make amends for the wrongs inflicted by its subjects or to restore what it has unjustly seized."[3]

To get to the idea of humanitarian intervention, we must shift our attention from wrongs done by one community to another to those done by a government to its own subjects, either directly or by permitting mistreatment. And if the justification of war is to prevent or punish wrongdoing, it is not hard to make this shift. Thomas More accomplishes it effortlessly when he reports that the Utopians go to war only "to protect their own land, to drive invading armies from the territories of their friends, or to liberate an oppressed people, in the name of humanity, from tyranny and servitude."[4] In the absence of a norm of nonintervention, no special justification for humanitarian intervention is needed. Even those who treat "the liberation of an oppressed people" as needing further justification will have an easier time making their case if the core justification for war is to "avenge wrongs."

One kind of oppression that medieval moralists saw as justifying intervention was the mistreatment of Christians in non-Christian ("infidel") kingdoms. Some realized that this one-sided concern could be generalized to include situations in which infidels injure one another, and even situations in which Christians injure infidels. In medieval discourse, the question of whether a Christian ruler might properly use force to protect the victims in these situations was eventually framed as a question of whether the pope, as the recognized universal authority, should intervene. Because the pope was responsible for seeing that all human beings obey God's laws, he could punish violations by anyone, infidel or Christian. Papal intervention, here, meant that the pope would authorize princes to intervene, just as UN intervention means that states are authorized to use armed force under its mandate.

A key figure in this discussion, on whom many sixteenth- and seventeenth-century moralists relied, is the thirteenth-century canon lawyer Sinibaldo Fieschi, who wrote authoritatively as Pope Innocent IV on relations between the papacy and non-Christian societies. The immediate context of Innocent's discussion was the Crusades, which raised the issue of whether it is morally justifiable for Christians to invade lands ruled by non-Christian princes. He argued that infidels, being rational creatures, are capable of making their own decisions, including forming civil societies and choosing rulers. Furthermore, infidels cannot be forcibly converted. But because the gospel is addressed to everyone, the pope must be concerned with infidel as well as Christian souls. And all people are under the jurisdiction of natural law.

Putting these arguments together, Innocent concludes that the pope has authority to act when infidels violate natural law. This might happen if infidel rulers violate this law, or if infidel subjects violate it and their rulers do not prevent or punish them. So, for example, if infidels practice idolatry or sodomy, which Innocent thinks are forbidden by natural law, Christians are justified in punishing them. Christians can also seek to promote the spiritual good of infidels by preaching the gospel among them. And should infidels interfere with Christian missionaries, their right to preach can be defended by armed force. Finally, force can be used to prevent persecution of Christians in infidel kingdoms. In short, the pope can intervene in any community to enforce natural law. Innocent IV, no naïf in these matters, knew that Christian rulers would twist these principles to justify the conquest of infidel societies. He therefore insisted that Christians could wage war against infidels to enforce natural law only with papal authorization.[5]

These principles were applied three centuries later by Francisco de Vitoria to the Spanish conquest of America. This brutal conquest was the subject of a long-running debate concerning the rights and conduct of the conquerors. But there was a new element in this debate, for Europeans saw the indigenous inhabitants not only as infidels but also as barbarians; that is, as uncivilized, even subhuman. These barbarians were distinguished from civilized peoples by their cannibalism and rituals of human sacrifice, practices that Europeans often invoked to justify subjecting them to Spanish rule.

Drawing explicitly upon Innocent IV, Vitoria considers whether cannibalism and human sacrifice provide grounds for the conquest. He argues that although natural law prohibits these acts, this does not necessarily justify war against those who practice them. Other crimes—adultery, sodomy, and theft, for example—also contravene natural law, but one cannot justly wage war against countries in which these crimes occur. "Surely," he writes, "it would be strange that fornication should be winked at in Christian society, but used as an excuse for conquering the lands of unbelievers!"[6] If armed intervention is a permissible response to cannibalism and human sacrifice, it must be because these crimes are especially evil. In such cases, outsiders are justified in defending the victims, even if they have not invited such assistance.

Like modern defenders of humanitarian intervention, Vitoria insists that a war to protect the innocent must be strictly limited. If the Spaniards wage war to suppress crimes against natural law, they cannot lawfully continue the war once it has achieved its goal, nor can they seize the property of the Indians or overthrow their governments. In other words, a lawful intervention cannot, without additional justification, become a lawful conquest. Moreover, if Europeans do, for whatever reason, come to rule the Indians, they must govern them for their own good.[7]

Some defenders of the conquest held that because the Indians were subhuman "brutes," it was lawful to hunt and kill them at will. Others argued that the barbarians, though human, were intellectually deficient and culturally primitive. These "brutish men" were what Aristotle had called "natural slaves"—human beings possessing enough reason to follow commands but not enough to assume responsibility for their own affairs. They were, moreover, slaves without masters, an anomaly for which the Spanish conquest seemed an obvious remedy. Vitoria rejects these claims. The Indians are not natural slaves. Even though their beliefs and conduct are strange and offensive, they have cities, laws, governments, and property, and in this respect are no different from other human beings. But even if the Indians were incapable of governing their own affairs, this would hardly justify killing, enslaving, or expropriating them. Like that of children, madmen, or the senile, their incapacity calls for paternal care.

Another defender of Indian rights, the missionary priest Bartolomé de las Casas, argues that the Spaniards were not justified in harming many to rescue a few. Such injury is disproportionate and, when its victims are innocent, inherently immoral. "In those provinces where unbelievers eat human flesh and sacrifice innocent persons, only a few persons commit these crimes, whereas innumerable persons . . . do not participate in these acts in any way."[8] The conquistadors wage war on the pretext of freeing the innocent, but they annihilate thousands of innocents. Luis de Molina, Domingo De Soto, and other contemporary critics of the conquest make similar points.

The Protestant Hugo Grotius is a key figure in debates over intervention to uphold natural law. The international morality he defends is one that permits such intervention but does not demand it. Grotius's "thin" or minimal morality requires human beings to refrain from injuring one another but does not require that they help one another. The basis for this morality, which he expounds in an unpublished early work, is self-preservation. Because the desire for self-preservation is inherent in their nature, human beings cannot be blamed for acting on it. And if they have a right to preserve themselves, they must also have the right to acquire the things needed for life and to defend their lives and possessions.[9]

These presocial rights, which are the foundation of natural law, in Grotius's view are enjoyed not only by natural persons but also by artificial persons, such as states, that coexist in a condition of nature. In such a condition, the first imperative is self-preservation. And because it rests on self-preservation, the law that governs this condition, the law of nature, is a law that prescribes mutual forbearance, not beneficence. Natural law requires only that we leave one another alone; it does not demand that we assist or protect one another. But we may assist or protect one another. It would contravene the teaching of Christ, Grotius argues, to say that Christians have nothing in common with non-Christians, for the injunction to love one's neighbor means that a Christian must love every human being. It follows that "the protection of infidels from injury (even from injury by Christians) is never unjust."[10] He concludes that the Dutch East India Company might justly wage war on the Portuguese for seeking to prevent the sultan of Johore from trading with the Dutch.[11] This conclusion may cause us to raise an eyebrow with respect to Grotius's motives, but it does not undermine his argument that justice may require forcibly protecting the rights of anyone who is the victim of unjust coercion.

In a subsequent work, Grotius asks whether a sovereign can rightly wage war to punish violations of natural law that do not affect him or his subjects. His answer is that sovereigns have the right to punish any acts that "excessively violate the law of nature or of nations in regard to any persons whatsoever." He invokes Innocent IV against those who argue that punishment is a civil power and therefore that a government has no right to wage war to defend persons over whom it has no legal jurisdiction.

If we accept this view, Grotius argues, no sovereign would be able to punish another for harming him or his subjects. The right to punish is based not on civil power but on the law of nature, which existed before there were civil societies. Therefore, wars are justly waged on those who "sin against nature" by engaging in cannibalism, piracy, and other barbaric practices. "Regarding such barbarians, wild beasts rather than men, one may rightly say . . . that war against them was sanctioned by nature; and . . . that the most just war is against savage beasts, the next against men who are like beasts."[12] Because Grotius does not distinguish between bestial men and bestial societies, sentences such as these justify punitive wars that go far beyond humanitarian intervention, narrowly defined. They point to deep worries about the threat that such societies pose to civilization itself, as Europeans understood it.

According to the new understanding of international relations that was emerging along with the idea of the sovereign state, any government has the right to enforce natural law against any other government that is guilty of violating it. In the "state of nature" postulated by Grotius and other seventeenth-century natural law theorists, there is no enforcing power superior to that of the sovereign of each state. Because in the state of nature unpunished violations of natural law by one sovereign harm every other sovereign by undermining natural law, any sovereign can punish such violations. A sovereign is even justified in punishing crimes that another commits against his own subjects, provided the offense is "very atrocious and very evident."[13] This general "right of punishment" owned by every sovereign in the international state of nature therefore justifies humanitarian intervention, at least in some situations.

The nonintervention principle, which became more and more important in international law during the eighteenth and nineteenth centuries, can be understood as a reaction against the view that every state has a right to enforce natural law. The chief objection to this doctrine was made by Samuel Pufendorf in works published during the 1670s. "We are not to imagine," Pufendorf writes, "that every man, even they who live in the liberty of nature, has a right to correct and punish with war any person who has done another an injury," for it is "contrary to the natural equality of mankind for a man to force himself upon the world for a judge and decider of controversies. . . . Any man might make war upon any man upon such a pretense."[14]

Nevertheless, according to Pufendorf, any person may justly assist any victim of oppression who invites assistance. "Kinship alone"—the mere fact of common humanity—"may suffice for us to go to the defense of an oppressed party who makes a plea for assistance, so far as we conveniently may."[15] For Pufendorf, to come to the aid of the oppressed is not only a right but in some cases a duty. It is, however, an "imperfect duty"—not a specific obligation like that prescribed by a contract but a duty of beneficence to be performed insofar as it can be performed without disproportionate inconvenience. The proviso that the victim must have invited assistance cannot, however, bear the weight Pufendorf gives it in distinguishing justifiable humanitarian intervention from unjustifiable interference by a sovereign who has usurped the office of judge over other sovereigns. Morally speaking, it is the act of oppression, not a request for assistance, that justifies an intervention.

The natural law argument for humanitarian intervention continued to erode during the eighteenth and nineteenth centuries as the view that international law is "positive law" based on the will of states emerged. The enlightenment philosopher Christian Wolff and his popularizer, Emmerich de Vattel, are among the last to treat international law as part of natural law (i.e., as belonging in effect to morality rather than to positive law), and both dismiss the classic argument justifying humanitarian intervention. According to Wolff, "A punitive war is not allowed against a nation for the reason that it is very wicked, or violates dreadfully the law of nature, or offends against God." And he explicitly asserts the principle of nonintervention, even when a sovereign abuses his subjects.[16] Vattel agrees, though he adds a qualification: If "by his insupportable tyranny" a prince "brings on a national revolt against him," any foreign power "may rightfully give assistance to an oppressed people who ask for its aid."[17] But in the absence of armed rebellion, intervention must be condemned; to say that one nation can use force to punish another for grave moral abuses is to open the door to war motivated by religious zealotry or economic ambition.[18]

Here we have a new principle, added to Pufendorf's requirement that the victims of oppression must request outside assistance: They must mount their own armed resistance. By the middle of the nineteenth century, this principle was being used to argue against humanitarian intervention. In his essay "A Few Words on Non-intervention," J. S. Mill argues that the subjects of an oppressive ruler must win their own freedom, without outside assistance, and they must suffer the consequences if their struggle is unsuccessful. Not even bloody repression can justify armed intervention by foreign powers, for were such intervention permissible, the idea of "self-determination," which Mill thinks is basic to political community, would be meaningless.[19]

Though he is a moralist, not an international lawyer, Mill perfectly articulates the view of humanitarian intervention we find in mainstream nineteenth-century international law. W. E. Hall, the author of a standard English work on international law at the end of that century, treats humanitarian intervention under the heading "Interventions in Restraint of Wrongdoing," a precise title, morally speaking. He argues that tyrannical oppression by a government of its own subjects, including religious persecution or massacres and brutality in a civil war, has nothing to do with relations between states. And he insists that we must not confuse outraged public opinion with the requirements of law. Some commentators, he writes, hold that states can lawfully intervene "to put an end to crimes and slaughter," but in the absence of consensus on this point, their judgment is not law.[20] If there is any legal basis for humanitarian intervention, it must rest not on principles of international morality but on agreement among states to recognize such principles as law. Hall here invokes the doctrine—a keystone of legal positivism—that international law is enacted by the joint will of sovereign states. Just as legislation is the criterion of law within each state, so agreement between states is the criterion of international law. The age of natural law had come to an end.

COMMON MORALITY AND THE DUTY TO PROTECT

Though banished from the realm of positive law, natural law did not simply disappear. It continued to march under the banner of morality. To distinguish this latter-day natural law, stripped of its religious and legal connotations, from the mores of particular communities, we may speak of a "common morality" binding on all human beings. Common morality assumes that human beings are thinking, choosing agents, and that everyone has an equal right to think and choose. It therefore requires us to recognize the inherent capacity of each person to make choices of his or her own. The foundation of common morality, then, is the principle that each person must respect the agency of every other. This is Kant's "principle of respect."[21] The more specific precepts of common morality are interpretations of this basic principle.

We must distinguish common morality from the mores of particular communities. Its principles constitute a common moral world in which human beings have rights not as members of this or that community but as members of the human community. Common morality rests neither on positive law nor on custom. It is, rather, the product of critical reflection on laws and customs, and in this sense may be said to be known by "reason." Its principles provide a standard "by which everybody ought to live, no matter what the mores of his neighbors might be."[22]

The principles of common morality—such as those that prohibit murder and deliberate harm to innocents and teach friendship, cooperation, and fairness—are basic to civilized life and are in fact recognized in most communities and traditions. This broad recognition is of immense practical importance, for it means that in appealing to common morality the moralist is appealing to principles whose authority has already been granted, implicitly if not explicitly, by a great many people. There are certainly people who do not belong to the common moral world, but one should not underestimate the degree to which its principles are generally acknowledged.[23] It is important to emphasize, however, that although the principles of common morality may be "common" in the sense that they are recognized in different communities, their validity does not depend on such recognition. They are required by a conception of the person and of what is owed to persons, not by convention. Common morality is a critical morality possessing wider authority than the moral practices of particular communities, and for this reason it provides a standard by which to criticize these practices. Like the idea of human rights, the idea of common morality is opposed to communitarian ethical theories that ground moral duties on custom and consent.

The relevance of common morality to humanitarian intervention should by now be apparent. Humanitarian intervention is a response to grave human rights violations, and the most basic human rights are universal moral rights—rights, in other words, that rest on the principles of common morality. There are, then, good reasons for grounding the ethics of humanitarian intervention in common morality and not in particular religious or national moralities, or even in international law, which rests on custom and agreement, not moral reasoning.

Unlike some ethical traditions, common morality does not regulate every aspect of life. In any situation, there is always a wide range of morally permissible responses, and common morality is for the most part unconcerned with choosing among them. Common morality is a minimal morality, and for this reason it must be distinguished from religious and other traditions that make a broad range of concerns a matter of moral duty.[24] It regulates the choices we make as rational agents, not as adherents of this or that tradition. But precisely because it rests on a view of human beings as rational agents, common morality permits us considerable freedom to choose as we will. It imagines a human community in which individuals pursue their own self-chosen ends, and it seeks to regulate this pursuit so that the actions of one do not unjustly interfere with the actions of others.

Common morality forbids us to use other human beings coercively to achieve our ends. Using force, without good reason, violates the principle of respect. This explains not only why murder and slavery are wrong but also why self-defense is morally justifiable. But common morality does not limit the use of force to self-defense. It also permits us to defend the rights of others when those rights are threatened. We are therefore justified in using force to thwart violence against other persons, provided those persons are morally "innocent"—that is, not themselves engaged in unjust violence. Using force to resist those who attack the innocent does not violate the attackers' rights as free persons because they have, by their own actions, lost the moral right to act as they

choose. It is even permitted to kill attackers, if necessary, to protect their victims. We are justified in using as much force as is needed to thwart the attack,
but not more—bearing in mind that precise calculations about such matters are
impossible.[25]

Though derived ultimately from the principle of respect, the right to use
force to defend the innocent from violence rests more immediately on the idea
of beneficence, which is the idea that human beings should support one another
in appropriate ways. To respect other human beings as rational agents means
not only that we must not interfere with their freedom but also that we should
assist them in achieving their ends. Common morality is at its core a morality
of constraint, but its precepts are not limited to those that constrain us. It
also asks us to advance the well-being of others—by being cooperative, helpful,
charitable, and the like—in ways that are morally permissible and not disproportionately costly. In other words, in helping others we are forbidden to do
wrong for their sake and we are not required to do more than we can reasonably
afford.

Given the principle of beneficence, common morality may require us to act
when others are in danger of serious injury, whether by accident or as victims
of wrongdoing. This requirement is expressed in the parable of the Good
Samaritan (Luke 10:29–37) and, more pointedly, in the divine command that
you must not stand idly by when lives are in danger (Lev. 19:16). The principle
of beneficence, which this command invokes, leaves us free to decide how to
promote the well-being of others. Nevertheless, if we are able to provide immediate assistance to someone who needs it, we should provide that assistance.
And this implies that we must not allow anyone to be harmed by violence if we
can reasonably prevent it. In short, assuming that the costs are not too high, it
is "not merely permissible but a duty to employ force against the violent if their
victims cannot otherwise be protected."[26] This is the fundamental principle
underlying humanitarian intervention.[27]

The principle addresses three aspects of the decision to act on behalf of
persons threatened by violence. First, we must ask under what circumstances
such action is morally called for. Who should be protected (who is my "neighbor"), and from which harms? Second, who should intervene? Who is the
"thou" who is forbidden to stand idly by when another is in danger? And third,
what must we do to avoid the charge that we are standing idly by? And what
must we not do—what constraints, in other words, must we observe in providing aid?

We can use these questions to illuminate the morality of humanitarian intervention. But in doing so, we must remember that principles alone cannot determine complex foreign policy decisions. Moral principles can provide broad
goals to guide deliberation, and they prescribe constraints on what choices can
be made. But they cannot more precisely determine those goals and choices.

Humanitarian action may require anything from ending a massacre to rebuilding a society whose institutions have failed. Deciding which of several morally permissible courses of action to pursue in a particular situation demands judgment and prudence, but this task belongs to politics, not moral philosophy.

WHEN IS HUMANITARIAN INTERVENTION PERMISSIBLE?

For Maimonides, the biblical injunction is to "save" another, and the implication is that the victim's life is endangered. If humanitarian intervention means acting to protect human rights, many such rights besides the right to life might be threatened, including rights against torture, arbitrary detention, and racial discrimination. But usually only the gravest violations, such as genocide and ethnic cleansing, are held to justify armed intervention. Such acts affect the lives of many people and the fate of entire communities. In the classic phrase, they "shock the conscience of humankind."

It is consistent with common morality to argue that humanitarian intervention is justified, in principle, in a wide range of situations, but that practical considerations usually override this justification.[28] Yet one can also justify limiting intervention to the gravest abuses by invoking considerations that arise from the aims of civil association. The state as a coercive institution is morally justifiable because, in principle, it enables human beings to fulfill their potentialities by living together according to common rules. Once a state has been established, however, its citizens must obey the laws it adopts for this purpose, assuming these laws are not substantially unjust. And a substantially just state is entitled to respect by other states, which are morally barred from interfering with its government.

The nonintervention principle is therefore basic to relations between states. It is not a mere custom of the international system. There are moral reasons why a state must be recognized as having rights, in particular the right that outsiders respect its independence and boundaries. But the same principles that justify the nonintervention principle justify exceptions to the principle. If a government seriously violates the moral rights of those it governs, others may defend those rights, using force if necessary. The nonintervention principle is not a shield behind which an unjust state can hide while it violates the moral rights of its subjects. Such violations, if serious enough, permit forcible humanitarian intervention and may even demand it. But respect for the rights of a political community requires that those violations be truly grave.

Christian tradition holds explicitly that all human beings are "neighbors." Vitoria, for example, writes that "the barbarians are all our neighbors, and therefore anyone, and especially princes, may defend them from . . . tyranny and oppression."[29] Common morality, also, holds every human being is in principle my neighbor and therefore entitled to assistance, though practically speaking I may be limited to helping those with whom I am connected in some way. It follows that humanitarian intervention is governed by the same principles of nondiscrimination that govern all conduct. It would, for example, be discriminatory in a way that deserves moral condemnation if Western governments acted to redress gross violations of human rights in Europe but remained indifferent to equivalent or graver harms suffered by Africans. To be sure, Europeans today do not necessarily have the same duty to intervene in Africa as in Europe, for there may be special obligations or practical constraints that distinguish the situations. But the case must be made carefully. No people can be arbitrarily excluded from humanitarian concern in ways that amount to prejudicial discrimination.

WHO SHOULD INTERVENE?

Humanitarian intervention is traditionally defined as the use of force by states to protect human rights. This definition presumes that states should do the intervening. It is sometimes argued that the traditional definition is obsolete because humanitarian intervention is increasingly a matter of collective action under UN auspices, not action undertaken by states acting on their own authority.[30]

However, to say that humanitarian intervention should be collective is simply to offer a different answer to the question of who should intervene. The moral principle is general: *You* shall not stand idly by, whoever you are, if you can provide effective assistance at reasonable cost and without neglecting other duties. There are practical reasons for suggesting that the international community should authorize humanitarian interventions. Such interventions may, for example, be more likely than unilateral actions to benefit from collective wisdom and to gain wide support.[31] But to insist on such authorization is to presume a degree of justice and effectiveness at the supranational level that the world has not yet achieved.

There are, however, moral reasons why states should adhere to international law and therefore why unilateral intervention should be condemned if international law forbids it. It is regrettable that NATO's decision to intervene in Kosovo had to be made outside the framework of the United Nations and in a manner not explicitly provided for by its own charter, which requires its members to defend one another if attacked, but says nothing about intervention or peacekeeping that is unrelated to collective defense. But if unilateral intervention is illegal and procedures exist for collective action, and yet the international community as a whole is unable to act effectively, must individual states also "stand idly by"? As UN secretary-general Kofi Annan implies in discussing the world's failure to act in Rwanda, to say "yes" is to repudiate common morality.

Some moralists argue that only a government that respects human rights is entitled to intervene to protect human rights.[32] There are reasons for favoring such a requirement in many cases, but the principle is not part of common morality. A murderer is not forbidden to save a drowning child. The objectionable character of the Vietnamese government in 1979 does not mean that its intervention in Cambodia, which ended the genocide there, was morally wrong.[33]

WHAT MEANS OF PROTECTION ARE CALLED FOR?

Common morality prescribes that we must not stand idly by when human lives are threatened, but this is a very broad injunction. As we have seen, coercive action is not immoral if it is aimed at those who are themselves acting immorally, and provided we do not pursue good ends by immoral means. Clearly, this means that forces conducting humanitarian interventions must comply with the laws of war, as these laws are understood both in the just war tradition and in international law. It means in particular that such forces must respect the principle of noncombatant immunity, which is that innocent persons may not be directly attacked either as an end or as a means to an end, and that the costs of indirect injury must not be unfairly distributed.[34]

The responses we might choose are not limited to those requiring military force. War is an extreme remedy. The label "humanitarian intervention" is sometimes applied to transnational charitable efforts to relieve human suffering as well as to forcible interventions to protect human rights. Those who see armed intervention as a kind of just war sometimes protest that using a common label muddies the waters by linking modes of international assistance that raise different issues and should be handled in different ways. Common morality certainly recognizes as morally relevant the distinction between coercive and noncoercive assistance. But it also prescribes assisting fellow human beings in any effective and morally permissible manner. It therefore allows a wide range of responses to situations in which lives are endangered, while recognizing that responses involving the use of force require additional justification. It also reminds us that military action cannot be assumed to be effective and that the only force that is morally justifiable is the minimum necessary to accomplish its purpose.

In considering what to do, an intervening state is not barred from considering the costs and from deciding not to act if those costs are too high. Although beneficence is a duty, it is what moralists sometimes call an imperfect duty. Like an individual person, a state is not obligated to intervene at great cost to itself. Risking all to save others may be praiseworthy, even saintly, but common morality does not demand it.[35] But if no country can be asked to seriously harm its own interests to assist another, what can we reasonably ask it to do? If I save someone's life, I am not supposed to have taken on a long-term obligation to care for that person.

However, the injunction to "save" my neighbor, if my neighbor is a community, might entail continued involvement. Armed intervention to halt a massacre is likely to be only the first of many measures needed to restore order to a chaotic society and prevent subsequent massacres. If prevention is important, the challenge for humanitarian policy is to move from responding to humanitarian crises to forestalling them. And if common morality requires civil association and the rule of law, a policy of progressively strengthening civil institutions at the international level may itself be morally required, as Kant long ago argued in "Perpetual Peace."[36] It is perhaps no coincidence that the greatest theorist of common morality was also concerned with the conditions of a just and peaceful international order.

In sum, common morality suggests that humanitarian intervention is justifiable under three conditions. First, it must be an extraordinary remedy, chosen in response to grave human rights abuses that cannot be ended by diplomatic means. This limitation recognizes that the legal rights of states cannot be lightly set aside, and that military intervention is an uncertain remedy, which has great costs of its own.

Second, interventions should be approved by a recognized international authority acting in accordance with reasonably just international laws. But if such an authority does not exist or is substantially unjust or ineffective, either in general or in a given situation, states may act without its approval. Whether the UN is a just and effective international authority is a judgment that those contemplating intervention will have to make—and defend.

Third, any intervention must be conducted by effective and morally permissible means. It must respect domestic and international laws unless there is good reason to override them because they are manifestly unjust or because the relevant governments or international authorities are ineffective. But above all, those who intervene must respect the moral laws that forbid harming innocent people as a means to an end and that require a fair distribution of risk (by prescribing attention to considerations of "proportionality" and "due care") between the intervening forces and those they aim to assist.

Decisions about whether and how to intervene will always involve a wide range of contingencies, for states have no duty to intervene unless they can do so successfully and at reasonable cost to themselves and to others. It follows that selectivity in the choice of occasions for intervention is both inevitable and potentially justifiable.

These conclusions are neither novel nor especially controversial. This should be taken as an encouraging sign, for it suggests that the contribution of common morality to the debate over humanitarian intervention is to help us clarify the rational foundation of views whose cogency is already widely acknowledged. Its contribution is to indicate, from the standpoint of a carefully articulated and intellectually powerful position, where, morally speaking, arguments over particular interventions can and cannot go.

CONCLUSION

I began by briefly contrasting two traditions of thought on humanitarian intervention. One, embedded in modern international law and the UN Charter, sees intervention as inherently problematic, given the importance the law attaches to preserving the political independence and territorial integrity of states. The other, which belongs to the tradition of natural law or common morality, sees humanitarian intervention as an expression of the basic moral duty to protect the innocent from violence. The tension between them raises the question of how we can reconcile the complex institutional duties prescribed by international law with the more primitive, noninstitutional duties of common morality. Common morality achieves its reconciliation by requiring that we respect institutions established through the free exercise of human capacities—the family, property, the state, and international law—provided these institutions are reasonably effective and just.

The problem of humanitarian intervention, then, is analogous to the problem of political obligation. The question "Are citizens morally obligated to obey the laws of the civil society in which they live?" becomes "Are states obligated to obey the law of international society?" Precisely how ineffective or unjust the relevant laws and institutions must be before states are entitled to override the nonintervention principle or to ignore the UN Charter is a practical question to which no general answer can be given. But it is helpful to see that this is the right question to ask in debating humanitarian intervention. Moral guidance can be obtained neither by asserting existing law, as if its authority were unquestionable, nor by asserting moral principles, as if in obeying humanitarian imperatives no attention need be given to respecting laws, but only by giving careful attention to the claims of each in the particular situations to which the international community is called to respond.

As I have emphasized, common morality does not prescribe answers to many of the practical questions raised by particular interventions, except within very wide limits. It has little to say about whether acts of beneficence, and therefore humanitarian interventions, should be unilateral or collective, beyond requiring that collective procedures be respected, where they exist and are not ineffective or unjust. Although it forbids us to deny any human being the status of neighbor, it leaves us wide latitude in deciding whom we can assist, by what means we can assist them, and how much assistance we can provide. What common morality does provide is a way of viewing the ethics of humanitarian intervention that is rooted in a widely shared and rationally defensible conception of human dignity, and which for these reasons is relatively independent of the contingencies of particular situations. It follows that the moral principles underlying humanitarian intervention do not need to be rethought "in the post–Cold War world" or "after Kosovo." These principles have been known for centuries, if not millennia. They will acquire new meanings in each new situation to which they are applied, and because this requires judgment, they will often be misapplied. But the principles themselves will not soon be replaced.

NOTES

This essay first appeared in *Ethics & International Affairs* 16, no. 1 (2002): 57–70. It was revised in 2008. Earlier versions of this essay were presented at the Travers Ethics Conference, held at the University of California, Berkeley, in December 1999; at a symposium sponsored by the Center for Global Peace and Conflict Studies at the University of California, Irvine, in May 2000; at the Annual Meeting of the International Studies Association in February 2001; and at conferences hosted by the Center for European Studies and the Carr Center for Human Rights Policy at Harvard University in January and September 2001. I am grateful to the participants in these events and to the editors and reviewers of *Ethics & International Affairs* for helpful criticism and advice.

1. Alan Donagan, *The Theory of Morality* (Chicago: University of Chicago Press, [1977] 1979).

2. Saint Thomas Aquinas, *Summary of Theology* II–II, Q. 40, a. 1, in *On Law, Morality, and Politics*, ed. William P. Baumgarth and Richard J. Regan (Indianapolis, IN: Hackett Publishing Company, 1988), 221.

3. Augustine, *Questions on the Heptateuch* 6.10, quoted in Aquinas, *On Law, Morality and Politics*, 221.

4. Thomas More, *Utopia* (1516), ed. George M. Logan and Robert M. Adams (Cambridge: Cambridge University Press, 1989), 87–88.

5. James Muldoon, *Popes, Lawyers, and Infidels: The Church and the Non-Christian World 1250–1550* (Philadelphia: University of Pennsylvania Press, 1979), 10–11, 12.

6. Francisco de Vitoria, "On Dietary Laws, or Self-Restraint" (1537), in *Political Writings*, ed. Anthony Pagden and Jeremy Lawrance (Cambridge: Cambridge University Press, 1991), 230.

7. Vitoria, "On Dietary Laws," 225–226; and Vitoria, "On the American Indians" (1539), in *Political Writings*, ed. Pagden and Lawrance, 288.

8. Bartolomé de las Casas, *In Defense of the Indians* (1552), trans. Stafford Poole (DeKalb: Northern Illinois University Press, 1992), 207.

9. Hugo Grotius, *De jure praedae* (1604), published in English as Commentary on the *Law of Prize and Booty*, trans. Gwladys L. Williams (Oxford: Clarendon Press, 1950), 10.

10. Grotius, *De jure praedae*, 315.

11. Richard Tuck, *The Rights of War and Peace: Political Thought and the International Order from Grotius to Kant* (New York: Oxford University Press, 1999), 93–94.

12. Hugo Grotius, *De jure belli ac pacis* (1625), *On the Law of War and Peace* (1646), trans. Francis W. Kelsey (New York: Oxford University Press, 1925), 504–6.

13. Grotius, *De jure belli ac pacis*, 508.

14. Samuel von Pufendorf, *Of the Law of Nature and Nations* (1672), trans. C. H. Oldfather and W. A. Oldfather (Oxford: Clarendon Press, 1934), 847. I have modernized the spelling and punctuation.

15. Samuel von Pufendorf, *On the Duty of Man and Citizen*, ed. James Tully (Cambridge: Cambridge University Press, 1991), 170.

16. Christian von Wolff, *The Law of Nations Treated According to a Scientific Method* (1748), trans. Joseph D. Drake (New York: Oxford University Press, 1934), section 637; sections 258 and 1011.

17. Emmerich de Vattel, *The Law of Nations, or Principles of Natural Law Applied to the Conduct and Affairs of Nations and Sovereigns* (1758), trans. Charles G. Fenwick (Washington, DC: Carnegie Institution, 1916), 131; see also 340.

18. de Vattel, *Law of Nations*, 116.

19. J. S. Mill, *Dissertations and Discussions*, 2nd ed. (London: Longmans, 1867), vol. 3, 153–178. The essay was first published in 1859.

20. William Edward Hall, *A Treatise on International Law*, 6th ed. (New York: Oxford University Press, 1909), 284, 287–88.

21. Immanuel Kant, *Foundations of the Metaphysics of Morals* (1785), trans. Lewis White Beck (Indianapolis, IN: Bobbs-Merrill, 1959), 66–67.

22. Donagan, *Theory of Morality*, 1. My sketch of common morality draws freely on Donagan and on Michael Walzer, *Just and Unjust Wars: A Moral Argument with Historical Illustrations*, fourth edition (New York: Basic Books, [1977] 2006). On the connection between the arguments of these works, see Joseph Boyle, "Casuistry and the Boundaries of the Moral World," *Ethics & International Affairs* 11 (1997): 83–98.

23. Two recent and especially cogent explorations of the relationship between universal and communal moral views are Amartya Sen, "Human Rights and Asian Values," 16th Morgenthau Memorial Lecture on Ethics and Foreign Policy, Carnegie Council, New York City, May 25, 1997; and Michael Walzer, "Universalism and Jewish Values," 20th Morgenthau Memorial Lecture, May 15, 2001. Both lectures are available online via www.cceia.org/resources/publications/morgenthau/index.html.

24. Grotius offers a statement of this distinction in Christian tradition when he writes that in the "holy law" of the New Testament, "a greater degree of moral perfection is enjoined upon us than the law of nature . . . would require" (*Law of War and Peace*, 27).

25. Donagan, *Theory of Morality*, 85–87.

26. Ibid., 86.

27. Since the original version of this essay was published, I have come to understand that humanitarian intervention is grounded not only on the principle of beneficence but also, and independently, on a duty to resist violence. This is a duty of justice, not humanity. The failure to intervene is a failure to resist violence and therefore to condone the injustice it represents. We have a duty to cooperate in resisting violence not only for the sake of the victims but also to uphold everyone's right not to be violently harmed. In resisting violence we defend that right as well as the victim. For a fuller statement of this argument, see Terry Nardin, "International Political Theory and the Question of Justice," *International Affairs* 82 (2006): 449–66.

28. Jerome Slater and Terry Nardin, "Nonintervention and Human Rights," *Journal of Politics* 48 (1986): 86–96.

29. Vitoria, "On the American Indians," 288.

30. For criticism of the traditional definition, see Oliver Ramsbotham and Tom Woodhouse, *Humanitarian Intervention in Contemporary Conflict* (Cambridge: Polity Press, 1996), 113–14.

31. Stephen A. Garrett, *Doing Good and Doing Well: An Examination of Humanitarian Intervention* (Westport, CN: Praeger, 1999), chap. 7.

32. Fernando R. Tesón, *A Philosophy of International Law* (Boulder, CO: Westview Press, 1998), 59.

33. Nicholas J. Wheeler, *Saving Strangers: Humanitarian Intervention in International Society* (New York: Oxford University Press, 2001), 110.

34. Walzer provides a clear explanation of the principle of discrimination, and related ideas like double effect and due care, in *Just and Unjust Wars*, 151–59.

35. Walzer, in his preface to the third edition of *Just and Unjust Wars* (2000), agrees that intervention is an "imperfect duty," but he is bitter about it: "the massacres go on, and every country that is able to stop them decides that it has more urgent tasks" (xiii).

36. Immanuel Kant, *Political Writings*, ed. Hans Reiss, second edition (Cambridge: Cambridge University Press, 1991).

Chapter 6

Responsibility to Protect or Trojan Horse?

The Crisis in Darfur and Humanitarian Intervention after Iraq

Alex J. Bellamy

THE WORLD'S FAILURE to prevent or halt the Rwandan genocide was described as a "sin of omission" by UN secretary-general Kofi Annan.[1] British prime minister Tony Blair promised that "if Rwanda happens again we would not walk away as the outside has done many times before," and insisted that international society had a "moral duty" to provide military and humanitarian assistance to Africa whenever it was needed.[2] The United States labeled as "rogues" states that "brutalize their own people and squander their natural resources for the personal gain of their rulers."[3] Since 2003, the Sudanese government and its notorious Janjaweed militia have conducted a brutal campaign of mass killing and ethnic cleansing in response to an uprising by the Sudanese Liberation Army and the Justice and Equality Movement, who have themselves attacked civilians in the Darfur region, though on a much smaller scale.[4] Recent surveys place the number of deaths caused by direct violence between 73,700 and 172,154.[5] Deaths from malnutrition and preventable disease in internally displaced persons camps stood at 108,588 in January 2005, with approximately 25,000 more having died in inaccessible regions.[6] The British Parliament's International Development Committee put the total casualty figure at around 300,000.[7] At least 1.8 million more had been forced to flee their homes.[8] Following a unanimous vote by the U.S. Congress in July 2004, Colin Powell took the unprecedented step of labeling the violence "genocide."

Despite professed commitments to prevent future man-made humanitarian catastrophes, the world's response to the Darfur crisis has been muted. At the time of writing, a small, underfunded and understaffed African Union mission (AMIS) is deployed in Darfur. Although it has a mandated size of approximately 3,300, there are fewer than 1,500 AMIS peacekeepers on the ground. The force has proven unable to halt sporadic escalations of violence or prevent the humanitarian situation from deteriorating.[9] The UN Security Council has taken an ambivalent position. On the one hand, it has to date failed to impose serious sanctions on Sudanese officials and has not contemplated using force to protect civilians or humanitarian aid. On the other hand, while it has yet to decide whether the UN Mission to Sudan (UNMIS), created recently to support, monitor, and verify the comprehensive peace agreement between the government of Sudan and the Sudan People's Liberation Movement/Army (SPLM/A) in the south, will play an active role in Darfur, there is a distinct possibility that it could.[10] Moreover, on March 31, 2005, the council took the momentous step of referring the Darfur case to the International Criminal Court (ICC).[11]

This article explores what international engagement with Darfur tells us about the norm of humanitarian intervention since the 2003 war in Iraq. Do states and regional organizations recognize that they have a "responsibility to protect" civilians at risk, as the International Commission on Intervention and State Sovereignty (ICISS) argued? Or is humanitarian intervention perceived as a "Trojan horse" used by the powerful to legitimize their interference in the affairs of the weak? I examine whether the Iraq war has shifted the balance between these two positions, posing the question: Is there more or less likelihood of global consensus on armed responses to "supreme humanitarian emergencies"?[12] My response proceeds in two parts. The first provides a brief overview of the norm of humanitarian intervention, focusing on *The Responsibility to Protect* and on debates about the impact of the "war on terror" and the war in Iraq on it. The second offers a detailed study of the international response to Darfur.

I argue that the situation in Darfur reveals two subtle changes to the humanitarian intervention norm. First, although the level of consensus about humanitarian intervention has not perceptively shifted, the debates on Darfur lend credence to the thesis that the Iraq war has undermined the standing of the United States and the United Kingdom as norm carriers.[13] According to Martha Finnemore and Kathryn Sikkink, new norms only replace old ones after a period of contestation between advocates of the old and the new.[14] If the credibility of those most associated with the new norm is undermined by perceptions that they have abused it or raised it for primarily self-serving purposes, the process of normative change is likely to be slowed or reversed.[15] Traditional advocates of the new norm will find that their arguments have less resonance among skeptics. The problem is compounded by military overstretch on the part of key advocates of humanitarian intervention, in particular the United States and the United Kingdom. In short, it has become harder for these states to persuade others to act decisively in humanitarian emergencies at precisely the moment when those states themselves are less able to bear the costs of acting outside the world's institutional framework. From the American and British perspectives there is no feasible alternative to collective action through the UN or AU in addressing the situation in Darfur, but they have been unable to build consensus about collective action at least in part, I would suggest, because of their diminished credibility as norm carriers.

Second, the Darfur debates have been deeply infused with the language of a "responsibility to protect." The meaning of that language, however, has been hotly contested. Changing the language of the intervention debate has done little to forge consensus or overcome the struggle between sovereignty and human rights. In the debates I examine, "responsibility to protect" talk was used to oppose international activism as much as to support it. If we accept Quentin Skinner's argument that actors will not act in ways that they cannot justify by reference to the prevailing normative context, it could be claimed that the brief period of acquiescence to humanitarian interventions in the 1990s was at least partly due to the absence of plausible arguments *against* them. This claim is made more compelling when the absence of plausible arguments against intervention is set against the global consensus that horrors such as the Rwandan genocide should not have been permitted.[16] In the Darfur case, as I will show, "responsibility to protect" language has now enabled *anti-interventionists* to legitimize arguments against action by claiming that primary responsibility in certain contested cases still lies with the state, and not (yet) with an international body. Given the credibility crisis confronting some of the leading advocates of humanitarian intervention, there is a real danger that appeals to a responsibility to protect will evaporate amid disputes about where that responsibility lies.

THE NORM OF HUMANITARIAN INTERVENTION

It is widely accepted that the Security Council has a legal right to authorize humanitarian intervention under Chapter VII of the UN Charter.[17] There is also a partial consensus among some liberal states that there is a moral right to intervene without council authorization in extreme cases.[18] It is highly unlikely that the Security Council would have objected had others used force to halt the 1994 Rwandan genocide.[19] Throughout the Security Council's deliberations about Rwanda, no state publicly argued that either the ban on force (Article 2[4]) or the nonintervention rule (Article 2[7]) ought to prohibit armed action to halt the bloodshed.[20] Moreover, as Simon Chesterman has argued, there is little evidence to suggest that sovereignty concerns inhibit states from saving strangers when they have the means and desire to do so.[21] Throughout the 1990s, the Security Council expanded its interpretation of "international peace and security," authorizing interventions to protect civilians in so-called safe areas (Bosnia), maintain law and order, protect aid supplies (Somalia), and restore an elected government toppled by a coup (Haiti). However, two questions remain hotly contested: First, who has the authority to sanction humanitarian intervention when the Security Council is blocked by the veto? Second, when should a humanitarian crisis trigger potential armed intervention? I argue in the following sections that although a partial consensus on these questions was established during the 1990s, there is now deep division about how to interpret the effects of the "war on terror" and the invasion of Iraq on that consensus.

The Partial Consensus on Humanitarian Intervention

As mentioned earlier, in the past few years many liberal states have begun to accept the proposition that intervention not authorized by the Security Council could be legitimate. NATO's intervention in Kosovo was a watershed in this regard. A commission of experts found the intervention to be "illegal but legitimate," meaning that while it did not satisfy international society's legal rules, it was "sanctioned by its compelling moral purpose."[22] This finding implies a degree of consensus around the idea that states have a moral right to intervene to save strangers in supreme humanitarian emergencies. A Russian draft Security Council resolution condemning the intervention was rejected by twelve votes to three (Russia, China, and Namibia).[23] While the failure of the Russian draft did not constitute retrospective authorization, it does add credence to the idea that there is a moral consensus among liberal states and some others about the right of intervention in supreme humanitarian emergencies.[24] The claim that the consensus extended beyond Western liberal states in the Kosovo case is further demonstrated by the Organization of the Islamic Conference's support for the intervention, which was communicated to the Security Council in a letter stating, "A decisive international action was necessary to prevent humanitarian catastrophe and further violations of human rights" in Kosovo.[25] This is a *partial* consensus, however, because many, if not most, of the world's states do not subscribe to the view that in exceptional circumstances unauthorized intervention may be legitimate. In addition to the well-recorded hostility of Russia, China, and India, the Non-Aligned Movement responded to Kosovo by declaring its rejection of "the so-called right of humanitarian intervention, which has no legal basis."[26]

Further evidence of a developing moral consensus about humanitarian intervention in supreme humanitarian emergencies has emerged since Kosovo. Article 4(h) of the AU's Constitutive Act, signed on July 11, 2000, awarded the new organization "the right . . . to intervene in a Member State pursuant to a decision by the Assembly in respect of grave circumstances, namely: war crimes, genocide and crimes against humanity."[27] And in 2001, Kofi Annan used his Nobel lecture to argue, "The sovereignty of states must no longer be used as a shield for gross violations of human rights."[28] In the same period there were myriad authorized and unauthorized interventions.[29]

In 2001, the Canadian government gave the high-profile ICISS the task of establishing common ground on the question of humanitarian intervention.[30] The ICISS recommended replacing the atavistic terminology of humanitarian intervention (sovereignty vs. human rights) with the new language of the "responsibility to protect." It called for an approach that looked at the problem from the victim's point of view. It insisted that the primary responsibility to protect civilians lay with the host state and that outside intervention could only be contemplated if the host state proved either unwilling or unable to fulfill its responsibilities.[31]

On the question of when to intervene, the ICISS adopted the commonly held view that intervention should be limited to "extreme" cases—in other words, Wheeler's "supreme humanitarian emergencies" and Tom Farer's "spikes."[32] Outside intervention, it argued, was warranted in cases in which there was large-scale loss of life or ethnic cleansing, whether deliberately caused by the state or facilitated by neglect or incapacity. The question of authority proved thornier. The ICISS proposed a three-layered distribution of responsibility. Primary responsibility lay with the host state. Secondary responsibility lay with the domestic authorities working in partnership with outside agencies. If the primary and secondary levels failed to ameliorate the humanitarian emergency, international organizations would assume responsibility. At this third level of responsibility, the ICISS accepted the view that primary legal authority for action was vested in the Security Council. If the Security Council was dead-locked, it argued that potential interveners should approach the General Assembly under the Uniting for Peace mechanism and, if that failed, work through regional organizations. In an attempt to increase the chances of consensus in the council, the ICISS recommended that its permanent members commit themselves to a series of criteria relating to the use of force in humanitarian emergencies. It was suggested that states always seek Security Council authorization before using force; that the council commit itself to dealing promptly with humanitarian emergencies involving large-scale loss of life; that the permanent members should commit themselves to not casting a veto to obstruct humanitarian action unless their vital national interests are involved; and that Security Council members should recognize that if they fail to fulfill their responsibility to protect, other states and organizations may take it upon themselves to act.[33] The commission insisted that the question of military intervention should be placed firmly on the Security Council's agenda if two "just cause thresholds" (large-scale loss of life and ethnic cleansing) and four "precautionary principles" (right intention, last resort, proportional means, and reasonable prospects) were satisfied.[34]

Reactions to the ICISS report were generally positive, though there were notable signs of dissent. It was received most favorably by states, such as Canada, Japan, Germany, and (to a lesser extent) the United Kingdom, that had, since the intervention in Kosovo, been exploring the potential for developing criteria to guide global decision making about humanitarian intervention.[35] When the Security Council discussed the report at its annual informal retreat in May 2002, almost all of the permanent members expressed disquiet with the idea of formalizing criteria for intervention. The United States rejected them on the grounds that it could not offer precommitments to engage its military forces where it had no national interests, and that it would not bind itself to criteria that would restrain its right to decide when and where to use force.[36] China had opposed the idea throughout the ICISS process, and while Russia was generally supportive, it insisted that no action should be taken without Security Council approval, a position that was unacceptable to the United States, the United Kingdom, and France.[37] For their part, the United Kingdom and France, two advocates of the ICISS principles among the Permanent Five, expressed concern that formulating criteria to govern humanitarian intervention would not produce the missing ingredients of political will and consensus.[38]

The U.S. intervention in Afghanistan seemed to support the idea of a partial moral consensus on the importance of humanitarianism in war. The U.S. administration felt obliged to argue that Operation Enduring Freedom would improve humanitarian conditions inside Afghanistan, even though it was widely recognized as a legitimate act of self-defense.[39] The 2003 invasion of Iraq, however, proved much more problematic. In this case, the political leaders of all the major troop contributors (the United States, the United Kingdom, and Australia) gave considerable weight to the humanitarian case for war in their public justifications, though the formal legal justification was based on the enforcement of existing Security Council resolutions.[40] Although the humanitarian argument received support in some quarters, it was widely rejected.[41] Whereas in the Kosovo case NATO could point to a moral consensus among liberal states and some others about the need to act, there was a much smaller consensus in the Iraq case, with many liberal states (such as Canada, Germany, and France) opposing the war.

The Effect of the "War on Terror" and the Invasion of Iraq
What impact has the so-called war on terror and the invasion of Iraq had on the partial consensus on the norm of humanitarian intervention? There are, broadly, three positions. The first group can be described as "optimists."[42] This view accepts that states will only intervene in humanitarian emergencies when vital national interests are at stake; it makes a virtue of this, however, by arguing that since September 11 interests and humanitarianism have merged for many Western states.[43] Two factors contributed to this merger. On the one hand, Afghanistan demonstrates all too clearly the linkage between terrorism and state failure. The strategic imperative to prevent terrorism therefore entails a humanitarian imperative to prevent state failure. As such, Western states are potentially more likely to respond decisively to humanitarian crises than they were prior to September 11.[44] On the other hand, the U.S. response to September 11, especially the so-called Bush doctrine of preemption, has reduced the normative significance of sovereignty. This, Farer argues, should lead us to expect more rather than fewer interventions.[45] The post-September 11 record does not fully support these claims. For instance, the West's contribution to UN peace operations remains paltry, the United States has not made a significant troop contribution

to reconstruction efforts in Afghanistan, and it played only a marginal role in alleviating the crises in Liberia and Haiti.[46]

The second perspective, shared by some involved with the ICISS, is that the "sun has set" on the humanitarian intervention agenda. This claim is arrived at from two directions. Thomas Weiss, the commission's director of research, argued that the United States and the United Nations' political will to act in humanitarian emergencies has "evaporated" because of their obsession with Afghanistan, Iraq, and the war on terror.[47] This position is helpful inasmuch as it highlights the fact that the overstretched American and British militaries are unlikely to be used in frontline roles, and that strategic considerations related to the "war on terror" are likely to trump humanitarian concerns when the two collide. On the other hand, it overstates the extent of humanitarian interventionism prior to September 11. In the 1990s, the world failed to "save strangers" in the Balkans, Rwanda, and elsewhere, and the legitimacy of humanitarian intervention remained hotly contested.[48] Indeed, the Security Council has yet to authorize humanitarian intervention against a fully functioning state without the latter's consent.[49]

The second way of arriving at the conclusion that the "sun has set" on humanitarian intervention suggests that the use of humanitarian justifications to defend the invasion of Iraq was widely perceived as "abuse." ICISS co-chair Gareth Evans argued that the "poorly and inconsistently" argued humanitarian justification for the war in Iraq "almost choked at birth what many were hoping was an emerging new norm justifying intervention on the basis of the principle of 'responsibility to protect.'"[50] This view is widely held among critics: Ian Williams argued that the Iraq war brought "humanitarian intervention into disrepute"; Richard Falk lamented that the war risked undermining consensus at the UN; Karl Kaiser insisted that "Washington has lowered [consensus on] the humanitarian intervention approach to an unprecedented level"; John Kampfner suggested that "there has been no better time for dictators to act with impunity"; and The Fund for Peace project collating regional responses to humanitarian intervention found that in the one consultation conducted immediately before the Iraq war, in Europe, participants were reluctant to support humanitarian intervention for fear of tacitly legitimizing the invasion of Iraq.[51] David Clark, a former special adviser to the British Foreign Office, argued that "Iraq has wrecked our case for humanitarian wars. As long as U.S. power remains in the hands of the Republican right, it will be impossible to build a consensus on the left behind the idea that it can be a power for good. Those who continue to insist that it can, risk discrediting the concept of humanitarian intervention."[52] The key question, however, is whether states share this view.

The answer to this is difficult to gauge precisely. Of course, as noted earlier, many states opposed the ICISS agenda before Iraq. There is evidence, however, that some states that were initially supportive of humanitarian intervention have become less so as a result of perceived abuse in the Iraq case. Immediately after the Iraq war began, a forum of social-democratic political leaders rejected sections of a draft communiqué proposed by Prime Minister Blair supporting the idea that the "responsibility to protect" ought to override sovereignty in supreme humanitarian emergencies. At least one of these states, Germany, had previously supported the ICISS agenda. German chancellor Gerhard Schroeder reportedly rejected the communiqué because he feared that any doctrine of unauthorized humanitarian intervention would be used by the United States and the United Kingdom to justify the Iraq war.[53] There is also clear evidence that in the Darfur case the Sudanese government linked American activism in Darfur with its actions in Iraq, portraying it both as oil-oriented and anti-Islamic, and that this strategy helped to reinforce African and Middle Eastern hostility to the idea of Western enforcement.[54] Importantly, neither of these cases clearly indicates an increased reluctance to support humanitarian intervention per se. Sudan may have adopted its strategy regardless of events in Iraq, while Germany's position was directed more against the potential uses of criteria for intervention than against the idea of humanitarian intervention itself.

A subtle variation on this theme holds that while the Iraq war has not directly affected the norm of humanitarian intervention, it has impacted negatively on the ability of the United States and its allies to act as norm carriers. According to one analyst, the U.S. administration sacrificed its international credibility over Iraq and is therefore not well placed to lead in Darfur and elsewhere.[55] Similarly, at least one article in the British press suggested that were Prime Minister Blair to advocate intervention in the Sudan, "oil [would] be the driving factor."[56] Such skepticism is what led Kenneth Roth of Human Rights Watch to predict that one of the most troubling consequences of the attempts to justify the Iraq war in humanitarian terms was that "it will be more difficult next time for us to call on military action when we need it to save potentially hundreds of thousands of lives."[57]

A third perspective suggests that the ICISS criteria for intervention should be viewed as constraints that will limit states' ability to abuse humanitarian justifications rather than as enablers for intervention. Ramesh Thakur, another ICISS commissioner, argues that the moral consensus about the "responsibility to protect" is likely to be strengthened in the wake of Iraq as states come to realize that it provides a language that can be used to oppose legitimate intervention. According to Thakur, consensus on criteria will make it more, not less, difficult for states to claim a humanitarian mantle for their interventions.[58]

The impact of the "war on terror" and the war in Iraq on the norm of humanitarian intervention is therefore hotly contested. There is certainly evidence that prior to the war in Iraq there was a general consensus about the necessity of intervention in supreme humanitarian emergencies when authorized by the Security Council, and a consensus among some liberal states that unauthorized intervention may be legitimate if the council is deadlocked. However, there are at least three plausible explanations for the direction the norm has taken since the Iraq war. As I will demonstrate in the remainder of the article, the Darfur case lends support to the idea that the humanitarian intervention norm has subtly changed in two ways. First, the credibility of the United States and the United Kingdom as norm carriers has diminished. Second, "responsibility to protect" language can be mobilized to legitimate opposition to intervention in humanitarian emergencies as well as to support it.

INITIAL ENGAGEMENT TO THE DEPLOYMENT OF ARMS

For much of 2003, the international response to the Darfur crisis was limited to the delivery of humanitarian aid. The main political effort during this period focused on the Naivasha process aimed at resolving the civil war between the Sudanese government and the SPLM/A. In early 2004, Mukesh Kapila, the UN's coordinator for Sudan, accused Arab militia backed by the government of "ethnic cleansing" and warned that if left unchecked the humanitarian catastrophe in Darfur would be comparable to that in Rwanda.[59] Secretary-General Annan used a Rwandan anniversary speech to the UN Human Rights Commission to observe that unfolding events in Darfur "leave me with a deep sense of foreboding." He continued:

> Whatever term it uses to describe the situation, the international community cannot stand idle. . . . The international community must be prepared to take swift and appropriate action. By "action" in such situations I mean a continuum of steps, which may include military action.[60]

In May 2004, Germany informally proposed the deployment of UN peacekeepers to Darfur, and it was widely rumored that Norway had offered to command such a force.[61] The *New York Times* ran a series of articles exposing the massive human rights abuses there and calling for U.S. action, earning criticism from the Sudanese embassy.[62] Human Rights Watch, Amnesty International, and the International Crisis Group also actively lobbied for action in Darfur.

In April 2004, the UN Human Rights Commission dispatched a fact-finding team to Darfur. The team found "a disturbing pattern of disregard for basic principles of human rights and humanitarian law, which is taking place in Darfur for which the armed forces of the Sudan and the Janjaweed are responsible." It concluded that "it is clear that there is a reign of terror in Darfur," and that the government and its proxies were almost certainly guilty of widespread crimes.[63] Before the commission could vote on a resolution based on the draft report, its content was leaked to the press. Pakistan and Sudan condemned the leak and called for an immediate inquiry.[64] Unwilling to force the issue, and concerned that a strongly worded resolution would be rejected by the commission's African and Asian members, the EU members watered down a draft resolution they were preparing. The redrafted resolution neither condemned Sudan nor mentioned its crimes. It was passed with fifty votes in favor and only three against (the United States, Australia, and Ukraine).[65]

The underlying dynamics of the Security Council's attitude to Darfur became apparent when it met on June 11, 2004, to pass unanimously Resolution 1547, expressing the council's willingness to authorize a peace operation to oversee the comprehensive peace agreement in Sudan's south. Although the resolution did not relate to Darfur, some council members nevertheless reaffirmed Sudanese sovereignty and expressed deep skepticism about humanitarian intervention. Pakistan reminded the council:

> The Sudan is an important member of the African Union, the Organization of the Islamic Conference and the United Nations. As a United Nations Member State, the Sudan has all the rights and privileges incumbent under the United Nations Charter, including to sovereignty, political independence, unity and territorial integrity—the principles that form the basis of international relations.[66]

That this was not the view of an isolated minority in the council was demonstrated by the fact that the resolution's drafters felt it necessary to doff their caps to Sudanese sovereignty by inserting a passage "*reaffirming* its commitment to the sovereignty, independence and unity of Sudan."[67] Pakistan, China, and Russia believed that the scale of human suffering in Darfur was insufficient to provoke serious reflection on whether responsibility to Sudan was fulfilling its responsibilities to its citizens, and the United States, the United Kingdom, and France were reluctant to force them to do so. All three of the Western democracies that contributed to the June 11, 2004, debate made pointed remarks about the Darfur emergency and tacitly referred to the commission of crimes against humanity and war crimes, yet none cast doubts on Sudanese sovereignty. Germany, for instance, noted that peace in Sudan was indivisible and required "an end to the sweeping and widespread human rights violations" without suggesting how this might be achieved. Similarly, the United States pointed toward a litany of human rights abuses in Darfur but simply confirmed its support for AU initiatives.[68]

This pattern was repeated on July 30, 2004, when the council met to pass Resolution 1556.[69] Three positions were put forward during the council's deliberations, which saw the first injection of "responsibility to protect" language into the debate. The first view, put forward by the Philippines, was that Sudan had failed in its duty to protect its citizens and that international action was warranted. The reference to the ICISS could not have been clearer:

> Sovereignty also entails the responsibility of a State to protect its people. If it is unable or unwilling to do so, the international community has the responsibility to help that State achieve such capacity and such will and, in extreme necessity, to assume such responsibility itself.[70]

At the other end of the spectrum, China, Pakistan, and Sudan all rejected talk of intervention, while Brazil and Russia exhibited reluctance to even contemplate the question. China abstained in the vote, complaining that the resolution alluded to "mandatory measures" against the Sudanese government, while Pakistan argued that it "did not believe that the threat or imposition of sanctions against . . . Sudan was advisable."[71] The Sudanese government itself made a classic "Trojan horse" argument, even referring to the Greek legend. The ambassador wondered,

> if the Sudan would have been safe from the hammer of the Security Council even if there had been no crisis in Darfur, and whether the Darfur humanitarian crisis might not be a Trojan horse? Has this lofty humanitarian objective been adopted and embraced by other people who are advocating a hidden agenda?[72]

The resolution's sponsors and their supporters adopted a line between these two positions. The United States, the United Kingdom, Germany, Chile, and Spain invoked the language of the "responsibility to protect" without suggesting that the responsibility ought to pass from the Sudanese government to the Security Council. They referred to the AU as bearing the primary responsibility for action should Sudan fail in its responsibilities. This tension between, on the one hand, a genuine concern for human suffering in Darfur and, on the other hand, a reluctance to press for action was most clearly expressed by the United States:

> Many people who are concerned about Darfur would say that this resolution does not go far enough. Last week, the Congress of the United States passed resolutions referring to the atrocities in Darfur as genocide. Many people would want the Security Council to do the same. *Perhaps they are right.* But it is important that we not become bogged down over words. It is essential that the Security Council act quickly, decisively and with unity. We need to fix this humanitarian problem now.[73]

This debate produced an understandably Janus-faced resolution that invoked Chapter VII and condemned human rights abuses, but stopped short of sanctioning or even condemning the Sudanese government. Resolution 1556 gave the government thirty days to disarm the Janjaweed and punish human rights abusers, threatening economic sanctions if it failed to do so. For some, such as China and Pakistan, the resolution went too far; for others, it did not go far enough.[74]

The initial international response to events in Darfur was therefore characterized by three contradictory trends. First, there was clear recognition on the part of Western journalists, human rights organizations, and some states of a responsibility to protect the people of Darfur. Second, however, there were significant doubts about which organization should bear that responsibility (the

UN, AU, or Sudan?), and a deep reluctance on the part of key Western states to assume responsibility by arguing that the Sudanese government was either unable or unwilling to protect Darfurians. Third, many states expressed deep disquiet at any potential violation of Sudanese sovereignty.

FROM AMIS TO UNMIS

The intervention debate crystallized around the question of *who* had the responsibility to protect Darfurians. Embedded in this debate were concerns about the deployment of AMIS and its relationship with the UN, the question of whether sanctions should be imposed on Sudan, the prosecution of war criminals, and the composition and mandate of a UN force (UNMIS) to oversee the peace agreement in the south of Sudan.

This section is divided into two parts. The first focuses on the AU's involvement in Darfur. Against this backdrop, the second returns to the Security Council debates about intervention.

African Union Mission in Sudan

In July 2004, the AU began to discuss the possibility of deploying a small force to protect its civilian monitors in Darfur, who had been sent to El Fashir to monitor the cease-fire agreement of June 9, 2004. At the same time, the Sudanese government stated that it would "strongly resist all [UN Security Council] resolutions calling for dispatching international forces to Darfur" and threatened to use force against peacekeepers.[75] Initially, an AU force of approximately 3,000 troops drawn from nine states was envisaged.[76] In mid-August, Rwanda deployed an advance party of 154 troops, and President Kagame insisted that they would use force to protect civilians if necessary.[77] Although the AU indicated in a communiqué to the Security Council that its troops would indeed fulfill this role, some AU members expressed reservations. The Sudanese government itself rejected Kagame's interpretation of the mandate. Foreign affairs minister Abdelwahad Najeb insisted, "The mission for those forces is very clear: protection of the monitors. As far as the civilians, this is the clear responsibility of the government of Sudan."[78] When Nigeria deployed the first 153 of an intended 1,500 troops, President Obasanjo of Nigeria insisted that his forces would only protect AU observers and operate with the consent of the Sudanese government.[79] With Sudan refusing to consent to a broad civilian protection mandate, a compromise was found whereby AMIS troops would only protect vulnerable civilians in their vicinity.[80] The compromise mandate, to which the government of Sudan consented, insisted that AMIS would "protect civilians whom it encounters under imminent threat and in the immediate vicinity, within resources and capability, it being understood that the protection of the civilian population is the responsibility of the [government of Sudan]."[81]

It soon became clear, however, that the AU lacked the necessary financial and logistical resources to deploy even the modest 3,000 peacekeepers originally intended. In late September 2004, with still only 300 troops deployed, Secretary-General Annan called for international assistance to expand AMIS, and President Obasanjo lamented that although the AU was willing to deploy more peacekeepers, it was unable to do so without international assistance.[82] On the ground, AMIS was constrained by the Sudanese government, which, among other things, prevented AU helicopters from flying by denying them fuel as well as repeatedly insisting that AMIS troops were monitors, not peacekeepers.[83]

On October 20, the AU's Peace and Security Council announced its intention to increase the overall size of its mission to 3,320, including some 2,341 troops.[84] A week later, Rwandan and Nigerian reinforcements began arriving in Darfur, assisted by the U.S. Air Force. However, AMIS remained unable to do much more than report cease-fire breaches. On December 20, Nigeria's General Okonkwo reported that government forces had attacked villages using aircraft.[85] Days later, Secretary-General Annan complained that the world's peacekeeping strategy in Darfur was "not working," and that AMIS had failed to protect civilians or prevent the crisis from deteriorating because it "has not been able to put in as many (military) forces as we had hoped."[86] The situation did not improve in 2005. In February, Jan Pronk, the secretary-general's special representative for Sudan (who was appointed in June 2004), complained that AMIS was too small and its deployment too slow to afford real protection to Darfur's civilians.[87] Others grumbled that the AMIS deployment was "chaotic," characterized by "poor logistical planning" and a "lack of trained personnel, funds and experience in intervening to protect civilians."[88]

Return to the Council

Was AMIS merely "a fig leaf to cover the world's inaction," as one commentator lamented?[89] The key question for the remainder of this section is why the Security Council and supporters of the "responsibility to protect" agenda did not take measures either to coerce the Sudanese government into compliance or to improve the effectiveness of AMIS.

Resolution 1556 and the Question of Sanctions. Resolution 1556 had imposed a thirty-day deadline in July 2004 for the Sudanese government to comply with the Security Council's demands and had threatened sanctions if it failed to comply. In informal consultations immediately after its passage, the United States gauged potential support for sanctions, including an arms embargo and travel ban on government officials in the event of Sudanese noncompliance. During these consultations a consensus against sanctions began to emerge. Pakistan opposed sanctions in principle (because they violated Sudanese sovereignty), and the Arab League joined the chorus by issuing a statement opposing sanctions in any circumstances.[90] Other council members (most notably China and Russia) had mixed motives for opposing sanctions: a combination of principle and economic interests.[91] Crucially, the United Kingdom also informally opposed sanctions. A senior Foreign Office official told reporters that the United Kingdom had two problems with sanctions. First, expressing concerns about undermining the Naivasha process, the British were "wary of giving the impression that the international community is beating up on the government of Sudan." Second, invoking the "responsibility to protect," they believed that "the best way to deliver security to the people of Darfur is to get those with primary responsibility for it to do it . . . the government of Sudan."[92] U.K. officials apparently worried that coercion could inflame the situation in Darfur and undermine the peace agreement without delivering security owing to the logistical difficulties that a Darfur deployment would entail.

On September 2, 2004, Pronk observed that the Sudanese government's compliance with Resolution 1556 was mixed. He claimed that the AU Ceasefire Commission had reported that government forces had not breached the cease-fire, a claim hotly disputed by the United States.[93] Pronk also noted, however, that the government had failed to stop Janjaweed attacks or disarm and prosecute the militia's members. Nevertheless, he endorsed the emerging Security Council consensus that the Sudanese government had primary responsibility for ending the crisis. Indeed, he implied that the crisis had barely gone beyond the first level of responsibility identified by the ICISS (that is, of the host government) when he argued that "if the government is unable to fully protect its citizens by itself" it should "request and accept assistance from the international community."[94] This view was supported by the secretary-general's representative on internally displaced persons, Francis Deng—the author of the "sovereignty as responsibility" concept that preceded the "responsibility to protect."[95] Paradoxically, Deng argued that although the government "probably" lacked the will and capacity to disarm the Janjaweed, it retained primary responsibility for doing so. Moreover, Deng argued that the government had indicated its strong preference for cooperating with the AU and "was fearful of any direct international involvement" to such an extent that it "would probably resist it, either directly or through other means." He concluded that international intervention would "complicate and aggravate" the crisis by increasing the level of violence and causing the government to withdraw its cooperation.[96] The best way forward, he argued, was to encourage the AU to increase its presence in the region in collaboration with the government.

Resolution 1564 and the Failure of a Robust Approach. Although there was an emerging Security Council consensus that primary responsibility for alleviating the crisis lay with the Sudanese government in cooperation with the AU, the United States continued to push for stronger measures, propelled by its finding that the government and its allies were committing genocide in Darfur.[97] In mid-September 2004, it circulated a draft resolution finding Sudan to be in material breach of Resolution 1556 and calling for an expanded AU force, international overflights to monitor the situation, moves to prosecute those responsible for genocide, a no-fly zone for Sudanese military aircraft, and targeted sanctions (such as travel bans) against the ruling elite.[98] Resolution 1564 contained many of these measures but in a much-diluted form. It called for an expanded AU presence, reiterated earlier demands for respect for the cease-fire and for the government to disarm and prosecute the Janjaweed, invited the secretary-general to create a commission of inquiry to investigate reported crimes, and indicated its intention to "consider" further measures if the government failed to comply.[99] The resolution failed to find Sudan in breach of Resolution 1556, impose measures upon it, or even criticize the government. Once again, three positions were apparent.

First, many states expressed deep skepticism about the legitimacy of enforcement measures against Sudan. Explaining its abstention, Algeria argued that while "certain measures that might have been unacceptable assaults on Sudan's sovereignty" (such as overflights) had been dropped from the original U.S. draft, the resolution was still problematic because it failed to recognize Sudan's cooperation with the AU and UN. Russian, Chinese, and Pakistani opposition to sanctions were partly principled objections to sanctions, partly instrumental objections predicated on the view that the situation in Darfur was improving. Although it supported the resolution, Brazil expressed disquiet at what it described as the "excessive" use of Chapter VII, which, it feared, "runs the risk of misleading all parties concerned."[100] These views were widely endorsed outside the council. For instance, a communiqué issued by an "African mini-summit" on Darfur led by Libya and Egypt reaffirmed a commitment to preserve Sudanese sovereignty and expressly rejected "any foreign intervention by any country, whatsoever in this pure African issue."[101]

At the other end of the spectrum, two states spoke out in favor of a more robust approach. The Philippines reiterated its view that if a state is unable or unwilling to protect its citizens, "the Security Council has the moral and legal authority to enable that State to assume that responsibility." Romania endorsed this view more pointedly, implying that the council had not yet fulfilled its responsibilities:

> There should be no moral hesitation in the Council in taking up its responsibilities. While it may be true that it is not for the Council to make legal findings, it is certainly within its political, legal and moral obligations to ring the alarm bell and foster—and indeed, urge—proper consideration of such acts in the appropriate venues.[102]

As before, the United States and the United Kingdom adopted a public position midway between the other two. While the United States noted that progress had been made, it insisted that the Sudanese government remained in breach of Resolution 1556. Nevertheless, it stopped short of specifically criticizing the

Sudanese government or calling for further measures. Likewise, the United Kingdom noted ceasefire violations by all parties to the conflict and reiterated its view that "ultimate responsibility lies with the Government of Sudan and the rebel groups."[103]

What is remarkable is not so much that the resolution was toned down to secure a Security Council consensus, but that the United States especially chose not to argue along the lines of Romania and the Philippines that the council should assume the "responsibility to protect." This is most striking in the U.S. case, because its Congress and secretary of state had publicly declared a genocide in Darfur and because it had attempted to develop a more activist approach during the Security Council's informal consultations. The United States found itself faced with two options. It could act as it had over Kosovo and Iraq and adopt a robustly activist line in the council. It could also declare itself willing to act outside the council if that body was unable to reach a consensus. Because of its military overstretch, however, the latter course would have been a politically infeasible strategy. The alternative was to pursue a consensus within the council. Council consensus remained very fragile owing to the deep skepticism expressed toward anything but AU interventionism by states including Russia, China, Pakistan, and Algeria, as well as many key AU members and the League of Arab States. As such, American diplomats may have felt unable to take a more robust public stance for fear of undermining the council's fragile consensus.

Resolutions 1590, 1591, and 1593: Compromises on Darfur. The situation in Darfur deteriorated soon after Resolution 1564 was passed. As noted earlier, evidence grew of AMIS's inability to protect civilians. Human Rights Watch pointed to renewed clashes between rebels and government forces.[104] Jan Pronk reported that government compliance was going backward, telling the Security Council of "numerous" cease-fire breaches by all parties and militia attacks on civilians.[105] At the end of October 2004, the UN estimated that the number of people needing aid in Darfur had increased by as much as 10 percent in the previous month alone and reported that militia and government forces were harassing displaced persons and preventing the timely delivery of aid.[106] In his monthly report to the Security Council on Darfur, Secretary-General Annan noted a string of cease-fire breaches by all parties, very slow progress on disarmament, and almost no progress on apprehending Janjaweed militia. Tellingly, he advised that the "Security Council may wish to consider creative and prompt action" to ensure effective implementation of its demands.[107]

The U.S. ambassador to the UN expressed doubts, however, about whether sanctions would ever be implemented, and suggested that "carrots" not "sticks" would be used to alleviate the problem.[108] As two observers persuasively put it, while the UN had "unsurprisingly . . . epitomized paralysis," the U.S. administration had also decided to "take a pass on Darfur," owing to military overstretch and a "tarnished image in the Muslim world."[109] Following this analysis, the fact that the United States had been forced to seek a consensus—one it then failed to reach—on enforcement measures against Sudan could plausibly be attributed, at least in part, to a diminishing of its status as a humanitarian intervention norm carrier. Further weight is given to this explanation by the positions taken by Germany, the AU, and the League of Arab States described above. Lest there be any doubt, even the SPLM/A ruled out "foreign" (non-African) intervention, specifically pointing to the Iraq experience. A spokesman for a Sudanese opposition organization comprising the SPLM/A, Farouk Abu Eissa, insisted, "We are against foreign military intervention in Darfur. We have before us the case of Iraq. We do not want a similar situation to develop in Darfur, or Sudan."[110]

In early 2005, Pronk reported that increased violence in Darfur had "seeped into the [internally displaced persons] camps themselves." December, he noted, had seen an arms buildup, numerous attacks by all sides, including government aircraft, the spread of violence into West Kordofan, and the emergence of new rebel groups.[111] The only way to improve the situation, Pronk argued, was to deploy more international personnel into the region. This recommendation represented an important policy change for Pronk, who had previously endorsed AU primacy. Now, Pronk tacitly recognized the AU's inability to protect civilians in Darfur and suggested that other agencies be deployed.

From this point onward, the sanctions debate was complicated by two further interrelated debates. First, there was a debate about whether to refer the case of Darfur to the ICC. Second, the conclusion of the peace agreement for the south of Sudan initiated a debate about whether the UN force created to police the peace agreement would be a Chapter VI or Chapter VII mission, and whether it would also deploy in Darfur. Importantly, in both debates the United States attempted to further its case for stronger measures to protect Darfurians. In the first, it eventually succumbed to European pressure and agreed to refer the case of Darfur to the ICC despite its continuing grave concerns about the court. In the second, it led an informal push to give the new UN mission a role in Darfur.

On January 25, 2005, the UN Commission of Inquiry concluded that while the Sudanese government did not have a policy of genocide, it was implicated in numerous war crimes and crimes against humanity. Moreover, the commissioners wrote, "In some instances individuals, including government officials, may commit acts with genocidal intent."[112] However, it judged that only a competent court would be able to determine whether specific crimes were genocidal. The report sparked a heated debate about the appropriate venue in which to prosecute accused war criminals. EU states, including the United Kingdom, argued that the Security Council should refer the matter to the ICC. The British ambassador to the UN insisted that the ICC referral was "nonnegotiable." The United States argued that the Security Council should create a special tribunal in Arusha to indict and prosecute war criminals. Nigeria offered a compromise in the form of an AU tribunal. The EU states rejected the Nigerian proposal, fearing that any compromise on the ICC would fatally undermine the court.[113] For more than two months, the debate hamstrung efforts to create a UN force, as the Europeans insisted on the ICC referral being part of any authorizing resolution.

The deadlock was broken in late March when the two issues were decoupled. On March 31, the council passed Resolution 1593, referring the case of Darfur to the ICC. Explaining its decision to abstain in the vote, the United States reaffirmed its fundamental objection to the ICC, which, it claimed, "strikes at the essence of the nature of sovereignty," but noted the importance of a unified response to Darfur and the need to end impunity in the region.[114] The United States had very few options in Darfur, and was ultimately forced to accept the ICC referral as the only alternative to inaction or unilateralism.

The debate about the role and nature of UNMIS was similarly long-winded. States were divided on the mission's rules of engagement and its zone of operations. In February 2005, the secretary-general recommended a traditional peacekeeping force under Chapter VI of the Charter. However, the UN's Department of Peacekeeping Operations found few states willing to contribute troops. Though a group of liberal states that had come together to form a Multi-National Stand-By High Readiness Brigade expressed a willingness to contribute forces, most wanted a Chapter VII resolution giving them authority to use force to protect themselves and endangered civilians.[115] After protracted negotiation, the council agreed to authorize a Chapter VII operation.

The council remained divided, however, on the question of whether UNMIS could be "rerouted" to Darfur. The United States wanted a clear statement authorizing UNMIS to deploy in Darfur, but this was informally opposed by Russia, China, and Algeria. In the end, Resolution 1590 authorized a Chapter VII peace operation mandated to observe the cease-fire and protect civilians, using force if necessary. The resolution avoided pronouncing on whether UNMIS would be deployed to Darfur, and invited the secretary-general to investigate the types of assistance that UNMIS could offer to AMIS, identifying "technical and logistical" assistance as two potential areas.[116]

No consensus emerged on the question of sanctions, however. In mid-February 2005, the United States circulated a draft resolution coupling UNMIS and oil sanctions.[117] After a protracted round of informal consultations, the United States dropped the oil embargo in favor of the imposition of travel bans and asset freezing on suspected war criminals. Russia and China, however, rejected both the asset freezing and the linkage between sanctions and UNMIS. The United States revised its draft further, and on March 29 the Security Council passed Resolution 1591, imposing a travel ban on suspected war criminals. Russia, China, and Algeria abstained—Algeria because it believed that the draft failed to recognize the significant progress that the Sudanese government had made, and Russia and China because they remained opposed to sanctions. Tanzania argued that while it supported Resolution 1591, it believed that the post–

peace agreement government in Khartoum "should not be subjected to a sanctions regime less than three months from now."[118]

At the time of writing, the UN was preparing to deploy UNMIS to the south of Sudan, ICC prosecutors were investigating crimes in Darfur, and the AU was continuing to expand its presence in Darfur. On the other hand, the Sudanese government remained in breach of Resolution 1556 but had avoided enforcement measures, violence in Darfur continued, and the numbers of dead and displaced continued to rise.

MINOR SETBACKS OF THE HUMANITARIAN INTERVENTION NORM

The Darfur experience suggests that the claims that either the "sun has set" on humanitarian intervention or that, after September 11, the West is likely to be more interventionist are both misplaced. The first overestimates the strength of the humanitarian intervention norm prior to the September 11 attacks and the subsequent wars in Afghanistan and Iraq—as well as those wars' impact on the norm in general.

If we accept the view that prior to the Iraq war there was a partial consensus that the Security Council has a right to authorize humanitarian intervention and a moral consensus among liberal states that unauthorized intervention may be a legitimate response to supreme humanitarian emergencies, the world's response to Darfur suggests that neither of these consensuses has been eroded. This was evidenced by the widespread political support offered to AMIS and by the fact that in the West, at least, there was little suggestion that an AU intervention required either an authorizing Security Council resolution or the Sudanese government's consent. Although AMIS subsequently received Sudanese government consent for its limited civilian protection role, it is significant that when Rwanda unilaterally gave its peacekeepers a civilian protection role prior to the revised AMIS mandate, liberal states did not criticize it for doing so.

The second view overestimates the link between humanitarian crises and security concerns, such as weapons of mass destruction and international terrorism. Although there was clear linkage in the Afghanistan case, there was no such link with respect to Darfur. What the Darfur case suggests, then, is that changes to the norm of humanitarian intervention after the Iraq war have been more subtle and complex. Two changes in particular can be identified.

First, debates about how to respond to the crisis in Darfur lend weight to the thesis that the credibility of the United States and the United Kingdom as humanitarian intervention norm carriers has significantly diminished as a result of the Iraq war. Throughout discussions on Darfur, some states and organizations expressly rejected American- and British-led activism in the Security Council, while endorsing the AU intervention and calling for its expansion. This view was expressed by AU members, the League of Arab States, the Organization of the Islamic Conference, and several Security Council members (such as Pakistan and Algeria). There were also signs that in a context where they were unable to act outside the Security Council because of their military overstretch problems, the United States and the United Kingdom appeared to recognize that their diminished credibility as norm carriers would make it harder for them to take a lead in building a council consensus on action. By autumn 2004, British officials were informally expressing the view that it would be imprudent for Britain to push the sanctions issue. Although the United States continued in its attempts to bring pressure to bear on the Sudanese government, and American officials frequently expressed their frustration at being unable to do so, it refrained from taking a robust line in the council's public deliberations (as the Philippines and Romania did), and the possibility of unauthorized action was never seriously raised, even after Congress and Colin Powell described Darfur as genocide. It is too early to offer definitive insights about precisely why the United States adopted this position. Given military overstretch, however, unauthorized military action was probably considered infeasible, leaving a consensus-based approach through the Security Council as the only viable alternative. The problem here was that America's and Britain's likely diminished status as norm carriers meant that an aggressive diplomatic push for coercive measures would probably have been counterproductive.

Second, the Darfur case supports Thakur's argument that the "responsibility to protect" criteria could constrain as well as enable intervention. It casts serious doubt, however, on Thakur's presumption that this furthers the cause of global humanitarianism. "Responsibility to protect" language was used by both advocates and opponents of intervention. It enabled opponents of intervention to legitimate their actions by reference to the prevailing normative order. In effect, it allowed traditional opponents of intervention to replace largely discredited "sovereignty-as-absolute"-type arguments against intervention in supreme humanitarian emergencies with arguments about who had the primary responsibility to protect Darfur's civilians. The Sudanese government, the AU, the League of Arab States, UN officials on occasion, and in at least one instance the United Kingdom argued that the Sudanese government had primary responsibility, though for different reasons.[119] In the context of the ongoing debate, this argument was used to reject external involvement other than that endorsed by the government of Sudan. Occasionally, AU members and UN officials suggested that the government had proven itself either unable or unwilling to protect Darfur's citizens and that international organizations, particularly the AU, should assist it. Only the Philippines and Romania argued that the Security Council should accept primary responsibility for protecting Darfurians, and that argument enjoyed very little support.

According to the ICISS report, the transfer of the "responsibility to protect" from the host state to the Security Council should be guided by what it portrays as a simple empirical test: when the host state is unable or unwilling to protect its citizens. In practice, this threshold was hotly disputed. Few states publicly reject the idea that the Security Council should act to halt genocide or mass murder, but it has proven difficult to forge a consensus on when the threshold is crossed. With Darfur, as with Kosovo, opponents of intervention argued that military action would probably worsen the situation. Repeatedly, they argued that the situation in Darfur was improving and had not reached the threshold necessary to validate intervention.

The point here is that while Thakur was correct to argue that "responsibility to protect" language could reduce the likelihood of humanitarian justifications being abused, his line of reasoning reveals a deeper problem with the ICISS agenda: changing the language of humanitarian intervention (from sovereignty vs. human rights to levels of responsibility) has not changed its underlying political dynamics. As such, "responsibility to protect" language may also be used to inhibit the emergence of consensus about action in genuine humanitarian emergencies. As was the case with Kosovo, the debate over Darfur boils down to the question of whether enough states can be persuaded to act. The key difference is that in the Kosovo case many liberal states were prepared to act outside the Security Council if necessary.

In the Kosovo case, the existence of this alternative route enabled advocates of intervention to take a more robust diplomatic line in the Security Council, forcing traditional opponents of intervention to acknowledge the humanitarian catastrophe in Kosovo when the council identified Serbian ethnic cleansing as a threat to international peace and security and imposed economic and other sanctions on the Belgrade regime.[120] Sadly, due to a combination of military overstretch and the United States' and the United Kingdom's diminished credibility as norm carriers, that alternative was not available in the Darfur case. As a result, little such pressure has been brought to bear on traditional opponents of intervention, who, in turn, have been able to legitimate their opposition to intervention in terms of the responsibility to protect. While the ICISS was right to be concerned about reducing the danger that states might abuse humanitarian justifications to legitimate unjust wars, it evidently should have paid more attention to the danger that responsibility to protect language could itself be abused by states keen to avoid assuming any responsibility for saving some of the world's most vulnerable people.

NOTES

This essay appeared in *Ethics & International Affairs* 19, no. 2 (2005): 31–53. I would like to thank Paige Arthur, Mark Beeson, Ian Clark, Nicholas J. Wheeler, Paul D. Williams, Ramesh Thakur, two anonymous reviewers, and especially Sara Davies for their help and advice.

1.   "UN Chief's Rwanda Genocide Regret," *BBC News*, March 26, 2004.

2.   Tony Blair, speech given to the Labour Party Conference, Brighton, England, October 2, 2001. I am grateful to Nick Wheeler for bringing this to my attention.

3.   "National Security Strategy of the United States of America," September 17, 2002, sec. V, www.whitehouse.gov/nsc/nss.pdf.

4.   According to Alex de Waal, the government of Sudan has "consistently franchised its counter-insurgency operations to militia," in this case the Janjaweed. The government provides the militia with arms, intelligence, and air support and allows them to operate with complete impunity, creating an "ethics-free zone." Alex de Waal, "Briefing: Darfur, Sudan: Prospects for Peace," *African Affairs* 104, no. 414 (2005): 129.

5.   These figures were offered in a detailed study by Jan Coebergh, "Sudan: Genocide Has Killed More Than the Tsunami," *Parliamentary Brief* 9, no. 7 (2005): 5–6. The lower figure is extrapolated from a Médecins Sans Frontières survey and the upper one from a U.S. Department of State report.

6.   Ibid. These figures are extrapolated from data provided by the United States Agency for International Development (USAID) and the World Health Organization (WHO).

7.   House of Commons International Development Committee, Darfur, *Sudan: The Responsibility to Protect*, fifth report of session 2004–2005, vol. 1 (HC 67–1), March 30, 2005, 3.

8.   UN News Centre, "UN Refugee Agency Withdraws Staff from South Darfur Over Sudanese Restrictions," November 11, 2004.

9.   See Thalif Deen, "New UN Force for Sudan Will Skirt Darfur Crisis," Inter Press Service, February 9, 2005. It is widely recognized that after an initial respite, the humanitarian situation has actually deteriorated despite AMIS.

10.   UNSC Res. 1590, March 24, 2005.

11.   UNSC Res. 1593, March 31, 2005. Passed with eleven in favor and four abstentions (Algeria, Brazil, China, and the United States).

12.   This is Wheeler's term. See his *Saving Strangers: Humanitarian Intervention in International Society* (New York: Oxford University Press, 2001), 34.

13.   See also Nicholas J. Wheeler and Justin Morris, "Justifying Iraq as a Humanitarian Intervention: The Cure is Worse Than the Disease," in *The Iraq Crisis and World Order: Structural, Institutional, and Normative Challenges*, ed. Ramesh Thakur and Waheguru Pal Singh Sidhu (Tokyo: United Nations University Press, 2006). I owe the "norm carriers" idea to them.

14.   A process they describe as "norm cascade." See Martha Finnemore and Kathryn Sikkink, "International Norm Dynamics and Political Change," *International Organization* 52, no. 4 (1998): 887–918.

15.   Ward Thomas, for instance, argues that a new norm's vitality depends on its advocates being seen to practice it in good faith. Ward Thomas, *The Ethics of Destruction: Norms and Force in International Relations* (Ithaca, NY: Cornell University Press, 2001), 34–35.

16.   The idea of "acquiescence" to the West's humanitarian agenda is taken from Wheeler and Morris, "Justifying Iraq as a Humanitarian Intervention," 15. My argument draws on Quentin Skinner, "Analysis of Political Thought and Action," in *Meaning and Context: Quentin Skinner and His Critics*, ed. James Tully (Cambridge: Polity Press, 1988), 116–117. I am grateful to Nick Wheeler for suggesting this.

17.   Nicholas J. Wheeler, "The Humanitarian Responsibilities of Sovereignty: Explaining the Development of a New Norm of Military Intervention for Humanitarian Purposes in International Society," in *Humanitarian Intervention and International Relations*, ed. Jennifer M. Welsh, (New York: Oxford University Press, 2004).

18.   The debates among liberal states about whether to intervene in Kosovo provide the best demonstration of this moral consensus. See Alex J. Bellamy, *Kosovo and International Society* (London: Palgrave Macmillan, 2002). The best theoretical expression of this liberal

consensus can be found in Michael Walzer, "The Politics of Rescue," in *Arguing about War* (New Haven, CT: Yale University Press, 2004).

19.   It is important to note, however, that five states abstained when France requested a Security Council mandate to launch Operation Turquoise in Rwanda, most citing concerns about France's motives. See Wheeler, *Saving Strangers*, 232.

20.   See Michael Barnett, *Eyewitness to a Genocide: The United Nations and Rwanda* (Ithaca, NY: Cornell University Press, 2002); and Wheeler, *Saving Strangers*, 231–41.

21.   Simon Chesterman, *Just War or Just Peace? Humanitarian Intervention and International Law* (New York: Oxford University Press, 2001), 231.

22.   Independent International Commission on Kosovo, *Kosovo Report: Conflict, International Response, Lessons Learned* (New York: Oxford University Press, 2000), 4; and Ian Clark, *Legitimacy in International Society* (New York: Oxford University Press, 2005), 212.

23.   It is remarkable that even traditionally conservative states such as Malaysia chose to side with NATO rather than to abstain. UNSC 3989th meeting, S/PV.3989, March 26, 1999.

24.   Nicholas J. Wheeler, "The Legality of NATO's Intervention in Kosovo," in *The Kosovo Tragedy: The Human Rights Dimensions*, ed. Ken Booth (London: Frank Cass, 2001), 156.

25.   S/1999/363, March 31, 1999, annex.

26.   See Final Document of the XIII Ministerial Conference of the Movement of Non-Aligned Countries, Cartagena, Colombia, April 8–9, 2000, 41–42, www.nam.gov.za/xiiimin conf/index.html. It should be noted that the Non-Aligned Movement itself did not achieve a consensus on this position.

27.   Constitutive Act of the African Union, www.africa-union.org/About_AU/ AbConstitutive_Act.htm.

28.   Kofi Annan, speech given to the Nobel Foundation, Oslo, Norway, December 10, 2001, www.nobel.se/peace/laureates/2001/annanlecture.html.

29.   Most of the unauthorized interventions were conducted with host nation consent, sometimes coerced. For a definitive list of these operations (up to February 2005), see tables 1 and 2 in Alex J. Bellamy and Paul D. Williams, "Who's Keeping the Peace? Regionalization and Contemporary Peace Operations," *International Security* 29, no. 4 (2005): 35–36.

30.   Gareth Evans and Mohamed Sahnoun, "Foreword," in International Commission on Intervention and State Sovereignty (ICISS), *The Responsibility to Protect* (Ottawa: IDRC, 2001), viii.

31.   ICISS, *Responsibility to Protect*, 17.

32.   "Supreme humanitarian emergencies" and "spikes" refer to the idea that mass killing is either ongoing or imminent at the time of the intervention. See Wheeler, *Saving Strangers*, 34; and Tom Farer, "Cosmopolitan Humanitarian Intervention: A Five-Part Test," *International Relations* 19, no. 2 (2005): 216–17.

33.   ICISS, *Responsibility to Protect*, paras. 4.19, 6.11, 6.29–6.40, and xii–xiii.

34.   Ibid., xii.

35.   See Nicholas J. Wheeler, "Legitimating Humanitarian Intervention: Principles and Procedures," *Melbourne Journal of International Law* 2, no. 2 (2001): 552–54.

36.   Jennifer M. Welsh, "Humanitarian Intervention after 11 September," in *Humanitarian Intervention*, ed. Welsh, 180.

37.   Ian Williams, "Writing the Wrongs of Past Interventions: A Review of the International Commission on Intervention and State Sovereignty," *International Journal of Human Rights* 6, no. 3 (2002): 103.

38.   Welsh, "Humanitarian Intervention," 204, n. 4.

39.   See Colin McInnes, "A Different Kind of War? September 11 and the United States' Afghan War," *Review of International Studies* 29, no. 2 (2003): 165–84; Nicholas J. Wheeler, "Humanitarian Intervention after September 11, 2001," in *Just Intervention*, ed. Anthony F. Lang, Jr. (Washington, DC: Georgetown University Press, 2003); and Simon Chesterman, "Humanitarian Intervention and Afghanistan," in *Humanitarian Intervention*, ed. Welsh.

40.   See Adam Roberts, "Law and the Use of Force after Iraq," *Survival* 45, no. 2 (2003): 48.

41.   Michael Ignatieff, an ICISS commissioner, was an early supporter; see Ignatieff, "Why Are We in Iraq? (And Liberia? And Afghanistan?)," *New York Times Magazine*, September 7, 2003, 38ff. Kenneth Roth wrote one of the most detailed rejections in Ken Roth, "War in Iraq: Not a Humanitarian Intervention," *Human Rights Watch World Report 2004: Human Rights and Armed Conflict*; see also David Vesel, "The Lonely Pragmatist: Humanitarian Intervention in an Imperfect World," *BYU Journal of Public Law* 18, no. 1 (2004): 56. It is also worth noting that the humanitarian argument was not raised in the Security Council's formal proceedings.

42.   This terminology is drawn from Nicholas J. Wheeler and Alex J. Bellamy, "Humanitarian Intervention in World Politics," in *The Globalization of World Politics: An Introduction to International Relations*, ed. John Baylis and Steve Smith, third edition (New York: Oxford University Press, 2005), 572.

43.   I am grateful to Nick Wheeler for this formulation.

44.   See Chesterman, "Humanitarian Intervention and Afghanistan"; and Wheeler, "Humanitarian Intervention after September 11."

45.   Tom Farer, "Humanitarian Intervention before and after 9/11: Legality and Legitimacy," in *Humanitarian Intervention: Ethical, Legal, and Political Dilemmas*, ed. J. L. Holzgrefe and Robert O. Keohane (Cambridge: Cambridge University Press, 2003), 80.

46.   See Richard Bruneau, "Selfishness in Service of the Common Good: Why States Participate in UN Peacekeeping" (unpublished ms.), 3.

47.   Thomas G. Weiss, "The Sunset of Humanitarian Intervention? The Responsibility to Protect in a Unipolar Era," *Security Dialogue* 35, no. 2 (2004): 135; and James Traub, "Never Again, No Longer?" *New York Times*, July 18, 2004.

48.   See Wheeler, *Saving Strangers*, 295.

49.   A point developed in Paul D. Williams and Alex J. Bellamy, "The Responsibility to Protect and the Crisis in Darfur," *Security Dialogue* 36, no. 1 (2005): 41.

50.   Gareth Evans, "When Is It Right to Fight?" *Survival* 46, no. 3 (2004): 59–82.

51.   Respectively, Ian Williams, "Intervene with Caution," *In These Times*, July 28, 2003; Richard Falk, "Humanitarian Intervention: A Forum," *Nation*, July 14, 2003; Karl Kaiser, "A European Perspective on the Post Iraq New International Order," paper presented at the Center for Strategic and International Studies, Jakarta, Indonesia, July 29, 2003; John Kampfner, interviewed by Tim Dunne; available at www.ex.ac.uk/shipss/news/kampfner .htm; and *The Fund for Peace, Neighbors on Alert: Regional Views on Humanitarian Intervention*, Summary Report of the Regional Responses to Internal War Program, October 2003, 6.

52.   David Clark, "Iraq Has Wrecked Our Case for Humanitarian Wars," *Guardian*, August 12, 2003.

53.   See Agence France-Presse, "British PM Urges Tougher Stance against Brutal Regimes," July 14, 2003; and Kevin Ward, "Process Needed so Countries Know When to Intervene to Protect Human Rights," *CBS News* (Canada), July 13, 2003.

54.   Cheryl O. Igiri and Princeton N. Lyman, "Giving Meaning to 'Never Again': Seeking an Effective Response to the Crisis in Darfur and Beyond," Council on Foreign Relations Special Report 5 (2004), 21.

55. Scott Straus, "Darfur and the Genocide Debate," *Foreign Affairs* 84, no. 1 (2005): 128.

56. John Laughland, "The Mask of Altruism Disguising a Colonial War," *Guardian*, August 2, 2004.

57. Kenneth Roth, "The War in Iraq: Justified as Humanitarian Intervention?" Joan B. Kroc Institute Occasional Paper 25 (2004), 2–3.

58. Ramesh Thakur, "Iraq and the Responsibility to Protect," *Behind the Headlines* 62, no. 1 (2004): 1–16; and Ramesh Thakur, "Developing Countries and the Intervention-Sovereignty Debate," in *The United Nations and Global Security*, ed. Richard M. Price and Mark W. Zacher (New York: Palgrave Macmillan, 2004).

59. Cited in "Mass Rape Atrocity in West Sudan," *BBC News*, March 19, 2004.

60. SG/SM/9197 AFR/893 HR/CN/1077, April 7, 2004.

61. See Human Rights Watch, "Darfur Destroyed: Ethnic Cleansing by Government and Militia Forces in Western Sudan," May 2004, 56–57; and "UN Peacekeeping Mission for Sudan Prepared," *Afrol News*, May 28, 2004.

62. See, e.g., John Prendergast, "Sudan's Ravines of Death," *New York Times*, July 15, 2004; and Embassy of the Republic of Sudan, "The New York Times Faulted Sudan," April 13, 2004.

63. E/CN.4/2005/3, May 7, 2004, 3.

64. Human Rights Watch, "Darfur Destroyed," 55.

65. E/CN.4/2004.L11/Add7, April 23, 2004.

66. UNSC 4988th meeting, S/PV.4988, June 11, 2004, 4.

67. UNSC Res. 1547 (2004), June 11, 2004; emphasis in original.

68. UNSC 4988th meeting, S/PV.4988, June 11, 2004, 4.

69. Passed with thirteen affirmative votes and two abstentions (China and Pakistan).

70. UNSC 5015th meeting, S/PV.5015, July 30, 2004, 10–11.

71. Ibid., 10.

72. Ibid., 13.

73. Ibid., 4; emphasis added.

74. Simon Tisdall described it as a "dark study in disillusion." Simon Tisdall, "Brave Talk but No Action: Darfur Gets a Familiar Response from the West," *Guardian*, August 3, 2004. I am grateful to Paul Williams for bringing this to my attention.

75. "Australia May Join Darfur Mission," *Daily Telegraph*, July 28, 2004. I am grateful to Sara Davies for bringing this to my attention.

76. "African Union Sending Military Force to Darfur," *CBC News*, July 6, 2004; and Reuters, "African Union to Send Troops to Darfur," July 5, 2004.

77. Human Rights Watch, "Darfur: Rwandan Troops to Protect Civilians," *Human Rights News*, August 17, 2004.

78. Quoted in Eric Reeves, "The Meaning of AU Forces Deployment to Darfur," *Sudan Tribune*, October 26, 2004.

79. Human Rights Watch, "Darfur: African Union Must Insist on More Troops," *Human Rights News*, August 20, 2004.

80. Duncan Woodside, "Mandate Unclear as AU Troops Head for Darfur," *Business Day* (South Africa), October 29, 2004, 12.

81. African Union Peace and Security Council Communiqué PSC/PR/Comm. (XVII), Peace and Security Council, 17th meeting, October 20, 2004, Addis Ababa, Ethiopia, para. 6, 2.

82. UN News Centre, "World is Responsible for Ending 'Terrible Violence' in Sudan, Annan Says," September 24, 2004.

83. "Thousands More Troops for Darfur," *BBC News*, October 1, 2004.

84. S/2004/881, November 2, 2004, para. 57.

85. Reuters, "Troops Attack in Darfur as a Deadline Passes," December 20, 2004.

86. Quoted in Thalif Deen, "UN Admits Sudan Policies Failing," Inter Press Service, December 22, 2004. Also see Leslie Lefkow, "No Justice for Sudan," *Guardian*, January 10, 2005.

87. Quoted in Deen, "New UN Force for Sudan Will Skirt Darfur Crisis."

88. Waranya Moni, "The UN Report on Darfur: What Role for the AU?" *Pambazuka News*, February 10, 2005.

89. Eric Reeves, "Genocide by Attrition," *In These Times*, February 16, 2005.

90. Amil Khan and Mohamed Abdellah, "Arab League Rejects Sudan Embargo," Reuters, August 9, 2004.

91. Russia had recently sold MiG aircraft to Sudan and feared that the government would use any potential sanctions as a justification for defaulting on its payments. China has important oil interests in Sudan. See Scott Peterson, "Sudan's Key Ties at the UN," *Christian Science Monitor*, August 31, 2004.

92. Quoted in "Security Council Disagrees over Sudan Sanctions," *Sunday Standard* (Nairobi), August 22, 2004.

93. S/PV.5027, September 2, 2004, 2. U.S. ambassador John Danforth argued that Annan's report was wrong to suggest that there was no evidence of attacks by government forces and that the AU Ceasefire Commission had in fact reported two such incidents. Cited in UN News Centre, "Sudan: Annan Calls for Expanded International Presence to Stop Darfur Attacks," September 3, 2004.

94. UNSC 5027th meeting, S/PV.5027, September 2, 2004, 3.

95. Francis M. Deng et al., *Sovereignty as Responsibility: Conflict Management in Africa* (Washington, DC: Brookings Institution, 1996).

96. E/CN.4/2005/8, September 27, 2004, paras. 22, 26, and 36.

97. For an excellent account of why the United States has adopted an activist role in the Darfur debate, see Samantha Power, "Dying in Darfur: Can the Ethnic Cleansing in Sudan Be Stopped?" *New Yorker*, August 30, 2004, 270–87.

98. "Powell Declares Genocide in Sudan," *BBC News*, September 9, 2004.

99. UNSC Res. 1564, September 18, 2004, paras. 2, 3, 7, 9, 12, and 14.

100. S/PV.5040, September 18, 2004, 2–3, 5, 7, and 10.

101. By "foreign" the communiqué evidently meant non-African. "Final Communiqué: African Mini-Summit on Darfur," Tripoli, Libya, October 17, 2004, 2.

102. S/PV.5040, September 18, 2004, 12.

103. Ibid., 10.

104. Human Rights Watch, "Darfur: Donors Must Address Atrocities Fueling Crisis," *Human Rights News*, September 27, 2004.

105. UN News Centre, "Sudan Has Failed to Disarm Militias or Prevent More Attacks in Darfur—UN Envoy," October 5, 2004.

106. UN News Centre, "Sudan: UN Reports 10 Percent Jump in Number of People in Darfur Who Need Aid," October 22, 2004; and UN News Centre, "Humanitarian Aid in Sudan Limited by Insecurity, Road Closures, Says UN Mission," October 27, 2004.

107. S/2004/881, November 2, 2004, paras. 5 and 16.

108. Cited in "Prompt Action Needed in Darfur," *BBC News*, November 4, 2004.

109. Christian W. D. Bock and Leland R. Miller, "Darfur: Where is Europe?" *Washington Post*, December 9, 2004.

110.   Quoted in Gamal Nkrumah, "Darfur in Flames," *Al-Ahram* (Cairo), April 29–May 5, 2004.

111.   S/PV.5109, January 11, 2005, pp. 2–3.

112.   "Report of the International Commission of Inquiry on Darfur to the United Nations Secretary-General," January 25 2005.

113.   See Peter Heinlein, "UN Security Council Deadlocked over Darfur," *Voice of America*, March 18, 2005.

114.   UNSC 5158th meeting, S/PV.5158, March 31, 2005, 3.

115.   "Sudan Peace Agreement Signed 9 January Historic Opportunity, Security Council Told," UN Press Release, SC/8306, February 8, 2005.

116.   UNSC Res. 1590, March 24, 2005, paras. 4 and 5.

117.   Reuters, "US Resolution Calls for UN Peacekeeping Mission in Sudan," February 15, 2005.

118.   UNSC 5153th meeting, S/PV.5153, March 29, 2005, 2–5.

119.   As noted earlier, the United Kingdom's position was influenced by a mixture of prudential considerations and dependence on Security Council consensus.

120.   For a discussion, see Bellamy, *Kosovo and International Society*, 68.

Chapter 7

Ecological Intervention
Prospects and Limits

Robyn Eckersley

VIOLENCE IN CIVIL CONFLICTS in the post–Cold War period has ignited a heated debate about the morality, legality, and legitimacy of humanitarian intervention. Recriminations continue against the failure of the UN Security Council to prevent massacres in Bosnia, Rwanda, and Darfur. But should the international community also be concerned about massacres perpetrated against critically endangered species? Must it stand by and allow a deliberate massacre of, say, the last surviving population of mountain gorillas by poachers? In considering this and other scenarios of grave environmental harm, this essay seeks to extend the already controversial debate about humanitarian intervention by critically exploring the morality, legality, and legitimacy of ecological intervention and its corollary, ecological defense. By "ecological intervention" I mean the threat or use of force by a state or coalition of states within the territory of another state *and without the consent of that state* in order to prevent grave environmental damage.[1] By "ecological defense" I mean the preventive use of force in response to the threat of serious and immediate environmental harm flowing into the territory of a "victim" state.

If the legacy of the Holocaust was the Nuremberg trials and acceptance of a new category of "crimes against humanity," an emerging norm of humanitarian intervention, and, most recently, the creation of an international criminal court, then might the willful or reckless perpetration of mass extinctions and massive ecosystem destruction be regarded as "crimes against nature" such as to support a new norm of ecological intervention and an international environmental court?[2] If the international community condemns genocide, might it one day be ready to condemn ecocide?

In 2001 the International Commission on Intervention and State Sovereignty (ICISS), an independent, international, twelve-member body established by the government of Canada to reconcile the international community's commitment to upholding humanitarian norms with the principle of state sovereignty, argued that sovereignty carries with it responsibilities, and that all states have "a responsibility to protect" their citizens.[3] In cases of serious harm, such as genocide and gross human rights violations, the commission argued that the international community has the responsibility to step in and prevent abuses where the responsible state is unable or unwilling to do so. In the words of the commission, in these circumstances, "the principle of non-intervention yields to the international responsibility to protect."[4] This essay explores the analogous but more controversial argument that state sovereignty carries with it not only the right to control and develop territory but also the responsibility to protect it, and that states' responsibilities over their territories should be understood as fiduciary rather than proprietary.

The international community has already endorsed the basic idea that states have a responsibility to protect the environment in a wide range of environmental treaties, declarations, and action programs. Apart from environmental war crimes, however, states have so far declined to underpin their individual and collective environmental responsibilities with a minimal code of acceptable environmental behavior, the breach of which might in appropriate circumstances justify the use of force and/or prosecution in an international court. Yet it seems odd that the international community should accept environmental criminal prosecutions for "scorched earth" environmental atrocities committed during times of war but not in times of peace, even though some forms of environmental harm generated during peacetime may be no less grave and imminent—and there is not even the defense of "military necessity."[5] Indeed, we should expect standards of environmental protection to be higher during times of peace than times of war. The international customary law principle of state responsibility for environmental harm imposes a duty on states to pay reparations to neighboring states for transboundary environmental harm, but there are no mechanisms that enable states to force the cessation of such harm.

WHY CONSIDER MILITARY FORCE?

Although there is now a widespread literature on ecological security and an emerging literature on ecological peacekeeping, the question of military intervention to secure environmental protection has so far received only limited treatment by international lawyers and even less attention from political theorists and moral philosophers interested in global sustainability and environmental justice.[6] This is not surprising, given that most ecological problems rarely constitute a high level of threat, offer only a short period of warning, *and* require the need for a rapid military-style response.[7] While global warming, for example, has been designated a "weapon of mass destruction" because its harmful consequences are likely to be at least as severe as those of nuclear, chemical, and biological weapons, the threat is not immediate and military intervention is a singularly inappropriate means of responding to such a complex problem.[8]

This is typical of most environmental problems, which are normally diffuse, transboundary, and unintended; evolve and continue over a fairly long time frame; implicate a wide range of actors; and usually require painstaking dialogue to move toward cooperation and resolution.[9] More generally, it has been shown that shared ecological problems present peacemaking opportunities.[10] Indeed, many environmental scholars see very little advantage, and considerable dangers, in "securitizing" our understanding of ecological problems in order to elevate them to the status of "high politics." Daniel Deudney, who has spearheaded this critique, has suggested that "for environmentalists to dress their programs in the blood-soaked garments of the war system betrays their core values and creates confusion about the real tasks at hand."[11] These "real" (and more mundane) tasks include more concerted environmental capacity building (in the form of green aid packages and environmental technology transfer), more robust environmental treaties that equitably distribute the benefits and burdens of cooperation, and fairer international trading and credit rules.

The foregoing arguments provide very good reasons for approaching the question of the use of military force to secure environmental protection with great caution. Nonetheless, there are at least two reasons why an exploration of the case for ecological intervention (and ecological defense) is a worthwhile exercise. First, while most ecological problems are not amenable to any kind of military response, there are still *some* ecological problems and risks that do constitute environmental emergencies in the sense that they are grave and imminent and require a military or paramilitary response if they are to be avoided or minimized. Suppose, for example, that a chain reaction has commenced in an outdated nuclear reactor in Ukraine that is threatening to grow beyond control, with the imminent threat of a Chernobyl-style nuclear explosion. Suppose, too, the Ukrainian government has refused international technical assistance, even though European experts warn that Ukraine lacks the technical capacity and human resources to bring the potential emergency under control. Under such circumstances, military intervention may be the only means of preventing an imminent transboundary ecological disaster.

We can also expect that the number of environmental disasters and emergencies is likely to grow rather than lessen over time, given increasing economic interconnectedness, increasing pressures on natural resources and ecosystems, rising populations, and new technologies. Anticipating such emergencies and encouraging a debate about an appropriate principled response may head off the possible proliferation of unilateral military action to protect the environment, such as when Canadian naval forces seized a Spanish fishing vessel on the high seas in 1995 in an effort to prevent overfishing of migratory stocks that were central to the viability of the Canadian fishing industry.[12]

Apart from environmental emergencies that threaten public safety, there are other categories of environmental harm that may not necessarily have transboundary effects but might still constitute a high level of threat and offer only a short period of warning, thereby possibly warranting a rapid military-style response. For example, if the Rwandan government were unable and/or unwilling to protect its dwindling population of mountain gorillas from illegal hunting and poaching, then a swift response by multilateral forces might be the only remaining effective measure that would prevent the total extinction of these great apes.[13]

Second, exploring the use of military force for environmental protection enables a useful stocktaking and clarification of the relationship between new ecological norms and the fundamental political and legal norm of nonintervention and its corollary, self-determination. Such an inquiry provides one significant gauge of the extent to which sovereignty has been, or may be, "greened."[14] The international human rights discourse is complicated, controversial, and mostly aspirational, but support can now be found for the idea that there should be certain minimal standards of human decency, the breach of which should entail the temporary forfeiting of certain prerogatives associated with the principle of state sovereignty. In the light of three major environmental summits and an expanding body of mutually reinforcing environmental treaties, declarations, and strategies, it is timely to explore whether it is possible to piece together a basic set of nonderogable environmental norms (that is, norms that cannot be abrogated by any state) that must be observed during times of war and peace.

THE LEGALITY, MORALITY, AND LEGITIMACY OF MILITARY INTERVENTION

Given the potential mischief associated with any kind of military intervention, the case for ecological intervention should pass a fairly stiff test. Ideally, it must be consistent with, or at least find a precedent in, international law; it must qualify as a just cause (and the remaining requirements of *jus ad bellum*, such as the proportionality criterion, must also be satisfied); and it should be widely accepted as legitimate or "rightful" by most states, which means that it must transcend the cultural and political proclivities of powerful states and reflect norms that are common to developed and developing countries alike. While the requirements of legality, morality, and political legitimacy can overlap in practice and are sometimes mutually informing and constraining, they are analytically distinct and often diverge. For example, moral claims are normative claims about what ought to be done according to the demands of justice, whereas claims that certain actions are politically legitimate are based on social and political conventions that are derived from particular political communities (in this case, the society of states).[15] To expect a neat convergence among legality, morality, and legitimacy in order to justify military intervention is, therefore, rather a tall order, given that learned interpretations of international law, understandings about justice and morality, and political judgments about what is appropriate behavior are rarely clear, settled, and in perfect alignment. Yet it is the slippages and discrepancies among legal, moral, and political norms that create openings for normative innovation, and it is these openings that I wish to explore and exploit in the discussion that follows.

Shifts in morality or political understandings of appropriate behavior can sometimes lead to shifts in law (and vice versa). Humanitarian intervention has only an "emergent" rather than "settled" status as an international norm precisely because the legal, moral, and political arguments have yet to coalesce. For example, the Independent International Commission on Kosovo concluded that NATO's intervention in Kosovo was "legitimate" (in this case, meaning morally just because it sought to put a stop to human rights abuses) though not strictly "legal," and it recommended the legal codification of the doctrine of humanitarian intervention to bridge the gap between law and justice and provide greater clarity.[16] Many developing countries, however, wish to uphold the principle of nonintervention embedded in the UN Charter as an important political principle because, among other reasons, it provides an important bulwark against unilateral interventions by powerful states. My strategy, then, is to assess the legality, morality, and political legitimacy of ecological intervention in order to pinpoint where the blockages and possible openings for innovation may be found. This means that my analysis will be partly legal, partly normative, and partly sociological. My task is to explore and, where possible, exploit precedents, analogies, and anomalies in order to present the case for ecological intervention in its best light, and also to assess its general prospects.

To focus the discussion, I explore the potential scope of ecological intervention and defense in relation to three different categories of environmental harm: (1) major environmental emergencies with transboundary spillover effects that threaten public safety in the wider region; (2) ecocide or crimes against nature that also involve genocide or serious human rights violations (irrespective of spillover effects); and (3) ecocide or crimes against nature that are confined within the territory of the offending state and which involve no serious human rights violations. I consider the prospects for multilateral action (by the Security Council), as well as unilateral action by one or more states.

Environmental Emergencies with Transboundary Spillover Effects

The UN Charter upholds the principle of the sovereign equality of its member states and expressly forbids any state to use or threaten to use force against "the territorial integrity or political independence of any State," except for the purposes of individual or collective self-defense against an armed attack.[17] The quality of the global environment was not a concern of the drafters of the Charter, and the word "environment" makes no appearance in the text. Nonetheless, the United Nations, through the General Assembly and the UN Environmental Program, has facilitated the development of a range of significant multilateral environmental declarations and treaties, particularly over the last three decades in response to mounting environmental problems. There are also increasing cross-references among treaties, declarations, and strategies and a growing degree of convergence in many of the principles embodied in these environmental multilateral instruments. The 1992 Rio Declaration brings together these shared understandings, including the recognition that "peace, development and environmental protection are interdependent and indivisible."[18] In the post–Cold War period, it has become increasingly recognized that environmental degradation is a potential threat to peace and security.

The Security Council has the power to determine what constitutes a threat to the peace, a breach of the peace, or an act of aggression, and to authorize military intervention under Chapter VII of the UN Charter in order to restore international peace and security. Although peace and security are undefined in the Charter, it does not require any great stretch of the imagination to classify an environmental emergency or imminent environmental disaster with international ramifications, such as an imminent nuclear explosion, as a threat to peace and security.[19] Indeed, British prime minister John Major, speaking as president of the UN Security Council, declared in 1992 that "non-military sources of instability in the economic, social, humanitarian and ecological fields have become threats to peace and security."[20] Given this acknowledgment, and the Security Council's preparedness to authorize the use of force in response to other nonmilitary sources of insecurity in the post–Cold War period, such as humanitarian crises, it would seem inconsistent for the Security Council not to respond to environmental emergencies that also undermine human security, especially when such emergencies threaten to cause significant loss of human life and suffering on a larger scale than humanitarian crises that are confined to one state. Environmental emergencies of this kind represent one situation when the principle of nonintervention ought to yield to the international responsibility to protect. Indeed, it is hard to think of a credible moral or political argument against intervention in our "Chernobyl" scenario. After all, nuclear radiation is nuclear radiation, irrespective of whether it emanates from a failed nuclear power plant or a nuclear bomb. Ecological intervention in these circumstances would uphold the principle of collective security enshrined in the UN Charter, which represents one of the most significant renovations to the Westphalian system in the twentieth century.

If the Security Council declined to act because of the exercise of the veto power by one or more permanent members, it could be argued that in a Chernobyl-like scenario neighboring states, or NATO, would be entitled to take control of the reactor as an act of self-defense in order to guarantee the health and safety of their citizens. Article 51 of the Charter explicitly preserves the right of states to use force in "self-defense" against an attack, and this has been interpreted to extend to the use of preemptive measures when a serious threat or attack is imminent and likely to be overwhelming and leave no room for choice.[21] Direct and major incursions of pollution or hazardous substances into the territory of neighboring states are analogous to an "armed attack" with chemical, biological, or nuclear weapons; they enter or threaten to enter the territory of the victim state without its consent and with equally grave consequences. Ecological defense may therefore be understood as representing an appropriate response to a wrongful *intervention* in the "territorial integrity or political independence" of the defending state within the meaning of Article 2(4) of the Charter. "Territorial integrity" can readily be interpreted to include "ecosystem integrity"; and "political independence" includes the political autonomy of nation-states to determine their own levels of environmental quality and not have them undermined by the willful or reckless actions of other states. On this interpretation, the act of ecological defense would reinforce rather than undermine the fundamental principle of nonintervention.

The foregoing interpretations would also overcome the limitations in the current state remedies available under the customary law principle relating to transboundary environmental harm, according to which no state may use its territory in ways that cause serious injury to the territory, property, or population of another state.[22] This principle has been interpreted not to permit unilateral preemptive measures or even injunctive relief in the World Court on the part of victim states to head off serious environmental damage, but merely to permit compensation for tangible damage suffered.[23] For example, in the French nuclear tests case brought before the International Court of Justice by Australia and New Zealand against atmospheric nuclear testing in the Pacific, it was admitted by Judge Ignacio-Pinto that Australia and New Zealand could not legally prohibit another state from using its territory in ways that exposed them to the future likelihood of nuclear fallout.[24] All they could do was to wait for the incursion and then seek reparations for actual damages suffered. Such a situation provides small comfort to victim states and their residents (such as residents of Mururoa Atoll), who may suffer from radiation sickness.

Taking preemptive measures to prevent massive harm from an imminent environmental disaster emanating from a neighboring state probably represents one of the few instances where unilateral military action might be legally, morally, and politically justified in the name of environmental protection in circumstances where the UN Security Council was unable or unwilling to respond to the crisis. Such action would, of course, need to be reported to the Security Council and respect the laws of war and the just war tradition (including the requirements of necessity and proportionality in the case of self-defense).

Ecocide Involving Serious Human Rights Violations

Genocide is universally condemned and the prohibition against genocide is considered to be *jus cogens* and therefore nonderogable.[25] Serious human rights abuses, such as torture, are also widely condemned by the international community, notwithstanding the ongoing philosophical and political disagreement about the justification of human rights claims. Insofar as ecocide also produces direct, immediate, and grave consequences for humans, involving large numbers of deaths and/or significant human suffering on a par with genocide or crimes against humanity, then the moral case for ecological intervention need only ride on the coattails of the moral case for humanitarian intervention. The decimation of the marsh region, the homeland of the Ma'dan, or Marsh Arabs, by Saddam Hussein's Baathist government is a case in point. The large-scale, government-sponsored drainage of the marsh region has been ecologically cata-strophic and directly implicated in human rights abuses against the Marsh Arabs.[26] The Marsh Arabs were also the most persecuted of the Shia Muslims in Iraq. The brutal murder, torture, imprisonment, forced expulsion, and disap-pearance of Marsh Arabs has clearly constituted genocide and crimes against humanity.[27] Upholding the human rights of Marsh Arabs therefore provides one indirect means of protecting the marsh region, and vice versa. We might therefore call military intervention to stop ecocide that also involves genocide "eco-humanitarian intervention."

To the extent that grave environmental harm is often associated with serious human rights violations, there are obvious advantages in developing these link-ages and building on existing humanitarian law, along with the existing pro-grams of UN agencies. Many well-recognized human rights also have an ecological dimension, such as the right to life and security of the person (which presupposes the absence of major ecological risks that threaten human health and well-being, such as a contaminated environment produced by radiation or toxic chemicals), but new developments are also under way.[28] A further general advantage of linking ecological intervention with humanitarian intervention is that it will ensure that human rights abuses, including social discrimination, are not committed in the name of ecological intervention. Conversely, separating the observance of human rights from the preservation of ecosystems could potentially provide a license for "coercive conservation" and other misan-thropic practices.[29] Given the difficult military capacity issues associated with mounting swift and successful humanitarian interventions, there is the predict-able concern that a broader case for ecological intervention (where no harm to humans is imminent) might divert scarce resources away from humanitarian crises. Eco-humanitarian intervention would avoid this problem by bringing together the arguments for humanitarian and ecological intervention.

Humanitarian intervention is, as we have noted, only an "emerging" rather than settled norm. If the case for eco-humanitarian intervention is to ride on the back of the case for humanitarian intervention, then it must address the familiar challenges that confront supporters of humanitarian intervention. Most of these challenges arise less from moral disagreement about the importance of human rights and more from significant asymmetries in the power of states to decide when to intervene, which tends to match asymmetries in military and economic power. The key political challenge is how to avoid a replay of the colonial past and address the suspicion among non-Western states that humani-tarian and, by extension, eco-humanitarian interventions are just Western imperial projects dressed up to appear "universal."[30]

The colonial legacy continues to shape the environmental values, priorities, and practices of developed and developing countries in multiple ways. Developing countries have shown considerable hostility toward new forms of "green conditionality" attached to trade, aid, and debt relations imposed by powerful states in the North upon states in the South, which they view as just another verse in the same old colonial song. The double-barreled "responsibility to protect" underlying the norm of eco-humanitarian intervention—to observe certain minimal requirements of human decency as well as minimal standards of environmental conduct—is likely to be rejected by developing states as a further encroachment on their right of self-determination, including the right to develop according to their own priorities. I address these concerns in more detail below in the discussion of the duty to protect biodiversity.

International lawyers and various states are also divided over whether the UN Security Council has the legal power to authorize humanitarian intervention. Those adopting a literal reading of the Charter (what we might call the "legal classicists") argue that such intervention contravenes the plain language of Article 2(4) of the UN Charter. In contrast, "legal realists" adopt a more flexible, contextual approach that interprets the Charter in the light of contemporary geopolitical needs and realities.[31] The legal realists also point to the broad discretion conferred on the Security Council in Article 39 to determine what constitutes "a threat to the peace." Upholding human rights is also one of the basic tenets of the UN Charter, and the Security Council has on a number of occasions (Rwanda, Somalia, and Haiti) already considered that it has the power under Chapter VII to authorize the use of force to prevent major human rights violations.[32] Clearly, the case for eco-humanitarian intervention would likewise rest on a legal realist interpretation of the UN Charter.

The case for eco-humanitarian intervention by a single state or "a coalition of the willing" is likely to be mired in the same legal, moral, and political controversies as unilateral humanitarian intervention. Based on a strict interpretation of the Charter, unilateral humanitarian intervention by a single state or "a coalition of the willing" is illegal. The NATO intervention in Kosovo, for example, is widely considered to be illegal, and this view has indeed been reiterated by many states, particularly from the developing world.[33] Moreover, Michael Byers and Simon Chesterman have argued that it is extremely unlikely that workable criteria for *unilateral* humanitarian intervention could be developed to the satisfaction of more than a handful of states.[34]

In the event of strong resistance to eco-humanitarian intervention by any permanent members of the Security Council, advocates of eco-humanitarian intervention face a now familiar but unpalatable choice: resignation to a paralyzed and ineffective Security Council dominated by the geopolitical interests of the permanent members, or the pursuit of action outside the UN Charter that threatens to undermine the principles and institutions of international law. In the light of this dilemma, Byers and Chesterman argue that "coalitions of the willing" should concede that their actions are prima facie contrary to international law, but to offer a special "plea in mitigation" based on extraordinary, exculpatory circumstances. They reject the alternative, which is to offer new and creative interpretations of the existing rules, as merely an effort to mold the law to suit the practices of a small handful of powerful states.[35] Thomas Franck has pushed this argument in favor of "exceptional illegality" one step further in pointing out how pleas in mitigation can play a positive role in the evolution of international law by helping to bridge the gap between strict adherence to the letter of the law and common notions of what is just and necessary. Jane Stromseth has likewise defended what she calls an "excusable breach" of the UN Charter as providing an important "safety valve" that reduces the tension between legality and legitimacy, although she argues that it is preferable to defend the action as a legal exception in accordance with an emerging norm of customary international law.[36]

If we accept the foregoing arguments as an appealing "middle way," then proponents of eco-humanitarian intervention, either by a particular state or a coalition of states, would need to pick their test case of "exceptional illegality" extremely carefully; that is, they would need to be confident that they are on strong moral grounds, to know they have at least the tacit support of a significant number of states, and to show that the law is seriously lagging behind morality and legitimacy. The very different reactions of the international community to NATO's intervention in Kosovo and the U.S.-led military adventure in Iraq are revealing in this respect. As Franck points out, "the reactions of the UN system to such 'off-Charter' uses of force may be bellwethers of evolution in Charter interpretations."[37] The acceptance of the case for eco-humanitarian intervention would be seriously set back by an ill-considered unilateral adventure that attracted strong international condemnation.

Ecocide, Crimes Against Nature, and the Protection of Biodiversity

Military intervention to prevent ecocide or "crimes against nature" involving no serious harm to humans represents the most challenging case because it directly appeals to a moral referent beyond humanity. Humanitarian law rests on the bedrock humanist idea that all humans matter, that they matter equally, and therefore that each person is equally entitled to physical security, sustenance, and a life of dignity and respect. For full-blooded liberal cosmopolitans, such as Jean Bethke Elshtain, the basis of humanitarian intervention should shift from rescuing victims as an act of charity or pity to upholding civic security as a matter of justice, based on the elementary international justice principle of equal regard and inviolable human dignity.[38] For communitarians, such as Michael Walzer, the duty of humanitarian intervention in response to genocide and crimes against humanity is a moral duty simply because human atrocities of this kind shock the conscience of *all* communities and are universally condemned as morally repugnant.[39] For communitarians generally (whether liberal, leftist, or conservative), we might say that the idea of crimes against humanity reminds us of our membership in a common human family and implicitly uses nonhuman species as the necessary point of differentiation. What distinguishes us humans from other species is our moral capacities, so that mass atrocities committed by some humans against others reflect badly on us all.

If we accept that we humans are members of a broader web of life, however, then major environmental atrocities also reflect badly on us all. The ecological crisis and the rise of environmental activism have spawned a revolution in Western ethics that has challenged what David Ehrenfeld called "the arrogance of humanism," or what has since become known as anthropocentrism or human chauvinism.[40] This is the widely held idea that humans are the center of the universe, the apex of evolution, and the only beings that matter from a moral point of view. Nonanthropocentric environmental philosophers have argued that anthropocentrism legitimates a purely instrumental posture toward the nonhuman world, which diminishes nonhuman nature (along with humanity) while also rendering it completely valueless and dispensable unless it serves some useful human purpose. Nonanthropocentric moral discourses share the conviction that the dominant political ideologies that have helped to shape the modern world (most notably, liberalism and Marxism) have elevated and celebrated humanity at the expense of nonhuman nature, and that this has helped to sanction the domination and destruction of nonhuman nature. The ethical quest has been to develop a new moral vocabulary that recognizes human membership in a larger moral community and respects the value of nonhuman species "for their own sake." The political and legal quest has been to develop new policies and laws that enable the *mutual* flourishing of the human and nonhuman world, rather than the flourishing of humans at the expense of the nonhuman world. If the idea of "crimes against nature" is to have any meaning beyond eco-humanitarianism, then an ethical and political development along these lines would seem to be necessary to provide a warrant for the rescue of the endangered mountain gorillas or other endangered species and habitats.

Nonanthropocentric environmental philosophers divide over how much of nonhuman nature should be admitted into Kant's kingdom of ends, however, and whether moral considerability should be confined to individual organisms or extended to ecological communities. Utilitarian (e.g., Peter Singer) and Kantian (e.g., Tom Regan) liberal philosophers concerned with the welfare of animals work from an atomistic ontology and consider only individual animals, or sentient creatures, as worthy of having their interests considered in any utilitarian moral calculus or of possessing rights.[41] Both have argued that an animal need not be a fully competent moral *agent* (equipped with powers of moral reasoning) in order to be recognized as a worthy moral *subject*—that is, as a being that is entitled to moral consideration. If we accept that morally incompetent humans are nonetheless morally considerable, then there is no good reason for not accepting nonhuman others as morally considerable on the grounds that they too are ends in themselves or otherwise capable of suffering or being harmed. Failure to consider the interests of animals is symptomatic of species-ism—an unwarranted prejudice against nonhuman others *just because they are not human*. Whereas biocentric philosophers take these arguments one step further by extending moral recognition to all living things, ecocentric philosophers work from a relational ontology and are concerned with the integrity of not only populations and species but also broader ecological communities at multiple levels of aggregation.[42] Despite their significant differences, however, animal liberationists, biocentrists, and ecocentrists all generally support the protection of species habitat and biological diversity, either for their own sake or because they are essential for the survival and well-being of animals, sentient creatures, and/or individual living organisms.

One adventurous attempt to extend moral consideration to nonhuman species in the international sphere, which builds on liberal moral arguments, is the International Great Ape Project. Supporters of this project argue that great apes—the chimpanzee, bonobo (pygmy chimpanzee), gorilla, and orangutan—should be included in the human "community of equals." Rather than invoke a new biocentric ethic, however, the project's "Declaration of Great Apes" self-consciously builds on the human rights tradition—particularly the Universal Declaration of Human Rights of 1948—in claiming that great apes belong to the same moral community as humans and are entitled to a right to life, a right to the protection of their liberty, and a right to be free from torture.[43] Robert Goodin, Carole Pateman, and Roy Pateman have extended this argument by defending the idea of "simian sovereignty" in the form of internationally protected, autonomous trust territories for great apes.[44] Building on the precedent of protectorates and mandated territories, initially set up by the League of Nations, they suggest that a body or state with an interest in the well-being of great apes could be empowered by international law to secure great ape communities by resisting incursions (whether from inside or outside the relevant state) into their homeland.[45] All of this has become thinkable, they argue, because the concept of sovereignty is becoming more flexible in the wake of globalization. Moreover, apes are recognized as having their own "authority structures," so providing great apes with limited rights of *internal* self-determination in relation to their homelands is consistent with a range of arguments for the self-determination of nations that fall short of state sovereignty. In short, human communities are shown to be not the only communities or "tribes" entitled to self-determination.

Yet the idea of human rights for apes raises a strategic and moral dilemma for those interested in the preservation of biodiversity and ecosystem health and resilience in general. On the one hand, in employing familiar moral arguments and legal precedents, the Great Ape Project provides an argument for building political support for the protection of great apes that is directly analogous with humanitarian intervention. Whether the threatened decimation of our "close relatives" is sufficiently "conscience-shocking" to warrant international condemnation and support for a military response is an open question. Indeed, we can expect the argument to unsettle established moral hierarchies. More generally, however, the arguments underpinning the Great Ape Project have limited ecological mileage because they cannot be readily extended beyond the great ape community to species who are not "like us." The ecological reach of this argument is therefore minimal. Indeed, it could be argued that the relevant crime here on the part of gorilla poachers is still a crime against humanity (or a "crime against great apes" as a "community of equals") rather than a crime against nature, because it still rests on a *humane* rather than *ecological* ethic.

What, then, of the more controversial case for ecological intervention to prevent major assaults on biological diversity?[46] The legal concept of "common heritage of humankind" has not been extended to include biodiversity *within* the territory of nation-states, even though it has been designated a "common concern of humankind."[47] Traditionally, biodiversity has been understood to form part of the natural resource assets of states and therefore subject to the principle of permanent sovereignty over natural resources, which is widely regarded as a basic constituent of the right to self-determination.[48] The template for the general notion of state dominion over territory came from Roman private law, which gave the property owners complete and exclusive control over their property.[49] In more recent times, states have gradually expanded their dominion over territory by negotiating a range of agreements that extend their sovereign rights beyond the "territorial sea" to include maritime "exclusive economic zones" (which include most of the world's fish catch) and to plant and animal genetic resources.[50]

The principle of permanent sovereignty over natural resources has formed an important plank in the "negative sovereignty" discourse of postcolonial states. The 1962 UN Resolution on Permanent Sovereignty over Natural Resources declared that "the rights of peoples and nations to permanent sovereignty over their natural wealth and resources must be exercised in the interest of their national development and of the well-being of the People of the State concerned."[51] While this principle had originally been formulated as a *human* right belonging to peoples or nations that had been subjected to colonial rule to freely dispose of their natural wealth, since the 1972 Stockholm Conference on the Human Environment it is more typically formulated as a right belonging to sovereign *states*.[52] As it happens, most of the earth's richest areas of biodiversity lie in tropical and subtropical regions in developing states. The argument that biodiversity should be considered part of the common asset of humankind held in trust by states, rather than as exploitable resources, would be widely regarded by developing states as yet another imperialist scheme by the North to deny former colonies the right to make use of their natural resources for the benefit of their people.

The question of the *wrongful appropriation* of natural resources or biodiversity by colonial or former colonial powers, however, is analytically distinct from the question of their *appropriate* management and protection by states. In any event, the principle of permanent sovereignty over natural resources was formulated in a waning colonial context that predates most of the significant developments in international environmental law and policy. The 1972 Stockholm Declaration and the 1992 Rio Declaration marked significant turning points in the general evolution of the development prerogatives and environmental responsibilities of states. The Rio Declaration, which represents the most up-to-date encapsulation of international environmental norms, seeks to artfully balance the principle of permanent sovereignty over natural resources with states' responsibility for avoiding transboundary environmental harm in Principle 2.[53] More significantly, the Rio Declaration also makes clear that states have environmental responsibilities in relation to their *own* territories. Principle 3 provides that "the right to development must be fulfilled so as to equitably meet developmental and environmental needs of present and future generations"; while Principle 4 declares that "in order to achieve sustainable development, environmental protection shall constitute an integral part of the development process and cannot be considered in isolation from it." Although the UN Convention on Biological Diversity reaffirms that states have sovereign rights over their biological resources, it also recognizes the intrinsic value of biological diversity and affirms that its conservation is a "common concern of humankind."[54]

Curiously, very little has been written by political philosophers about the *moral* basis of the state's right to control its territory and natural resources, as distinct from the people inhabiting or moving through its territory.[55] The significant exception are liberal cosmopolitans, such as Charles Beitz, who consider the distribution of natural resources among states to be even more morally arbitrary than the distribution of natural talents among individuals; such arbitrariness is seen to justify the application of Rawls's difference principle on a global scale.[56] However, international legal recognition of the territorial rights of states is based on the fact of possession and the power to assert control and to defend a territorial claim rather than on any moral entitlement—as indigenous peoples around the world have painfully learned. Indeed, the means by which most states have acquired their territory has been anything but morally exemplary. The acquisition of territory by seizure, military conquest, or negotiation under duress by powerful states has been eventually accepted and legally recognized by the international community, albeit sometimes "after a suitable mourning period."[57] Yet if it is accepted that the right of sovereign states to control *people* should be subject to certain minimal moral strictures, then why should not the right of sovereign states to control their *territories* be likewise subject to minimal moral strictures? As we have seen, the international community has made it clear in the Rio Declaration that the right of states to exploit their territory is not unlimited. States may not cause transboundary environmental harm; states must serve the development and environment needs of present *and* future generations; and environmental protection should form an integral part of the development process.

The international customary law principle of state responsibility for environmental harm, also derived from Roman law, goes some way toward regulating the external duties of states. This principle merely seeks to qualify state territorial user rights, however, rather than to protect victims or ecosystems per se. The principle is based on a presumption in favor of territorial rights, which places the onus on the victim state to prove tangible damage, causation, and a lack of due diligence. Moreover, as we saw in the French nuclear tests case, the customary rule provides no mechanisms that enable states to bring about the cessation of such harm. Indeed, reparations could simply be factored into the costs of doing business on the part of the culprit state. Nor does this customary principle prevent states from causing serious harm to their *own* environment if the consequences are confined within the territory of the state.

Environmental customary law has been increasingly overshadowed by environmental treaty law, however, and the broad trend in treaty law is to move away from a construction of the state as owner or overlord of its territory and toward that of caretaker or trustee of territory, with multiple "responsibilities to protect" vis-à-vis different classes of environmental beneficiaries.[58] Although treaty law is binding only on the parties, there is an increasing convergence of international opinion around certain key environmental norms.[59] We may think of the trustor as the international community (the bestower of recognition of territorial rights), and the primary beneficiaries as the citizens of the state (in relation to the state's internal duties) and the international community and global commons (in relation to the state's external responsibilities and matters of "common concern").[60]

Of course, clarifying the general environmental responsibilities of states is a different exercise from determining what might amount to a serious dereliction of responsibility sufficient to warrant internationally sanctioned military intervention in the absence of any serious transboundary environmental harm. If the conservation of biological diversity, including the preservation of species, is a "common concern" of humankind, then what categories of harm might serve as minimal, nonderogable standards of conduct to shore up this common concern? Given that genocide and crimes against humanity perform this role in the field of humanitarian law, then the obvious candidates in the field of environmental law are ecocide and crimes against nature. Building on humanitarian precedents,[61] ecocide may be defined as intentional and systematic acts that cause "widespread, long-term and severe damage to the natural environment."[62] This formulation has already been accepted by the international community in the case of environmental war crimes, and there seems to be no good reason not to extend it to times of peace as well to enable the prosecution of the perpetrators in an international criminal court. If the category of crimes against nature is to have any independent meaning over and above the category of ecocide, then it may be understood as intentional and systematic acts that cause the extinction of a species. The willful and systematic extermination of a species may be considered especially "conscience-shocking" because the effects are irreversible. In both cases (ecocide and crimes against nature), it should not be necessary that the damage to the natural environment or the extinction of species constitute the *primary* purpose of the acts. Rather, it should be enough that the acts themselves are willful and systematic, and that the environmental damage or extinction is a clearly foreseeable consequence of the acts. A clear wartime case is Iraq's willful setting fire to Kuwait's oil wells, which led to immense smoke clouds, a ten-degree Celsius drop in temperature in Kuwait, and massive pollution of coastal stretches resulting from the considerable influx of crude oil into the sea.[63]

It could be argued that the prohibitions against ecocide and crimes against nature ought to constitute legal duties that are nonderogable and owed to the international community as a whole.[64] In effect, this would require the enlargement of the trustor-trustee-beneficiary relationship sketched above to include nonhuman species as direct rather than merely indirect beneficiaries of the trust relationship. If this argument is accepted, then military intervention by UN-sanctioned forces to prevent these crimes may be defended as intervention for a "just cause," assuming, of course, that the remaining criteria of *jus ad bellum* can be satisfied (for example, that intervention did not make matters worse).[65] This is a big "if," however, and it remains an open question whether these basic prohibitions—particularly crimes against nature—would attract a cross-cultural consensus among states. There are certainly many non-Western indigenous cultures and religions that value nature in noninstrumental terms, but these traditional orientations have tended to be overshadowed by state-sponsored practices of economic development. It is possible that the wide range of instrumental arguments for the protection of ecosystems and biological diversity may, over time, prove to be sufficient to ground a general agreement over "critical ecological thresholds" and/or forms of ecocide that "shock the conscience" of the international community. Until such time as these norms take hold, the gorillas in our fictitious scenario would remain at the mercy of poachers.

CONCLUSION

Advocates of the use of military force for environmental protection face a heavy political onus, especially now that skepticism toward military intervention of any kind is running high in the shadow of the Anglo-American intervention in Iraq. If anything, the norm of nonintervention has become more rather than less politically important over time with the proliferation of non-European states, which regard nonintervention as an important principle of justice in an unequal world.[66] States with limited military capacity have been unable to play any prominent rule in deciding when military intervention may be warranted.[67] There is also the danger that the case for ecological intervention might provide a license for powerful states to act as global green action heroes or military missionaries in furtherance of their own environmental values and priorities that may not be widely shared. Moreover, the state with the greatest military power has hardly been exemplary when it comes to ratifying and implementing key international environmental treaties to protect biological diversity or to mitigate global warming (which is expected to accelerate rates of species extinction). Finally, military intervention itself can often result in heavy civilian casualties and environmental damage, which is one of the many factors that lie behind the general pacifist orientation of most environmentalists.[68] These factors conspire to make military intervention politically hazardous, even in circumstances where the moral case might otherwise seem compelling. The advantage of ecological defense over ecological intervention is that it avoids these hazards by reinforcing rather than challenging the prevailing norm of nonintervention. More generally, military intervention should always be a last resort, even in cases of imminent ecocide or crimes against nature, and the consequences should always be carefully assessed against the consequences of nonmilitary forms of intervention, whether coercive (such as trade sanctions), semi-coercive (such as "green conditionality" attached to loans), or consensual (such as ecological peacekeeping with the consent of the relevant state).

I have shown that the minimalist argument for ecological intervention—multilateral intervention in the case of environmental emergencies with transboundary spillover effects—is also the strongest because it is likely to satisfy all three tests of legality, morality, and legitimacy. "Eco-humanitarian intervention" (to prevent ecocide and crimes against nature involving serious human rights violations) is, however, like humanitarian intervention, still particularly shaky on the question of political legitimacy, especially from the point of view of many developing countries. The most challenging case of all—the military rescue of nonhuman species—conflicts with deeply entrenched international legal and political norms concerning state territorial rights. Nonetheless, the moral case cannot be dismissed, and I have suggested that some of the legal norms of territoriality have, appropriately, started to fray to the point where extending the idea of "the responsibility to protect" to include biological diversity is no longer unthinkable.

NOTES

This essay appeared in *Ethics & International Affairs* 21, no. 3 (2007): 293–316. An earlier version was presented as a seminar paper to the Department of International Relations at the Australian National University on October 12, 2005. I am grateful to the participants for their feedback, and especially to Bob Goodin, as well as to several anonymous reviewers, for constructive suggestions. This essay is the subject of an online Carnegie Council symposium featuring Mathew Humphrey, Simon Dalby, Clare Palmer, and Mark Woods, which can be accessed at www.cceia.org/resources/journal/21_3/feature_and_symposium/index.html.

1.   This definition represents an adaptation of J. L. Holzgrefe's definition of humanitarian intervention in "The Humanitarian Intervention Debate," in *Humanitarian Intervention: Ethical, Legal, and Political Dilemmas*, ed. Robert O. Keohane and J. L. Holzgrefe (Cambridge: Cambridge University Press, 2003), 15–52. A less restrictive interpretation might also include nonmilitary coercive measures, such as sanctions, or ecological peacekeeping, which is usually carried out with state consent, but my primary concern here is to explore the circumstances when military force might be justifiable.

2.   This is the objective of the International Court of the Environment Foundation (ICEF), a nongovernmental organization founded in Rome in 1992 under the directorship of Judge Amedeo Postiglione of the Italian Supreme Court. See www.icef-court.org/icef/about.htm.

3.   International Commission on Intervention and State Sovereignty, *The Responsibility to Protect* (Ottawa: International Development Research Center, 2001).

4.   Ibid., xi.

5.   I should add that no state has ever been held accountable for environmental damage during wartime and no individual has been criminally prosecuted. See Tara Weinstein, "Prosecuting Attacks that Destroy the Environment: Environmental Crimes or Humanitarian Atrocities?" *Georgetown International Environmental Law Review* 17, no. 4 (2005): 698.

6.   For a comprehensive overview of this literature, see Lorraine Elliott, "Imaginative Adaptations: A Possible Environmental Role for the UN Security Council," *Contemporary Security Policy* 24, no. 2 (2003): 47–68. See also Markku Oksanen, "Humanitarian Military Intervention Versus Nature: An Environmental Ethical Perspective" (paper presented to the workshop on "A New Generation of Green Thought," 7th Nordic Environmental Social Science Research Conference, Gothenburg University, Sweden, June 15–17, 2005).

7.   Mark F. Imber, *Environment, Security, and UN Reform* (New York: St. Martin's Press, 1994), 19.

8.   John Houghton, "Global Warming Is Now a Weapon of Mass Destruction," *Guardian*, July 28, 2003.

9.   Daniel H. Deudney, "The Case against Linking Environmental Degradation to National Security," *Millennium* 19, no. 3 (1990): 461–76.

10.   Ken Conca and Geoffrey D. Dabelko, eds., *Environmental Peacemaking* (Baltimore: Johns Hopkins University Press, 2002).

11.   Daniel H. Deudney, "Environmental Security: A Critique," in *Contested Grounds: Security and Conflict in the New Environmental Politics*, ed. Daniel H. Deudney and Richard A. Matthew (Albany, NY: SUNY Press, 1999), 214.

12.   Derrick M. Kedziora, "Gunboat Diplomacy in the Northwest Atlantic: The 1995 Canada–EU Fishing Dispute and the United Nations Agreement on Straddling and High Migratory Fish Stocks," *Northwestern Journal of International Law and Business* 17, no. 2/3 (1996): 1132.

13.   I hasten to add that this is a hypothetical situation designed to force a confrontation with the environmental ethical issues at stake. The Rwandan government has an active program to save the mountain gorillas.

14.   Karen T. Litfin, ed., *The Greening of Sovereignty in World Politics* (Cambridge, MA: MIT Press, 1998).

15. I use the term *political legitimacy* here to refer to sociological legitimacy, while *morality* refers to normative legitimacy. The former refers to social and political conventions of rightful conduct in a particular community (observable by an anthropologist or sociologist), while the latter refers to normative claims of justice (which may vary according to particular moral or religious frameworks).

16. Independent International Commission on Kosovo, *Kosovo Report* (New York: Oxford University Press, 2000), 187–98.

17. UN Charter, Articles 2(4) and 51.

18. Rio Declaration on Environment and Development, Principle 25.

19. See Linda A. Malone, "'Green Helmets': A Conceptual Framework for Security Council Authority in Environmental Emergencies," *Michigan Journal of International Law* 17 (1996): 515–36; and Michael Murphy, "Achieving Economic Security with Swords as Ploughshares: The Modern Use of Force to Combat Environmental Degradation," *Virginia Journal of International Law* 39 (1999): 1197.

20. UN Security Council, Note by the President of the Security Council, S/23500, January 31, 1992, 3.

21. The customary international law of preemptive defense, according to the "Caroline criteria," requires that there must be "a necessity of self-defence, instant, overwhelming, leaving no choice of means and no moment for deliberation," and the action taken must not be "unreasonable or excessive." See Michael Byers, "Iraq and the 'Bush Doctrine' of Preemptive Self-Defence," Crimes of War Project, August 20, 2002; available at www.crimesof war.org/expert/bush-byers.html.

22. *Trail Smelter* Case (*United States v. Canada*), Arbitral Tribunal, Montreal, April 16, 1938, and March 11, 1941; *UN Reports of International Arbitral Awards* 3 (1947), 1905.

23. Moreover, the victim state must show causation and a lack of due diligence on the part of the offending state, a test that rests on the prevailing understanding of what is "reasonable use of territory."

24. Nuclear Tests Case (*Australia v. France*), *ICJ Reports*, 1973, 99; (*New Zealand v. France*), *ICJ Reports*, 1974, 135. As it turned out, France voluntarily agreed to halt nuclear testing, so the ICJ was not required to make a determination on the specific claim.

25. A *jus cogens* norm may not be violated by any state, including states that object to the norm, which means that it can override ordinary customary law (which is based on consent).

26. The marsh region is located at the confluence of the Tigris and Euphrates rivers in southeastern Iraq and once formed the largest system of wetlands and lakes in the Middle East, covering an area of around 20,000 square kilometers. Not only do the marshlands contain rich deposits of oil, but they also provided a refuge for political opponents of Saddam Hussein's regime ("The Iraqi Government Assault on the Marsh Arabs," Human Rights Watch Briefing Paper, January 2003, www.hrw.org/backgrounder/mena/marsharabs1.htm). See also Sayyed Nadeem Kazmi and Stuart Leiderman, "Twilight People: Iraq's Marsh Inhabitants," *Human Rights Dialogue* 2, no. 11 (2004).

27. According to Human Rights Watch, the population of the Marsh Arabs in their ancestral homeland has been reduced from around 250,000 in 1991 to around 20,000 in 2003, with an estimated minimum of 100,000 internally displaced in Iraq ("The Iraqi Government Assault on the Marsh Arabs"). See also Aaron Schwabach, "Ecocide and Genocide in Iraq: International Law, the Marsh Arabs, and Environmental Damage in Non-International Conflicts," *Colorado Journal of International Environmental Law & Policy* 15, no. 1 (2004): 1–28.

28. For example, the UN Sub-Commission on Prevention of Discrimination and Protection of Minorities (working with the U.S.-based Sierra Club Legal Defense Fund) has produced a Draft Declaration of Principles on Human Rights and the Environment, which is

incorporated into the Sub-Commission's Final Report. Final Report on Human Rights and the Environment, Commission on Human Rights, Sub-commission on Prevention of Discrimination and Protection of Minorities, UN ESCOR, 46th Sess., UN Doc. E/CN.4/Sub.2/1994/9 (1994), 74–77.

29.   See, e.g., Nancy Lee Peluso, "Coercing Conservation: The Politics of State Resource Control," in *The State and Social Power in Global Environmental Politics*, ed. Ronnie D. Lipschutz and Ken Conca (New York: Columbia University Press, 1993), 46–70.

30.   See, e.g., Tzvetan Todorov, "Right to Intervene or Duty to Assist?" in *Human Rights, Human Wrongs: The Oxford Amnesty Lectures*, ed. Nicholas Owen (New York: Oxford University Press, 2001); and Mohammed Ayoob, "Humanitarian Intervention and State Sovereignty," *International Journal of Human Rights* 6, no. 1 (2002): 81–102.

31.   For a more detailed discussion of these differences, see Holzgrefe, "The Humanitarian Intervention Debate," in *Humanitarian Intervention*, eds. Keohane and Holzgrefe.

32.   Ibid., 41–43.

33.   Michael Byers and Simon Chesterman, "Changing the Rules about Rules? Unilateral Humanitarian Intervention and the Future of International Law," in *Humanitarian Intervention*, eds. Keohane and Holzgrefe.

34.   Ibid., 202.

35.   Ibid.

36.   Jane Stromseth, "Rethinking Humanitarian Intervention: The Case for Incremental Change," in *Humanitarian Intervention*, eds. Keohane and Holzgrefe, 243–44. For example, NATO did not plead exceptional illegality for its intervention in Kosovo; rather, it justified its actions as legally exceptional in order to prevent genocide.

37.   As Thomas M. Franck goes on to point out, while some illegal acts of intervention have been roundly condemned, others have been greeted with "mute, but evident satisfaction," while still others have received retrospective validation through the authorization of a UN presence. See Thomas M. Franck, "Interpretation and Change in the Law of Humanitarian Intervention," in *Humanitarian Intervention*, eds. Keohane and Holzgrefe.

38.   Jean Bethke Elshtain, "International Justice as Equal Regard and the Use of Force," *Ethics & International Affairs* 17, no. 2 (2003): 63–75.

39.   Michael Walzer, *Just and Unjust Wars: A Moral Argument with Historical Illustrations*, fourth edition (New York: Basic Books, [1977] 2006), 107; *Thick and Thin: Moral Argument at Home and Abroad* (Notre Dame, IN: University of Notre Dame Press, 1994), 15–19; and "The Politics of Rescue," *Dissent* (Winter 1995): 35–41; also available in his *Arguing About War* (New Haven, CT: Yale University Press, 2004).

40.   David Ehrenfeld, *The Arrogance of Humanism* (New York: Oxford University Press, 1981).

41.   Peter Singer, *Animal Liberation: A New Ethics for Our Treatment of Animals* (New York: The New Review, 1975); Tom Regan, *The Case for Animal Rights* (Berkeley and Los Angeles: University of California Press, 1983); and Paola Cavalieri and Peter Singer, eds., *The Great Ape Project: Equality Beyond Humanity* (New York: St. Martin's Press, 1994).

42.   For a defense of ecocentrism, see Robyn Eckersley, *Environmentalism and Political Theory: Toward an Ecocentric Approach* (Albany, NY: SUNY Press, 1992). For a general stocktaking of nonanthropocentric discourses, see Robyn Eckersley, "Ecocentric Discourses: Problems and Future Prospects for Nature Advocacy," in *Debating the Earth: The Environmental Politics Reader*, ed. John S. Dryzek and David Schlosberg, 2nd ed. (New York: Oxford University Press, 2005), 364–81.

43.   Great Ape Project, "Declaration of Great Apes"; available at www.greatapeproject .org/declaration.html; accessed October 4, 2005.

44.   Robert E. Goodin, Carole Pateman, and Roy Pateman, "Simian Sovereignty," *Political Theory* 25, no. 6 (1997): 821–49.

45.   Ibid., 834–35.

46.   Biodiversity is used in the 1992 UN Convention on Biological Diversity to encompass all aspects of variability evident within the living world, including diversity within and between individuals; within populations; within species; and within communities and ecosystems on land and water.

47.   The preamble to the 1992 UN Convention on Biological Diversity recognizes that the conservation of biological diversity is a common concern of humankind. Similarly, the preamble to the UN Framework Convention on Climate Change also acknowledges "that change in the Earth's climate and its adverse effects are a common concern of humankind." See Frank Biermann, "'Common Concern of Humankind': The Emergence of a New Concept of International Environmental Law," *Archiv des Völkerrechts* 34 (1996): 426–81.

48.   Franz Xaver Perrez, "The Relationship between 'Permanent Sovereignty' and the Obligation Not to Cause Transboundary Environmental Damage," *Environmental Law* 26 (1996): 1207.

49.   Friedrich Kratochwil, "Sovereignty as Dominium: Is There a Right of Humanitarian Intervention?" in *Beyond Westphalia? National Sovereignty and International Intervention*, ed. Gene M. Lyons and Michael Mastanduno (Baltimore: Johns Hopkins University Press, 1995), 25.

50.   See the 1982 UN Convention on the Law of the Sea, Article 56; the 1992 Convention on Biological Diversity, Article 15; and the Food and Agricultural Organization's International Treaty on Plant Genetic Resources for Food and Agriculture, Article 10.1. Peter H. Sand, "Sovereignty Bounded: Public Trusteeship for Common Pool Resources?" *Global Environmental Politics* 4, no. 19 (2004): 47–48.

51.   Article 1, GA resolution 1803 (XVII), December 14, 1962.

52.   Nico Schrijver, *Sovereignty Over Natural Resources: Balancing Rights and Duties* (Cambridge: Cambridge University Press, 1997), 369–70.

53.   Principle 2 of the Rio Declaration provides that "States have, in accordance with the Charter of the United Nations and the principles of international law, the sovereign right to exploit their own resources pursuant to their own environmental and developmental policies, and the responsibility to ensure that activities within their jurisdiction or control do not cause damage to the environment of other States or of areas beyond the limits of national jurisdiction."

54.   See note 47.

55.   A. John Simmons, "On the Territorial Rights of States," in *Social, Political, and Legal Philosophy*, ed. Ernest Sosa and Enrique Villanueva (Boston: Blackwell, 2001), 301.

56.   See Charles R. Beitz, *Political Theory and International Relations*, revised edition (Princeton, NJ: Princeton University Press, [1979] 1999).

57.   Simmons, "On the Territorial Rights of States," 303.

58.   Robyn Eckersley, *The Green State: Rethinking Democracy and Sovereignty* (Cambridge, MA: MIT Press, 2004).

59.   Examples include the polluter pays principle; the precautionary principle; the principle of sustainable development, which incorporates the principle of intra- and intergenerational equity; and the principle of "common but differentiated responsibilities," which acknowledges the different capacities and abilities of developed and developing countries to respond to global environmental change and pursue sustainable development strategies.

60.   This trustee relationship is adapted from Peter Sand, "Sovereignty Bounded," 55.

61. Genocide involves the intentional and systematic killing of large numbers of people on the basis of their social, political, religious, or ethnic status, whereas crimes against humanity are defined as a range of acts (such as murder, extermination, enslavement, and torture) "committed as part of a widespread or systematic attack directed against any civilian population, with knowledge of the attack." See Articles 6 and 7 of the Rome Statute of the International Criminal Court.

62. The phrase "widespread, long-term and severe damage to the natural environment" is taken from Article 8(b)(iv) of the Rome Statute of the International Criminal Court, dealing with war crimes (in this case, environmental war crimes).

63. Eva M. Kornicker Uhlmann, "State Community Interests, *Jus Cogens* and Protection of the Global Environment: Developing Criteria for Peremptory Norms," *Georgetown International Environmental Law Review* 11 (1998): 120.

64. In this respect, the prohibitions approximate the status of *jus cogens* or *erga omnes* obligations. The definition of *jus cogens* in section 53 of the Vienna Convention is rather general, but it has been fleshed out by Eva M. Kornicker Uhlmann as requiring the satisfaction of the following four criteria: (1) The norm must transcend the individual interests of states and serve the entire community of states or "state community interests"; (2) it must have a foundation in morality; (3) the norm must be absolute or overriding; and (4) it must command the agreement of the vast majority of states. See Kornicker Uhlmann, "State Community Interests," 104.

65. The remaining requirements are last resort, right intention, proportionality, proper authority, and reasonable hope of success. In the wake of the U.S.-led invasion of Iraq, we might add an assessment of the prospects for successful postintervention institution building.

66. Jennifer M. Welsh, "Taking Consequences Seriously: Objections to Humanitarian Intervention," in *Humanitarian Intervention and International Relations*, ed. Jennifer M. Welsh (New York: Oxford University Press, 2004), 66.

67. Most multilateral and unilateral humanitarian interventions have been carried out against small, weak, or failed states. No such interventions have taken place in nuclear states or powerful and rich states, and the majority of states do not have the military capacity to act unilaterally. Smaller states do have the opportunity to influence intervention decisions, however, when they take a turn as a nonpermanent member on the Security Council.

68. Of course, these factors should always form part of the general pragmatic assessment as to whether military intervention is likely to make matters better or worse, all things considered.

PART THREE

~

Governance, Law, and Membership

What should we expect of global governance institutions, such as the United Nations? By what standard can international institutions claim to be legitimate? Can and should they be democratic? In what circumstances and to what extent may such institutions interfere with the domestic affairs of states? What roles can global actors and cosmopolitan norms claim in reshaping domestic political structures? To what extent should liberal peoples tolerate diverse practices abroad? And at what point does toleration endanger the rights of women or minorities? What, if anything, justifies differential treatment of citizens and noncitizens? Do states have a right to control immigration, or are they morally obliged to admit those who seek to enter?

Chapter 8

The Legitimacy of Global Governance Institutions

Allen Buchanan and Robert O. Keohane

"Legitimacy" has both a normative and a sociological meaning. To say that an institution is legitimate in the normative sense is to assert that it has *the right to rule*—where ruling includes promulgating rules and attempting to secure compliance with them by attaching costs to noncompliance and/or benefits to compliance. An institution is legitimate in the sociological sense when it is widely *believed* to have the right to rule.[1] When people disagree over whether the World Trade Organization (WTO) is legitimate, their disagreements are typically normative. They are not disagreeing about whether they or others *believe* that this institution has the right to rule; they are disagreeing about whether it *has* the right to rule.[2] This essay addresses the normative dimension of recent legitimacy discussions.

We articulate a global public standard for the normative legitimacy of global governance institutions. This standard can provide the basis for principled criticism of global governance institutions and guide reform efforts in circumstances in which people disagree deeply about the demands of global justice and the role that global governance institutions should play in meeting them. We stake out a middle ground between an increasingly discredited conception of legitimacy that conflates legitimacy with international legality understood as state consent, on the one hand, and the unrealistic view that legitimacy for these institutions requires the same democratic standards that are now applied to states, on the other.

Our approach to the problem of legitimacy integrates conceptual analysis and moral reasoning with an appreciation of the fact that global governance institutions are novel, still evolving, and characterized by reasonable disagreement about what their proper goals are and what standards of justice they should meet. Because both standards and institutions are subject to change as a result of further reflection and action, we do not claim to *discover* timeless necessary and sufficient conditions for legitimacy. Instead, we offer a principled *proposal* for how the legitimacy of these institutions ought to be assessed—for the time being. Essential to our account is the idea that to be legitimate a global governance institution must possess certain *epistemic* virtues that facilitate the ongoing critical revision of its goals, through interaction with agents and organizations outside the institution. A principled global public standard of legitimacy can help citizens committed to democratic principles to distinguish legitimate institutions from illegitimate ones and to achieve a reasonable congruence in their legitimacy assessments. Were such a standard widely accepted, it could bolster public support for valuable global governance institutions that either satisfy the standard or at least make credible efforts to do so.

"Global governance institutions" covers a diversity of multilateral entities, including the WTO, the International Monetary Fund (IMF), various environmental institutions, such as the climate change regime built around the Kyoto Protocol, judges' and regulators' networks, the UN Security Council, and the new International Criminal Court (ICC).[3] These institutions are like governments in that they issue rules and publicly attach significant consequences to compliance or failure to comply with them—and claim the authority to do so. Nonetheless, they do not attempt to perform anything approaching a full range of governmental functions. These institutions do not seek, as governments do, to monopolize the legitimate use of violence within a permanently specified territory, and their design and major actions require the consent of states.

Determining whether global governance institutions are legitimate—and whether they are widely perceived to be so—is an urgent matter. Global governance institutions can promote international cooperation and also help to construct regulatory frameworks that limit abuses by nonstate actors (from corporations to narcotraffickers and terrorists) who exploit transnational mobility. At the same time, however, they constrain the choices facing societies, sometimes limit the exercise of sovereignty by democratic states, and impose burdens as well as confer benefits. For example, states must belong to the WTO in order to participate effectively in the world economy, yet WTO membership requires accepting a large number of quite intrusive rules, authoritatively applied by its dispute settlement system. Furthermore, individuals can be adversely affected by global rules—for example, by the blacklists maintained by the Security Council's Sanctions Committee[4] or the WTO's policies on intellectual property in "essential medicines." If these institutions lack legitimacy, then their claims to authority are unfounded and they are not entitled to our support.

Judgments about institutional legitimacy have distinctive practical implications. Generally speaking, if an institution is legitimate, then this legitimacy should shape the character of both our responses to the claims it makes on us and the form that our criticisms of it take. We should support or at least refrain from interfering with legitimate institutions. Further, agents of legitimate institutions deserve a kind of impersonal respect, even when we voice serious criticisms of them. Judging an institution to be legitimate, if flawed, focuses critical discourse by signaling that the appropriate objective is to reform it, rather than to reject it outright.

It is important not only that global governance institutions be legitimate, but that they are perceived to be legitimate. The perception of legitimacy matters, because, in a democratic era, multilateral institutions will only thrive if they are viewed as legitimate by democratic publics. If one is unclear about the appropriate standards of legitimacy or if unrealistically demanding standards are assumed, then public support for global governance institutions may be undermined and their effectiveness in providing valuable goods may be impaired.

ASSESSING LEGITIMACY

The Social Function of Legitimacy Assessments

Global governance institutions are valuable because they create norms and information that enable member states and other actors to coordinate their behavior in mutually beneficial ways.[5] They can reduce transaction costs, create opportunities for states and other actors to demonstrate credibility, thereby overcoming commitment problems, and provide public goods, including rule-based, peaceful resolutions of conflicts.[6] An institution's ability to perform these valuable functions, however, may depend on whether those to whom it addresses its rules regard them as binding and whether others within the institution's domain of operation support or at least do not interfere with its functioning. It is not enough that the relevant actors agree that *some* institution is needed; they must agree that *this* institution is worthy of support. So, for institutions to perform their valuable coordinating functions, a higher-order coordination problem must be solved.[7]

Once an institution is in place, ongoing support for it and compliance with its rules are sometimes simply a matter of self-interest from the perspective of states, assuming that the institution actually achieves coordination or other benefits that all or at least the more powerful actors regard as valuable.[8] Similarly, once the rule of the road has been established and penalties for violating it are in place, most people will find compliance with it to be rational from a purely self-interested point of view. In the latter case, no question of legitimacy arises, because the sole function of the institution is coordination and the choice of the particular coordination point raises no issues on which people are likely to disagree. Global governance institutions are not pure coordination devices in the way in which the rule of the road is, however. Even though all may agree that some institution or other is needed in a specific domain (the regulation of global trade, for example), and all may agree that any of several particular institutions is better than the noninstitutional alternative, different parties, depending upon their differing interests and moral perspectives, will find some feasible institutions more attractive than others. The fact that all acknowledge that it is in their interest to achieve coordinated support for some institution or other may not be sufficient to assure adequate support for any particular institution.

The concept of legitimacy allows various actors to coordinate their support for particular institutions by appealing to their common capacity to be moved by *moral reasons*, as distinct from purely strategic or exclusively self-interested reasons. If legitimacy judgments are to perform this coordinating function, however, actors must not insist that only institutions that are *optimal* from the standpoint of their own moral views are acceptable, since this would preclude coordinated support in the face of diverging normative views. More specifically, actors must not assume that an institution is worthy of support only if it is *fully just*. We thus need a standard of legitimacy that is both accessible from a diversity of moral standpoints and less demanding than a standard of justice. Such a standard must appeal to various actors' capacities to be moved by moral reasons, but without presupposing more moral agreement than exists.

Legitimacy and Self-Interest

It is one thing to say that an institution promotes one's interests and another to say that it is legitimate. As Andrew Hurrell points out, the rule-following that results from a sense of legitimacy is "distinguishable from purely self-interested or instrumental behaviour on the one hand, and from straightforward imposed or coercive rule on the other."[9] Sometimes self-interest may speak in favor of treating an institution's rules as binding; that is, it can be in one's interest to take the fact that an institution issues a rule as a weighty reason for complying with it, independently of a positive assessment of the content of particular rules. This would be the case if one is likely to do better, from the standpoint of one's own interest, by taking the rules as binding than one would by evaluating each particular rule as to how complying with it would affect one's interests. Yet clearly it makes sense to ask whether an institution that promotes one's interests is legitimate. So legitimacy, understood as the right to rule, is a moral notion that cannot be reduced to rational self-interest. To say that an institution is legitimate implies that it has the right to rule even if it does not act in accordance with the rational self-interest of everyone who is subject to its rule.

There are advantages in achieving coordinated support for institutions on the basis of moral reasons, rather than exclusively on the basis of purely self-interested ones. First, the appeal to moral reasons is instrumentally valuable in securing the benefits that only institutions can provide because, as a matter of psychological fact, moral reasons matter when we try to determine what practical attitudes should be taken toward particular institutional arrangements. For example, we care not only about whether an environmental regulation regime reduces air pollutants and thereby produces benefits for all, but also whether it fairly distributes the costs of the benefits it provides. Given that there is widespread disagreement as to which institutional arrangement would be optimal, we need to find a shared evaluative perspective that makes it possible for us to achieve the coordinated support required for effective institutions without requiring us to disregard our most basic moral commitments. Second, and perhaps most important, if our support for an institution is based on reasons other than self-interest or the fear of coercion, it may be more stable. What is in our self-interest may change as circumstances change and the threat of coercion may not always be credible, and moral commitments can preserve support for valuable institutions in such circumstances.

For questions of legitimacy to arise there must be considerable moral disagreement about how institutions should be designed. Yet for agreement about legitimacy to be reached, there must be sufficient agreement on the sorts of moral considerations that are relevant for evaluating alternative institutional designs. The practice of making legitimacy judgments is grounded in a complex belief—namely, that while it is true that institutions ought to meet standards more demanding than mere mutual benefit (relative to some relevant noninstitutional alternative), they can be worthy of our support even if they do not maximally serve our interests and even if they do not measure up to our highest moral standards.[10]

Legitimacy requires not only that institutional agents are justified in carrying out their roles, but also that those to whom institutional rules are addressed have content-independent reasons to comply with them, and that those within the domain of the institution's operations have content-independent reasons to support the institution or at least to not interfere with its functioning.[11] One has a content-independent reason to comply with a rule if and only if one has a reason to comply regardless of any positive assessment of the content of that rule. For example, I have a content-independent reason to comply with the rules of a club to which I belong if I have agreed to follow them and this reason is independent of whether I judge any particular rule to be a good or useful one. If I acknowledge an institution as having authority, I thereby acknowledge that there are content-independent reasons to comply with its rules or at least to not interfere with their operation. Legitimacy disputes concern not merely what institutional agents are morally permitted to do but also whether those to whom the institution addresses its rules should regard it as having authority.

The debate about the legitimacy of global governance institutions engages both the perspective of states and that of individuals. Indeed, as recent mass protests against the WTO suggest, politically mobilized individuals can adversely affect the functioning of global governance institutions, both directly, by disrupting key meetings, and indirectly, by imposing political costs on their governments for their support of institutional policies. Legitimacy in the case of global governance institutions, then, is the right to rule, understood to mean both that institutional agents are morally justified in making rules and attempting to secure compliance with them and that people subject to those rules have moral, content-independent reasons to follow them and/or to not interfere with others' compliance with them.

If it becomes widely believed that an institution does not measure up to standards of legitimacy, then the result may be a lack of coordination, at least until the institution changes to conform to the standards or a new institution that better conforms to them replaces it. Thus, it would be misleading to say simply that the function of legitimacy judgments is to achieve coordinated support for institutions; rather, their function is to make possible coordinated support based on moral reasons, while at the same time supplying a critical but realistic minimal moral standard by which to determine whether institutions are *worthy* of support.

Justice and Legitimacy

The foregoing account of the social function of legitimacy assessments helps clarify the relationship between justice and legitimacy. Collapsing legitimacy into justice undermines the valuable social function of legitimacy assessments. There are two reasons not to insist that only just institutions have the right to rule. First, there is sufficient disagreement on what justice requires that such a standard for legitimacy would thwart the eminently reasonable goal of securing coordinated support for valuable institutions on the basis of moral reasons. Second, even if we all agreed on what justice requires, withholding support from institutions because they fail to meet the demands of justice would be self-defeating from the standpoint of justice itself, because progress toward justice requires effective institutions. To mistake legitimacy for justice is to make the best the enemy of the good.

COMPETING STANDARDS OF LEGITIMACY

Having explicated our *conception* of legitimacy, we now explore *standards* of legitimacy: the conditions an institution must satisfy in order to have the right to rule. In this section we articulate three candidates for the appropriate standard of legitimacy—state consent, consent by democratic states, and global democracy—and argue that each is inadequate.

State Consent

The first view is relatively simple. Global governance institutions are legitimate if (and only if) they are created through state consent. In this conception, legitimacy is simply a matter of legality. Legally constituted institutions, created by states according to the recognized procedures of public international law and consistent with it, are ipso facto legitimate or at the very least enjoy a strong presumption of legitimacy.[12] Call this the International Legal Pedigree View (the Pedigree View, for short). A more sophisticated version of the Pedigree View would require the periodic reaffirmation of state consent, on the grounds that states have a legitimate interest in determining whether these institutions are performing as they are supposed to.[13]

The Pedigree View fails because it is hard to see how state consent could render global governance institutions legitimate, given that many states are non-democratic and systematically violate the human rights of their citizens and are for that reason themselves illegitimate. State consent in these cases cannot transfer legitimacy for the simple reason that there is no legitimacy to transfer. To assert that state consent, regardless of the character of the state, is sufficient for the legitimacy of global governance institutions is to regress to a conception of international order that fails to impose even the most minimal normative requirements on states. Indeed, once we abandon that deeply defective conception of international order, it is hard to see why state consent is even a *necessary* condition for legitimacy.

It might be argued, however, that even though the consent of illegitimate states cannot itself make global governance institutions legitimate, there is an important instrumental justification for treating state consent as a necessary condition for their legitimacy: doing so provides a check on the tendency of stronger states to exploit weak ones. In other words, persisting in the fiction that all states—irrespective of whether they respect the basic rights of their own citizens—are moral agents worthy of respect serves an important value. This conception of the state, however, is not a fiction that those who take human rights seriously can consistently accept.

The proponent of state consent might reply as follows: "My proposal is not that we should return to the pernicious fiction of the Morality of States. Instead, it is that we should agree, for good cosmopolitan reasons, to regard a global governance institution as legitimate only if it enjoys the consent of all states." Withholding legitimacy from global governance institutions, no matter how valuable they are, simply because not all states consent to them, however, would purport to protect weaker states at the expense of giving a legitimacy veto to tyrannies. The price is too high. Weak states are in a numerical majority in multilateral institutions. Generally speaking, they are less threatened by the dominance of powerful states within the institutions than they are by the actions of such powerful states acting outside of institutional constraints.

The Consent of Democratic States

The idea that state consent confers legitimacy is much more plausible when restricted to democratic states. On reflection, however, the mere fact of state consent, even when the state in question is democratic and satisfies whatever other conditions are appropriate for state legitimacy, is not sufficient for the legitimacy of global governance institutions.

From the standpoint of a particular weak democratic state, participation in global governance institutions such as the WTO is hardly voluntary, since the state would suffer serious costs by not participating. Yet "substantial" voluntariness is generally thought to be a necessary condition for consent to play a legitimating role.[14] Of course, there may be reasonable disagreements over what counts as substantial voluntariness, but the vulnerability of individual weak states is serious enough to undercut the view that the consent of democratic states is by itself sufficient for legitimacy.

There is another reason why the consent of democratic states is not sufficient for the legitimacy of global governance institutions: the problem of reconciling democratic values with unavoidable "bureaucratic discretion" that plagues democratic theory at the domestic level looms even larger in the global case. The problem is that for a modern state to function, much of what state agents do will not be subject to democratic decisions, and saying that the public has consented in some highly general way to whatever it is that state agents do is clearly inadequate. The difficulty is not in identifying chains of delegation stretching from the individual citizen to state agents, but rather that at some point the impact of the popular will on how political power is used becomes so attenuated as to be merely nominal. Given how problematic democratic authorization is in the modern state and given that global governance institutions require lengthening the chain of delegation, democratic state consent is not sufficient for legitimacy.

Still, the consent of democratic states may appear to be necessary, if not sufficient, for the legitimacy of global governance institutions. Indeed, it seems obvious that for such an institution to attempt to impose its rules on democratic states without their consent would violate the right of self-determination of the people of those states. Matters are not so simple, however. A democratic people's right of self-determination is not absolute. If the majority persecutes a minority, the fact that it does so through democratic processes does not render the state in question immune to sanctions or even to intervention. One might accommodate this fact by stipulating that a necessary condition for the legitimacy of global governance institutions is that they enjoy the consent of states that are democratic *and* that do a credible job of respecting the rights of all their citizens.

This does not mean that all such states must consent. A few such states may willfully seek to isolate themselves from global governance (Switzerland only joined the UN in 2002). Furthermore, democratic states may engage in wars that are unnecessary and unjust, and resist pressures from international institutions to desist. It would hardly delegitimize a global governance institution established to constrain unjust warfare that it was opposed by a democratic state that was waging an unjust war. A more reasonable position would be that there is a *strong presumption* that global governance institutions are illegitimate unless they enjoy the ongoing consent of democratic states. Let us say, then, that ongoing consent by rights-respecting democratic states constitutes *the democratic channel* of accountability.[15]

However valuable the democratic channel of accountability is, it is not sufficient. First, as already noted, the problem of bureaucratic discretion that attenuates the power of majoritarian processes at the domestic level seems even more serious in the case of global bureaucracies. Second, not all the people who are affected by global governance institutions are citizens of democratic states, so even if the ongoing consent of democratic states fosters accountability, it may not foster accountability to *them*. If—as is the case at present—democratic states tend to be richer and hence more powerful than nondemocratic ones, then the requirement of ongoing consent by democratic states may actually foster a type of accountability that is detrimental to the interests of the world's worst-off people. From the standpoint of any broadly cosmopolitan moral theory, this is a deep flaw of domestic democracies as ordinarily conceived: government is supposed to be responsive to the interests and preferences of the "sovereign people"—*the people whose government it is*—not all people or even all people whose legitimate interests will be seriously affected by the government's actions.[16] For these reasons, the consent of democratic states seems insufficient. The idea that the legitimacy of global governance institutions requires democracy on a grander scale may seem plausible.

Global Democracy

Because democracy is now widely thought to be the gold standard for legitimacy in the case of the state, it may seem obvious that global governance institutions are legitimate if and only if they are democratic. And since these institutions increasingly affect the welfare of people everywhere, surely this must mean that they ought to be democratic in the sense of giving everyone an equal say in how they operate. Call this the Global Democracy View.

The most obvious difficulty with this view is that the social and political conditions for democracy are not met at the global level and there is no reason to think that they will be in the foreseeable future. At present there is no global political structure that could provide the basis for democratic control over global governance institutions, even if one assumes that democracy requires little direct participation by individuals. Any attempt to create such a structure in the form of a global democratic federation that relies on existing states as federal units would lack legitimacy, and hence could not confer legitimacy on global governance institutions, because, as has already been noted, many states are themselves undemocratic or lack other qualities necessary for state legitimacy. Furthermore, there is at present no global public—no worldwide political community constituted by a broad consensus recognizing a common domain as the proper subject of global collective decision making and habitually communicating with one another about public issues. Nor is there consensus on a normative framework within which to deliberate together about a global common interest. Indeed, there is not even a global consensus that some form of global government, much less a global democracy, is needed or appropriate. Finally, once it is understood that it is *liberal* democracy, democracy that protects individual and minority rights, that is desirable, the Global Democracy View seems even more unfeasible. Democracy worth aspiring to is more than elections; it includes a complex web of institutions, including a free press and media, an active civil society, and institutions to check abuses of power by administrative agencies and elected officials.

Global governance institutions provide benefits that cannot be provided by states and, as we have argued, securing those benefits may depend upon these institutions being regarded as legitimate. The value of global governance institutions, therefore, warrants being more critical about the assumption that they must be democratic *on the domestic model* and more willing to explore an alternative conception of their legitimacy. In the next section we take up this task.

A COMPLEX STANDARD OF LEGITIMACY

Desiderata for a Standard of Legitimacy

Our discussion of the social function of legitimacy assessments and our critique of the three dominant views on the standard of legitimacy for global governance institutions (state consent, democratic state consent, and global democracy) suggest that a standard of legitimacy for such institutions should have the following characteristics:

1. It must provide a reasonable public basis for coordinated support for the institutions in question, on the basis of moral reasons that are widely accessible in spite of the persistence of significant moral disagreement—in particular, about the requirements of justice.
2. It must not confuse legitimacy with justice but nonetheless must not allow that extremely unjust institutions are legitimate.
3. It must take the ongoing consent of democratic states as a presumptive necessary condition, though not a sufficient condition, for legitimacy.
4. Although the standard should not make authorization by a global democracy a necessary condition of legitimacy, it should nonetheless *promote* the key values that underlie demands for democracy.
5. It must properly reflect the dynamic character of global governance institutions: the fact that not only the means they employ, but even their goals, may and ought to change over time.
6. It must address the two problems we encountered earlier: the problem of bureaucratic discretion and the tendency of democratic states to disregard the legitimate interests of foreigners.

The standard of legitimacy must therefore incorporate mechanisms for accountability that are both more robust and more inclusive than that provided by the consent of democratic states.

Moral Disagreement and Uncertainty

The first desideratum of a standard of legitimacy is complex and warrants further explication and emphasis. We have noted that a central feature of the circumstances of legitimacy is the persistence of disagreement about, first, what the proper goals of the institution are (given the limitations imposed by state sovereignty properly conceived), second, what global justice requires, and third, what role if any the institution should play in the pursuit of global justice. Moral disagreement is not unique to global governance institutions, but extends also to the appropriate role of the state.

There are two circumstances in the case of global governance institutions, however, that exacerbate the problem of moral disagreement. First, in the case of the state, democratic processes, at least ideally, provide a way of accommodating these disagreements, by providing a public process that assures every citizen that she is being treated as an equal, through the electoral process, while, as we have seen, democracy is unavailable at the global level. Second, although there is a widespread perception, at least among cosmopolitans broadly speaking, that there is serious global injustice and that the effective pursuit of global justice requires a significant role for global institutions, it is not possible at present to provide a principled specification of the division of institutional labor for pursuing global justice. In part the problem is that there is no unified system of global institutions within which a fair and effective allocation of institutional responsibilities for justice can be devised. How responsibilities for justice ought to be allocated among global institutions and between states and global institutions depends chiefly on the answers to two questions: What are the proper responsibilities of states in the pursuit of global justice, taking into account the proper scope of state sovereignty (because this will determine how extensive the role of global institutions should be), and what are the capabilities of various global institutions for contributing to the pursuit of global justice? But neither of these questions can be answered satisfactorily at present, in part because global governance institutions are so new and in part because people have only recently begun to think seriously about achieving justice on a global scale. So the difficulty is not just that there is considerable moral disagreement about the proper goals of global governance institutions and about the role these institutions should play in the pursuit of global justice; there is also moral *uncertainty*.[17] A plausible standard of legitimacy for global governance institutions must somehow accommodate *the facts of moral disagreement and uncertainty*.

Three Substantive Criteria

We begin with a set of institutional attributes that have considerable intuitive appeal: minimal moral acceptability, comparative benefit, and institutional integrity.

Minimal Moral Acceptability. Global governance institutions, like institutions generally, must not persist in committing serious injustices. If they do so, they are not entitled to our support. On our view, the primary instance of a serious injustice is the violation of human rights. We also believe that the most plausible conception of human rights is what might be called the basic human interest conception. This conception, which we can only sketch in broad outlines here, builds on Joseph Raz's insight that rights generally are normative relations (in particular, duties and entitlements), which, if realized, provide important protections for interests.[18] On this view, to justify the claim that R is a right, one must identify an interest, support the claim that the interest is of sufficient moral importance to ground duties, explain why the duties are owed to the right holders, and make the case that if the normative relations in question are satisfied, significant protection for the interest will be achieved. Certain rights are properly called human rights because the duties they entail provide especially important protections for basic human interests, given the standard threats to those interests in our world.

What the standard threats are can change over time. For example, when human societies create legal systems and police and courts to enforce laws, they also create new opportunities for damaging basic human interests. For this reason, the content of particular human rights, and even which rights are included among the human rights, may also change, even though the basic interests that ground them do not. For example, all human beings, regardless of where or when they exist, have a basic interest in physical security, but in a society with a legal system backed by the coercive power of the state, adequate protection of this interest requires rights of due process and equal protection under the law.

There is disagreement among basic interest theorists of human rights as to exactly what the list of human rights includes and how the content of particular rights is to be filled out. There is agreement, however, that the list includes the rights to physical security, to liberty (understood as at least encompassing freedom from slavery, servitude, and forced occupations), and the right to subsistence. Assuming that this is so, we can at least say this much: global governance institutions (like institutions generally) are legitimate only if they do not persist in violations of the least controversial human rights. This is a rather minimal moral requirement for legitimacy. Yet in view of the normative disagreement and uncertainty that characterize our attitudes toward these institutions, it might be hard at present to justify a more extensive set of rights that all such institutions are bound to respect. It would certainly be desirable to develop a more meaningful consensus on stronger human rights standards. What this suggests is that we should require global governance institutions to respect minimal human rights, but also expect them to meet higher standards as we gain greater clarity about the scope of human rights.

For many global governance institutions, it is proper to expect that they should respect human rights, but not that they should play a major role in *promoting* human rights. Nonetheless, a theory of legitimacy cannot ignore the fact that in some cases the dispute over whether a global governance institution is legitimate is in large part a disagreement over whether it is worthy of support if it does not actively promote human rights. A proposal for a standard of legitimacy for global governance institutions must take into account the fact

that some of these institutions play a more direct and substantial role in securing human rights than others.

When we see the injustices of our world and appreciate that ameliorating
them requires institutional actions, we are quick to attribute obligations to institutions and then criticize them for failing to fulfill those obligations. It is one
thing to say that it would be a good thing if a particular global governance
institution took on certain functions that would promote human rights, however, and quite another to say that it has a duty to do so and that this duty is of
such importance that failure to discharge it makes the institution illegitimate.
There are two mistakes to be avoided here. The first is "duty dumping," that is,
arbitrarily assuming that some particular institution has a duty simply because
it has the resources to fulfill it and no other actor is doing so.[19] Duty dumping
not only makes unsupported attributions of institutional responsibility; it also
distracts attention from the difficult task of determining what a fair distribution
of the burdens—among individuals and institutions—for protecting the human
rights in question would be. The second error derives from the first: if one
uncritically assumes that the institution has a duty to provide X and also
assumes that X is a central matter of justice (as is the case with human rights),
then one may conclude that the institution's failure to provide X is such a
serious injustice as to rob the institution of legitimacy. But the fact that an
institution could provide X and the fact that X is a human right does not imply
that in refraining from providing X the institution commits a serious injustice.
That conclusion would only follow if it were established that the institution has
a duty of justice to provide X. Merely pointing out that the institution could
provide X—or even showing that it is the only existing institution that can do
so—is not sufficient to show that it has a duty of justice or any duty at all to
provide X.

We seem to be in a quandary. Contemporary institutions have to operate in
an environment of moral disagreement and uncertainty, which limits the
demands we can reasonably place on them to respect or protect particular
human rights. Furthermore, to be sufficiently general, an account of legitimacy
must avoid moral requirements that only apply to some global governance institutions. These considerations suggest the appropriateness of something like the
minimal moral acceptability requirement, understood as refraining from violations of the least controversial human rights. On the other hand, the standard
of legitimacy should somehow reflect the fact that part of what is at issue in
disputes over the legitimacy of some of these institutions is whether they should
satisfy more robust demands of justice. In other words, the standard should
acknowledge the fact that where the issue of legitimacy is most urgent, there is
likely to be deep moral disagreement and uncertainty.

In our view, the way out of this impasse is to build the conditions needed
for principled, informed deliberation about moral issues *into the standard of
legitimacy itself*. The standard of legitimacy should require minimal moral

acceptability, but should also accommodate and even encourage the possibility of developing more determinate and demanding requirements of justice for at least some of these institutions, as a principled basis for an institutional division of labor regarding justice emerges.

Comparative Benefit. This second substantive condition for legitimacy is relatively straightforward. The justification for having global governance institutions is primarily if not exclusively instrumental. The basic reason for states or other addressees of institutional rules to take them as binding and for individuals generally to support or at least to not interfere with the operation of these institutions is that they provide benefits that cannot otherwise be obtained. If an institution cannot effectively perform the functions invoked to justify its existence, then this insufficiency undermines its claim to the right to rule.

"Benefit" here is comparative. The legitimacy of an institution is called into question if there is an institutional alternative, providing significantly greater benefits, that is feasible, accessible without excessive transition costs, and meets the minimal moral acceptability criterion. The most difficult issues, as discussed below, concern trade-offs between comparative benefit and our other criteria. Legitimacy is not to be confused with *optimal* efficacy and efficiency. The other values that we discuss are also important in their own right; and in any case, institutional stability is a virtue. Nevertheless, if an institution steadfastly remains instrumentally suboptimal when it could take steps to become significantly more efficient or effective, this could impugn its legitimacy in an indirect way: it would indicate that those in charge of the institution were either grossly incompetent or not seriously committed to providing the benefits that were invoked to justify the creation of the institution in the first place. For instance, as of the beginning of 2006 the United Nations faced the issue of reconstituting a Human Rights Commission that had been discredited by the membership of states that notoriously abuse human rights, with Libya serving as chair in 2003.[20]

Institutional Integrity. If an institution exhibits a pattern of egregious disparity between its actual performance, on the one hand, and its self-proclaimed procedures or major goals, on the other, its legitimacy is seriously called into question. The UN Oil-for-Food scandal is a case in point. The Oil-for-Food Program was devised to enable Iraqi oil to be sold, under strict controls, to pay for food imports under the UN-mandated sanctions of the 1990s. The purpose was both to prevent malnutrition in Iraq and to counter Iraqi propaganda holding the UN responsible for the deaths of hundreds of thousands of Iraqi children, without relieving the pressure on Saddam Hussein's regime to get rid of its supposed weapons of mass destruction. Yet it led to a great deal of corruption. Oil-for-Food became a huge program, permitting the government of Iraq to sell $64.2 billion of oil to 248 companies, and enabling 3,614 companies to sell $34.5 billion of humanitarian goods to Iraq. Yet more than half of the companies involved paid illegal surcharges or kickbacks to Saddam and his cronies, resulting in large profits for corporations and pecuniary benefits for some program administrators, including at least one high-level UN official.[21] The most damning charge is that neither the Security Council oversight bodies nor the Office of the Secretary-General followed the UN's prescribed procedures for accountability. At least when viewed in the light of the historical record of other, perhaps less egregious failures of accountability in the use of resources on the part of the UN, these findings have raised questions about the legitimacy of the Security Council and the secretariat.

It also appears that an institution should be presumed to be illegitimate if its practices or procedures predictably undermine the pursuit of the very goals in terms of which it justifies its existence. Thus, for example, if the fundamental character of the Security Council's decision-making process renders that institution incapable of successfully pursuing what it now acknowledges as one of its chief goals—stopping large-scale violations of basic human rights—this impugns its legitimacy. To take another example, Randall Stone has shown that the IMF during the 1990s inconsistently applied its own standards with respect to its lending, systematically relaxing enforcement on countries that had rich and powerful patrons.[22] Similarly, if the WTO claims to provide the benefits of trade liberalization to all of its members, but consistently develops policies that exclude its weaker members from the benefits of liberalization, this undermines its claim to legitimacy. If an institution fails to satisfy the integrity criterion, we have reason to believe that key institutional agents are either untrustworthy or grossly incompetent, that the institution lacks correctives for these deficiencies, and that the institution is therefore unlikely to be effective in providing the goods that would give it a claim to our support.

Integrity and comparative benefit are related but distinct. If there are major discrepancies between an institution's behavior and its prescribed procedures and professed goals, then we can have little confidence that it will succeed in delivering the benefits it is supposed to provide. Integrity, however, is a more forward-looking, dynamic virtue than comparative benefit, which measures benefit solely in terms of the current situation. If an institution satisfies the criterion of integrity, there is reason to be confident that institutional actors will not only deliver the benefits that are now taken to constitute the proper goals of institutional activity, but also that they will be able to maintain the institution's effectiveness if its goals change.

Epistemic Aspects of Legitimacy

Minimal moral acceptability, comparative benefit, and institutional integrity are plausible presumptive substantive requirements for the legitimacy of global governance institutions. It would be excessive to claim that they are necessary conditions *simpliciter*, because there might be extraordinary circumstances in which an institution would fail to satisfy one or two of them, yet still reasonably be regarded as legitimate. This might be the case if there were no feasible and

accessible alternative institutional arrangement, if the noninstitutional alternative were sufficiently grim, and if there was reason to believe that the institution
had the resources and the political will to correct the deficiency. How much we
expect of an institution should depend, inter alia, upon how valuable the benefits it provides are and whether there are acceptable, feasible alternatives to it.
For example, we might be warranted in regarding an institution as legitimate
even though it lacked integrity, if it were nonetheless providing important protections for basic human rights and the alternatives to relying on it were even
less acceptable. In contrast, the fact that an institution is effective in incremen-
tally liberalizing trade would not be sufficient to rebut the presumption that it
is illegitimate because it abuses human rights.[23]

Our three substantive conditions are best thought of as what Rawls calls
"counting principles": the more of them an institution satisfies, and the higher
the degree to which it satisfies them, the stronger its claim to legitimacy.[24]

There are two limitations on the applicability of these three criteria, however. The first is *the problem of factual knowledge*: being able to make reasonable judgments about whether an institution satisfies any of the three
substantive conditions requires considerable information about the workings
of the institution and their effects in a number of domains, as well as about
the likely effects of feasible alternatives. Some institutions may not only fail to
supply the needed information, however; they may, whether deliberately or
otherwise, make such information either impossible for outsiders to obtain or
make obtaining it prohibitively costly. Even if the institution does not try to
limit access to the relevant information, it may not be accessible, in suitably
integrated, understandable form.

The second difficulty with taking the three substantive conditions as jointly
sufficient for legitimacy is *the problem of moral disagreement and uncertainty*
noted earlier. Even if there is sufficient agreement on what counts as the violation of basic human rights, there are ongoing disputes about whether some
global governance institutions should meet higher moral standards. As emphasized above, there is not only disagreement but also uncertainty as to the role
that some of these institutions should play in the pursuit of global justice,
chiefly because we do not have a coherent idea of what the institutional division
of labor for achieving global justice would look like.

Furthermore, merely requiring that global governance institutions not violate
basic human rights is unresponsive to the familiar complaint that rich countries
unfairly dominate them, and that even if they provide benefits to all, the richer
members receive unjustifiably greater benefits. Although all parties may agree
that fairness matters, however, there are likely to be disagreements about what
fairness would consist of, disputes about whether fairness would suffice or
whether equality is required, and about how equality is to be understood and
even over what is to be made equal (welfare, opportunities, resources, and so
on). So, quite apart from the issue of what positive role, if any, these institutions

should play in the pursuit of global justice, there is disagreement about what standards of fairness they should meet internally. There is also likely to be disagreement about how unfair an institution must be to lack legitimacy. A proposal for a public global standard of legitimacy must not gloss over these disagreements.

In the following sections we argue that the proper response to both the problem of factual knowledge and the problem of moral disagreement and uncertainty is to focus on what might be called the *epistemic–deliberative* quality of the institution, the extent to which the institution provides reliable information needed for grappling with normative disagreement and uncertainty concerning its proper functions. To lay the groundwork for that argument we begin by considering two items that are often assumed to be obvious requirements for the legitimacy of global governance institutions: accountability and transparency.

Accountability. Critics of global governance institutions often complain that they lack accountability. To understand the strengths and limitations of accountability as a gauge of legitimacy, we start with a skeletal but serviceable analysis of accountability. Accountability includes three elements: first, standards that those who are held accountable are expected to meet; second, information available to accountability holders, who can then apply the standards in question to the performance of those who are held to account; and third, the ability of these accountability holders to impose sanctions—to attach costs to the failure to meet the standards. The need for information about whether the institution is meeting the standards accountability holders apply means that a degree of transparency regarding the institution's operations is essential to any form of accountability.

It is misleading to say that global governance institutions are illegitimate because they lack accountability and to suggest that the key to making them legitimate is to make them accountable. Most global governance institutions, including those whose legitimacy is most strenuously denied, include mechanisms for accountability.[25] The problem is that existing patterns of accountability are morally inadequate. For example, the World Bank has traditionally exhibited a high degree of accountability, but it has been accountability to the biggest donor countries, and the Bank therefore has to act in conformity with their interests, at least insofar as they agree. This kind of accountability does not ensure meaningful participation by those affected by rules or due consideration of their legitimate interests.[26] A high degree of accountability in this case may serve to perpetuate the defects of the institution.

So accountability per se is not sufficient; it must be the right sort of accountability. At the very least, this means that there must be effective provisions in the structure of the institution to hold institutional agents accountable for acting in ways that ensure satisfaction of the minimal moral acceptability and comparative benefit conditions. But accountability understood in this narrow way is not sufficiently *dynamic* to serve as an assurance of the legitimacy of global governance institutions, given that in some cases there is serious disagreement about what the goals of the institution should be and, more specifically, about what role if any the institution should play in the pursuit of global justice. The point is that what the *terms of accountability* ought to be—what standards of accountability ought to be employed, who the accountability holders should be, and whose interests the accountability holders should represent—cannot be definitively ascertained without knowing what role, if any, the institution should play in the pursuit of global justice.

Therefore, what might be called narrow accountability—accountability without provision for contestation of the terms of accountability—is insufficient for legitimacy, given the facts of moral disagreement and uncertainty. Because what constitutes appropriate accountability is itself subject to reasonable dispute, the legitimacy of global governance institutions depends in part upon whether they operate in such a way as to facilitate principled, factually informed deliberation about the terms of accountability. There must be provisions for revising existing standards of accountability and current conceptions of who the proper accountability holders are and whose interests they should represent.

Transparency. Achieving transparency is often touted as the proper response to worries about the legitimacy of global governance institutions.[27] But transparency by itself is inadequate. First, if transparency means merely the *availability* of accurate information about how the institution works, it is insufficient even for narrow accountability—that is, for ensuring that the institution is accurately evaluated in accordance with the current terms of accountability. If information about how the institution operates is to serve the end of narrow accountability, it must be (a) accessible at reasonable cost, (b) properly integrated and interpreted, and (c) directed to the accountability holders; furthermore, (d) the accountability holders must be adequately motivated to use it properly in evaluating the performance of the relevant institutional agents. Second, if, as we have suggested, the capacity for critically revising the terms of accountability is necessary for legitimacy, information about how the institution works must be available not only to those who are presently designated as accountability holders, but also to those who may contest the terms of accountability.

Broad transparency is needed for critical revisability of the terms of accountability. Both institutional practices and the moral principles that shape the terms of accountability must be revisable in the light of critical reflection and discussion.[28] Under conditions of broad transparency, information produced initially to enable institutionally designated accountability holders to assess officials' performance may be appropriated by agents *external* to the institution, such as nongovernmental organizations (NGOs) and other actors in transnational civil society, and used to support more fundamental criticisms, not only of the institution's processes and structures, but even of its most fundamental goals and its role in the pursuit of global justice.

One especially important dimension of broad transparency is *responsibility for public justification*.[29] Institutional actors must offer public justifications of at least the more controversial and consequential institutional policies and must facilitate timely critical responses to them. Potential critics must be in a position to determine whether the public justifications are cogent, whether they are consistent with the current terms of accountability, and whether, if taken seriously, these justifications call for revision of the current terms of responsibility. To help ensure this dimension of broad transparency, it may be worthwhile to draw on, while adapting, the notice and comment procedures of administrative law at the domestic level.[30]

Earlier we noted that although comparative benefit, minimal moral acceptability, and integrity are reasonable presumptive necessary conditions for legitimacy, it may be difficult for those outside the institution to determine whether these conditions are satisfied. We suggest that broad transparency can serve as a proxy for satisfaction of the minimal moral acceptability, comparative benefit, and integrity criteria. For example, it may be easier for outsiders to discover that an institution is not responding to demands for information relevant to determining whether it is violating its own prescribed procedures, than to determine whether in fact it is violating them. Similarly, it may be very difficult to determine whether an institution is comparatively effective in solving certain global problems, but much easier to tell whether it generates—or systematically restricts access to—the information outsiders would need to evaluate its effectiveness. If an institution persistently fails to cooperate in making available to outsiders the information that would be needed to determine whether the three presumptive necessary conditions are satisfied, that by itself creates a presumption that it is illegitimate.

Legitimate global governance institutions should possess three epistemic virtues. First, because their chief function is to achieve coordination, they must generate and properly direct reliable information about coordination points; otherwise they will not satisfy the condition of comparative benefit. Second, because accountability is required to determine whether they are in fact performing their current coordinating functions efficiently and effectively requires narrow transparency, they must at least be transparent in the narrow sense. They must also have effective provisions for integrating and interpreting the information current accountability holders need and for directing it to them. Third, and most demanding, they must have the capacity for *revising the terms of accountability*, and this requires broad transparency: institutions must facilitate positive information externalities to permit inclusive, informed contestation of their current terms of accountability. There must be provision for ongoing deliberation about what global justice requires and how the institution in question fits into a division of institutional responsibilities for achieving it.

Overcoming Informational Asymmetries

A fundamental problem of institutional accountability is that insiders generally have better information about the institution than outsiders. Outsiders can determine whether institutions enjoy the consent of states, and whether states are democratic; but it may be very difficult for them to reach well-informed conclusions about the minimal moral acceptability, comparative benefit, and integrity conditions. Our emphasis on epistemic institutional virtues is well suited to illuminate these problems of asymmetrical information.

First, if institutional agents persist in failing to provide public justifications for their policies and withhold other information critical to the evaluation of institutional performance, we have good reason to believe the institution is not satisfying the substantive criteria for legitimacy.[31] Second, there may be an asymmetry of knowledge in the other direction as well, and this can have beneficial consequences for institutional accountability. Consider issue areas such as human rights and the environment, which are richly populated with independent NGOs that seek to monitor and criticize national governments and global governance institutions and to suggest policy alternatives. Suppose that in these domains there is a division of labor among external epistemic actors. Some individuals and groups seek information about certain types of issues, while others focus on other aspects, each drawing on distinct but in some cases overlapping groups of experts. Still others specialize in integrating and interpreting information gathered by other external epistemic actors.

The fact that the information held by external epistemic actors is dispersed will make it difficult for institutional agents to know what is known about their behavior or to predict when potentially damaging information may be integrated and interpreted in ways that make it politically potent. The institutional agents' awareness of this asymmetry will provide incentives for avoiding behavior for which they may be criticized. A condition of *productive uncertainty* will exist: although institutional agents will know that external epistemic actors do not possess the full range of knowledge that they do, they will know that there are many individuals and organizations gathering information about the institution. Further, they will know that some of the information that external epistemic actors have access to can serve as a reliable proxy for information they cannot access. Finally, they will also know that potentially damaging information that is currently harmless because it is dispersed among many external epistemic agents may at any time be integrated and interpreted in such a way as to make it politically effective, but they will not be able to predict when this will occur. Under these conditions, institutional agents will have significant incentives to refrain from behavior that will attract damning criticism, despite the fundamental asymmetry of knowledge between insiders and outsiders.

This is not to say that the effects of transparency will always be benign. Indeed, under some circumstances transparency can have malign effects. As

David Stasavage points out, "open-door bargaining . . . encourages representatives to posture by adopting overly aggressive bargaining positions that increase the risks of breakdown in negotiations."[32] When issues combine highly charged symbolic elements with the need for incentives, conflicts between transparency and efficiency may be severe. Our claim is not that outcomes are necessarily better the more transparent institutions are. Rather, it is that the dispersal of information among a plurality of external epistemic actors provides some counterbalance to informational asymmetries favoring insiders. There should be a very strong but rebuttable presumption of transparency, because the ills of too much transparency can be corrected by deeper, more sophisticated public discussion, whereas there can be no democratic response to secret action by bureaucracies not accountable to the public.

Furthermore, if national legislatures are to retain their relevance—if what we have called the democratic accountability channel is to be effective—they must be able to review the policies of global governance institutions.[33] For legislatures to have information essential to performing these functions, they need a flow of information from transnational civil society. Monitoring is best done pluralistically by transnational civil society, whereas the sanctions aspects of accountability are more effectively carried out by legislatures. With respect both to the monitoring and sanctioning functions, broad transparency is conducive to the principled revisability of institutions and to their improvement through increasingly inclusive criticism and more deeply probing discussion over time.

Institutional agents generally have incentives to prevent outsiders from getting information that may eventually be interpreted and integrated in damaging ways and to deprive outsiders of information that can serve as a reliable proxy to assess institutional legitimacy. The very reasons that make the epistemic virtues valuable from the standpoint of assessing institutional legitimacy may therefore tempt institutional agents to ensure that their institutions do not exemplify these virtues. But institutional agents are also aware that it is important for their institutions to be widely regarded as legitimate. Outsiders deprived of access to information are likely to react as does the prospective buyer of a used car who is prevented from taking it to an independent mechanic. They will discount the claims of the insiders and may conclude that the institution is illegitimate. So if there is a broad consensus among outsiders that institutions are not legitimate unless they exemplify the epistemic virtues, institutional agents will have a weighty reason to ensure that their institutions do so.

Contestation and Revisability: Links to External Actors and Institutions

We have argued that the legitimacy of global governance institutions depends upon whether there is ongoing, informed, principled contestation of their goals and terms of accountability. This process of contestation and revision depends upon activities of actors outside the institution. It is not enough for the institutions to make information available. Other agents, whose interests and commitments do not coincide too closely with those of the institution, must provide a check on the reliability of the information, integrate it, and make it available in understandable, usable form to all who have a legitimate interest in the operations of the institution. Such activities can produce positive feedback, in which appeal to standards of legitimacy by the external epistemic actors not only increases compliance with existing standards but also leads to improvements in the quality of these standards themselves. For these reasons, in the absence of global democracy, and given the limitations of the democratic channel described earlier, legitimacy depends crucially upon not only the epistemic virtues of the institution itself but also on the activities of *external epistemic actors*. Effective linkage between the institution and external epistemic actors constitutes what might be called the *transnational civil society channel of accountability*.

The needed external epistemic actors, if they are effective, will themselves be institutionally organized.[34] Institutional legitimacy, then, is not simply a function of the institution's characteristics; it also depends upon the broader institutional environment in which the particular institution exists. To borrow a biological metaphor, ours is an ecological conception of legitimacy.

All three elements of our complex standard of legitimacy are now in place. First, global governance institutions should enjoy the ongoing consent of democratic states. That is, the democratic accountability channel must function reasonably well. Second, these institutions should satisfy the substantive criteria of minimal moral acceptability, comparative benefit, and institutional integrity. Third, they should possess the epistemic virtues needed to make credible judgments about whether the three substantive criteria are satisfied and to achieve the ongoing contestation and critical revision of their goals, their terms of accountability, and ultimately their role in a division of labor for the pursuit of global justice, through their interaction with effective external epistemic agents.

The Complex Standard frames the legitimacy of global governance institutions as both dynamic and relational. Its emphasis on the conditions for ongoing contestation and critical revision of the most basic features of the institutions captures the exceptional moral disagreement and uncertainty that characterize the circumstances of legitimacy for this type of institution. While acknowledging the facts of moral disagreement and uncertainty, the Complex Standard includes provisions for developing more robust moral requirements for institutions over time. The Complex Standard also makes it clear that whether the institution is legitimate does not depend solely upon its own characteristics, but also upon the epistemic–deliberative relationships between the institution and epistemic actors outside it.

A Place for Democratic Values in the Absence of Global Democracy

Earlier we argued that it is a mistake to hold global governance institutions to the standard of democratic legitimacy that is now widely applied to states. We now want to suggest that when the Complex Standard of legitimacy we propose is satisfied, important democratic values will be served. For purposes of the present discussion we will assume, rather than argue, that among the most important democratic values are the following: first, equal regard for the fundamental interests of all persons; second, decision making about the public order through principled, collective deliberation; and third, mutual respect for persons as beings who are guided by reasons.

If the Complex Standard of legitimacy we propose is satisfied, all three of these values will be served. To the extent that connections between the institutions and external epistemic actors provide access to information that is not restricted to certain groups but available globally, it becomes harder for institutions to continue to exclude consideration of the interests of certain groups, and we move closer toward the ideal of equal regard for the fundamental interests of all. Furthermore, by making information available globally, networks of external epistemic actors are in effect addressing all people as individuals for whom moral reasons, not just the threat of coercion, determine whether they regard an institution's rules as authoritative. Finally, if the Complex Standard of legitimacy is satisfied, every feature of the institution becomes a potential object of principled, informed, collective deliberation, and eligibility for participation in deliberation will not be restricted by institutional interests.[35]

Consistency with Democratic Sovereignty

One source of doubts about the legitimacy of global governance institutions is the worry that they are incompatible with democratic sovereignty. Our analysis shows why and how global governance *should* constrain democratic sovereignty. The standard of legitimacy we propose is designed inter alia to help global governance institutions correct for the tendency of democratic governments to disregard the interests and preferences of those outside their own publics. It does this chiefly in two ways. First, the emphasis on the role of external institutional epistemic actors in achieving broad accountability helps to ensure more inclusive representation of interests and preferences over time. Second, the requirement of minimal moral acceptability, understood as nonviolation of basic human rights, provides an important protection for the most vulnerable: if this condition is met, democratic publics cannot ignore the most serious "negative externalities" of their policy choices. Global governance institutions that satisfy our standard of legitimacy should not be viewed as undermining democratic sovereignty, but rather as enabling democracies to function justly.

A legitimate global order will include human rights institutions that promote the conditions for the proper functioning of democracy (the right to basic education, the right to freedom of expression and association, and so on) in countries that are democratizing and help sustain these conditions in countries that already have democratic institutions. Critics of global governance institutions that claim they are illegitimate because they constrain democratic sovereignty either beg the question by assuming that the "will of the people" should not be constrained so as to take into account the interests of those outside their polity or they underestimate the extent to which democracy depends upon global governance institutions.

Having articulated the Complex Standard, and indicated how it reflects several key democratic values, we can now show, briefly, how it satisfies the desiderata for a standard of legitimacy we set out earlier.

1. The Complex Standard provides a reasonable basis for coordinated support of institutions that meet the standard, support based on moral reasons that are widely accessible in the circumstances under which legitimacy is an issue. To serve the social function of legitimacy assessments, the Complex Standard only requires a consensus on the importance of not violating the most widely recognized human rights, broad agreement that comparative benefit and integrity are also presumptive necessary conditions of legitimacy, and a commitment to inclusive, informed deliberation directed toward resolving or at least reducing the moral disagreement and uncertainty that characterize our practical attitudes toward these institutions. In other words, the Complex Standard steers a middle course between requiring more moral agreement than is available in the circumstances of legitimacy and abandoning the attempt to construct a more robust, shared moral perspective from which to evaluate global governance institutions. In particular, the Complex Standard acknowledges that the role that these institutions ought to play in a more just world order is both deeply contested and probably not knowable at present.

2. In requiring only minimal moral acceptability at present, the Complex Standard acknowledges that legitimacy does not require justice, but at the same time affirms the intuition that extreme injustice, understood as violation of the most widely recognized human rights, robs an institution of legitimacy.

3. The Complex Standard takes the ongoing consent of democratic states to be a presumptive necessity, though not a sufficient condition for legitimacy.

4. The Complex Standard rejects the assumption that global governance institutions cannot be legitimate unless there is global democracy, but at the same time promotes some of the key democratic values, including informed, public deliberation conducted on the assumption that every individual has standing to participate and the requirement that key institutional policies must be publicly justified.

5. The Complex Standard reflects a proper appreciation of the dynamic, experimental character of global governance institutions and of the fact that not only the means they employ but even the goals they pursue may and probably should change over time.

6. The Complex Standard's requirement of a functioning transnational civil society channel of accountability—an array of overlapping networks of external epistemic actors—helps to compensate for the limitations of accountability through democratic state consent.

The central argument of this essay can now be summarized. The Complex Standard provides a reasonable basis for agreement in legitimacy assessments of global governance institutions. When the comparative benefit condition is satisfied, the institution provides goods that are not readily obtainable without it. These goods, however, can be reliably provided only if coordination is achieved, and achieving coordination without excessive costs requires that the relevant agents regard the institution's rules as presumptively binding—that is, that they take the fact that the rule is issued by the institution as a content-independent reason for compliance. The instrumental value of institutions that satisfy the comparative benefit condition also gives individuals generally a content-independent reason not to interfere with the functioning of the institutions. Satisfaction of the minimal moral acceptability condition rules out the more serious moral objections that might otherwise undercut the instrumental reasons for supporting the institution. Satisfaction of the other conditions of the Complex Standard, taken together, provides moral reasons to support or at least not interfere with the institution. Among the most important of these reasons is that the institution has epistemic virtues that facilitate the development of more demanding standards and the progressive improvement of the institution itself. Thus, when a global governance institution meets the demands of the Complex Standard, there is justification for saying that it has the right to rule, not merely that it is beneficial.

CONCLUSION

In this essay we have offered a *proposal* for a public standard of legitimacy for global governance institutions. These institutions supply important benefits that neither states nor traditional treaty-based relationships among states can provide, but they are quite new, often fragile, and still evolving. Politically mobilized challenges to the legitimacy of these institutions jeopardize the support they need to function effectively, in spite of the fact that these challenges are typically unprincipled and possibly grounded in unrealistic demands that confuse justice with legitimacy. A principled global public standard of legitimacy could facilitate more responsible criticism while at the same time providing guidance for improvement, through a process of institutionalized, collective learning, both about what it is reasonable to expect from global governance institutions and about how to achieve it. Our hope is that the proposal offered in this paper serves these purposes.

NOTES

This essay appeared in *Ethics & International Affairs* 20, no. 4 (2006): 405–37. We are grateful to Sahar Akhtar, Christian Barry, Thomas Christiano, Michael Doyle, Nicole Hassoun, Andrew Hurrell, Nan Keohane, Avery Kolers, Joseph S. Nye, John Tasioulas, and two anonymous referees for their helpful comments on earlier versions of this paper, and to William Alford, Ryan Goodman, and Gerald L. Neuman for valuable criticisms and suggestions when such a version was presented at Harvard Law School, November 3, 2005. We are particularly grateful to comments by Charles Beitz and a number of other colleagues made at a workshop on the normative and empirical evaluation of global governance, Princeton University, February 17–18, 2006. Further useful comments were made at the conference on "Legitimacy and International Law" at the Max Planck Institute for Comparative Public Law and International Law, Heidelberg, Germany, June 13–14, 2006.

1.   A thorough review of the sociological literature on organizational legitimacy can be found in Mark C. Suchman, "Managing Legitimacy: Strategic and Institutional Approaches," *Academy of Management Review* 20, no. 3 (1995): 571–610.

2.   For an excellent discussion of the inadequacy of existing standards of legitimacy for global governance institutions, see Daniel Bodansky, "The Legitimacy of International Governance: A Coming Challenge for International Environmental Law?" *American Journal of International Law* 93, no. 3 (1999): 596–624. For an impressive earlier book on the subject, see Thomas Franck, *The Power of Legitimacy among Nations* (New York: Oxford University Press, 1990). Franck's account focuses on the legitimacy of rules more than institutions and in our judgment does not distinguish clearly enough between the normative and sociological senses of legitimacy.

3.   A large and growing literature exists on global governance. See, for example, Aseem Prakash and Jeffrey A. Hart, eds., *Globalization and Governance* (London: Routledge, 1999); Joseph S. Nye and John D. Donahue, eds., *Governance in a Globalizing World* (Washington, DC: Brookings Institution Press, 2000); and David Held and Anthony McGrew, eds., *Governing Globalization: Power, Authority, and Global Governance* (London: Polity Press, 2002).

4.   Erika de Wet, "The Security Council as Legislator/Executive in Its Fight against Terrorism and against Proliferation of Weapons of Mass Destruction: The Question of Legitimacy" (presentation at the conference "Legitimacy and International Law," Max Planck Institute for Comparative Public Law and International Law, Heidelberg, Germany, June 14, 2006).

5.   The emphasis here on the coordinating function should not be misunderstood: global governance institutions do not merely coordinate state actions in order to satisfy *preexisting* state preferences. As our analysis will make clear, they can also help shape state preferences and lead to the development of new norms and institutional goals.

6.   Robert O. Keohane, *After Hegemony: Cooperation and Discord in the World Political Economy* (Princeton, NJ: Princeton University Press, [1984] 2005).

7.   James D. Fearon, "Bargaining, Enforcement, and International Cooperation," *International Organization* 52, no. 2 (1998): 269–306.

8.   This is a major theme of Russell Hardin, *Liberalism, Constitutionalism, and Democracy* (New York: Oxford University Press, 1999).

9.   Andrew Hurrell, "Legitimacy and the Use of Force: Can the Circle Be Squared?" *Review of International Studies* 31, supp. S1 (2005): 16.

10.   Legitimacy can also be seen as providing a "focal point" that helps strategic actors select one equilibrium solution among others. For the classic discussion of focal points, see

Thomas C. Schelling, *The Strategy of Conflict* (Cambridge, MA: Harvard University Press, 1960), ch. 3. For a critique of theories of cooperation on the basis of focal point theory, and an application to the European Union, see Geoffrey Garrett and Barry Weingast, "Ideas, Interests, and Institutions: Constructing the European Community's Internal Market," in *Ideas and Foreign Policy: Beliefs, Institutions and Political Change*, ed. Judith Goldstein and Robert O. Keohane (Ithaca, NY: Cornell University Press, 1993), esp. 178–85.

11. Most contemporary analytic philosophical literature on legitimacy tends to focus exclusively on the legitimacy of the *state* and typically assumes a very strong understanding of legitimacy. In particular, it is assumed that legitimacy entails (1) a content-independent moral *obligation* to comply with all institutional rules (not just content-independent moral reasons to comply and/or a content-independent moral obligation to not interfere with others' compliance), (2) being justified in using *coercion* to secure compliance with rules, and (3) being justified in *using coercion to exclude* other actors from operating in the institution's domain. (See, for example, Christopher Heath Wellman and A. John Simmons, *Is There a Duty to Obey the Law? For and Against* [Cambridge: Cambridge University Press, 2005]). It is far from obvious, however, that this very strong conception is even the only conception of legitimacy appropriate for the state, given what is sometimes referred to as the "unbundling" of sovereignty into various types of decentralized states and the existence of the European Union. Be that as it may, this state-centered conception is too strong for global governance institutions, which generally do not wield coercive power or claim such strong authority. For a more detailed development of this point, see Allen Buchanan, "The Legitimacy of International Law," in *The Philosophy of International Law*, ed. Samantha Besson and John Tasioulas (New York: Oxford University Press, forthcoming).

12. This view was forcefully expressed by Professor Yoram Dinstein of Tel Aviv University, in comments on a draft of this essay.

13. For a more detailed discussion, see Allen Buchanan, *Justice, Legitimacy and Self-Determination: Moral Foundations for International Law* (New York: Oxford University Press, 2003), esp. ch. 5.

14. For a perceptive discussion of how consent to new international trade rules in the Uruguay Round (1986–1994) was merely nominal, since the alternatives for poor countries were so unattractive, see Richard H. Steinberg, "In the Shadow of Law or Power? Consensus-based Bargaining and Outcomes in the GATT/WTO," *International Organization* 56, no. 2 (2002): 339–374.

15. How the requirement of ongoing consent should be operationalized is a complex question we need not try to answer here; one possibility would be that the treaties creating the institution would have to be periodically reaffirmed.

16. Buchanan, "The Legitimacy of International Law."

17. For a valuable discussion that employs a different conception of normative uncertainty, see Monica Hlavac, "A Developmental Approach to the Legitimacy of Global Governance Institutions" (unpublished paper).

18. See Joseph Raz, *The Morality of Freedom* (New York: Oxford University Press, 1986), n. 17.

19. Allen Buchanan and Matthew DeCamp, "Responsibility for Global Health," *Transnational Medicine* 27, no. 1 (2006): 95–114.

20. In March 2005, Secretary-General Kofi Annan called for the replacement of the Commission on Human Rights (fifty-three members elected from slates put forward by regional groups) with a smaller Human Rights Council elected by a two-thirds vote of members of the General Assembly (see his report "In Larger Freedom," A/59/2005, para. 183).

21.   For the report of the Independent Inquiry Committee into the UN Oil-for-Food Program (the Volcker Committee), dated October 27, 2005, see www.iic-offp.org/story 27oct05.htm.

22.   Randall W. Stone, "The Political Economy of IMF Lending in Africa," *American Political Science Review* 98, no. 4 (2004): 577–591. See also Randall W. Stone, *Lending Credibility: The International Monetary Fund and the Post-Communist Transition* (Princeton, NJ: Princeton University Press, 2002).

23.   We are indebted to Andrew Hurrell for this example.

24.   John Rawls, *A Theory of Justice* (Cambridge, MA: Harvard University Press, 1971).

25.   Ruth W. Grant and Robert O. Keohane, "Accountability and Abuses of Power in World Politics," *American Political Science Review* 99, no. 1 (2005): 29–44. See also Robert O. Keohane and Joseph S. Nye, "Redefining Accountability for Global Governance," in *Governance in a Global Economy: Political Authority in Transition*, ed. Miles Kahler and David A. Lake (Princeton, NJ: Princeton University Press, 2003).

26.   For a discussion, see Ngaire Woods, "Holding Intergovernmental Institutions to Account," *Ethics & International Affairs* 17, no. 1 (2003): 69–80.

27.   Ann Florini, *The Coming Democracy: New Rules for Running a New World* (Washington, DC: Island Press, 2003).

28.   For a discussion of the role of critical revisability in practical reasoning, with parallels to theoretical reasoning, see Allen Buchanan, "Revisability and Rational Choice," *Canadian Journal of Philosophy* 5, no. 3 (1975): 395–408.

29.   For an illuminating account of the legitimacy of health care institutions that emphasizes responsibility for justifications, see Norman Daniels and James Sabin, "Limits to Health Care: Fair Procedures, Democratic Deliberation, and the Legitimacy Problem for Insurers," *Philosophy & Public Affairs* 26, no. 4 (1997): 303–50.

30.   See Richard B. Stewart, "Administrative Law in the Twenty-First Century," *New York University Law Review* 78, no. 2 (2003): 437–60; and Benedict Kingsbury, Nikon Kirsch, and Richard B. Stewart, "The Emergence of Global Administrative Law," *Law and Contemporary Problems* 68, nos. 3 and 4 (2005). See also Daniel Esty, "Toward Good Global Governance: The Role of Administrative Law" (paper presented at a conference on global administrative law, New York University, April 21–23, 2005). See also John Wickham, "Toward a Green Multilateral Investment Framework: NAFTA and the Search for Models," *Georgetown International Environmental Law Review* 12, no. 3 (2000): 617–46; James Salzman, "Labor Rights, Globalization, and Institutions: The Role and Influence of the Organization for Economic Cooperation and Development," *Michigan Journal of International Law* 21, no. 4 (2000): 769–848; and OECD, *Getting to Grips with Globalization: The OECD in a Changing World* (Paris: OECD Publications, 2004).

31.   The analogy in the economics of information is to the market for used cars. A potential buyer of a used car would be justified in inferring poor quality if the seller were unwilling to let him have the car thoroughly examined by a competent mechanic. See George A. Akerlof, "The Market for Lemons: Quality Uncertainty and the Market Mechanism," *Quarterly Journal of Economics* 84, no. 3 (1970): 488–500.

32.   David Stasavage, "Open-Door or Closed-Door? Transparency in Domestic and International Bargaining," *International Organization* 58, no. 4 (2004): 667–704.

33.   On the role of legislatures with respect to the legitimacy of an international legal order, see Rudiger Wolfrum, "Legitimacy in International Law: Some Introductory Considerations" (paper prepared for the conference "Legitimacy in International Law" at the Max Planck Institute for Comparative Public Law and International Law, Heidelberg, Germany, June 13–14, 2006).

34.   We use the term "external epistemic actor" here broadly, to include individuals and groups outside the institution in question who gain knowledge about the institution, interpret and integrate such knowledge, and exchange it with others, in ways that are intended to influence institutional behavior, whether directly or indirectly (through the mediation of the activities of other individuals and groups).

35.   On our view, the legitimacy of global governance institutions, at present at least, does not require participation in the critical evaluation of institutional goals and policies by all who are affected by them; but if the standard of legitimacy we recommend were accepted, opportunities for participation would expand.

Chapter 9

On the Alleged Conflict between Democracy
and International Law

Seyla Benhabib

IT IS DECEMBER 12, 1960. Israeli secret agents have captured Adolf Eichmann,
and the Israeli government has declared its intention to put Eichmann on trial.
Karl Jaspers writes to Hannah Arendt: "The Eichmann trial is unsettling . . .
because I am afraid Israel may come away from it looking bad no matter how
objective the conduct of the trial. . . . Its significance is not in its being a legal
trial but in its establishing of historical facts and serving as a reminder of those
facts for humanity."[1] For the next several months and eventually years an
exchange ensues between Hannah Arendt and her teacher and mentor, Karl
Jaspers, about the legality or illegality of the Eichmann trial, about institutional
jurisdiction, and about the philosophical foundations of international law and
in particular of "crimes against humanity."

Arendt replies that she is not as pessimistic as Jaspers is about "the legal basis
of the trial."[2] Israel can argue that Eichmann had been indicted in the first trial
in Nuremberg and escaped arrest. In capturing Eichmann, Israel was capturing
an outlaw—a *hostis humani generis* (an enemy of the human race)—who had
been condemned of "crimes against humanity." He should have appeared
before the Nuremberg court, but since there was no successor court to carry out
its mission, Arendt thinks that Israeli courts have a plausible basis for assuming
jurisdiction.

According to Hannah Arendt, *genocide* is the one crime that truly deserves
the label "crime against humanity." "Had the court in Jerusalem," she writes,
"understood that there were distinctions between discrimination, expulsion,
and genocide, it would have become clear that the supreme crime it was confronted with, the physical extermination of the Jewish people, was a crime
against humanity, perpetrated upon the body of the Jewish people. . . ."[3]

If, however, there are crimes that can be perpetrated against humanity itself,
then the individual human being is considered not only as a being worthy of
moral respect but as having a legal status as well that ought to be protected by

international law. The distinguishing feature of this legal status is that it would take precedence over all existing legal orders and it would bind them.[4] *Crimes against humanity* are different from other crimes, which can only exist when there is a known and promulgated law that has been violated. But which are the laws that crimes against humanity violate, particularly if, as in the case of Eichmann and the Nazi genocide of the Jews, a state and its established legal system sanctify genocide, and even order it to be committed? A crime, as distinct from a moral injury, cannot be defined independently of posited law and a positive legal order.

Arendt is aware that on account of philosophical perplexities, there will be a tendency to think of crimes against humanity as "crimes against humanness" or "humaneness," as if what was intended was a moral injury that violated some kind of shared moral code. The Nuremberg Charter's definition of "crimes against humanity" (*Verbrechen gegen die Menschheit*) was translated into German as "*Verbrechen gegen die Menschlichkeit*" (crimes against humaneness), "as if," she observes, "the Nazis had simply been lacking in human kindness, certainly the understatement of the century."[5]

Although Jaspers is willing to accept Arendt's distinction between *crimes against humanity* versus *humaneness*, he points out that since international law and natural law are not "law in the same sense that underlies normal court proceedings,"[6] it would be most appropriate for Israel to transfer the competency to judge Eichmann either to the UN, to the International Court at The Hague, or to courts provided for by the UN Charter.

Neither Arendt nor Jaspers harbors any illusions that the UN General Assembly would rise up to this task.[7] The postscript to *Eichmann in Jerusalem* ends on an unexpected and surprising note: "It is quite conceivable that certain political responsibilities among nations might some day be adjudicated in an international court; what is inconceivable is that such a court would be a criminal tribunal which pronounces on the guilt or innocence of individuals."[8]

Why does Arendt deny that an International Criminal Court is conceivable? Does she mean that it is unlikely to come into existence, or rather that, even if it were to come into existence, it would be without authority? Her position is all the more baffling since her very insistence upon the juridical as opposed to the merely moral dimension of crimes against humanity suggests the need for a standing international body that would possess the jurisdiction to try such crimes committed by individuals.

COSMOPOLITAN NORMS OF JUSTICE

The Eichmann trial, much like the Nuremberg trials before it, captured some of the perplexities of the emerging norms of international and, eventually, cosmopolitan justice. It is my thesis that since the UN Declaration of Human Rights in 1948, we have entered a phase in the evolution of global civil society

that is characterized by a transition from *international* to *cosmopolitan* norm
of justice. While norms of international justice frequently emerge through treaty
obligations to which states and their representatives are signatories, cosmopoli
tan norms of justice accrue to individuals as moral and legal persons in a world
wide civil society. Even if cosmopolitan norms also originate through treatylike
obligations, such as the UN Charter can be considered to be for the signatory
states, their peculiarity is that they endow individuals with certain rights and
claims, and often against the will of the states that are themselves signatories
This is the uniqueness of the many human rights agreements signed since World
War II. They signal an eventual transition from international law based on
treaties among states to cosmopolitan law understood as public law that bind
and bends the will of sovereign nations.[9]

The rise of multiple human rights regimes causes both the collusion and
confluence of international and domestic law. By an "international human
rights regime," I understand a set of interrelated and overlapping global and
regional regimes that encompass human rights treaties as well as customary
international law or international soft law.[10] The consequence is a complex sys
tem of interdependence that gives the lie to Carl Schmitt's dictum that "there
is no sovereign to force the sovereign."[11] As Gerald Neuman observes, "National
constitutions vary greatly in their provisions regarding the relationship between
international and domestic law. Some are more or less dualist, treating interna
tional norms as part of a distinct legal system. . . . Others are more or less
monist, treating international law and domestic law as a single legal system
often giving some category of international norms legal supremacy over domes
tic legislation."[12] The transformation of human rights norms[13] into generalizable
norms that ought to govern the behavior of sovereign states and in some cases
their incorporation into domestic constitutions is one of the most promising
aspects of contemporary political globalization processes.

We are witnessing this development in at least three related areas:

Crimes against Humanity, Genocide, and War Crimes. The concept of *crime*
against humanity, first articulated by the Allied powers in the Nuremberg trials
of Nazi war criminals, stipulates that there are certain norms in accordance with
which state officials as well as private individuals are to treat one another, even
and precisely under, conditions of extreme hostility and war. Ethnic cleansing
mass executions, rape, cruel and unusual punishment of the enemy, such as
dismemberment, which occur under conditions of a "widespread or systematic
attack," are proscribed and can all constitute sufficient grounds for the indict
ment and prosecution of individuals who are responsible for these actions, even
if they are or were state officials, or subordinates who acted under orders. The
refrain of the soldier and the bureaucrat—"I was only doing my duty"—is no
longer an acceptable ground for abrogating the rights of humanity in the person
of the other, even when, and especially when, the other is your enemy.

During the Nuremberg trials, "crimes against humanity" was used to refer to crimes committed during international armed conflicts.[14] Immediately after the Nuremberg trials, *genocide* was also included as a crime against humanity, but was left distinct, due its own jurisdictional status, which was codified in Article II of the Convention on the Prevention and Punishment of the Crime of Genocide (1948). *Genocide* is the knowing and willful destruction of the way of life and existence of a collectivity through acts of total war, racial extinction, or ethnic cleansing. It is the supreme crime against humanity, in that it aims at the destruction of human variety, of the many and diverse ways of being human. Genocide does not only eliminate individuals who may belong to this or another group; it aims at the extinction of their way of life.[15]

War crimes, as defined in the Statute of the International Criminal Tribunal for the Former Yugoslavia (1993), initially only applied to *international conflicts*. With the Statute of the International Criminal Tribunal for Rwanda (1994), recognition was extended to *internal armed conflict* as well. "War crimes" now refers to international as well as internal conflicts that involve the mistreatment or abuse of civilians and noncombatants, as well as one's enemy in combat.[16]

Thus, in a significant development since World War II, crimes against humanity, genocide, and war crimes have all been extended to apply not only to atrocities that take place in international conflict situations but also to events *within* the borders of a sovereign country that may be perpetrated by officials of that country and/or by its citizens during peacetime.

The continuing rearticulation of these three categories in international law, and in particular their extension from situations of international armed conflict to civil wars within a country and to the actions of governments against their own people, has in turn encouraged the emergence of the concept of "humanitarian interventions."

Humanitarian Interventions. The theory and practice of humanitarian interventions, to which the United States and its NATO allies appealed in order to justify their actions against ethnic cleansing and continuing crimes against the civilian population in Bosnia and Kosovo, suggest that when a sovereign nation-state egregiously violates the basic human rights of a segment of its population on account of their religion, race, ethnicity, language, or culture there is a *generalized moral obligation* to end actions such as genocide and crimes against humanity.[17] In such cases, human rights norms trump state sovereignty claims. No matter how controversial in interpretation and application they may be, humanitarian interventions are based on the growing consensus that the sovereignty of the state to dispose over the life, liberty, and property of its citizens or residents is not unconditional or unlimited.[18] State sovereignty is no longer the ultimate arbiter of the fate of citizens or residents. The exercise of state sovereignty even within domestic borders is increasingly subject to internationally recognized norms that prohibit genocide, ethnocide, mass expulsions, enslavement, rape, and forced labor.

Transnational Migration. The third area in which international human rights norms are creating binding guidelines upon the will of sovereign nation-states is that of international migration. *Humanitarian interventions* deal with the treatment by nation-states of their citizens or residents; *crimes against humanity* and *war crimes* concern relations among enemies or opponents in nationally bounded as well as extraterritorial settings. *Transnational migrations,* by contrast, pertain to the rights of individuals not insofar as they are considered members of concrete bounded communities, but insofar as they are human beings *simpliciter,* when they come into contact with, seek entry into, or want to become members of territorially bounded communities.

The Universal Declaration of Human Rights recognizes the right to freedom of movement across boundaries, a right to emigrate—that is, to leave a country—but not a right to immigrate, a right to enter a country (Article 13). Article 14 anchors the right to enjoy asylum under certain circumstances, while Article 15 proclaims that everyone has "the right to a nationality." The second half of Article 15 stipulates that "No one shall be arbitrarily deprived of his nationality nor denied the right to change his nationality."

Yet the declaration is silent on states' *obligations* to grant entry to immigrants, to uphold the right of asylum, and to permit citizenship to alien residents and denizens. These rights have no specific addressees, and they do not appear to anchor *specific* obligations on the part of second and third parties to comply with them. Despite the cross-border character of these rights, the declaration upholds the sovereignty of individual states. A series of internal contradictions between universal human rights claims and territorial sovereignty are thereby built right into the logic of the most comprehensive international law document in our world.

The Geneva Convention of 1951 Relating to the Status of Refugees, and its Protocol added in 1967, is the second most important international legal document after the Universal Declaration of Human Rights. Nevertheless, neither the existence of this document nor the creation of the UN High Commissioner for Refugees has altered the fact that this convention and its protocol are binding on signatory states alone and can be brazenly disregarded by nonsignatories and, at times, even by signatory states themselves.

Some lament the fact that as international human rights norms are increasingly invoked in immigration, refugee, and asylum disputes, territorially delimited nations are challenged not only in their claims to control their borders but also in their prerogative to define the "boundaries of the national community." Others criticize the Universal Declaration for not endorsing "institutional cosmopolitanism," and for upholding an "interstatal" rather than a truly cosmopolitan international order.[19] Yet one thing is clear: the treatment by states of their citizens and residents within their boundaries is no longer an unchecked prerogative. One of the cornerstones of Westphalian sovereignty—namely, that states enjoy ultimate authority over all objects and subjects within heir circumscribed territory—has been delegitimized through international aw.

The evolution of cosmopolitan norms, however, is rife with a central contra-liction: while territorially bounded states are increasingly subject to interna-ional norms, states themselves are the principal signatories as well as enforcers of the multiple and varied human rights treaties and conventions through which nternational norms spread. In this process, the state is both sublated and rein-orced in its authority. Throughout the international system, as long as territori-ily bounded states are recognized as the sole legitimate units of negotiation and epresentation, a tension, and at times even a fatal contradiction, is palpable: the modern state system is caught between *sovereignty* and *hospitality*, between the prerogative to choose to be a party to cosmopolitan norms and human rights reaties, and the obligation to extend recognition of these human rights to all.

In a Kantian vein, by "hospitality" I mean to refer to all human rights claims hat are cross-border in scope.[20] The tension between sovereignty and hospital-ty is all the more real for liberal democracies since they are based on the fragile but necessary negotiation of constitutional universalism and territorial sovereignty.

THE PARADOX OF DEMOCRATIC LEGITIMACY

Ideally, democratic rule means that all members of a sovereign body are to be respected as bearers of human rights, and that the consociates of this sovereign freely associate with one another to establish a regime of self-governance under which each is to be considered both author of the laws and subject to them. This ideal of the original contract, as formulated by Jean-Jacques Rousseau and adopted by Immanuel Kant, is a heuristically useful device for capturing the logic of modern democracies. Modern democracies, unlike their ancient coun-terparts, conceive of their citizens as rights-bearing consociates. The rights of the citizens rest upon the "rights of man." "Les droits de l'homme et du citoyen" do not contradict one another; quite to the contrary, they are coimpli-cated. This is the idealized logic of the modern democratic revolutions following the American and French examples.

The democratic sovereign draws its legitimacy not merely from its act of constitution, but equally significantly, from the conformity of this act to univer-sal principles of human rights, which are in some sense said to precede and antedate the will of the sovereign and in accordance with which the sovereign undertakes to bind itself. "We, the people" refers to a particular human com-munity, circumscribed in space and time, sharing a particular culture, history, and legacy; yet this people establishes itself as a democratic body by acting in the name of the "universal." The tension between universal human rights claims and particularistic cultural and national identities is constitutive of dem-ocratic legitimacy. Modern democracies act in the name of universal principles, which are then circumscribed within a particular civic community. This is the "Janus face of the modern nation," in the words of Jürgen Habermas.[21]

Since Rousseau, however, we also know that the will of the democratic people may be legitimate but unjust, unanimous but unwise. "The general will" and "the will of all" may not overlap either in theory or in practice. Democratic rule and the claims of justice may contradict one another. The democratic precommitments expressed in the idealized allegiance to universal human rights—life, liberty, and property—need to be reactualized and renegotiated within actual polities as democratic intentions. Potentially, there is always a conflict between an interpretation of these rights claims that precede the declared formulations of the sovereign and the actual enactments of the democratic people that could potentially violate such interpretations. We encounter this conflict in the history of political thought as the conflict between liberalism and democracy, and even as the conflict between constitutionalism and popular sovereignty. In each case the logic of the conflict is the same: to assure that the democratic sovereign will uphold certain constraints upon its will in virtue of its precommitment to certain formal and substantive interpretations of rights. Liberal and democratic theorists disagree with one another as to the proper balance of this mix: while strong liberals want to bind the sovereign will through precommitments to a list of human rights, strong democrats reject such a prepolitical understanding of rights and argue that they must be open to renegotiation and reinterpretation by the sovereign people—admittedly within certain limits.

Yet this paradox of democratic legitimacy has a corollary that has been little noted: every act of self-legislation is also an act of self-constitution. "We, the people" who agree to bind ourselves by these laws are also defining ourselves as a "we" in the very act of self-legislation. It is not only the general laws of self-government that are articulated in this process; the community that binds itself by these laws defines itself by drawing boundaries as well, and these boundaries are territorial as well as civic. The will of the democratic sovereign can only extend over the territory that is under its jurisdiction; democracies require borders. Empires have frontiers, while democracies have borders. Democratic rule, unlike imperial dominion, is exercised in the name of some specific constituency and binds that constituency alone. Therefore, at the same time that the sovereign defines itself territorially, it also defines itself in civic terms. Those who are full members of the sovereign body are distinguished from those who "fall under its protection," but who do not enjoy "full membership rights." Women and slaves, servants, propertyless white males, non-Christians and non-white races were historically excluded from membership in the sovereign body and from the project of citizenship. They were, in Kant's famous words, "mere auxiliaries to the commonwealth."[22]

In addition to these groups are those residents of the commonwealth who do not enjoy full citizenship rights either because they do not possess the requisite identity criteria through which the people defines itself, or because they belong to some other commonwealth, or because they choose to remain as outsiders. These are the "aliens" and "foreigners" amid the democratic people. They are different from second-class citizens, such as women and workers, as well as from slaves and tribal peoples. Their status is governed by mutual treaties among sovereign entities—as would be the case with official representatives of a state power upon the territory of the other; and if they are civilians, and live among citizens for economic, religious, or other cultural reasons, their rights and claims exist in that murky space defined by respect for human rights on the one hand and by international customary law on the other. They are refugees from religious persecution, merchants and missionaries, migrants and adventurers, explorers and fortune seekers.

I have circumscribed in general theoretical terms the paradox of democratic legitimacy. The paradox is that the republican sovereign should undertake to bind its will by a series of precommitments to a set of formal and substantive norms, usually referred to as "human rights."

I want to argue that while this paradox can never be fully resolved in democracies, its impact can be mitigated through the renegotiation and reiteration of the dual commitments to human rights and sovereign self-determination. Popular sovereignty is not identical with territorial sovereignty, although the two are closely linked, both historically and normatively. Popular sovereignty means that all full members of the demos are entitled to have a voice in the articulation of the laws by which the demos governs itself. Democratic rule extends its jurisdiction to those who can view themselves as the authors of such rule. There never was a perfect overlap between the circle of those who stand under the law's authority and those recognized as full members of the demos. Every democratic demos has disenfranchised some, while recognizing only certain individuals as full citizens. Territorial sovereignty and democratic voice have never matched completely. Yet presence within a circumscribed territory, and in particular continuing residence within it, brings one under the authority of the sovereign—whether democratic or not. The new politics of cosmopolitan membership is about negotiating this complex relationship between rights of full membership, democratic voice, and territorial residence. While the demos, as the popular sovereign, must assert control over a specific territorial domain, it can also engage in reflexive acts of self-constitution, whereby the boundaries of the demos can be readjusted.

The evolution of cosmopolitan norms, from crimes against humanity to norms extending to regulate refuge, asylum, and immigration, have caught most liberal democracies within a network of obligations to recognize certain rights claims. Although the asymmetry between the "demos" and the "populus," the democratic people and the population as such, has not been overcome, norms of hospitality have gone far beyond what they were in Kant's understanding: the status of alienage is now protected by civil as well as international laws; the guest is no longer a guest but a resident alien, as we say in American parlance, or a "foreign co-citizen," as Europeans say. In a remarkable evolution of the norms of hospitality, within the European Union in particular, the rights of third-country nationals are increasingly protected by the European Convention on Fundamental Rights and Freedoms, with the consequence that citizenship, which was once the privileged status entitling one to rights, has now been disaggregated into its constituent elements.[23]

TESTING THE PARADOX: THE CASE OF GERMANY

I want to concretize these considerations by turning to a decision of the German Supreme Court on alien suffrage rights in order to illustrate some of the conceptual issues involved in a concrete institutional setting.

On October 31, 1990, the German Constitutional Court ruled against a law passed by the provincial assembly of Schleswig-Holstein on February 21, 1989, that changed the qualifications for participating in local municipal and district-wide elections.[24] According to Schleswig-Holstein's election laws in effect since May 31, 1985, all those who were defined as German in accordance with Article 116 of the Basic Law, who had reached the age of eighteen and who had resided in the electoral district for at least three months were eligible to vote. The law of February 21, 1989, proposed to amend this as follows: all foreigners residing in Schleswig-Holstein for at least five years, who possessed a valid permit of residency or who were in no need of one, and who were citizens of Denmark, Ireland, The Netherlands, Norway, Sweden, or Switzerland, would be able to vote in local and district-wide elections. The choice of these six countries was made on the grounds of reciprocity. Since these countries permitted their foreign residents to vote in local, and in some cases regional, elections, the German provincial legislators saw it appropriate to reciprocate.

The claim that the new election law was unconstitutional was brought by 224 members of the German Parliament, all of them members of the conservative Christian Democratic and Christian Social Union (CDU/CSU) party; it was supported by the Federal Government of Germany. The court justified its decision with the argument that the proposed change of the electoral law contradicted "the principle of democracy," as laid out in Articles 20 and 28 of Germany's Basic Law, and according to which "All state power [Staatsgewalt] proceeds from the people."[25] Furthermore,

> The people [das Volk], which the Basic Law of the Federal Republic of Germany recognizes to be the bearer of the authority [Gewalt] from which issues the constitution, as well as the people which is the subject of the legitimation and creation of the state, is the German people. Foreigners do not belong to it. Membership in the community of the state [Staatsverband] is defined through the right of citizenship. . . . Citizenship in the state [Staatsangehörigkeit] constitutes a fundamentally indissoluble personal right between the citizen and the state. The vision [or image—Bild]

of the people of the state [*Staatsvolkes*], which underlies this right of belonging to the state, is the political community of fate [*die politische Schicksalsgemeinschaft*], to which individual citizens are bound. Their solidarity with and their embeddedness in [*Verstrickung*] the fate of their home country, which they cannot escape [*sich entrinnen können*], are also the justification for restricting the vote to citizens of the state. They must bear the consequences of their decisions. By contrast, foreigners, regardless of however long they may have resided in the territory of the state, can always return to their homeland.[26]

This resounding statement by the court can be broken down into three components: first, a disquisition on the meaning of *popular sovereignty* (all power proceeds from the people); second a *procedural* definition of how we are to understand *membership* in the state; third, a philosophical explication of the nature of the bond between the state and the individual, based on the vision of a "*political community of fate.*" The court argued that according to the principle of popular sovereignty, there needed to be a "congruence" between the principle of democracy, the concept of the people, and the main guidelines for voting rights, at all levels of state power—namely, federal, provincial, district, and communal. Different conceptions of popular sovereignty could not be employed at different levels of the state. Permitting long-term resident foreigners to vote would imply that popular sovereignty would be defined in different fashion at the district-wide and communal levels than at the provincial and federal levels. In an almost direct repudiation of the Habermasian discursive democracy principle, the court declared that Article 20 of Germany's Basic Law does not imply that "the decisions of state organs must be legitimized through those whose interests are affected [*Betroffenen*] in each case; rather, their authority must proceed from the people as a group bound to each other as a unity [*das Volk als eine zur Einheit verbundene Gruppe von Menschen*]."[27]

The provincial parliament of Schleswig-Holstein challenged the court's understanding and argued that neither the principle of democracy nor that of the people excludes the rights of foreigners to participate in elections: "The model underlying the Basic Law is the construction of a democracy of human beings, and not that of the collective of the nation. This basic principle does not permit that one distinguish in the long-run between the people of the state [*Staatsvolk*] and an association of subservients [*Untertanenverband*]."[28]

The German Constitutional Court eventually resolved this controversy about the meaning of popular sovereignty by upholding a unitary and functionally undifferentiated version of it, but it did concede that the sovereign people, through its representatives, could change the definition of citizenship. Procedurally, "the people" simply means all those who have the requisite state membership. If one is a citizen, one has the right to vote; if not, not. "So the Basic Law . . . leaves it up to the legislator to determine more precisely the rules for the acquisition and loss of citizenship and thereby also the criteria of belonging to the people. The law of citizenship is thus the site at which the legislator can do justice to the transformations in the composition of the population of the Federal Republic of Germany." This can be accomplished by expediting the acquisition of citizenship by all those foreigners who are long-term permanent residents of Germany.[29]

The court here explicitly addresses what I have called the paradox of democratic legitimacy—namely, that those whose rights to inclusion or exclusion from the demos are being decided upon will not themselves be the ones to decide upon these rules. The democratic demos can change its self-definition by altering the criteria for admission to citizenship. The court still holds to the classical model of citizenship according to which democratic participation rights and nationality are strictly bundled together, but by signaling the procedural legitimacy of changing Germany's naturalization laws, the court also acknowledges the power of the democratic sovereign to alter its self-definition such as to accommodate the changing composition of the population. The line separating citizens and foreigners can be renegotiated by the citizens themselves.

Yet the procedural democratic openness signaled by the court stands in great contrast to the conception of the democratic people, also adumbrated by the court, and according to which the people is viewed as "a political community of fate," held together by bonds of solidarity in which individuals are embedded (*verstrickt*). Here the democratic people is viewed as an *ethnos*, as a community bound together by the power of shared fate, memories, solidarity, and belonging. Such a community does not permit free entry and exit. Perhaps marriage with members of such a community may produce some integration over generations; but, by and large, membership in an ethnos—in a community of memory, fate, and belonging—is something that one is born into, although as an adult one may renounce this heritage, exit it, or wish to alter it. To what extent should one view liberal democratic polities as *ethnoi* communities? Despite its emphatic evocation of the nation as a "community of fate," the court also emphasizes that the democratic legislature has the prerogative to transform the meaning of citizenship and the rules of democratic belonging. Such a transformation of citizenship may be necessary to do justice to the changed nature of the population. The demos and the ethnos do not simply overlap.

Written in 1990, this decision of the German Constitutional Court appears in retrospect as a swan song to a vanishing ideology of nationhood.[30] In 1993 the Treaty of Maastricht, or the Treaty on the European Union, established European citizenship, which granted voting rights and rights to run for office for all citizens of the fifteen, and now twenty-five, members of the signatory states residing in the territory of other member countries. Of the six countries to whose citizens Schleswig-Holstein wanted to grant reciprocal voting rights— Denmark, Ireland, The Netherlands, Norway, Sweden, and Switzerland—only

Norway and Switzerland remained nonbeneficiaries of the Maastricht Treaty since they were not EU members.

In the years following, an intense process of democratic iteration unfolded in the now-unified Germany, during which the challenge posed by the Federal Constitutional Court to the democratic legislature of bringing the definition of citizenship in line with the composition of the population was taken up, rearticulated, and reappropriated. The city-state of Hamburg, in its parallel plea to alter its local election laws, stated this very clearly: "The Federal Republic of Germany has in fact become in the last decades a country of immigration. Those who are affected by the law that is being attacked here are thus not strangers but cohabitants [*Inländer*], who only lack German citizenship. This is especially the case for those foreigners of the second and third generation born in Germany."[31] The demos is not an *ethnos*, and those living in our midst who do not belong to the ethnos are not strangers either; they are rather "cohabitants," or as later political expressions would have it, "our co-citizens of foreign origin" [*Ausländische Mitbürger*]. Even these terms, which may sound odd to ears not accustomed to any distinctions besides those of citizens, residents, and nonresidents, suggest the transformations of German public consciousness in the 1990s. This intense and soul-searching public debate finally led to an acknowledgment of the *fact* as well as the *desirability* of immigration. The need to naturalize second- and third-generation children of immigrants was recognized, and the new German citizenship law was passed in January 2000.

Ten years after the German Constitutional Court turned down the election law reforms of Schleswig-Holstein and the city-state of Hamburg on the grounds that resident foreigners were not citizens and were thus ineligible to vote, Germany's membership in the European Union led to the disaggregation of citizenship rights. Resident members of EU states can vote in local as well as EU-wide elections; furthermore, Germany now accepts that it is a country of immigration; immigrant children become German citizens according to *jus soli* and keep dual nationality until the age of twenty-four, at which point they must choose either German citizenship or that of their country of birth. Furthermore, long-term residents who are third-country nationals can naturalize if they wish to do so. The democratic people can reconstitute itself through such acts of democratic iteration so as to enable the extension of democratic voice. Aliens can become residents, and residents can become citizens. Democracies require porous borders.

The constitution of "we, the people" represents a fluid, contentious, contested, and dynamic process. All people possess a dual identity as an *ethnos*, as a community of shared fate, memories, and moral sympathies, on the one hand, and as the demos, as the democratically enfranchised totality of all citizens, who may or may not belong to the same ethnos, on the other. All liberal democracies that are modern nation-states exhibit these two dimensions. The politics of

peoplehood consists in their negotiation. The presence of so many guest workers in Germany is a reflection of the economic realities of Germany since World
War II, just as the presence of so many migrants from Algeria, Tunisia, and
Morocco, as well as from central Africa, today testifies to France's imperial
past and conquests. Some would even argue that without their presence, the
post–World War II German miracle would not have been conceivable.[32] Peoplehood is dynamic and not a static reality.

The presence of others who do not share the dominant culture's memories
and morals poses a challenge to democratic legislatures to rearticulate the meaning of democratic universalism. Far from leading to the disintegration of the
culture of democracy, such challenges reveal the depth and the breadth of the
culture of democracy. Only polities with strong democracies are capable of such
universalist rearticulation, through which they refashion the meaning of their
own peoplehood.

Let me anticipate some objections against the considerations developed
above: in view of the resurgence of anti-immigration sentiment throughout
Europe, from Denmark to France to Germany and to Italy; in view of the anti-
Muslim backlash in all European countries, The Netherlands and France in
particular; in view of the mobilization of deeply nationalist sentiments in Germany against Turkey's admission to membership talks with the European
Union in particular, isn't the account I have presented above one that flies in
the face of historical realities? Far from cosmopolitanism, we are experiencing
the rise of tribalism, nationalism, and civilizational wars.

I want to suggest that in an odd fashion, but in ways that are not unfamiliar
to us from previous episodes of history, universalism and particularism may
incite, invite, and even provoke one another's articulation. Europe's migrants,
and particularly European Muslims, have becomes symbols for Europe's own
"othering," its gradual transformation from a continent of nation-states into a
continent of pooled sovereignty, guided by cosmopolitan principles of universalist human rights. Europe's peoples may not be, and I believe definitely are
not, ready for some of these transformations. The Muslim immigrants, with
their visible otherness displayed through their modes of dress, dietary laws,
habits of prayer, and generally repressive family and sexual ethic, are all too
striking symbols of the loosening of the boundaries of the nation.

The transition to a political entity whose identity is as yet undefinable generates anxiety: Is the European Union a republican federation, a supersized
nation-state, a free trading zone, or some sort of postnationalist condominium
in which increasingly more functions of sovereignty are pooled? Whatever its
precise future form, one thing is certain: the Europeans are set upon a path
through which they have sublated the nation-state with all its paradoxical consequences. The condition of Europe's third-country nationals is a sorry reminder
to them both of cultural othering and of the obsolescence of the nation. Not

surprisingly, therefore, like the phoenix rising from the ashes, French nationalism returns to defend "Muslim girls against their patriarchal oppressors." As
the Bernard Stasi report on the headscarves "affair" self-servingly proclaims,
"The Republic cannot remain deaf to these girls' cry for help."[33]

In Germany, where the very concept of *Kultur* had been sullied by its associations with the racializing overtones of the concept of the *Kulturnation*, socialist
historians of the past, such as Hans-Ulrich Wehler, find it possible to recycle
this old German set of ideas against the Turks, whose "culture" of militarism,
the extermination of the Armenians, and intolerance toward the property of
Christian churches is said to set them apart from Europe forever. Of course,
many silently think of Germany what the Germans think of the Turks, once we
substitute Jews for Armenians and Christians in these formulations. But the
attempt of some German intellectuals and politicians to redefine Europe as a
Christian cultural commonwealth has failed, precisely because of Germany's
own constitutional and legal commitments to the Treaty of Europe and the
European Charter of Human Rights and Fundamental Freedoms. A slim majority, but a majority nevertheless, supported Turkey's entry into the European
Union precisely on the basis of commitments that transcended German excep-
tionalism. It is this tension between cosmopolitan universalism and repressive
secular nationalism that we must disentangle in today's Europe.

Let me end by returning once more to the philosophical questions raised by
cosmopolitan norms.

THE NEW POLITICAL CONDITION

After the capture of Eichmann by Israeli agents in 1960, Arendt and Jaspers
initiated a series of reflections on the status of international law and norms of
cosmopolitan justice. Their queries can be summarized with three questions:
(1) What is the ontological status of cosmopolitan norms in a postmetaphysical
universe? (2) What is the authority of norms that are not backed by a sovereign
with the power of enforcement? and (3) How can we reconcile cosmopolitan
norms with the fact of a divided mankind?

My answer to the third question, of how to reconcile cosmopolitanism with
the unique legal, historical, and cultural traditions and memories of a people, is
that we must respect, encourage, and initiate multiple processes of democratic
iteration. By democratic iterations I mean social, cultural, legal, and political
processes of struggle and contestation, as well as deliberation and argumenta-
tion, through which jurisgenerative politics develops.[34] Jurisgenerative politics
are those cases of legal and political contestation when the meaning of rights
and other fundamental constitutional principles are reposited, resignified, and
reappropriated by new and excluded groups, or by the citizenry in the face of
unprecedented hermeneutic challenges and meaning constellations.

Universalist norms are thereby mediated with the self-understanding of local communities. The availability of cosmopolitan norms in the general public sphere raises the threshold of justification to which formerly exclusionary practices must now be submitted. Exclusions take place, but the threshold for justifying them is now higher. This higher threshold of justification triggers an increase in democratic reflexivity. It becomes increasingly more difficult to justify practices of exclusion against foreigners and others by democratic legislatures simply because their decisions express the will of the people; such decisions are now subject not only to constitutional checks and balances in domestic law but in the international arena as well. Reflexive grounds must be justifiable through reasons that would be valid for all. This means that such grounds can themselves be recursively questioned for failing to live up to the threshold set in their own very articulation.

To Arendt's and Jaspers's second question as to the authority of cosmopolitan norms, my answer is: *the democratic power of global civil society.* Of course, the global human rights regime by now has its agencies of negotiation, articulation, observation, and monitoring. In addition to processes of naming, shaming, and sanctions that can be imposed upon sovereign nations in the event of egregious human rights violations, the use of power by the international community, as authorized by the UN Security Council and the General Assembly, remains an option.

I come then to the final question: what is the ontological status of cosmopolitan norms in a postmetaphysical universe? Briefly, such norms and principles are morally constructive: they create a universe of meaning, values, and social relations that had not existed before in that they change the normative constituents and evaluative principles of the world of "objective spirit," to use Hegelian language. They found a new order—a *novo ordo saeclorum.* They are thus subject to all the paradoxes of revolutionary beginnings. Their legitimacy cannot be justified through appeal to antecedents or to consequents: it is the fact that there was no precedent for them that makes them unprecedented; likewise, we can only know their consequences once they have been adopted and enacted.

The act that "crimes against humanity" has come to name and to interdict was itself unprecedented in human history; that is, the mass murder of a human group on account of its race, and not its deeds, through an organized state power with all the legal and technological means at its disposal. Certainly, massacres, group murders, and tribal atrocities were known and practiced throughout human history. The full mobilization of state power, with all the means of a scientific-technological civilization at its disposal, in order to extinguish a human group on account of its claimed racial characteristics, was wholly novel.

In conclusion: although Hannah Arendt was skeptical that international criminal law could ever be codified and properly reinforced, she in fact praised and commended the judges who sought to extend existing categories of international law to the criminal domain. She wrote:

If genocide is an actual possibility of the future, then no people on earth
. . . can feel reasonably sure of its continued existence without the help
and the protection of international law. Success or failure in dealing with
the hitherto unprecedented can lie only in the extent to which this dealing
may serve as a valid precedent on the road to international penal law. . . .
In consequence of this as yet unfinished nature of international law, it has
become the task of ordinary trial judges to render justice without the
help of, or beyond the limitation set upon them through, positive, posited
laws.[35]

However fragile their future may be, cosmopolitan norms have evolved beyond
the point anticipated and problematized by Arendt. An International Criminal
Court exists, although the Bush administration has rescinded the decision of
former president Clinton to sign the Rome Treaty legitimizing it. The spread of
cosmopolitan norms, from interdictions of war crimes, crimes against humanity, and genocide, to the increasing regulation of cross-border movements
through the Geneva Conventions and other accords, has yielded a new political
condition: the local, the national, and the global are all imbricated in one
another. Future democratic iterations will make their interconnections and
interdependence deeper and wider. Rather than seeing this situation as an
undermining of democratic sovereignty, we can view it as promising the emergence of new political configurations and new forms of agency, inspired by
the interdependence—never frictionless but ever promising—of the local, the
national, and the global.

NOTES

This essay appeared in *Ethics & International Affairs* 19, no. 1 (2005): 85–100. It is based in
part on my Tanner Lectures, delivered at the University of California, Berkeley, in March
2004. My Tanner Lectures, including portions of this essay, later appeared as *Another Cosmopolitanism* (New York: Oxford University Press, 2006), a volume edited and introduced by
Robert Post, with commentaries by Bonnie Honig, Will Kymlicka, and Jeremy Waldron.

1.   Lotte Kohler and Hans Saner, eds., *Hannah Arendt–Karl Jaspers Correspondence: 1926–
1969*, trans. Robert and Rita Kimber (New York: Harcourt Brace Jovanovich, 1992), 409–410.
2.   Ibid., 414.
3.   Hannah Arendt, *Eichmann in Jerusalem: A Report on the Banality of Evil* (New York:
Penguin Books, [1963] 1994), 269.
4.   Kohler and Saner, eds., *Hannah Arendt–Karl Jaspers Correspondence*, 414.
5.   Arendt, *Eichmann in Jerusalem*, 275; and Kohler and Saner, eds., *Hannah Arendt–Karl
Jaspers Correspondence*, 423, 431.
6.   Kohler and Saner, eds., *Hannah Arendt–Karl Jaspers Correspondence*, 424.
7.   Arendt, *Eichmann in Jerusalem*, 270.
8.   Ibid., 298.
9.   See Anne-Marie Slaughter's lucid statement, in "Leading Through Law," *Wilson
Quarterly* (Autumn 2003): 42–43: "International law today is undergoing profound changes

that will make it far more effective than it has been in the past. By definition international law is a body of rules that regulates relations among states, not individuals. Yet over the course of the 21st century, it will increasingly confer rights and responsibilities directly on individuals. The most obvious example of this shift can be seen in the explosive growth of international criminal law."

10.   Such examples would include the UN treaty bodies under the International Covenant on Civil and Political Rights; the International Covenant on Economic, Social and Cultural Rights; the International Convention on the Elimination of All Forms of Racial Discrimination; the Convention on the Elimination of All Forms of Discrimination Against Women; the Convention Against Torture and Other Cruel, Inhuman or Degrading Treatment or Punishment; and the Convention on the Rights of the Child. The establishment of the European Union has been accompanied by a Charter of Fundamental Rights and by the formation of a European Court of Justice. The European Convention for the Protection of Human Rights and Fundamental Freedoms, which encompasses states that are not EU members as well, permits the claims of citizens of adhering states to be heard by the European Court of Human Rights. Parallel developments can be seen on the American continent through the establishment of the Inter-American System for the Protection of Human Rights and the Inter-American Court of Human Rights. See Gerald Neuman, "Human Rights and Constitutional Rights: Harmony and Dissonance," *Stanford Law Review* 55, no. 5 (2003): 1863–1901. By "soft law" is meant an international agreement that is not concluded as a treaty and therefore not covered by the Vienna Convention on the Law of Treaties. Such an agreement is adopted by states that do not want a treaty-based relationship and do not want to be governed by treaty or customary law in the event of a breach of their obligations.

11.   Carl Schmitt, *The Concept of the Political*, trans., intro., and notes by George Schwab (Chicago: University of Chicago Press, [1927] 1996).

12.   Neuman, "Human Rights and Constitutional Rights," 1875.

13.   I use the term "human rights norms" rather than "human rights" in this context for an important reason. Human rights need to be interpreted, concretized, and codified by each society's own democratic constitutions according to their own legal, constitutional, political, and cultural traditions. I distinguish between *the principle of rights* and *the schedule of rights*. While the principle of rights establishes that a democratic constitution ought to incorporate basic or fundamental rights to which all are entitled, the schedule of rights means that the precise concretization of these rights occurs through a process of collective self-determination. Of course, there will need to be a permissible range of interpretation and determination, for it is quite possible for countries with autocratic and illiberal traditions to claim that there is a schedule of "Asian rights" or "Islamic rights" that would not recognize the equal rights of women to divorce and inheritance, for example, as their male counterparts. In such cases, a contentious dialogue ensues between those upholding the general human rights norms enshrined in various human rights treaties and existing governments that choose to interpret them in a specific way. This is an example of "democratic iterations" that I discuss below.

14.   Charter of the International Military Tribunal, 1945, Art. 6 (c), as cited in Steven R. Ratner and Jason S. Abrams, *Accountability for Human Rights Atrocities in International Law: Beyond the Nuremberg Legacy*, second edition (New York: Clarendon Press, 2002), 26–45; and William A. Schabas, *An Introduction to the International Criminal Court* (Cambridge: Cambridge University Press, 2001), 6–7.

15.   Ratner and Abrams, *Accountability for Human Rights Atrocities*, 35–36.

16.   Ibid., 80–110; and Schabas, *Introduction to the International Criminal Court*, 40–53.

17.   Allen Buchanan, "From Nuremberg to Kosovo: The Morality of Illegal International Legal Reform," *Ethics* 111 (July 2001): 673–705.

18.   Michael W. Doyle, "The New Interventionism," in *Global Justice*, ed. Thomas Pogge (Malden, MA: Blackwell, 2001).

19.   For the first position, see David Jacobson, *Rights Across Borders: Immigration and the Decline of Citizenship* (Baltimore: Johns Hopkins University Press, 1997), 5; for the second, see Onora O'Neill, *Bounds of Justice* (Cambridge: Cambridge University Press, 2000), 180.

20.   For further discussion, see Seyla Benhabib, *The Rights of Others: Aliens, Citizens, and Residents* (Cambridge: Cambridge University Press, 2004), ch. 2.

21.   Jürgen Habermas, "The European Nation-State: On the Past and Future of Sovereignty and Citizenship," in *The Inclusion of the Other: Studies in Political Theory*, ed. Ciaran Cronin and Pablo de Greiff (Cambridge, MA: MIT Press, 1998), 115.

22.   Immanuel Kant, "Die Metaphysik der Sitten in zwei Teilen" [1797], in *Immanuel Kants Werke*, ed. Ernst Cassirer (Berlin: Cassirer, 1912), 121; *The Metaphysics of Morals*, trans. and ed. Mary Gregor (Cambridge: Cambridge University Press, 1996), 140.

23.   For a more detailed discussion of institutional developments, particularly within the European context leading to the disaggregation of citizenship rights, see Benhabib, *The Rights of Others*, ch. 4.

24.   A similar change in its election laws was undertaken by the free state of Hamburg such as to enable those of its foreign residents of at least eighteen years of age to participate in the election of local municipal assemblies. Since Hamburg is not a federal province but a free city-state, with its own constitution, some of the technical aspects of this decision are not parallel to those in the case of Schleswig-Holstein. I chose to focus on the latter case alone. It is nonetheless important to note that the federal government, which had opposed Schleswig-Holstein's electoral reforms, supported those of Hamburg. See *Bundesverfassungsgericht* (Federal Constitutional Court; abbreviated hereafter as *BVerfGe*) 83, 60, II, No. 4, 60–81; and *BVerfGe* 83, II, No. 3, 37. All translations from the German are mine.

25.   *BVerfGe* 83, 37, No. 3, 39.

26.   Ibid., 39–40.

27.   Ibid., 51.

28.   Ibid., 42.

29.   Ibid., 52.

30.   I do not mean to suggest that nationalist ideologies and sentiments vanished from the unified Germany. Unlike in many of Germany's neighboring countries, such as France and The Netherlands, however, they did lose institutional traction throughout the 1990s. The citizenship laws were passed by parliamentary majorities of Social Democrats, Greens, and Christian Democrats; but the price for the liberalization of citizenship was paid in terms of further restrictions on Germany's rather generous asylum laws. So these transitions were not without cost. Nationalism reappeared on the German scene first when one million signatures were collected in a referendum in Hesse against permitting dual citizenship of immigrant children, who are now entitled to this only until they reach age twenty-four; the second instance was the recent Iraq war and deep fear and dislike of the U.S. administration under George W. Bush; and the third case was the surprisingly racialized debate about Turkey's admission to membership talks in the European Union in the fall of 2004. For a representative sample of the positions in this debate, see Claus Leggewie, *Die Türkei und Europa* (Frankfurt: Suhrkamp, 2004).

31.   *BVerfGe* 83, 37, II, 42.

32.   James F. Hollifield, *Immigrants, Markets, and States: The Political Economy of Postwar Europe* (Cambridge, MA: Harvard University Press, 1992).

33. "Commission de Réflexion Sur l'Application du Principe du Laïcité dans la Republique" (Paris: Office of the President, December 11, 2003), 58.

34. For further elaboration of these themes, see Benhabib, *The Rights of Others*, ch. 5. The term "jurisgenerative politics" comes from Robert Cover, "Nomos and Narrative," *Harvard Law Review* 97, no. 1 (1983): 4–68; I am using the term here in a sense that is much indebted to Frank Michelman, "Law's Republic," *Yale Law Journal* 97, no. 8 (1998): 1493–1537.

35. Arendt, *Eichmann in Jerusalem*, 273–74.

Chapter 10

"Saving Amina"
Global Justice for Women and Intercultural Dialogue

Alison M. Jaggar

I dedicate this essay to the memory of Susan Moller Okin, whose work and friendship have been inspirational for me. Susan's dedication to justice for all women was unfailing both in her theoretical writings and in her life commitments. Before her death, Susan read this paper and graciously addressed its challenges.

ONE OF THE INNUMERABLE electronic petitions flashing across the Internet in the early months of 2003 held special interest for feminists. Carrying the name and logo of Amnesty International in Spanish, the petition asked recipients to sign electronically an appeal against the sentence of stoning to death handed down against Amina Lawal, a divorced Nigerian woman, who had had a baby outside marriage.[1] In August 2002, an Islamic court in Katsina state in northern Nigeria had convicted Lawal of adultery under Sharia law. The "save Amina" petition collected many thousands of electronic signatures from around the world, but in May 2003 it was followed by another e-communication with the subject line, "Please Stop the International Amina Lawal Protest Letter Campaigns." The second e-message was signed by Ayesha Imam and Sindi Medar-Gould, representing two Nigerian human rights organizations defending Lawal. Imam and Medar-Gould asserted that the "save Amina" petition in fact endangered Lawal and made the task of her Nigerian supporters more difficult, in part because the petition contained a number of factual errors, including a false assertion that execution of the sentence was imminent. They also observed: "There is an unbecoming arrogance in assuming that international human rights organizations or others always know better than those directly involved, and therefore can take actions that fly in the face of their express wishes."[2]

Electronic petitions have become a popular means by which Western feminists endeavor to "save" women in other countries. The petitions often use sensational language to denounce some non-Western culture for its inhumane treatment of women and girls. Worries about non-Western cultural practices

Amina Lawal with her baby in the Funtua Sharia court, Nigeria, July 2002.
Fred Noy/AFP/Getty Images

are not limited to those in the West who identify themselves as feminists. The popular press regularly runs stories about non-Western practices it finds disturbing, especially when these practices concern women's sexuality and/or are noticed to be occurring among immigrant groups. Recent news stories have raised the alarm about arranged marriage, "sexual slavery," dowry murder ("bride-burning"), "honor" killings, genital cutting ("circumcision," "mutilation"), sex-selective abortion, and female infanticide. Newspapers in the United States have also questioned whether female U.S. soldiers, stationed in Saudi Arabia, should be required when off base to conform to Saudi laws mandating covering their bodies and forbidding them to drive.

The perceived victimization of women by non-Western cultural practices has now also become a topic within Western philosophy. In this essay, I draw on the work of other feminist scholars to argue that conceiving injustice to poor women in poor countries primarily in terms of their oppression in "illiberal" cultures provides an understanding of the women's situations that is crucially incomplete. This incomplete understanding distorts our comprehension of our moral relationship to women elsewhere in the world and impoverishes our assumptions about the intercultural dialogue necessary to promote global justice for women.[3]

PHILOSOPHERS SAVING AMINA TWO INFLUENTIAL PHILOSOPHICAL TREATMENTS OF INJUSTICE TO WOMEN IN POOR COUNTRIES

The Debate in Women's Studies

The interdisciplinary literature in women's or feminist studies has discussed the perceived victimization of women in non-Western cultures for at least thirty years. In this academic context, two main positions have been opposed to each other. The first is global radical feminism, a perspective that made its appearance in the early years of second-wave Western feminism. The radical feminists wish to establish that women are a group subjected to a distinct form of oppression, and their earliest writings postulated the existence of a worldwide women's culture—one that lay "beneath the surface" of but was nonetheless colonized by "male" national, ethnic, and racial cultures.[4] Global radical feminism asserts the universality of "patriarchal" violence against women and sometimes advocates an ideal of global sisterhood.[5] Opposed to this position is postcolonial feminism, which asserts the diversity of forms of women's oppression across the world and emphasizes that this oppression is shaped by many factors, among which past colonialism and continuing neocolonialism are especially important. Postcolonial feminism charges that global feminist criticisms of cultural practices outside the West frequently are forms of "imperial feminism" or "feminist Orientalism," often exoticizing and sensationalizing non-Western cultural practices by focusing on their sexual aspects.[6] The polarized debate in women's studies has sometimes seemed to suggest that Western feminists who are concerned about the well-being of women across the world are confronted with a choice between colonial interference and callous indifference.[7]

Central to the women's studies debates has been the question of "essentialism," especially as it pertains to many Western feminist representations of women. This debate arose out of a concern that the supposedly universal "woman" invoked in much Western feminist writing in fact was a woman privileged along a number of dimensions. For instance, many theorists implicitly imagined her as white, middle class, heterosexual, able-bodied, and so on. The feminist literature on essentialism discusses how the relationships among various aspects of women's diverse "identities" should be conceptualized (are they additive or multiplicative, analytically separable or not?), and problematizes the whole idea of a universal woman.[8] The critique of essentialism is now widely accepted within the discipline of women's studies, where the term "essentialist" has become exclusively pejorative. The critique has been extremely valuable in revealing the biases lurking in many Western feminist generalizations about "women," although some theorists worry that denying that any essential characteristics can be attributed to women pulls the theoretical rug from under feminist activism.[9] Postcolonial feminists argue that universal generalizations about women are essentialist, because they reify gender by treating it as possessing immutable characteristics that are separable from the contingencies of class, ethnicity, race, age, and nationality in ways that the postcolonial critics regard as incoherent and mystifying. In one influential article, for example, Chandra Mohanty challenges the essentialist contrasts between Western women and "the average Third World woman" that she finds implicit in much Western feminist writing. Mohanty argues that this writing represents Western women "as educated, as modern, as having control over their own bodies and sexualities, and the freedom to make their own decisions," while depicting non-Western women as victimized and lacking in agency. She criticizes patronizing Western representations of "the typical Third World woman" that portray this woman as leading "an essentially truncated life based on her feminine gender (read: sexually constrained) and her being 'third world' (read: ignorant, poor, uneducated, tradition-bound, family-oriented, victimized)."[10]

The Debate in Philosophy

In the 1990s, academic debate about the gendered aspects of non-Western cultural practices moved out of the feminist fringe and into the mainstream of Western philosophy. This occurred primarily as a result of bold work by Martha Nussbaum and Susan Okin. The recent works of Nussbaum and of Okin diverge in important respects, but here I focus on some parallels between them.[11] In their discussions of poor women in poor countries (and of cultural minority women in rich countries), Nussbaum and Okin both turn away from earlier debates about the universality or otherwise of "patriarchy." They reframe the issues in terms of ongoing philosophical debates between liberalism and communitarianism, on the one hand, and liberalism and multiculturalism, on the other. Both take as their problem the question of how Western theorists should respond to non-Western cultural practices perceived as unjust to women, and both believe that answering this question requires addressing several current philosophical controversies. These include moral universalism and cultural relativism; the possibility of "external" as opposed to "internal" social criticism; and the question of whether liberal societies can tolerate illiberal cultural practices within their borders.

Nussbaum and Okin both identify themselves as liberal feminists, but both follow the radical feminists in staunchly opposing what they see as the oppression of women in non-Western cultures. They provide new arguments against postcolonial feminists, casting them as relativists who seek to avoid forthright condemnation of injustice to women in developing, or "Third World," countries. They also charge that the anti-essentialism advocated by postcolonial feminists rationalizes a disingenuous refusal to acknowledge forms of injustice that are distinctively gendered. Finally, Nussbaum and Okin suggest that women who seem content with unjust cultural practices suffer from adaptive preferences or learned desires for things that are harmful, a phenomenon called "false consciousness" by Western feminists influenced by the Marxist critique of ideology.

Nussbaum's work on this topic draws on Amartya Sen's concept of capabilities, which was developed originally as an alternative to welfarism and income metrics for measuring international levels of development. Nussbaum has modified the concept of capabilities and uses it to counter "cultural relativism," which she thinks often serves as a pretext for excusing outrageous injustice to women in poor countries. In a spate of books and articles published throughout the 1990s, Nussbaum defends the universal values that she believes are embodied in the capabilities, appealing to these values to condemn cultural practices that subordinate women. An early article provocatively defends "Aristotelian essentialism" against what Nussbaum regards as a "politically correct" anti-essentialism that rationalizes "ancient religious taboos, the luxury of the pampered husband, ill health, ignorance, and death."[12] In responding to the challenge that many people, including many poor women in poor countries, do not accept the capabilities that she identifies as universal values, Nussbaum invokes the concept of adaptive preferences.[13] She argues that existing desires and preferences may be corrupted or mistaken when they are adapted to unjust social circumstances; for example, women may sometimes fail to recognize that they are oppressed. More generally, Nussbaum contends that because preferences may be adaptive, existing desires provide an unreliable guide to justice and the good life, subverting intercultural agreement on universal values.[14]

Susan Okin has also addressed the situation of poor women in poor countries. Her analysis draws on her own earlier critique of Western practices of marriage and family, in which she argues persuasively that the traditional division of labor in marriage unjustly disadvantages Western women economically and in other ways.[15] Okin's analysis of the situation of poor women in poor countries is parallel to her analysis of the situation of Western women: in her view, "the problems of other women are 'similar to ours but more so.'"[16] Like Nussbaum, Okin challenges feminist anti-essentialism, quoting Nussbaum approvingly on this topic.[17] Also like Nussbaum, she worries that "false consciousness" arising from adaptive preferences and internalized oppression limits the usefulness of "interactive" or "dialogic" approaches to justice and advocates an alternative Rawlsian method of hypothetical dialogue in the original position. Okin's concern about cultural injustice to women emerges again in her contributions to the multiculturalism debate. In the discipline of philosophy, this debate focuses on the question of whether cultural minorities within liberal societies should enjoy special group rights.[18] Okin argues that the rights claimed by minority groups may conflict with liberalism's commitment to women's equality, so that a tension exists between multiculturalism and feminism.[19] In Okin's view, supporters of multiculturalism have failed to appreciate that illiberal cultural practices are often especially burdensome to women. In addition, she believes that some feminists have paid so much attention to differences among women that they have fallen into cultural relativism, ignoring the fact that "most cultures have as one of their principal aims the control of women by men."[20] Okin asks rhetorically, "When a woman from a more patriarchal culture comes to the United States (or some other Western, basically liberal, state), why should she be less protected from male violence than other women are?"[21]

Some Nonlogical Implications of Nussbaum's and Okin's Work

Okin and Nussbaum deserve great credit for drawing the attention of mainstream Western philosophers to issues they had previously neglected. Like all groundbreaking scholarship, Nussbaum's and Okin's work has shaped the subsequent literature in distinctive ways, highlighting some concerns and obscuring others. Specifically, their work has encouraged Western theorists to understand injustice to non-Western women as a matter of oppression caused by local cultural traditions. The issues that Nussbaum and Okin raise are crucial to understanding the injustices suffered by non-Western women. Here, however, I focus on the issues they have *not* raised, on their omissions and their silences. In other words, I am concerned here with what Cheshire Calhoun would call the nonlogical implications of Nussbaum's and Okin's work in this area, including the moral and political significance of their emphases and their lacunae.[22] In discussing the contributions that care ethics makes to moral theory, Calhoun argues that Western moral philosophy has produced a lopsided ideology of moral life and thought that reflects the moral preoccupations of propertied males and obscures the moral concerns of (among others) many women. Analogously, I argue that Nussbaum's and Okin's representations of the injustices suffered by poor women in poor countries are lopsided, reflecting some preoccupations while obscuring others. Calhoun suggests that the ethics of care, construed as a focus on hitherto neglected aspects of moral life and thought, can help to redress the gendered bias of moral theory. I suggest that a focus on certain aspects of the global political economy, hitherto largely neglected by Western philosophers, can help to present a fuller and fairer understanding of the injustices suffered by poor women in poor countries.

My concern is not that Nussbaum and Okin pay excessive attention to the sensationalized sexual issues that preoccupy the popular press. On the contrary, they take the poverty of many non-Western women extremely seriously, recognizing that poverty constrains women's autonomy and makes them vulnerable to a range of other abuses, such as violence, sexual exploitation, and overwork. Nussbaum's and Okin's discussions, however, give the impression that female poverty is attributable primarily to local cultural traditions, especially traditions of female seclusion.[23] For example, both treat as exemplary a study by Martha Chen, which explains that many women in India, especially female heads of households, are left destitute because the system of secluding women denies them the right to gainful employment outside the home.[24]

Nussbaum's and Okin's focus on the injustice of non-Western cultural traditions appears to lend credence to several theses that are commonly assumed to be true in popular Western discussions of the situation of poor women in poor countries. The first thesis, which I shall call the "injustice by culture" thesis, is that a major, perhaps *the* major, cause of suffering among women in poor countries is unjust treatment in accordance with local cultural traditions— traditions whose injustice is not necessarily recognized by the women involved. The second thesis, which I shall refer to as the "autonomy of culture" thesis, asserts that while the unjust local traditions that cause such suffering may resemble some Western practices, they are causally independent of them. The third thesis, which I shall designate as the "West is best for women" thesis, maintains that non-Western cultures are typically more unjust to women than is Western culture.

I doubt that either Nussbaum or Okin would assent to these theses, at least in the simple terms in which I have stated them. Nevertheless, I worry that both philosophers' preoccupation with opposing the perceived injustice of non-Western cultures encourages many of their readers to derive such nonlogical implications from their work. In addition, I worry that Nussbaum's and Okin's work in this area promotes too narrow a view of the task of those Western theorists who seek to explain injustice to poor women in poor countries. In other words, I am afraid it promotes a fourth thesis, which is that the task of Western theorists is to expose the injustices imposed on women by their local cultures and to challenge rationalizations of those injustices.

This thesis is the philosopher's version of the "save Amina" campaign. In the next section, I critically examine the first three of these theses; in the following section, I assess the fourth.

NON-WESTERN CULTURE AND INJUSTICE TO POOR WOMEN IN POOR COUNTRIES

Assessing claims about cultural injustice requires having some sense of what is meant by the term "culture," which Raymond Williams describes as "one of the two or three most complicated words in the English language."[25] The 1982 report of a UNESCO conference on cultural policy stated that, in the view of some delegates, "culture permeated the whole social fabric and its role was so preeminent and determining that it might indeed be confused with life itself."[26] In most contexts, however, the term "culture" is useful only if it is marked off against other areas of social life, so culture is often distinguished from politics and the economy.[27] Contemporary philosophical discussions of culture typically accept some version of this distinction. For example, Nancy Fraser contrasts concerns about cultural recognition with concerns about economic redistribution.[28] The items on Bhikhu Parekh's list of minority cultural practices in Britain all concern marriage, sexuality, dress, diet, education, body marking, and funeral customs.[29] In Okin's view, "the sphere of personal, sexual, and reproductive life provides a central focus of most cultures. . . . Religious or cultural groups are often particularly concerned with 'personal law'—the laws of marriage, divorce, child custody, division and control of family property, and inheritance."[30]

When culture is equated with dress, diet, sex, and family, it becomes an area of life that has special significance for women. Most of the practices on Parekh's list apply mainly or even exclusively to women and girls, and his last item is simply the "subordinate status of women and all it entails, including denial of opportunities for their personal development in some minority communities."[31] Thus, Okin's observation is uncontroversial:

> As a rule, then, the defense of "cultural practices" is likely to have much greater impact on the lives of women and girls than those of men and boys, since far more of women's time and energy goes into preserving and maintaining the personal, familial, and reproductive side of life. Obviously, culture is not only about domestic arrangements, but they do provide a major focus of most contemporary cultures. Home is, after all, where much of culture is practiced, preserved, and transmitted to the young.[32]

Seyla Benhabib writes, "Women and their bodies are the symbolic-cultural site upon which human societies inscribe their moral order."[33] Because women are typically seen as the symbols or bearers of culture, conflicts among cultural groups often are fought on the terrain of women's bodies, sometimes literally in the form of systematic rape.

The Limits of Injustice by Culture
The injustice by culture thesis asserts that local cultural traditions are a major, perhaps the major, source of the injustices suffered by women in poor countries.

Is this thesis correct? Certainly it is undeniable that many non-Western cultures are unjust to women. Striking evidence is provided by Sen's famous calculation that up to a hundred million women are "missing" as a result of Asian cultural practices, including both direct violence and systematic neglect.[34] It also seems indisputable that women in legally multicultural societies tend to suffer disproportionately from religious and cultural laws that apply only to members of specific religions or cultures within larger nation-states.[35] That injustice to women is inherent in many cultural traditions confirms the second-wave feminist arguments that the personal is political, and Okin's work on Western marriage and family has made a valuable contribution in drawing mainstream philosophers' attention to such injustices. The poverty and associated abuses suffered by poor women in poor countries, however, cannot be understood exclusively in terms of unjust local traditions.

To understand such poverty and abuse more fully, it is also necessary to situate these traditions in a broader geopolitical and geoeconomic context.

Contemporary processes of economic globalization, regulated by the Western-inspired and Western-imposed principles and policies of neoliberalism, have significantly affected the situation of many poor women in poor countries. Too often, these changes have been for the worse. The United Nations reports: "The majority of the 1.5 billion people living on one dollar a day or less are women. In addition, the gap between women and men caught in the cycle of poverty has continued to widen in the past decade, a phenomenon commonly referred to as 'the feminization of poverty.' Worldwide, women earn on average slightly more than 50 percent of what men earn."[36] Certainly some small women producers have benefited from the expansion, integration, and deregulation of the global market, and many more women have enjoyed increased economic independence as a result of the availability of paid work. Nevertheless, the Self Employed Women's Association observes, "While there are both positive and negative effects of globalisation on women in the informal sector, women have tended to be the least able to seize opportunities and the most likely to suffer from the changes involved."[37] On this view, "Globalization does not so much create difficulties for poor women where previously there were none as intensify some of the existing inequalities and insecurities to which poor women are subject. . . . For some unskilled women, it has meant loss of livelihoods. . . . For others, it has meant loss of labour rights (such as social benefits and the right to organize)."[38] In what follows, I offer a few examples of the impact of neoliberal globalization on many poor women in poor countries.

Most poor women in poor countries have traditionally made a living in small-scale and subsistence agriculture; even quite recently, 70 percent of the world's farmers were said to be women. The impact of neoliberal globalization, however, has made small-scale and subsistence agriculture increasingly unviable. One reason for this is the expansion of export agriculture, typically mandated by programs of structural adjustment, especially in South America and

Southeast Asia. Another reason is the refusal on the part of the wealthiest countries to conform to their own neoliberal principles. The United States and the
European Union currently spend far more on farm subsidies than they spend
on aid. As neoliberalism compels poor countries to open their markets, locally
grown agricultural products are unable to compete with the heavily subsidized
foods dumped by richer countries.[39]

The decline of small-scale and subsistence agriculture has driven many
women off the land and into the shantytowns that encircle most major cities
in developing countries. Here women struggle to survive in the informal economy, which is characterized by low wages or incomes, uncertain employment,
and poor working conditions. The informal economy is a shadow one whose
operations are not reflected in official records, whose workers typically do not
pay taxes, and whose jobs are unregulated by health and safety standards. It
covers a wide range of income-generating activities, including declining handi-
crafts, small-scale retail trade, petty food production, street vending, domestic
work, and prostitution, as well as home-based putting-out systems and contract work. Women predominate in the informal economy. Many become
street vendors or domestic servants. Those who remain landless in the country-
side are often forced to work as seasonal, casual, and temporary laborers at
lower wages than their male counterparts. Many women are driven into prostitution, accelerating the AIDS epidemic, which ravages the poorest women in
the poorest countries.[40]

Neoliberal globalization has also destroyed many traditional industries on
which poor women in poor countries once depended. More fortunate women
may obtain jobs in newer industries, especially the garment industry, which
produces the developing world's main manufactured exports and in which
women are the majority of workers. Indeed, women's participation in the paid
labor force has often given them increased autonomy and bargaining power.[41]
It has given women increased "power to choose," even within the many constraints that face "weak winners."[42] Nevertheless, conditions in the garment
industry are notoriously bad because poor countries, lacking capital, can compete in the global market only by implementing sweatshop conditions. The
situation for garment workers in poor countries is worsened by continuing
protectionism in the garment industry on the part of the United States and
the European Union. The most obviously unjust consequences of neoliberal
globalization for women are the worldwide cutbacks in social services, also often
mandated by programs of structural adjustment. These cutbacks have affected
women's economic status even more adversely than men's, because women's
responsibility for caring for children and other family members makes them
more reliant on such programs.[43] Reductions in social services have forced
women to create survival strategies for their families by absorbing these reductions with their own unpaid labor, and more work for women has resulted in
higher school dropout rates for girls. In addition, the introduction of school

fees in many Southern countries has made education unavailable, especially to girls. Less education and longer hours of domestic work contribute to women's impoverishment by making it harder for them to attain well-paying jobs.

The above examples are not intended to suggest that the poverty and poverty-related abuses that afflict many women in poor countries are caused exclusively by neoliberal globalization. Obviously, these problems result from interaction between factors that are both macro and micro, global and local. It is impossible to explain why women suffer disproportionately from the deleterious consequences of neoliberal globalization without referring to local cultural traditions. For example, if women were not assigned the primary responsibility of caring for children, the sick, and the old, the cutbacks in social services would not affect them disproportionately, nor would they find it harder than men to move to the locations of new industries. Only the injustice of cultural tradition seems to account for the fact that, within male-headed families, women and girls frequently receive less of such available resources as food and medical care. Nevertheless, the above examples do show that the poverty of poor women in poor countries cannot be attributed exclusively to the injustice of their local cultures. To assume this would be to adopt a one-sided analysis that ignored the ways in which the processes of neoliberal globalization have frequently exacerbated inequalities between men and women.

The Limits of the Autonomy of Culture

Faced with the evidence of the previous section, Nussbaum and Okin would undoubtedly acknowledge that neoliberal globalization bears considerable responsibility for women's poverty in poor countries, and they would surely condemn its injustices. Certainly it is reasonable for those wishing to address injustice to poor women in poor countries to focus sometimes on local rather than global problems and on cultural rather than economic injustices. When discussing issues of seeming injustice in non-Western cultures, however, it is problematic to write as though these cultures are self-contained or autonomous, as though their traditions have not been and do not continue to be shaped by Western interventions.

Theorists of the second wave of Western feminism sometimes inquired whether male dominance has existed in all societies or whether it was introduced to some societies by European colonizers.[44] Whatever the answer to this once hotly debated question, it is indisputable that many supposed cultural traditions in Asia, Latin America, and Africa have been strongly influenced by encounters with Western colonialism. For instance, Veena Oldenburg argues that the practice of dowry murder in India had imperial origins.[45] Moreover, non-Western cultural practices especially affecting women often gain new life as symbols of resistance to Western dominance. Dallas Browne, for example, shows how in Kenya "clitoridectomy became a political issue between the Kikuyu and Kenya's white settlers and missionaries, as well as a symbol of the struggle between African nationalists and British colonial power."[46] Uma Nara-yan describes how the supposed "Indian tradition" of *sati* (immolation of wid-ows) was likely "an *effect* of the extensive and prolonged debate that took place over the very issue of its status as tradition. As a result of this debate, *sati* came to acquire, for both British and Indians, and for its supporters as well as its opponents, an 'emblematic status,' becoming a larger-than-life symbol of 'Hindu' and 'Indian' culture."[47] Today, Leslye Amede Obiora writes, "Marginal-ized by exposure to an onslaught of conditions of modernity, the market econ-omy, and imperialistic transnational enterprises, distinct cultural groups tend to view themselves as being under pressure to demonstrate their ritual purity and allegiance to traditional high culture."[48] This sense of being economically and culturally beleaguered may help to explain the current worldwide flourish-ing of religious fundamentalisms, defined by Leti Volpp as modern political movements that use religion as a basis for their attempts to win or consolidate power and extend social control.[49] Contemporary fundamentalisms, Volpp points out, all "support the patriarchal family as a central agent of control and see women as embodying the moral and traditional values of the family and the whole community."[50]

Western culture is not merely a passive stimulus for gender-conservative reactions by those who have the authority to define "authentic" cultural tradi-tions. In addition, Western powers may reinforce or even impose gender-con-servative cultures on non-Western societies by supporting conservative factions of their populations. For most of the twentieth century, for example, the British and U.S. governments have supported a Saudi Arabian regime that practices gender apartheid. The Taliban government of Afghanistan, which also practiced gender apartheid, was installed after the United States provided extensive train-ing and aid to various mujahedeen forces opposing the then-communist but secular government. President Reagan described the mujahedeen as the moral equivalent of the Founding Fathers of the United States. Following its overthrow of the Taliban, the United States has installed a weak government in Afghanistan under which women's lives in many ways are just as precarious as they were under the Taliban. The burkha is no longer legally required, but most women are still afraid to remove it and they are not safe on the streets. Girls' schools are burned, families are threatened for sending girls to school, and three girls recently have been poisoned, apparently for attending school.[51] At present, the United States is trying to build an Iraqi government to succeed the Baathist regime it has overthrown. Under the Baathist regime, whatever its other faults, the conditions of Iraqi women were much better than those of women else-where in the region. Today, women are afraid to leave their homes,[52] and news media report that the United States is seeking political leadership for Iraq among its tribal and religious leaders—few of whom are women or whose prior-ities include improving the status of women.

Sharp contrasts between Western and non-Western cultures cannot ulti-mately be sustained. They rely characteristically on what Narayan calls cultural essentialist generalizations, which offer totalizing characterizations of whole cul-tures, treated as internally homogenous and externally sealed. Typically, such generalizations are quite inconsistent with empirical realities.[53] In the Anglo-American philosophical literature, it is becoming more common to observe that cultures are internally diverse and often conflict-ridden and that they are not autonomous relative to one another, but it is still unusual to note that they are only partially autonomous relative to political and economic structures. Yet, as the global political economy becomes more integrated, so too do its cultural manifestations. Thus, when multinational corporations exploit women in export-processing zones located in poor countries, it is impossible to say that this practice exclusively reflects either Western or non-Western culture. When Asian governments tempt multinational corporate investment with stereotypes of women workers as tractable, hardworking, dexterous, and sexy, it seems meaningless to ask whether these stereotypes are Western or non-Western or whether the super-exploitation and sexual harassment of these women repre-sents Western or non-Western cultural traditions. It seems equally meaningless to attribute the increasing sexualization of women worldwide to either Western or non-Western culture. Many women around the world have been drawn into some aspect of sex work. This includes a multibillion-dollar pornography indus-try and a worldwide traffic in women, in which the sex workers participate with varying degrees of willingness and coercion. It also includes servicing male workers in large plantations, servicing representatives of transnational corpora-tions, servicing troops around military bases, and servicing UN troops and workers. In some parts of Asia and the Caribbean, sex tourism is a mainstay of local economies. Prostitution has become a transnational phenomenon, shaped by global norms of feminine beauty and masculine virility.

In the new global order, local cultures interact and interpenetrate to the point where they often fuse. Some patterns seem discernible—for example, worldwide preferences for women as factory workers, sexual playthings, and domestic servants[54]—but these patterns shift and merge in an unending variety of particular combinations. Poor women in poor countries certainly are oppressed by local men whose power is rooted in local cultures, but they are also oppressed by global forces, including the forces of so-called development, which have reshaped local gender and class relations in varying and contradic-tory ways, simultaneously undermining and reinforcing them.[55] A new but still male-dominant global culture may be emerging, relying on the labor of a new transnational labor force that is feminized, racialized, and sexualized.[56]

Is the West Best for Women?
Much of the Western philosophical debate over multiculturalism discusses the relative situations of women in "liberal" and "illiberal" cultures. It tends to

equate Western with liberal culture and non-Western with illiberal culture, and it usually takes for granted that Western culture is more advanced than non-Western culture. Okin writes, "Many Third World families, it seems, are even worse schools of justice and more successful inculcators of the inequality of the sexes as natural and appropriate than are their developed world equivalents."[57] In her view, "the situation of some poor women in poor countries is different from—as well as distinctly worse than—that of most Western women today. It is more like the situation of the latter in the nineteenth century."[58]

As intercultural interactions accelerate, it becomes increasingly problematic to contrast whole cultures with each other. Culturally essentialist generalizations construct idealized and unrealistic images of cultures, which are typically designed to promote political agendas. What Narayan calls the colonialist stance presents Western cultures as dynamic, progressive, and egalitarian, while portraying non-Western cultures as backward, barbaric, and patriarchal. Colonialist representations characteristically engage in "culture blaming," for instance, by treating discrimination and violence against women as intrinsic parts of non-Western but not of Western cultures. While the West historically has blamed non-Western cultures for their backwardness, it has portrayed its own culture as staunchly committed to such values as liberty and equality, a "self-perception . . . untroubled by the fact that Western powers were engaged in slavery and colonization, or that they had resisted granting political and civil rights even to large numbers of Western subjects, including women."[59] Today, as Narayan notes, violence abounds in the United States, yet cross burnings, burnings of black churches, domestic violence murders, and gun deaths are not usually treated as manifestations of United States culture.[60] When cultural explanations are offered only for violence against poor women in poor countries, Narayan notes that the effect is to suggest that these women suffer "death by culture," a fate from which Western women seem curiously exempt.[61] Many continue to write as though Western culture is unambiguously liberal, ignoring Christian fundamentalism's influence on the present U.S. government, as well as its growth in several former Soviet bloc countries.[62] For instance, Parekh treats polygamy as an exclusively Muslim practice, ignoring its existence among Christian groups in the United States. It is true that what Parekh calls the public values of Western societies are mostly liberal,[63] but Western cultures certainly are not liberal all the way down—and illiberal values frequently rear above their surfaces.

Although the superiority of Western culture appears self-evident to most Westerners, non-Western women do not all agree. For instance, Western feminists have long criticized non-Western practices of veiling and female seclusion, but Leila Ahmed argues that the social separation of women from men on the Arabian Peninsula creates a space within which women may interact freely with one another and where they resist men's efforts to impose on them an ideology of inferiority and subservience.[64] Nussbaum and Okin suggest that non-Western women's acceptance of seemingly unjust cultural practices may be due to adaptive preferences or false consciousness. In Okin's view, not only do "many cultures oppress some of their members, in particular women . . . they are (also) often able to socialize these oppressed members so that they accept without question their designated cultural status."[65] To someone like myself, brought up in the British class system, this assertion seems indisputably true. But raising questions of false consciousness only with respect to non-Western women who defend their cultures could be read as suggesting that these women's moral perceptions are less reliable than the perceptions of Western women, whose consciousness is supposedly higher or truer. Such a suggestion reflects a second aspect of the colonialist stance—namely, the "missionary position," which supposes that "only Westerners are capable of naming and challenging patriarchal atrocities committed against Third-World women."[66] Nussbaum and Okin both recognize explicitly that non-Western women are perfectly capable of criticizing unjust cultural traditions and frequently do precisely that, but their practice of raising questions about adaptive preferences and false consciousness only when confronted by views that oppose their own encourages dismissing those views without considering them seriously. In fact, the question of the superiority of Western culture for women, especially poor women, is not as straightforward as Westerners often assume.

The thesis that the West is best for the poor women of the world is not necessarily true. Even if we set aside deep philosophical questions about how to measure welfare, development, or the quality of life and agree to assess cultures according to their success in preserving poor women's human rights, at least three sets of concerns cast doubt on the West-is-best thesis. First, it is of course true by definition that liberal cultures give a higher priority than illiberal cultures to protecting civil and political liberties. The ability to exercise these so-called first-generation human rights, however, can be enjoyed only in a context where second-generation social and economic rights are also guaranteed. As noted earlier, poverty makes women vulnerable to violations of their civil and political liberties, including assaults on their bodily integrity, and Western societies are very uneven in their willingness to address women's poverty. The feminization of poverty is especially conspicuous in the United States, where women continue to suffer extensive violence. Thus, it must be recognized that the human rights especially of poor women are routinely violated even in liberal Western societies, and on some accounts women fared better in the erstwhile Second World than in the First World, for much of the twentieth century.

Second, and turning to poor women in poor countries, it is hard to deny that Western powers are disproportionately responsible for designing, imposing, and enforcing a global economic order that continues to widen the staggering gap between rich and poor countries. Since gender inequality is strongly correlated with poverty, Western countries bear a considerable share of the responsibility for creating the conditions that make non-Western women vulnerable to local violations of their rights. Third, it must be acknowledged that some of the same Western powers that trumpet democracy and liberalism at home support undemocratic and gender-conservative regimes abroad, fomenting coups, dictatorships, and civil wars.[67] Poor women are disproportionately affected by these interventions. They suffer most from the absence of social programs cut to fund military spending, and they also suffer most from social chaos. They constitute the majority of war's casualties and a majority of the refugees dislocated by war.[68]

These three sets of concerns raise serious questions for the thesis that the West is best for women, especially for the vast majority of the world's poor women. I do not wish to romanticize non-Western cultures and traditions or to assert that Western culture is intrinsically violent and racist. Such reverse colonialist representations would be as essentialist and distorting as the claim that the West is best for women. In addition, suggesting that neocolonial domination is the cause of all the problems in poor countries would portray the citizens of those countries simply as passive victims, denying their agency and responsibility. My goal has been to challenge the images of both Western and non-Western cultures that are implicit in much of the most influential philosophical discussion on these topics.

Expanding our understanding of the causes of women's poverty in poor countries requires that we also expand our conception of our responsibility toward such women. Once we acknowledge that we share past, present, and future connections with poor women in poor countries, we see that we inhabit with them a shared context of justice. Westerners do not look at their problems from an Archimedean standpoint, as outsiders to their social world. Our involvement gives us a firmer moral standing for criticizing non-Western cultural practices, provided our criticisms are well informed and, in Onora O'Neill's words, "followable by" members of the society in question.[69] However, it also requires us to investigate how much moral responsibility should be attributed to the citizens of Western countries for the continuation of these practices, as well as for the unjust global order that traps many women in poor countries in grinding poverty.

RETHINKING GLOBAL JUSTICE FOR WOMEN WHAT'S ON THE AGENDA OF INTERCULTURAL DIALOGUE?

In Western classrooms, "cultural abuses" of women have become staple and sometimes titillating examples used to enliven discussion of such issues as moral relativism and the possibility of cross-cultural social criticism. Some moral and political theorists address perceived cultural injustice to women by recommending an aggressive cosmopolitanism; others promote a "culturally sensitive" relativism. Increasingly, however, they recognize that cultures are neither static nor hermetically sealed and they advocate intercultural dialogue.[70] In this section, I wish to suggest some items for inclusion on the agendas of intercultural dialogues about justice for women in poor countries.

Most obviously, such dialogues should not be regarded as opportunities for "saving" poor women in poor countries by proselytizing supposedly Western values or raising consciousness about the injustice of non-Western practices. It is always more pleasant to discuss other people's blind spots and faults than our own, but we need to think more carefully who these women are and from what or whom they need saving.

High on the agenda of intercultural dialogue about global justice for poor women in poor countries must be questions about the global basic structure, as well as the justice of those Western government policies that directly and indirectly affect poor women's lives. Important questions of economic justice include how to understand "natural" resources, when things like fossil fuels, sunny climates, coral beaches, or strategic locations become resources only within larger systems of economic production and social meaning; how to determine a country's "own" resources, when every country's boundaries have been drawn by force; what the meaning of "fair" trade is, and whether trade can be free in any meaningful sense when poor nations have no alternative to participating in an economic system in which they become ever poorer. Important topics of political justice include reexamining the Westphalian conception of sovereignty, at a time when the sovereignty of most countries is limited by the rules of world trade and the sovereignty of poor countries is rendered almost meaningless because of their domination by international financial institutions and trade organizations.[71] Although superficially ungendered, these topics in fact are all deeply gendered, most obviously because women suffer disproportionately from economic inequality and political marginalization.

Intercultural dialogue about global justice must also address the problem of militarism. Following and despite the end of the Cold War, arms expenditures rose and wars continued in many non-Western countries, exacerbating and exacerbated by the poverty associated with global neoliberalism. In the late 1990s, Spike Peterson and Anne Sisson Runyan note, "over half the nations of the world still provide higher budgets for the military than for their countries' health needs; 25 countries spend more on defense than on education; and 15 countries devote more funds to military programs than to education and health combined."[72] Since September 11, 2001, arms expenditures have increased still further. In today's world, the top arms exporters are the United States, Russia, and France, with the United States accounting for around 50 percent of sales.[73] The United States also maintains more than 200 permanent bases across the world; these distort local economies and foster the employment of many thousands of women as prostitutes.[74] As noted earlier, poor women and their children suffer disproportionately from war and militarism, and the expansion of these raises deep philosophical questions about the meanings of war, peace, and security—especially security for women.[75]

Another set of topics for intercultural dialogue about global justice for women concerns remedial justice, reparation, or compensation for past and continuing wrongs. Do countries that have expropriated resources or fought proxy wars in other countries owe reparations to those countries, and, if so, how should these be determined? Should wealthy countries compensate poor countries for the environmental destruction to which they have made a disproportionate contribution not only through militarism, which is the single largest cause of environmental destruction, but also through other destructive practices, including the careless extraction of resources from poor countries, the establishment of factories in poor countries with weak environmental standards, and extravagant patterns of consumption, especially the profligate burning of fossil fuels? The last produces carbon dioxide that causes acid rain and global warming, accompanied by devastating floods and hurricanes and a rise in sea levels that may cause some Southern countries to disappear entirely. Since poor women in poor countries suffer disproportionately from poverty, social chaos, and environmental destruction, they have the most to gain from an effective system of remedial justice.

Most of the above topics concern issues of justice among countries. Since such justice is likely to be slow in coming, intercultural dialogue about global justice might also address the question of how in the meantime individual citizens can directly assist poor women in poor countries. Imam and Medar-Gould note that not all victims of human rights violations can become international causes célèbres or subjects for letter-writing protests. They suggest that Western feminists who wish to help Lawal contribute to BAOBAB for Women's Human Rights or WRAPA, Women's Rights Advancement and Protection Agency, organizations that they respectively represent. Because money invariably comes with strings attached, promoting civil society initiatives in poor countries raises questions about the subversion of local democracies. Some critics argue that Northern-funded NGOs are a new form of colonialism, despite using the language of inclusion, empowerment, accountability, and grassroots democracy, because they create dependence on nonelected overseas funders and their locally appointed officials, undermining the development of social programs administered by elected officials accountable to local people.[76] In an integrated global economy, however, nonintervention is no longer an option; our inevitable interventions are only more or less overt and more or less morally informed. Although the foreign funding of women's NGOs has dangers, it is not necessarily imperialistic. Nira Yuval-Davis reports that many NGOs in the global South have been able to survive and resist local pressures through the aid provided from overseas, "as well as the more personal support and solidarity of feminist organizations in other countries." She observes, "It would be a westocentric stereotype to view women associated with NGOs in the South as puppets of western feminism."[77]

"Saving Amina"
The images of Amina Lawal that flashed around the world in 2004 show a beautiful African woman, holding a beautiful baby, looking to Christian eyes like an African Madonna. Her head is covered, however, her eyes are downcast, and she looks submissive, sad, and scared. Portrayed in bare feet and described as illiterate, she epitomizes the image of the oppressed "Third World woman" described by Mohanty. Her image has also been widely regarded as epitomizing the barbarity of Islamic fundamentalism. Such images encourage Western feminists to take up the supposed white man's burden of "saving brown women from brown men."[78]

Challenging the "Save Amina" petition and letter-writing campaign, Imam and Medar-Gould write:

> Dominant colonialist discourses and the mainstream international media have presented Islam (and Africa) as the barbaric and savage Other. Please do not buy into this. Accepting stereotypes that present Islam as incompatible with human rights not only perpetuates racism but also confirms the claims of right-wing politico-religious extremists in all of our contexts.[79]

They explain that when protest letters represent negative stereotypes of Islam and Muslims, they inflame local sentiments and may put victims of human rights abuses and their supporters in further danger.

Sensationalized criticisms of non-Western cultures reinforce Western as well as non-Western prejudices, promoting the impression that Western democracies are locked into a life-and-death "clash of cultures" with militant Islam.[80] Even philosophical criticisms sometimes have consequences outside the academy. Philosophy is often portrayed as an esoteric discipline practiced exclusively in ivory towers, but many moral and political philosophers intend also to influence the "real" world.[81] Philosophical criticism may be a political intervention and may be taken up outside academia in ways that its authors do not necessarily intend.[82] The Nation columnist Katha Pollitt, upset that militant Islamists had forced the Miss World pageant out of Nigeria, commented, "Not a good week for cultural relativism, on the whole."[83] Western criticism of non-Western cultural practices is not in principle patronizing or xenophobic, but critics should be aware that our colonial history and current geopolitical situation influence the interpretation and consequences of such criticisms; for instance, opponents of immigration cite non-Western cultural practices as reasons for closing the borders of the United States to immigrants from poor countries.[84] Given this context, Western moral and political theorists need to consider how their criticisms of non-Western cultural practices may be used politically. Amos and Parmar contend that racist British immigration policies were justified partly by invoking feminist opposition to arranged marriage.[85] President George W. Bush and his wife Laura both rationalized the bombing of Afghanistan by the

United States as necessary to save Afghan women from the oppression of the burkha.[86]

Philosophers wishing to help poor women in poor countries, such as Amina Lawal, certainly are at liberty to criticize cultural traditions in Nigeria and other places, and such criticisms are often well deserved. But it behooves us also to ask why these practices have become ensconced as cultural traditions. Nigeria is a country that enjoys huge oil revenues, yet its real per capita GDP declined by 22 percent between 1977 and 1998.[87] As we have seen, gender inequality is correlated with poverty, and, according to Thomas Pogge, the poverty suffered by most Nigerians is causally linked to the "resource privilege" that the existing international system accords to the de facto rulers of all countries. This encourages military coups, authoritarianism, and corruption in resource-rich countries such as Nigeria, which has been ruled by military strongmen for almost three decades and is listed near the bottom of Transparency International's chart of international corruption. In Pogge's view, "Corruption in Nigeria is not just a local phenomenon rooted in tribal culture and traditions, but encouraged and sustained by the international resource privilege."[88] In such circumstances, for philosophers to focus exclusively on the injustice of Nigerian cultural practices is to engage in a form of culture blaming that depoliticizes social problems and diverts attention from structural violence against poor populations.[89]

In addition to bearing in mind the larger context that sustains many unjust cultural practices in the global South, Western philosophers who criticize those practices should also remember that Southern women are not simply passive victims of their cultures—notwithstanding the images of Amina Lawal. On the contrary, many countries in the global South, including Nigeria, have longstanding women's movements, and Nigerian feminists remain active in struggles to democratize their cultures and to protect women's human rights.[90] Nigerian women are also active in struggles for justice against Western corporations; for instance, women from Itsekiri, Ijaw, Ilaje, and Urhobos are also currently challenging the activities of Shell Petroleum Development Company in the Niger Delta.[91] These women activists may have a better understanding of their own situation than that possessed by many of the Westerners who want to "save" them.

Westerners concerned about the plight of poor women in poor countries should not focus exclusively, and perhaps not primarily, on the cultural traditions of those countries. Since gender inequality is correlated so strongly with poverty, perhaps we should begin by asking why so many countries are so poor. To do so would encourage us to reflect on our own contribution to the plight of poor women, and this would be a more genuinely liberal approach because it would show more respect for non-Western women's ability to look after their own affairs according to their values and priorities.[92] Citizens and residents of countries (such as the United States and those of the European Union) that exert disproportionate control over the global order bear direct responsibility for how that order affects women elsewhere in the world. Rather than simply blaming Amina Lawal's culture, we should begin by taking our own feet off her neck.

NOTES

This essay appeared in *Ethics & International Affairs* 19, no. 3 (2005): 55–75. I would like to thank Abigail Gosselin for research assistance, Christian Barry for valuable editorial suggestions, two anonymous journal reviewers, and participants in the conference, "Global Justice and Intercultural Dialogue," Shanghai Normal University, Shanghai, China, January 8–12, 2004, especially Thomas Pogge, for helpful comments.

1.   The quotation in my title is taken from an article that appeared in *Essence* magazine in 2003, although the *Essence* article portrays Lawal's Nigerian woman lawyer, Hauwa Ibrahim, rather than Western feminists, as "saving Amina."

2.   Ayesha Imam and Sindi Medar-Gould, "Please Stop the International Amina Lawal Protest Letter Campaigns" (open letter, May 1, 2003).

3.   A note on my terminology: In this essay, "we" refers to moral and political theorists sympathetic to political feminism who work in North America or the European Union. I have in mind primarily citizens, but also, to a lesser extent, permanent residents. In speaking of countries' geopolitical and geoeconomic locations, feminist scholars have used a variety of terminologies—all problematic in some respects.

4.   Barbara Burris, "The Fourth World Manifesto," in *Radical Feminism*, ed. Anne Koedt, Ellen Levine, and Anita Rapone (New York: Quadrangle, 1973).

5.   Robin Morgan, ed., *Sisterhood Is Global: The International Women's Movement Anthology* (Garden City, NY: Anchor Press/Doubleday, 1984).

6.   See Valerie Amos and Pratibha Parmar, "Challenging Imperial Feminism," *Feminist Review* 17 (1984): 3–19; and Frederique Apffel-Marglin and Suzanne L. Simon, "Feminist Orientalism and Development," in *Feminist Perspectives on Sustainable Development*, ed. Wendy Harcourt (Atlantic Highlands, NJ: Zed Books, 1994).

7.   Alison M. Jaggar, "Western Feminism and Global Responsibility," in *Feminist Interventions in Ethics and Politics*, ed. Barbara S. Andrew, Jean Keller, and Lisa H. Schwartzman (Lanham, MD: Rowman & Littlefield, 2004).

8.   See, e.g., Hazel Carby, "White Women Listen!" in *Materialist Feminism: A Reader in Class, Difference, and Women's Lives*, ed. Rosemary Hennessy and Chrys Ingraham (New York: Routledge, 1997), 110–28; Diana Fuss, *Essentially Speaking: Feminism, Nature and Difference* (New York: Routledge, 1989); Elizabeth V. Spelman, *Inessential Woman: Problems of Exclusion in Feminist Thought* (Boston: Beacon Press, 1989); and Gayatri Chakravorty Spivak, "Can the Subaltern Speak?" in *Marxism and the Interpretation of Culture*, ed. Cary Nelson and Lawrence Grossberg (Urbana: University of Illinois Press, 1988), 271–313.

9.   See Jane Roland Martin, "Methodological Essentialism, False Difference, and Other Dangerous Traps," *Signs: Journal of Women in Culture and Society* 19, no. 3 (1994): 630–57.

10.   Chandra Mohanty, "Under Western Eyes: Feminist Scholarship and Colonial Discourse," in *Third World Women and the Politics of Feminism*, ed. Chandra Talpade Mohanty, Ann Russo, and Lourdes Torres (Bloomington: Indiana University Press, 1991).

11.   Philosophical disagreements between Nussbaum and Okin recently became more explicit. See Susan Moller Okin, "Poverty, Well-Being, and Gender: What Counts, Who's Heard?" *Philosophy & Public Affairs* 31, no. 3 (2003): 280–316; and Martha C. Nussbaum, "On

Hearing Women's Voices: A Reply to Susan Okin," *Philosophy & Public Affairs* 32, no. 2 (2004): 193–205.

12. Martha C. Nussbaum, "Human Functioning and Social Justice: In Defense of Aristotelian Essentialism," *Political Theory* 20, no. 2 (1992): 204.

13. Sen's concept of capabilities was designed in part to address the problem of adaptive preferences; he illustrated this problem by reference to Indian widows, who had learned to disregard their deprivation and bad health. See Amartya Sen, "Gender Inequality and Theories of Justice," in *Women, Culture and Development: A Study of Human Capabilities*, ed. Martha C. Nussbaum and Jonathan Glover (New York: Oxford University Press, 1995).

14. In defending the universality of the capabilities, Nussbaum's earlier work appealed to the Aristotelian method of critically refining the *eudoxa*, or reliable beliefs. Martha C. Nussbaum, "Public Philosophy and International Feminism," *Ethics* 108 (July 1998): 768. More recently, Nussbaum has developed a "non-Platonist substantive good" approach that allows her to postulate the capabilities as universal values even in the absence of expressed consensus. See Martha C. Nussbaum, *Women and Human Development: The Capabilities Approach* (Cambridge: Cambridge University Press, 2000). For critical discussion of this method, see Alison M. Jaggar, "Reasoning About Well-Being: Nussbaum's Methods of Justifying the Capabilities," *Journal of Political Philosophy* 14, no. 4 (2006): 301–22.

15. Susan Moller Okin, *Justice, Gender, and the Family* (New York: Basic Books, 1989).

16. Susan Moller Okin, "Gender Inequality and Cultural Differences," *Political Theory* 22, no. 1 (1994): 8.

17. Unlike Nussbaum, however, Okin argues against the essentialists that sexism can indeed be separated analytically from other categories of oppression, using empirical data to show that attention to gender is comparatively new to justice theories and development studies—and that it matters.

18. Will Kymlicka, *Multicultural Citizenship: A Liberal Theory of Minority Rights* (New York: Oxford University Press, 1995).

19. Susan Moller Okin, "Feminism and Multiculturalism: Some Tensions," *Ethics* 108 (July 1998): 661–684; and Susan Moller Okin, *Is Multiculturalism Bad for Women?* ed. Joshua Cohen, Matthew Howard, and Martha C. Nussbaum (Princeton, NJ: Princeton University Press, 1999).

20. Okin, *Is Multiculturalism Bad for Women?* 13.

21. Ibid., 20.

22. Cheshire Calhoun, "Justice, Care, Gender Bias," *Journal of Philosophy* 85, no. 9 (1988): 451–63.

23. Both Nussbaum and Okin identify their topics as philosophical problems about culture, specifically cultural relativism and multiculturalism. The term "culture" is also prominent in the titles of their writings about poor women in poor countries; one of Nussbaum's books is titled *Women, Culture, and Development*, and Okin's article analyzing the problems of poor women in poor countries is titled "Gender Inequality and Cultural Differences."

24. Martha Chen, "A Matter of Survival: Women's Right to Employment in India and Bangladesh," in *Women, Culture, and Development*, ed. Nussbaum and Glover. Martha Nussbaum regards Chen's study as evidence of the need for her universal capabilities approach ("Human Capabilities, Female Human Beings," *Women, Culture, and Development*, 62). Okin refers to Chen's work as evidence for her claims about cultural injustice to women (*Is Multiculturalism Bad for Women?* 15).

25. Raymond Williams, *Keywords: A Vocabulary of Culture and Society* (London: Fontana, 1983), 160.

26.   John Tomlinson, *Cultural Imperialism: A Critical Introduction* (Baltimore: Johns Hopkins University Press, 1991), 5.

27.   Ibid.

28.   Nancy Fraser, "From Redistribution to Recognition? Dilemmas of Justice in a 'Postsocialist' Age," in *Justice Interruptus: Critical Reflections on the "Postsocialist" Condition* (New York: Routledge, 1997).

29.   Bhikhu Parekh, *Rethinking Multiculturalism: Cultural Diversity and Political Theory* (Cambridge, MA: Harvard University Press, 2000), 264–65.

30.   Okin, *Is Multiculturalism Bad for Women?* 12–13.

31.   Parekh, *Rethinking Multiculturalism*, 265.

32.   Okin, *Is Multiculturalism Bad for Women?* 13.

33.   Seyla Benhabib, *The Claims of Culture: Equality and Diversity in the Global Era* (Princeton, NJ: Princeton University Press, 2002), 84.

34.   Amartya Sen, "More Than 100 Million Women Are Missing," *New York Review of Books* 37, no. 20 (1990): 61–66.

35.   Ayelet Shachar, "The Paradox of Multicultural Vulnerability: Individual Rights, Identity Groups, and the State," in *Multicultural Questions*, ed. Christian Joppke and Steven Lukes (New York: Oxford University Press, 1999); Ayelet Shachar, "On Citizenship and Multicultural Vulnerability," *Political Theory* 28 (2000): 64–89; and Ayelet Shachar, "The Puzzle of Interlocking Power Hierarchies: Sharing the Pieces of Jurisdictional Authority," *Harvard Civil Rights–Civil Liberties Law Review* 35, no. 2 (2000): 387–426.

36.   UN Dept. of Public Information, "The Feminization of Poverty," May 2000, www .un.org/womenwatch/daw/followup/session/presskit/fs1.htm

37.   Reema Nanavaty, "Making the Poor Women Reach Markets: SEWA's Journey" (Ahmedabad, India: SEWA, 2000); available via www.sewaresearch.org/books2.htm.

38.   UNIFEM, *Progress of the World's Women 2000* (New York: UNIFEM, 2000), 31.

39.   See, e.g., "Dumping Without Borders: How US Agricultural Policies Are Destroying the Livelihoods of Mexican Corn Farmers," Oxfam Briefing Paper, August 2003, www.oxfam .org/en/policy/briefingpapers/bp50_corn_dumping.pdf; and "Stop the Dumping: How EU Agricultural Subsidies Are Damaging Livelihoods in the Developing World," Oxfam Briefing Paper, October 2002, www.oxfam.org/en/files/pp020111_Stop_the_Dumping.pdf.

40.   The higher incidence of HIV among people living in the developing world has special significance for women's health, because women comprise a higher percentage of adults living with HIV/AIDS in these areas than they do in the wealthy countries. In sub-Saharan Africa, women account for 55 percent of all new cases of HIV. See Danielle Nierenberg, "What's Good for Women Is Good for the World," World Summit Policy Briefs (Washington, DC: Worldwatch Institute, 2002).

41.   Lourdes Beneria, *Gender, Development, and Globalization: Economics as if All People Mattered* (New York: Routledge, 2003), 78.

42.   Naila Kabeer, *Reversed Realities: Gender Hierarchies in Development Thought* (New York: Verso, 1994).

43.   See, e.g., UNRISD, *Gender Equality: Striving for Justice in an Unequal World* (Geneva: UNRISD, 2005), 46.

44.   Somewhat similarly, critics of recent Western-planned development projects have argued that these projects have often reinforced the subordination of women. See Esther Boserup, *Women's Role in Economic Development* (New York: St. Martin's Press, 1970); Kabeer, *Reversed Realities*; Nalini Visvanathan, "Introduction to Part I," in *The Women, Gender, and Development Reader*, ed. Nalini Visvanathan et al. (London: Zed Books, 1997).

45.   Veena Talwar Oldenburg, *Dowry Murder: The Imperial Origins of a Cultural Crime* (New York: Oxford University Press, 2002).

46.   Dallas L. Browne, "Christian Missionaries, Western Feminists, and the Kikuyu Clitoridectomy Controversy," in *The Politics of Culture*, ed. Brett Williams (Washington, DC: Smithsonian Institution Press, 1991), 262.

47.   Uma Narayan, *Dislocating Cultures: Identities, Traditions, and Third World Feminism* (New York: Routledge, 1997), 65.

48.   Leslye Amede Obiora, "Feminism, Globalization and Culture: After Beijing," *Journal of Global Legal Studies* 4 (1997): 355–406.

49.   Leti Volpp, "Feminism versus Multiculturalism," *Columbia Law Review* 101, no. 5 (2001): 1205, n. 108.

50.   Ibid.

51.   Greg Bearup, "Afghan Schoolgirls Poisoned," *Guardian Weekly*, May 6–12, 2004.

52.   Lauren Sandler, "Women Under Siege," *Nation*, December 29, 2003.

53.   Uma Narayan, "Essence of Culture and a Sense of History: A Feminist Critique of Cultural Essentialism," *Hypatia* 13, no. 2 (1998): 86–106.

54.   Bridget Anderson, *Doing the Dirty Work? The Global Politics of Domestic Labour* (London: Zed Books, 2000).

55.   Gita Sen and Caren Grown, *Development, Crises, and Alternative Visions: Third World Women's Perspectives* (New York: Monthly Review Press, 1987); Caroline O. N. Moser, "Gender Planning in the Third World: Meeting Practical and Strategic Needs," in *Gender and International Relations*, ed. Rebecca Grant and Kathleen Newland (Bloomington: Indiana University Press, 1991); and Kabeer, *Reversed Realities*.

56.   Hye-Ryung Kang, "Transnational Women's Collectivities as Agents of Global Justice Claims" (paper presented at the American Philosophical Association Pacific Division Meeting, March 2004).

57.   Okin, "Gender Inequality and Cultural Differences," 13.

58.   Ibid., 15.

59.   Narayan, *Dislocating Cultures*, 15.

60.   Ibid., 85.

61.   Ibid., 84–85.

62.   Inderpal Grewal and Caren Kaplan, *Scattered Hegemonies: Postmodernity and Transnational Feminist Practices* (Minneapolis: University of Minnesota Press, 1994), 24.

63.   Parekh, *Rethinking Multiculturalism*, 268–70.

64.   Leila Ahmed, "Western Ethnocentrism and Perceptions of the Harem," *Feminist Studies* 8 (1982): 530–34.

65.   Okin, *Is Multiculturalism Bad for Women?* 117.

66.   Narayan, *Dislocating Cultures*, 57, 59–60.

67.   Thomas Pogge, *World Poverty and Human Rights: Cosmopolitan Responsibilities and Reforms* (Cambridge: Polity Press, 2002), 153.

68.   Noleen Heyzer, "A Women's Development Agenda for the 21st Century," in *A Commitment to the World's Women*, ed. Noleen Heyzer (New York: United Nations, 1995), 47.

69.   Onora O'Neill, *Towards Justice and Virtue: A Constructive Account of Practical Reasoning* (Cambridge: Cambridge University Press, 1996).

70.   Parekh, *Rethinking Multiculturalism*; and Benhabib, *The Claims of Culture*. Fifteen years ago, Nussbaum and Sen already challenged sharp dichotomies between "internal" and "external" social criticism, noting the existence of extensive cross-cultural linkages. See Martha C. Nussbaum and Amartya Sen, "Internal Criticism and Indian Rationalist Traditions,"

in *Relativism: Interpretation and Confrontation*, ed. Michael Krausz (Notre Dame, IN: University of Notre Dame Press, 1989).

71. The institutions that govern the global economy are formally democratic, but in practice they are heavily influenced by a small group of wealthy countries. At both the World Bank and IMF, the number of votes a country receives is based on how much funding it gives the institution, so rich countries have disproportionate voting power. Each has about 150 members, with a Board of Executive Directors with twenty-four members. Five of these directors are appointed by five powerful countries: the United States, United Kingdom, France, Germany, and Japan. The president of the World Bank is elected by the board and traditionally nominated by the U.S. representative, while the managing director of the IMF is traditionally from the EU. The WTO is also formally democratic in that each of its member countries has one representative who participates in negotiations over trade rules, but democracy within the WTO is limited in practice in many ways. Wealthy countries have far more influence than poor ones, and numerous meetings are restricted to the G-7, the most powerful member countries, excluding the less powerful even when decisions directly affect them.

72. V. Spike Peterson and Anne Sisson Runyan, *Global Gender Issues* (Boulder, CO: Westview Press, 1999), 120.

73. Richard F. Grimett, "Conventional Arms Transfers to Developing Nations, 1996–2003" (Washington, DC: Congressional Research Service, 2004), 82. India and Pakistan are among the poorest of all countries, but India is the fifth largest importer of major conventional weapons, while Pakistan is the twelfth. Farrukh Saleem points out, "When the poverty-ridden East fills [the] West's craving for drugs, there is talk of 'supply control.' [However], the West remains . . . the largest seller of arms to the East." "Why Are We Poor?" *News International* (Pakistan), January 12, 2003.

74. Saundra Sturdevant, "Who Benefits? U.S. Military, Prostitution, and Base Conversion," in *Frontline Feminisms: Women, War, and Resistance*, ed. Marguerite R. Waller and Jennifer Rycenga (New York: Routledge, 2001).

75. In addition to the considerations mentioned earlier, women suffer most from militarism's environmental destruction and its promotion of a sexist and violent culture in which men are glorified as warriors while women are either degraded or portrayed as national resources. Rape is a traditional weapon of war, and military activity is usually associated with organized and sometimes forced prostitution.

76. Kalpana Mehta observes that, in India, "NGOs could be said to be running a parallel government in the country, with priorities determined abroad and with no accountability to the people." Quoted in Jael Silliman, "Expanding Civil Society, Shrinking Political Spaces: The Case of Women's Nongovernmental Organizations," in *Dangerous Intersections: Feminist Perspectives on Population, Environment, and Development*, ed. Jael Silliman and Ynestra King (Cambridge, MA: South End Press, 1999).

77. Nira Yuval-Davis, *Gender and Nation* (London: Sage Publications, 1997), 120–121. Western feminists may also support transnational feminist networks, such as the Latin American and Caribbean Women's Health Network, Women Living Under Muslim Laws, and ABANTU for Development. See Margaret E. Keck and Kathryn Sikkink, "Transnational Networks on Violence against Women," in *Activists Beyond Borders: Advocacy Networks in International Politics* (Ithaca, NY: Cornell University Press, 1998); and Christina Ewig, "The Strengths and Limits of the NGO Women's Movement Model: Shaping Nicaragua's Democratic Institutions," *Latin American Research Review* 34, no. 3 (1999): 83.

78. Spivak, "Can the Subaltern Speak?" 296.

79.   Imam and Medar-Gould, "Please Stop the International Amina Lawal Protest Letter Campaigns."

80.   Benjamin Barber, "Jihad vs. McWorld," *Atlantic Monthly* (March 1992): 53–63; and Samuel Huntington, *The Clash of Civilizations and the Remaking of World Order* (New York: Simon & Schuster, 1996).

81.   Nussbaum is one philosopher who is explicit about this. See, e.g., Nussbaum, *Women and Human Development.* That academic writing does indeed have an influence outside academia is shown by politically motivated attacks on ethnic and feminist studies, as well as more recent attacks on postcolonial and Middle Eastern studies.

82.   Linda Martine Alcoff, "The Problem of Speaking for Others," *Cultural Critique* (Winter 1991/92): 5–32.

83.   Katha Pollitt, "As Miss World Turns," *Nation*, December 15, 2002.

84.   A recent letter to the *Colorado Daily* stated, "First, we need a five year moratorium on all immigration into this country to give us a 'collective break' from the onslaught of foreign languages, diseases being imported, female genital mutilation practiced by Middle Eastern and African muslim immigrants that is barbaric." Frosty Wooldridge, Letter to the Editor, *Colorado Daily*, November 18, 2003.

85.   Amos and Parmar, "Challenging Imperial Feminism," 11.

86.   "The State of the Union," *New York Times*, January 20, 2002; and "Mrs. Bush Discusses Status of Afghan Women at UN," March 8, 2002, www.whitehouse.gov/news/releases/2002/03/20020308-2.html.

87.   UNDP, Human Development Report 2000: Human Rights and Human Development (New York: Oxford University Press, 2000), 185.

88.   Pogge, *World Poverty and Human Rights*, 114.

89.   Leti Volpp, "Blaming Culture for Bad Behavior," *Yale Journal of Law and Humanities* 12 (2000): 89–116. Charles L. Briggs and Carla Mantini-Briggs, in "'Bad Mothers' and the Threat to Civil Society: Race, Cultural Reasoning and the Institutionalization of Social Inequality in a Venezuelan Infanticide Trial," *Law and Social Inquiry* 25 (2000): 299–302, describe Venezuelan public health officials blaming cultural practices for high morbidity and mortality from cholera, thereby deflecting charges of institutional corruption, inefficiency, indifference, and genocide.

90.   Hussaina Abdullah, "Wifeism and Activism: The Nigerian Women's Movement," in *The Challenge of Local Feminisms: Women's Movements in Global Perspective*, ed. Amrita Basu (Boulder, CO: Westview Press, 1995).

91.   Sola Adebayo, "N-Delta Women Give Shell 10-Day Ultimatum on Demands," *Vanguard* (Lagos), November 14, 2002, www.allafrica.com/sustainable/stories/200211150838.html.

92.   "We demand the right to choose and struggle around the issue of family oppression ourselves, within our communities . . . without white feminists making judgments as to the oppressive nature of arranged marriages." See Amos and Parmar, "Challenging Imperial Feminism," 15.

Chapter 11

Who Should Get In?

The Ethics of Immigration Admissions

Joseph H. Carens

How SHOULD THE IMMIGRATION POLICIES of liberal democratic states be constrained, even when one assumes a broad sovereign right to control immigration? One might want to challenge the claim that states are generally entitled to control immigration, and I have done this elsewhere.[1] Nevertheless, since this entitlement is generally recognized in the practice of the international system and reflects moral views that are widely held by people in Western states, it is important to explore what can be said about the ethics of admissions without challenging it.

The conventional view is that acceptance of the state's broad general right to control immigration means that morality has little role to play with regard to admissions. As Michael Walzer, the most well-known defender of the conventional view, puts it, "The distribution of membership is not pervasively subject to the constraints of justice. Across a considerable range of the decisions that are made, states are simply free to take in strangers (or not)."[2] In practice, however, liberal democratic states do not treat their admissions decisions as morally unfettered. Many options that might seem attractive from a self-interested or even a majoritarian perspective are ruled out of bounds on moral grounds. Even a minimalist account of the moral limits widely accepted by liberal democratic states imposes much greater restrictions on the states' discretion with regard to immigration than the conventional view allows.

My goal here is to identify the norms and principles embedded in the immigration practices of liberal democratic states and reflect critically upon them. This is an immanent critique of immigration, rather than a foundationalist one. The idea is not to try to deduce principles for immigration from some general theory of justice, but instead plunge in medias res, exploring the connections of moral constraints on admissions to other familiar and widely accepted moral views. It is deliberately minimalist, in the sense of trying to appeal to moral views that are widely shared, not just in the United States but throughout North

America and across Europe. This does not mean that one cannot criticize particular practices or policies. But I will not attempt here to develop a more radical challenge to prevailing norms. I want only to show that, whatever moral limits ought to be placed on immigration policy, they ought at least to include the ones identified here, and that these are much more extensive than the conventional view would acknowledge.

One might object that control over immigration is so central to sovereignty that states must be permitted absolute discretion. To challenge a state's policies is to call the whole system of state sovereignty into question. In a related vein, one might insist that political communities must be able to decide who will be admitted and who will not because the determination of political membership is at the core of democratic self-determination. These objections confuse process and substance. There is a distinction between the question of who ought to have the power to make a decision and the question of whether the decision is right. It may be true that no international body ought to try to interfere with a state's immigration policies, but it does not follow that those policies cannot be subject to criticism, even external criticism, especially when the critics appeal to broad moral principles that the states themselves endorse.[3]

OBLIGATORY ADMISSIONS

It is common to hear people say that states are morally free to exclude whomever they choose. In fact, all liberal democratic states recognize moral obligations to admit noncitizens in two categories: the immediate family of current citizens and residents and refugees claiming asylum. Consider the former first. Even states that do not see themselves as countries of immigration admit people for purposes of joining immediate members of their family. It is particularly striking that states permit family reunification not only for citizens but also for noncitizen residents. For example, while many states in Europe ceased recruiting guest workers in the early 1970s and attempted to restrict other avenues of immigration, they continued to admit spouses and minor children of those who were already there. Why? After all, the families could have been reunited if the guest workers had gone home, as they were being encouraged to do. And for the most part these new admissions were not perceived as economically advantageous and were not politically popular. States did this nevertheless because they felt a moral obligation, sometimes acknowledged by government officials and sometimes pressed by court rulings about the implications of deep constitutional commitments. Indeed this right to bring in family members was and is often recognized even when the people bringing their families in do not have permanent resident status, so long as they are legally present for an extended period, for example as students, visiting professionals, or visiting workers. In states like Australia, Canada, and the United States that do see themselves as countries of immigration, acceptance of an immigrant normally entails acceptance of his or her immediate family for admission as well.

So liberal democratic states act as though they have a moral obligation to permit family reunification, even when they do not think it is in their interest to do so. How should this self-imposed requirement to permit family reunification be morally evaluated?[4] It must be kept in mind that family reunification is primarily about the moral claims of insiders, not outsiders. The state's obligation to admit outside family members is derived not so much from the claims of those seeking to enter as the claims of those they seek to join: citizens, residents, or others who have been admitted for an extended period. In a world of vast inequalities, many people would like access to rich liberal democratic states, but relatively few obtain it. If the comparison were simply between the relative moral urgency of claims put forward by outsiders seeking to join family members already inside and outsiders seeking to enter for other reasons, such as needy people seeking a chance at a better life, it is not obvious that the claims for family reunification would always be stronger. But I have already assumed that the state has a basic right to control entry. So, it is not a question here of a cosmopolitan challenge to the state's control over admissions but rather of the responsibilities of liberal democratic states toward those whom they govern. Even if it is assumed that liberal democratic states have very limited obligations toward outsiders, they do have an obligation to take the vital interests of their own members into account.

People clearly have a deep and vital interest in being able to live with their immediate family members. Peter Meilaender, who is generally a defender of the state's discretionary control over immigration, argues that this control is rightly limited by the claims of family:

> "We are bound to our family members through a more richly complex web of relationships, a mixture of love and dependence, than we share with any other people. These relationships give rise to especially intense feelings of mutual affection and concern. To deprive someone of these relationships is to deprive him of his richest and most significant bonds with other human beings. That is something we should do only in rare circumstances."[5]

Why must this interest in family life be met by admitting the family members? Could it not be satisfied just as well by the departure of the family members to join those abroad, assuming that the state where the other family members reside would permit this? Why is the state obliged to shape its admissions policies to suit the locational preferences of individuals?

In addition to their interest in family life, people also have a deep and vital interest in being able to continue living in a society where they have settled and sunk roots. Of course, people sometimes have good reasons of their own to leave and sometimes face circumstances that require them to make painful choices. If two people from different countries fall in love, for instance, they cannot both live in their home countries and live together. So, people must be free to leave. But no one should be forced by the state to choose between home and family. Whatever the state's general interest in controlling immigration, that interest cannot plausibly be construed to require a complete ban on the admission of noncitizens and cannot normally be sufficient to justify restrictions on family reunification. The qualifier "normally" is necessary because even basic rights are rarely absolute, and the right to family reunification cannot be conceived as absolute. States do not have an obligation to admit people whom they regard as a threat to national security, for example, even if they are family members. But the right of people to live with their family clearly sets a moral limit to the state's right simply to set its admissions policy as it chooses. Some special justification is needed to override the claim to family reunification, not merely the usual calculation of state interests.

So far the term "family" has been treated as though it were unproblematic, but the question of who should count as an immediate family member varies in practice and can be contested at the level of principle. For example, should it include people who are not legally married but have long-standing intimate relationships or common-law marriages? For some of those in such relationships, such as same-sex partners, marriage may not be a legal option, but being able to live with their partner may be just as vital and deep an interest for them as it is for people who are married. Some states recognize these relationships for purposes of family reunification, while others do not. What about multiple spouses, in practice, multiple wives, from polygamous relationships that are legally authorized in the country of origin but forbidden in the receiving country? France used to recognize polygamous marriages contracted before the date of immigration for purposes of family reunification but no longer does so, and most or all other states in Europe and North America refuse to recognize them. What about former spouses who share parenting responsibilities? In some cultures relatives who are not the biological parents may have roles and responsibilities comparable to those normally undertaken by parents in Europe and North America. Should these relationships entitle them to bring in children for whom they are responsible? Most states resist extending the rights of family reunification to either of these two categories of persons, although some make exceptions for special circumstances. For example a grandparent might be able to bring in a grandchild whose parents have died. Minor children clearly qualify for family reunification, but children who have already grown to adulthood usually do not. Some states permit adults to bring in their parents, and permission to do so becomes more likely if the parents are elderly, dependent, or without other children outside the destination country. On the other hand, almost no state pays attention to cultural differences between groups that may affect the character of the relationship between adult children and their parents.

All of these examples reflect a tension between an approach to the definition of family that is open to analogies, cultural variability, and functional equivalents and an approach that is fixed and relies on criteria from the dominant culture. The former leads to a more expansive definition and the latter to a more restrictive one. The merits of the alternative approaches are intimately connected to contemporary debates over multiculturalism, the neutrality of the state, and the moral relevance of minority cultures. From a minimalist perspective, no matter how narrowly one draws the category of family for admissions purposes, it clearly must include a spouse and minor children.

Liberal democratic states generally acknowledge the claims of family reunification, although some limit these claims or undermine them in ways that are morally problematic. For example, the United States gives a higher priority to citizens than to noncitizen residents with regard to the admission of spouses and minor children and even sets a numerical limit on the number of noncitizen immediate family members who are permitted to come.[6] Given the importance of family reunification, numerical limits on the entry of immediate family members are not morally defensible, and criteria that discriminate against noncitizen residents are even worse.

Often the obstacles to family reunification are not formal but administrative and procedural, which creates unjust practices even though the policy is formally just. In Canada, for example, there are frequent complaints that people with spouses and children in some areas of the world, such as South Asia, have to wait years for permission for their family members to immigrate because there is a huge backlog of applications. States have a moral obligation not only to respect the right of family reunification in principle but also to develop administrative procedures that ensure that the right will be substantive.

Another ethical problem arises in the ways that some states try to prevent the abuse of the right of family reunification. For many people, admission to the states of Europe and North America is a scarce and valuable opportunity. Since the ways to obtain admission are limited, some inevitably try to take advantage of points of access to which they are not entitled. Some people enter sham marriages with citizens or residents with whom they neither have nor aspire to have any intimate connection, simply for the sake of gaining admittance. If the state has the right to control immigration, it is clearly entitled to take measures to prevent this form of fraud. It must do so, however, within reason and not as an excuse for denying entry to legitimate spouses. For example, until recently the United Kingdom pursued a policy of refusing admittance to people if the "primary purpose" of their marriage to a U.K. resident was to immigrate. It then put the burden of proof on those seeking family reunification to establish that immigration to the United Kingdom was not the purpose of the marriage, which was a difficult standard to meet. The upshot of this policy was that the right of family reunification in the United Kingdom was more secure for EU citizens who were not British than for the British themselves because the claims of the former to family reunification were governed by EU law.[7] This sort of policy fails to respect the legitimate right of residents to family reunification. The claim that such a policy merely prevents fraudulent marriages is a thin disguise for an attempt to prevent an immigration flow that is politically unpopular but grounded in claims of justice.

REFUGEES

From the perspective of justice and immigration, one of the key issues is how to assess the ethical questions raised by people claiming to be refugees and seeking to immigrate for that reason. Remember, however, that such persons constitute only a tiny fraction of the world refugee population. Focusing on refugees as potential immigrants to advanced industrial societies entails leaving to one side a much broader set of issues about the responsibilities of states for the problems created by forced migration.

There are two categories of people to be considered under the heading of refugees. First are those who have been determined to be refugees by some formal process conducted by the UN High Commissioner for Refugees or a potential destination country and who are then selected for resettlement by that country. Here no question arises as to whether the people are really refugees. The questions are how many of them a state is obligated to admit and what criteria should be used in selecting them. The second category comprises people who arrive in one of the states of Europe or North America claiming to be refugees and asking for asylum. Here the first question is whether such people have a claim of justice to be admitted, even if they are acknowledged to be genuine refugees. If this question is answered affirmatively, one must ask who deserves to be classified as a refugee because states often deny admission to asylum claimants on the grounds that they are not genuine refugees, unlike the refugees seeking resettlement.

Resettlement

The number of refugees accepted for resettlement by liberal democratic states varies from country to country and year to year. Sweden and Canada have tended to take in the most on a per capita basis over the past few decades. In absolute numbers the United States generally accepts more than the rest of the world combined—averaging about 100,000 per year during the 1990s. States treat the admission of refugees for resettlement as entirely discretionary with regard to both the number accepted and the selection of particular individuals from among the much larger pool of refugees. This is not to say that there are no constraints, but rather that only the normal constraints that apply to discretionary admissions (for example, no use of racial criteria) apply. Canadian officials, for instance, use a points system to select for resettlement those refugees who they think are most likely to adapt successfully and contribute economically.

What should be made of this approach to resettlement from a moral perspective? On the one hand, the idea of choosing refugees for their economic potential strikes many people as perverse because refugees are in desperate need. On the other hand, people selected for resettlement have normally already found asylum outside their country, as a prerequisite to their being formally determined to be refugees.[8] For this reason, refugees awaiting or hoping for resettlement have escaped the immediate danger that caused them to become refugees, have some sort of safe haven, and cannot usually put forward a strong claim of justice to be admitted to a new country, given the background assumption of the right of states to control immigration. Thus, the argument for admitting refugees for resettlement is usually couched in humanitarian terms as something that is generous but not obligatory.

One minor qualification to this general picture is that states sometimes act as though they have a special obligation to admit particular groups of refugees when the state's own actions have contributed to the process by which the people have become refugees. For example, for a number of years after the end of the Vietnam War, the United States took in a very high number of refugees from Southeast Asia. Although the United States made no formal acknowledgment of any moral obligation to accept them, the public discussions surrounding the process made it clear that many Americans, opponents as well as supporters of the war, felt that acceptance of these refugees was a residual moral obligation from American involvement in the war that led to their displacement.

Asylum

Under the 1951 Geneva Convention Relating to the Status of Refugees and its 1967 Protocol, which all the states of Europe and North America have signed, people who arrive in a state and claim to be refugees must be given a fair hearing to determine whether they are in fact refugees and, if they are, must be permitted to stay. What is striking about this requirement is that it limits the normal right of the state to control the entry and term of residence of noncitizens. Legally this obligation derives from the decision by states to sign the Geneva Convention, but what about morally? Is it just a self-imposed limitation or does this reflect a deeper moral obligation toward those seeking asylum?

One of the puzzles here is why the obligations of states toward asylum seekers should be so much stronger than their obligation toward refugees seeking resettlement. Critics of contemporary asylum policies sometimes note that asylum seekers tend not to come from the worst off among the world's refugees. Refugees who arrive via asylum are more likely to be adult, male, well educated, and wealthy than the refugee population as a whole. It takes resources and knowledge for people to find their way to North America or Europe to make their claims. So from a moral perspective it can seem odd to give this subset among the world's refugees a stronger moral claim to entry.[9]

What gives asylum seekers a vital moral claim, however, is the fact that their arrival involves the state directly and immediately on their fate. It is one thing to leave someone languishing in a refugee camp, quite another to send a person back to the country of origin to be tortured or killed. Leaving people in refugee camps rather than offering them entry is not so different from leaving people in the living conditions of many countries rather than offering them entry. There are good reasons to criticize the injustice of a world order that permits such vast disparities in the life chances of people in different countries and allows so many to live their lives in desperate poverty, regardless of how one accounts for the causes of these conditions. In such a context, not offering entry to as many immigrants as possible may indeed be morally problematic. But if the state's general right to control immigration is taken as given, then leaving people in refugee camps once they have a safe haven does not violate any moral obligations.

By contrast if asylum seekers are denied entry and sent back, the state is directly involved in what happens to them. Those seeking to harm them could not do so if the destination state did not return them. That means that the moral responsibility for what happens to them is greater. Some would object that this argument rests upon a problematic distinction between acts and omissions.[10] But the distinction is not as flawed as some critics claim. We are indeed as responsible for the consequences of some of our omissions as for the consequences of our actions, but it is implausible to suppose that we should be held responsible for the consequences of every possible course of action that we do not pursue. What is required is a contextual account of responsibility. The degree of our responsibility depends both upon the ways in which our acts are connected to outcomes and upon the institutional contexts of our actions. Refusal of entry to a refugee seeking asylum leads directly to his or her suffering, whereas the refugee seeking resettlement is already safe.[11] So, the legal obligation of the Geneva Convention is not purely contingent but instead is grounded in a deep moral obligation that states have toward asylum seekers.

There can be no single bright line dividing those who deserve asylum from those who do not. There is instead a continuum of cases. At one end, with the strongest moral claim to asylum, stand those who suffer persecution, sometimes life-threatening persecution, from an oppressive regime. European Jews fleeing from Nazi Germany are the archetype of the genuine refugee. The tragic and shameful failure of many countries, including Canada and the United States, to accept Jews seeking asylum in the late 1930s and even the 1940s remains a vivid memory today and provides much of the moral impetus for the maintenance of a refugee regime that includes the right to asylum as one of its components.[12] At the other end, with no moral right to entry, are people who claim to be refugees but who face no real dangers at home. They want to improve their economic opportunities by migrating to advanced industrial states and use the filing of an asylum claim as a way of getting a foot in the door. Most asylum claimants are probably somewhere in between, having mixed motives for their flight and facing varying degrees of risk.

In deciding who will receive asylum and who will not, the destination countries have to construct categories that draw a line across this continuum.[13] Wherever that line is drawn, the cases of those just on one side of the line, who barely qualify as refugees, will resemble the cases of those just on the other side, who barely do not qualify, a lot more than either resembles the cases of people at the ends. That is inevitable, but we need to keep it in mind because even with the best possible definition and the best possible system for determining who fits under the definition, many of those who fail to gain recognition will be people who had some good reason to file a claim. Every refugee determination system, no matter how good, will have complex legal features that make the interpretation and application of the criteria to particular cases contestable and uncertain. So we should not assume that all failed claimants are acting in bad faith.

According to the Geneva Convention, a refugee is any person who, "owing to a well-founded fear of being persecuted for reasons of race, religion, nationality, membership of a particular social group or political opinion, is outside the country of his nationality and is unable to or, owing to such fear, unwilling to avail himself of the protection of that country. . . ." Almost every word in this definition is subject to interpretation and contestation. For example, what counts as a well-founded fear? Are the subjective feelings of the refugee claimant relevant or only the conditions in the country of origin? Must there be evidence that the claimant has been personally targeted for persecution, or is it sufficient if others similarly situated have been? To qualify as a refugee, is it necessary for the government itself to engage in persecution or is it sufficient if the government fails to prevent persecution by others, such as "private" death squads? What counts as "membership in a particular social group" for purposes of gaining refugee status? What harms are serious enough to qualify as persecution?

In practice each state has to implement the Geneva Convention through its own internal legislation, which means that it has to adopt the definition, sometimes in modified form, and then interpret and apply it through its own legal procedures. Some states adopt a much broader interpretation than others. A number of scholars have criticized the convention definition on the grounds that it focuses too narrowly on targeted political threats as opposed to other dangers to human well-being that are even greater and against which the state of origin provides little or no protection.[14] From a moral perspective, the great weakness of the definition is that it can be construed so narrowly that it excludes people from refugee status who clearly have fled in fear of their lives and need external assistance. For example, under many interpretations, people fleeing a violent civil war do not qualify as refugees under the convention, even if the war itself is profoundly marked by religious and ethnic conflict. Thus, people fleeing the war in Bosnia were often denied formal refugee status in Europe under the convention. From a moral perspective, what should matter the most is the seriousness of the danger and the extent of the risk, not the source of the threat or the motivation behind it. So, in principle, the definition should be revised to reflect this wider perspective. In practice, however, any attempt to modify the definition would be a mistake because, in the current political climate, any change would almost certainly lead to a contraction, not an expansion, of those covered.

DISCRETIONARY ADMISSIONS

The duties to admit immediate family members and refugees who come as asylum claimants are the only moral obligations that require people to be admitted by virtue of falling into particular categories, but they do not exhaust the ways in which immigration policies are morally constrained. How do liberal democratic states behave toward potential immigrants whom the state has no special obligation to admit, and how should they behave?

States' policies toward this sort of immigration vary widely. Some states, like Canada, Australia, and the United States, consider themselves to be countries of immigration. They expect to admit new immigrants every year, and they have policies and administrative arrangements in place designed to regulate this flow. Other states, like many of those in Europe, do not see themselves as countries of immigration. Even though they may feel obligated to take in some immigrants, perhaps even a substantial number, for reasons of family reunification and shelter of refugees, they try not to take in any immigrants whom they are not obliged to admit. Still other states fall somewhere in between, admitting a limited number beyond their obligations for specific purposes. Given the background assumption of this essay, states clearly are morally free to take in as many or as few of these immigrants as they choose. However, they are not morally free to use whatever criteria they want in deciding which ones to admit.

Some people may object to the use of any criteria whatsoever in deciding whom to admit, on the grounds that these criteria are inevitably discriminatory. In this view, states are entitled to set numerical limits but not otherwise to distinguish among those seeking entry. This is far too broad a constraint, however. In one sense of the term, it is true that any criterion of selection discriminates against those who do not have it, and any criterion of exclusion against those who do. But this merely uses the term "discrimination" to mean nonrandom choice. There are many areas of society quite apart from immigration in which there are more applicants than spaces, and we choose among applicants on the basis of criteria. Consider admission to universities or hiring for jobs. In these cases, we often select among applicants on the basis of some criteria that we regard as relevant to the position being filled; we do not reject all criteria and insist on a random selection process. Some criteria are regarded as morally permissible, such as test scores and grades, and others as morally impermissible, such as race, gender, or religion. So, the real question is what forms of discrimination (using the term in a broad sense) are morally acceptable, or, to put it another way, what forms of choosing are discriminatory (using the term in a narrow sense to refer to morally objectionable forms of choosing).

In choosing among potential immigrants whom they are not obliged to admit, what may states take into account? One may distinguish between criteria of exclusion and criteria of selection. The former are used to identify people who will not be admitted, the latter to choose who among those eligible for admission will be taken in.

Criteria of Exclusion

All states use some sort of security screen, denying admission to people perceived to be threats to national security. There is nothing problematic about this in principle; it reflects an important public interest. No state is obliged to admit saboteurs or subversives. In practice, of course, national security may be defined too broadly or interpreted too expansively, as was the case in the United States at the height of the Cold War. In the wake of September 11 a concern for national security has clearly become much more central to discussions of immigration in the United States, even though the perpetrators themselves were present as visitors rather than immigrants. Some people, including me, believe that the United States risks returning to the exclusionary excesses of the Cold War or has already done so, while others think it has not yet gone far enough in excluding threats to national security, but I cannot pursue this issue further here.

States also often prohibit people with significant criminal records from entering. There is obviously a public interest here, although the concern is public safety and the maintenance of law and order rather than national security. Again, use of this criterion is not unreasonable, so long as some attention is paid to context. For example, some states may use the criminal law to repress political dissent, and liberal states should be wary about reinforcing that practice by refusing admission to those so convicted.

If some criteria of exclusion are clearly morally permissible, others are just as clearly morally impermissible. No state may legitimately exclude potential immigrants on the basis of race, religion, or ethnicity. This is not just a hypothetical point. Canada, the United States, and Australia all used explicitly racial criteria to exclude potential immigrants in the past. The role of such criteria was not officially eliminated until the 1960s, and one can hear voices today advocating a return to such policies.[15] In the nineteenth century the immigration of Catholics and Jews was often portrayed as a dangerous threat to American society in language that was remarkably similar to the language used today to construct Muslim immigrants as threats to liberal democracy in Europe and

North America. Yet no plausible interpretation of liberal democratic principles is compatible with the exclusion of people on such grounds, and no liberal democratic state uses such criteria for exclusion today.

To this list of morally impermissible criteria should be added sexual orientation. For many years, homosexuality was grounds for declaring potential immigrants inadmissible to the United States. This is incompatible with respect for human freedom and human dignity. As with the case of race and religion, the use of homosexuality as a criterion of exclusion reflects deeply rooted prejudices that cannot be defended publicly as rationally related to the common good.

Two commonly used criteria of exclusion are more ambiguous: financial need and medical conditions. States like Canada and the United States that take in large numbers of immigrants routinely screen applicants for admission to determine whether they will be able to support themselves financially. If the immigrants have been selected because of their economic potential, this is not an issue, but many immigrants are admitted primarily because of their family connections. States often require domestic sponsors—people already in the country who can demonstrate that they have adequate economic resources for themselves and who will promise to support the immigrants if necessary so that they will not become dependent on the state's social welfare system. In practice, these guarantees have proven very difficult to enforce, but potential immigrants who cannot find domestic sponsors may not be accepted, even though they otherwise would be. Similarly, states often screen potential immigrants who have passed some preliminary hurdles to determine whether they suffer from illnesses, such as contagious diseases like tuberculosis or communicable ones like AIDS, that might harm the health of the existing population, or whether they have medical conditions, such as kidney disease requiring dialysis or a transplant, that might put unusually high demands upon the health care system.

Are these grounds for exclusion morally permissible? Let us distinguish first between objections to particular applications of this principle and objections to the principle itself. Sometimes people object that these sorts of criteria are being applied inappropriately or arbitrarily. For example, AIDS activists have objected that the risks of contracting HIV from someone who has AIDS are much smaller than the risks of contracting other equally dangerous diseases that are not seen as grounds for exclusion. Or people may object that the authorities are wrong to assume that a particular medical condition, such as a physical disability, creates a likelihood that the person affected will have unusually high medical costs compared with a range of other conditions that are not treated as grounds for exclusion. Although these immigrants have no specific moral claim to admittance, they still have a right to be treated fairly and not to be subject to a stigmatizing form of discrimination. That is why race, religion, and ethnicity cannot be used as criteria of exclusion. So, to the extent that the choice of these medical conditions as grounds for exclusion reflects popular prejudice and uninformed fear rather than a reasonable calculation of risks or burdens, those excluded on this basis have good grounds to complain that they are not being treated fairly.

What about the general principle, as opposed to its application to particular conditions? This involves giving decisive weight to the risks and burdens of those in the destination state in making decisions about whom not to admit, from a pool of applicants among whom none is morally entitled to be admitted. The use of such criteria is morally permissible because there is an important public interest at stake, and paying attention to this interest violates no moral claims that the applicants have. These considerations would not be sufficient to justify the exclusion of immediate family members or refugees seeking asylum, however. Because of the obligations to admit people in these categories, the justification for exclusion ought to pass a much higher threshold, such as a genuine threat to national security. In practice, however, states do employ both financial criteria and medical conditions as justifications for excluding immediate family members.

Criteria of Selection

Many with no moral entitlement to admission seek to enter, but few are chosen. What criteria do states use and what should they use in selecting these relative few? States often use family relationships, economic potential, cultural affinities, and ethnic ties in selecting among potential immigrants. "Family relationships" means connections to people who are already living in the destination society, whether citizens or not, but not connections that qualify the applicants for admission under the principle of family reunification. What counts as a close enough relationship to gain admission varies somewhat from one state to another, but typical examples would be siblings, grandparents, cousins, aunts, and uncles. Some states give no weight to these relationships in their admission policies, while others, like Canada, give them a little consideration, and still others, like the United States, give them quite a bit of emphasis. All of these approaches are morally permissible. This is an area in which states are morally free to exercise their discretion. Current members of a society do not have a vital enough interest in these secondary family ties for states to have a moral obligation to admit such family members. On the other hand, a state may decide that these less intimate connections will play a positive role in its admissions decisions perhaps on the grounds that it is easier for those with such connections to adjust to living in a new society or because the connections matter to people who are already members of the community. States violate no norm of justice and no obligation to the pool of potential immigrants in taking these relationships into account.

For example, American immigration policy gives unusually heavy weight to these sorts of family connections. This preference has been criticized on a number of grounds. First, some object that the emphasis on family ties leads to a selection of immigrants who are less likely to succeed economically than would be the case if the selection process focused more directly on factors relevant to economic success, as in the Canadian system, which gives only a little weight to such family ties and emphasizes instead qualities like education, training, and knowledge of the dominant languages.[16] Whether Canada's selection process really generates a pool of immigrants more likely to adapt successfully is a contested point, but it does not raise any issues of justice. Even if the American policy were inefficient or unwise from certain perspectives, that would not make it unjust.

A second objection is that the American emphasis on family ties is unjust because it discriminates against those who do not have relatives in the United States and is intended to reproduce the existing racial and ethnic makeup of the country, which is unfair to minorities. This criticism is not ultimately persuasive, although it has some merit. Again, any criterion may be construed as discriminating against those who do not possess it. That is the point of having a criterion in the first place. The question is whether the criterion is arbitrary or otherwise morally objectionable. The use of secondary family ties is not arbitrary because there are reasons for using it related to assumptions about what is good for the existing community and its members. To say that it discriminates against those without relatives in the United States is to overlook that the potential immigrants have no claim to be admitted. To discriminate on the basis of family connections is not self-evidently objectionable in the way that discriminating on the basis of race would be. The only plausible moral objection then is that this criterion perpetuates the racial and ethnic status quo, intentionally or not, so that the family preferences are a disguised form of racial and ethnic discrimination.

There is something to this objection. From the 1920s to the 1960s American immigration policy had a "national origins" quota that tied the number of spaces available for immigrants from other countries to the proportion of people from those countries already in the United States. This was explicitly intended to restrict the flow of immigrants from outside Europe and to maintain the ethnic and racial composition of the United States. This was indeed a racist and unjust policy. It is also true that the replacement of this policy in the mid-1960s with one that abolished overt forms of racial discrimination and introduced the system of family preferences was defended by its proponents on the grounds that it would perpetuate the patterns of the old policy without employing their explicitly invidious categories. So it may be right to condemn the intentions behind the policy as unjust. The policy did not work as intended, however, because relatively few people from Europe wanted to immigrate. So, the policy of family preferences gave rise to a pattern of chain migration in which the overwhelming proportion of new immigrants during the past three decades has come from Asia and Latin America. Indeed this is precisely what those who are opposed to the increasing ethnic and cultural diversity in the

United States object to in the current policy.[17] It is hard to maintain that the policy should be seen as unjustly discriminating on the basis of race and ethnicity.

A second commonly used criterion of selection is the immigrant's potential economic contribution. For example, the Canadian immigration process assesses potential immigrants in a complex calculation that gives weight to a number of factors, many of which, such as age, education, and work experience, are assumed to be indicators of the immigrant's potential for economic success in Canada. The United States also relies upon an assessment of economic potential in its selection of immigrants who do not have family ties. A number of European countries that have traditionally not had any formal programs for recruiting immigrants have begun to consider recruitment on this basis. As a general matter, this is another criterion that seems morally permissible. To be sure, the destination country is not acting altruistically in adopting this sort of immigration policy. It is selecting immigrants on the basis of its perception of the national interest. But since the country is morally free not to take any immigrants at all from the pool under consideration here, the fact that it is guided by its own interest in its selection of some for admission cannot be a decisive objection. Of course, states are equally free to adopt a more generous policy, taking in those whom they judge to be in greatest need. That is an admirable course, but it is not morally obligatory, given the initial assumption of this essay.

Sometimes immigrants are admitted because they possess particular skills that are in short supply in the domestic labor market, such as computer programming, or are willing to do certain kinds of work that local workers are unwilling to undertake, such as live-in caretaking. When immigrants are selected not for their general capacities but because of the specific labor needs of the destination country, their admission is often restricted in order to ensure that they really do perform these tasks, especially if the tasks are considered undesirable from the immigrant's perspective. The admission may be limited in duration as well. These sorts of restrictions create a clear gap between the rights of immigrants admitted conditionally and other members of civil society, including immigrants who are permanent residents. For that reason some people regard any such restrictions as deeply morally problematic. In my view, however, such arrangements are morally permissible, so long as they are strictly limited with regard to time and so long as the conditions imposed are reasonable. The time must be limited because the longer people stay and work in a society, the stronger their claims become to be treated equally. This is surely the lesson to be drawn from the European experience with guest workers in the 1960s and 1970s. The guest workers had been told from the outset that they could not stay permanently and had agreed to come under those terms. If consent were all that mattered, this should have made it legitimate to send them back when economic conditions changed and they were no longer needed. But the European states were unable to do this. In the face of their obvious deep connections to the places where they had moved, the original terms of admission had become irrelevant. As time passes, temporary residents are entitled to become permanent ones.

These restrictions on the kind of work that temporary workers do and where they do it are closely connected to the underlying rationale for having temporary workers in the first place—the need for a certain kind of labor in certain areas. One could not eliminate the restrictions altogether without eliminating the basic idea of temporary admissions. As I noted, some might think that is what justice requires. In my view, however, the restrictions are permissible, so long as they are not more restrictive than is necessary for the economic function.[18] Perhaps the greatest danger is that the unique restrictions that temporary workers face render them much more vulnerable to mistreatment by their employers than are ordinary workers, whatever the similarity of their formal legal rights. The risk is probably greatest when their permission to enter and work is limited to one particular employer rather than to a type of work, but even in the latter case their status renders them vulnerable.

A third criterion that is sometimes used in the selection of immigrants is cultural affinity. For example, Canada's system of selecting immigrants gives weight not only to economic potential but also to knowledge of Canada's official languages, English and French. The rationale behind this practice is that knowledge of the dominant language will facilitate economic and social integration. This is a reasonable view, well supported by empirical evidence. Moreover, knowledge of English and French is something that anyone can acquire and is not a covert marker of racial, ethnic, or religious identity. So, there is no reason for objecting to the use of linguistic competence as one factor in the selection of immigrants.

There are other aspects of culture whose use in selection would be far more problematic, however. One that would clearly be morally impermissible would be religious affiliation. It might be useful to ask why that is so. After all, the cultures of all European and North American states are deeply shaped by the Christian tradition. Moreover, it would probably be accurate as an empirical matter to say that a significant proportion of the population in many of these states would find it easier to accept Christian immigrants, other things being equal, than Muslim ones. Indeed a whole discourse has arisen, especially in Europe, that constructs Muslim immigrants as cultural threats to the receiving society.[19] Yet, no state in Europe or North America could announce that it was going to give preference to Christian immigrants or disfavor Muslim ones in its selection processes. The use of religion as a criterion of selection would violate deep liberal democratic norms about religious freedom and religious toleration. What these norms require is often contested, of course, but it is hard to imagine any plausible interpretation of them that would be compatible with systematically favoring one religious group or disadvantaging another in the selection of immigrants.[20]

Another criterion of selection that is used by some states in selecting immigrants and that is often seen as closely related to culture is ethnicity. It is important to distinguish here between ethnicity and family ties. Family ties involve personal relationships of descent or marriage: aunts and uncles, nieces and nephews, cousins, and so on. By contrast, an ethnic connection is something more distant, stretching back over generations and involving no specific link to a particular individual in the receiving country. Potential immigrants with ethnic ties to the dominant group in the destination society are given preference in selection, in part on the grounds that the existing population will find it easier to accept their arrival, in part on the assumption that it will be easier for these immigrants to adapt. Sometimes fellow ethnics are favored not only in the initial admission decision but also in forms of social support and in access to citizenship. In the past, the United States and Canada had immigration policies favoring those with ethnic ties, and Germany, Italy, Japan, and a number of other states still do today. Indeed, it may be denied that fellow ethnics are really immigrants at all, as was the case with Germany's postwar *Aussiedler* policy.

The use of ethnicity as a basis for immigrant selection is deeply problematic, although it may sometimes be justifiable in special circumstances. To give preferential treatment to people with a certain ethnic background is to establish that ethnic group as having a privileged position in relation to the political community as a whole. It implicitly calls into question the status of members of the society who come from other ethnic groups, all the more so when it is ethnicity alone that is the crucial factor. Under its *Aussiedler* policy, for example, Germany gave extensive social support and easy access to citizenship to people whose ancestors had left Germany hundreds of years before and who sometimes spoke no German, while it effectively excluded from citizenship other people who had lived in Germany their entire lives, such as the descendants of Turkish guest workers.[21] These policies were widely criticized both inside and outside Germany as being incompatible with liberal democratic commitments because they identified the political community with an ethnic group. Any morally satisfactory conception of liberal democracy has to construct the demos, the people of the political community, in such a way as to include all of those who are subject to its political authority over the long term, and cannot create special access for those who share only an ethnic link but no substantive social ties to members of the dominant ethnic group.[22]

The only justification for using ethnicity as a criterion for the selection of immigrants is when that ethnic identity is connected to a disadvantage elsewhere in the world. In that respect, West Germany's *Aussiedler* policy had a more plausible justification in decades past than it does today. In the period following World War II, people of German descent in Eastern Europe and the Soviet Union were subject to discrimination and worse. In that context, it may have been reasonable to give special preference to them if they sought entry to Germany. That has ceased to be a plausible rationale since 1990. In fact, German policy implicitly recognizes the increasing difficulty of defending that policy in the current context. Germany now limits the number of *Aussiedler* admitted each year and will phase out this special admissions track in the next decade. Moreover, Germany now requires more evidence of cultural affinity such as knowledge of the German language from those who are admitted in this category, which serves in part to make this appear more like selection on the basis of cultural affinity, although the ethnic tie remains fundamental.[23]

ETHICAL CONSTRAINTS ON IMMIGRATION

Even if one accepts the widely accepted premise that states have a right to control immigration, there are still significant moral constraints on how that control may be exercised. States are morally obligated to admit refugees seeking asylum and also to admit the immediate family of people who are already citizens or established residents. Moreover, in deciding whom to admit on a discretionary basis, states should not discriminate for or against applicants on the basis of such criteria as race, ethnicity, and religion, even as a proxy for national security. These moral constraints are not merely a theorist's construction of the world as it ought to be. They are already widely, if imperfectly, reflected in the practices of most states in Europe and North America.

NOTES

This essay appeared in *Ethics & International Affairs* 17, no. 1 (2003): 95–110. I thank Christian Barry and two anonymous reviewers for comments that greatly improved the text. An earlier version appeared in Spanish as "Inmigración y justicia: ¿A quién dejamos pasar?" in *Isegoria* 26 (June 2002):27.

1.   See Joseph H. Carens, "Aliens and Citizens: The Case for Open Borders," *Review of Politics* 49, no. 2 (1987): 251–73; and Joseph H. Carens, "Migration and Morality: A Liberal Egalitarian Perspective," in *Free Movement: Ethical Issues in the Transnational Migration of People and of Money*, ed. Brian Barry and Robert E. Goodin (Hemel Hempstead, UK: Harvester Wheatsheaf, 1992).

2.   Michael Walzer, *Spheres of Justice: A Defense of Pluralism and Equality* (New York: Basic Books, 1984), 61.

3.   For attempts to shield states from external criticism of their immigration policies, see Walzer, *Spheres of Justice*; and Peter C. Meilaender, *Toward a Theory of Immigration* (New York: Palgrave Macmillan, 2001).

4.   It may no longer be purely self-imposed. Meilaender cites evidence in support of the view that there is actually an emerging norm in international law that requires this. See Meilaender, *Toward a Theory of Immigration*, 280–81. But even if this is a norm, it is one that has emerged from practice and so it does not really change the question in the text.

5.   Meilaender, *Toward a Theory of Immigration*, 182.

6.   Hiroshi Motomura, "The Family and Immigration: A Roadmap for the Ruritanian Lawmaker," in *Immigration Admissions: The Search for Workable Policies in Germany and the*

United States, ed. Kay Hailbronner, David Martin, and Hiroshi Motomura (Oxford: Bergh-ahn Books, 1997).

7. Christian Joppke, *Immigration and the Nation-State: The United States, Germany, and Great Britain* (New York: Oxford University Press, 2000).

8. This oversimplifies things a bit because in a few key source countries (Cuba, the former Soviet Union, Vietnam, Haiti in the early 1990s) the United States has set up a process for determining whether people would qualify as refugees and for accepting them for resettle-ment even before they have left their country of origin. Although such people do not techni-cally meet the Geneva Convention definition of a refugee (which must be someone outside his or her home country), both the United States and the countries of origin in which these programs have been established have found this a more orderly way to manage a refugee flow that they anticipate would otherwise occur in a clandestine fashion. However, the United States never treats these programs as policies that it is morally obliged to pursue and certainly never suggests that any particular refugee has a moral right to be admitted to the United States.

9. Peter Singer and Renata Singer, "The Ethics of Refugee Policy," in *Open Borders? Closed Societies? The Ethical and Political Issues*, ed. Mark Gibney (New York: Greenwood Press, 1988).

10. Ibid., 120.

11. For a fuller development of this argument, see Joseph H. Carens, "Refugees and the Limits of Obligation," *Public Affairs Quarterly* 6, no. 1 (1992): 31–44.

12. Irving Abella and Harold Troper, *None Is Too Many: Canada and the Jews of Europe, 1933–1948* (Toronto: Lester & Orpen Dennys, 1982).

13. It is possible to construct more than one category, of course. For example, one can give some refugee claimants a more limited form of protection than others. See Joseph H. Carens, "The Philosopher and the Policymaker: Two Perspectives on the Ethics of Immigra-tion with Special Attention to the Problem of Restricting Asylum," in *Immigration Admis-sions*, ed. Hailbronner, Martin, and Motomura. Adding categories does not change the fundamental problem raised by the need to draw lines across a continuum, however.

14. Andrew Shacknove, "Who Is a Refugee?" *Ethics* 95, no. 2 (1985): 274–84; Aristide R. Zolberg, Astri Suhrke, and Sergio Aguayo, *Escape from Violence: Conflict and the Refugee Crisis in the Developing World* (New York: Oxford University Press, 1989); and David Martin, "The Refugee Concept: On Definitions, Politics, and the Careful Use of a Scarce Resource," in *Refugee Policy: Canada and the United States*, ed. Howard Adelman (Toronto: York Lanes Press, 1991).

15. Peter Brimelow, *Alien Nation: Common Sense about America's Immigration Disaster* (New York: Random House, 1995).

16. George J. Borjas, *Friends or Strangers: The Impact of Immigration on the U.S. Economy* (New York: Basic Books, 1990); and George J. Borjas, *Heaven's Door: Immigration Policy and the American Economy* (Princeton, NJ: Princeton University Press, 1999).

17. Brimelow, *Alien Nation*.

18. Since the original publication of this essay, I have modified my view about the acceptability of this sort of constraint. See Joseph H. Carens, "Live-In Domestics, Seasonal Workers, and Others Hard to Locate on the Map of Democracy," *Journal of Political Philoso-phy* 16, no. 4 (2008): 419–45.

19. For a critique of that discourse, see Joseph H. Carens and Melissa S. Williams, "Mus-lim Minorities in Liberal Democracies: The Politics of Misrecognition," in *The Challenge of Diversity: Integration and Pluralism in Societies of Immigration*, ed. Rainer Bauböck, Agnes Heller, and Aristide R. Zolberg (Aldershot, UK: Avebury Press, 1996).

20.   Israel's Law of Return presents a special case here because it employs a criterion that might be regarded as a hybrid of ethnicity and religion. This case involves so many other complex and contested issues that I cannot pursue it here.

21.   Daniel Kanstroom, "Wer Sind Wir Wieder? Laws of Asylum, Immigration, and Citizenship in the Struggle for the Soul of the New Germany," *Yale Journal of International Law* 18 (Winter 1993): 155–211; and William Barbieri, *Ethics of Citizenship: Immigration and Group Rights in Germany* (Durham, NC: Duke University Press, 1998).

22.   Ruth Rubio-Marín, *Immigration as a Democratic Challenge: Citizenship and Inclusion in Germany and the United States* (Cambridge: Cambridge University Press, 2000).

23.   Kanstroom, "Wer Sind Wir Wieder?"

PART FOUR

~

Global Economic Justice

Has globalization gone too far, not far enough, or has it been heading in the wrong direction? To what extent is global poverty a harm inflicted by the global economy? Does economic globalization lift all boats, or is it a modern form of empire? Is *globalization* another word for Americanization? Are its characteristic interactions and institutions exploitative, and, if so, does this generate moral duties? Do well-off peoples have to give up advantages and luxuries for the benefit of the global poor? What practical challenges and constraints do states and individuals face in responding to their global moral duties?

Models of International Economic Justice

Ethan B. Kapstein

A HOST OF ACTIVISTS, policymakers, and scholars have been asserting that today's international economic structure and its associated outcomes are fundamentally unfair or unjust to many people, especially the poor or least advantaged, and also to many countries, particularly those in the developing world. By questioning the morality and legitimacy of the contemporary multilateral system that governs world trade and finance, these critics have generated a widespread normative debate. But what, precisely, do these critics mean when they claim that the global economy is unjust or unfair?

In this essay I present three models, or frameworks, that seek to capture some of the central normative concerns that these critics have expressed about economic globalization (at least in its present form) and the empirical information that is relevant to assessing them. Beyond offering what I hope is a helpful taxonomic contribution, my aim is to join economic and moral theory in a way that promotes a positive research program. Assertions about economic justice can and should be matched to the extent possible with economic theories and empirical evidence—but they seldom are.[1] Closer attention to empirical evidence is important for theory as much as for practice. As a practical matter, empirical tools and data can help us to determine whether the global economy is becoming more or less fair over time, and to focus on those policies that are most likely to promote desirable ends. Articulating and examining the likely consequences of different theoretical and policy approaches to economic justice also serve to highlight potential trade-offs and conflicts among them, and help us to think more carefully about these trade-offs and what their consequences might be. Some of us, for example, might support a liberal free trade regime because we believe it promotes greater income equality among countries. But we might also reasonably assert that such a regime exacerbates economic injustices within some countries by causing dislocation and unemployment, particularly among vulnerable socioeconomic groups such as unskilled workers. Such reasoning, in turn, will help us to evaluate the approaches themselves.

In tackling problems of international economic justice, both theoretical work and policy analysis might benefit from closer collaboration between economists and political philosophers.[2] To date, these two groups of scholars have worked largely in isolation from one another, developing their own models and analytical approaches. This has certainly enriched the literature, but some cross-fertilization could, perhaps, prove rewarding, by matching theory and data in a way that advances our knowledge of the current state of the global economy and its impact on different countries and groups within them. Public policy recommendations that are informed by such collaborative work are likely to prove better targeted and more feasible to achieve.

This essay does not pretend to provide a theory of international economic justice. Its analysis of different models of international economic justice and of some of the data that may be relevant to them will hopefully help to provide a foundation for further research. The feeling that "something is wrong" with the international economy is widespread, and bringing clarity to the normative debate over globalization is one of the major contributions that moral philosophy can make to contemporary world politics.

The essay is divided into three sections. In the first section I present three ideal-typical approaches to the issue of international economic justice.[3] In the second section, I indicate the kinds of economic models and data sets that are relevant to determining whether and to what extent greater openness to global trade poses a threat to economic justice as conceived by each of these approaches. Specifically, I use these analytical tools in order to relate changes in openness to foreign trade to other social and economic outcomes, particularly changes in income inequality and poverty, which have tended to draw the attention of nearly all theorists of economic justice. In the third section, I characterize and critique the approach to economic justice that has been (implicitly) adopted by the major international institutions like the World Bank, International Monetary Fund (IMF), and World Trade Organization (WTO). I conclude with some policy implications and suggestions for further research in the area of international economic justice.

Let me make two methodological caveats to what follows. First, some readers will undoubtedly question the use of world trade as a proxy variable for globalization. After all, a country could be relatively open to world trade yet not very globalized; examples might include Saudi Arabia or even China. Further, even if we narrowed our focus to economic globalization, some readers might rightfully argue that investment and capital flows are equally if not more powerful influences in social arrangements. These concerns are well founded, but there are nevertheless three advantages to focusing on the trade data: it is widely available; existing models point toward its inter- and intranational distributive effects; and liberalization of trade policy has been a core recommendation of the international financial institutions for many years now, with their leading researchers even using trade variables to distinguish "globalizers" from "nonglobalizers." Finally, the WTO and the regime it governs have come to exemplify for many critics much of what is wrong with today's global economy. Second, I also recognize that some readers might find the emphasis on income inequality and poverty too restrictive from an ethical standpoint. Indeed, a fuller assessment of the effects of globalization would of course also require a comprehensive examination of additional variables such as the distribution of health care, education, or other highly valued goods and services that influence human capabilities. In many respects, these variables might give us a more adequate picture of how the disadvantaged are faring in reality than do the income data. Despite the limitations of income as an indicator of well-being, however, I will nonetheless use it here since it has the advantage of being widely available and widely used in terms of models that are available for assessing the distributive effects of economic policy change.

INTERNATIONAL ECONOMIC JUSTICE: MODELS AND DATA

Economic or distributive justice is fundamentally concerned with the principles and rules that determine how societies allocate goods, services, and incomes, and the patterns of allocation that result from such procedures.[4] Among the central issues that arise in this arena are what should be distributed, who should be the recipients, and how the allocations should be accomplished.[5]

Since the time of Aristotle, writing on economic justice has generally focused on distributive issues within the context of polities that are assumed to be more or less self-sufficient. John Rawls, for example, famously advocated a conception of justice that holds that a society's institutional arrangements ought to be assessed in terms of the shares of "social primary goods" (for example, income and wealth, opportunities, and liberties) that they engender for their least-advantaged members. His "difference principle" asserts that economic institutions are unjust insofar as the shares of income and wealth received by the least advantaged are smaller than they would be under feasible alternatives.[6]

Despite the fact that states have long been "globalized," at least in terms of their economic relations, the question of international economic justice has only recently been taken up in scholarly research.[7] To date, the assertions about international economic justice—or injustice—that are found in the literature (and, indeed, on the streets!) have taken at least three ideal-typical forms (see table 12.1).

Some critics of today's global economic order are primarily concerned with the effects of greater openness on domestic social and economic arrangements. These critics endorse what I will call a communitarian model of economic justice. Questions that are relevant to communitarians include: How has greater openness influenced poverty and the income distribution within countries, and particularly within "my" country? Has it closed income gaps or widened them?

Table 12.1   Models of International Economic Justice

Data	Policy goal	Theory	Level of analysis
Changes in income distribution within countries	Flatter income distribution within countries	Communitarian	Nation-state
Changes in income distribution among countries	Income convergence among countries	Liberal internationalist	Society of states; multilateral institutions
Changes in poverty rates among people	Global poverty eradication	Cosmopolitan/priority	Individuals

Who are the "winners" and "losers" from globalization within domestic societies? Can the losers be fairly and effectively compensated? What are the effects of greater openness on domestic fiscal and social policies—such as the state's capacity to maintain redistributive policies? These questions reflect a concern with the effects of global economic pressures on domestic societies, and with the capacity of the state to respond in a manner that preserves domestic distributive justice.

A second group of critics, whom I will refer to as liberal internationalists, emphasizes the consequences of today's international economic structure for the peace, prosperity, and stability of the "society of states," or "international community," as a whole. Advocates of this model are particularly concerned with the effects of increasing globalization (at least in its current form) on the legitimacy and stability of the international order, and on what states can do individually and collectively in order to maintain and strengthen a peaceful and prosperous system of exchange. Questions that are relevant to liberal internationalists include: How has openness influenced income distribution among countries? Have the gains from trade benefited some economies more than others? How can trade, aid, and investment be used most effectively as vehicles for promoting economic development and income convergence among countries? Such questions reflect a concern that the current global economic structure or regime is tilted against certain countries, threatening the multilateral arrangements that have been negotiated.

The third group of critics is composed of cosmopolitans, whose concern is with the effects of the prevailing international economic structure on the well-being of persons. In discussing this model, I will focus more narrowly on "prioritarian" cosmopolitans, who are particularly concerned with the effects of the international economic order on the poor and disadvantaged. Cosmopolitans of this type hold that global economic arrangements should be reformed so that they no longer bring about or permit such significant shortfalls from minimally adequate living conditions for so many people.[8] Questions that follow from this perspective include: Do contemporary international economic arrangements promote or harm the life chances of those who are most vulnerable, particularly the poor in developing countries, relative to feasible alternative arrangements? How can the international economic structure be reformed to meet the basic needs of the poor and least advantaged?

Common to all three of these approaches is a concern with the articulation and effects of the multilateral rules and procedures that govern international transactions. Is the existing set of international rules fair to all? Do these rules make for a level international playing field, or are they somehow "rigged" against certain countries or groups of persons? Indeed, if there is growing convergence among the different schools of thought with respect to where our policy attention ought to be focused, it is probably on the political structure of multilateral governance, which, it is argued, privileges the interests of rich and powerful states and the business interests within them, and perhaps the elites in developing countries as well. I will return to this point in the conclusion. Finally, these three models are not meant to be mutually exclusive. Most people give some weight to the central principles of each.

In order to examine whether criticisms of today's global economy by proponents of these three approaches are well founded, theories and data that relate changes in greater openness to trade to changes in poverty and income distribution within and among countries provide a useful starting point.[9]

THE COMMUNITARIAN MODEL GLOBALIZATION AND THE DOMESTIC SOCIAL IMPACT

The communitarian approach to international economic justice emphasizes the effects of greater openness on domestic social and economic arrangements. In this model, countries globalize in order to generate greater wealth, which is then distributed in a manner consistent with the domestic social compact. John Ruggie's "bargain of embedded liberalism"—the phrase he used to describe the postwar Bretton Woods order—offers perhaps the neatest expression of this position.[10] According to Ruggie, the challenge for the postwar leaders was to rebuild a global economy that would be consistent with welfare-state policies in Western Europe and North America. A dense network of domestic and international arrangements was crafted in order to ensure that global trade and investment did not undermine but rather promoted the goals of nationally based social policies, such as full employment and equal opportunity. Thus, international trade agreements included "escape clauses" to protect workers, and particular sectors such as agriculture were exempted from trade rules altogether. At the same time, the United States and other countries put into place "trade adjustment assistance" and other compensatory mechanisms to support those who were hurt by economic change. In short, greater openness was meant to be consistent with and to reinforce the domestic social compact. For a while, many had some reason to remain confident in this model. The increase in global trade after the World War II, for example, was accompanied by the wholesale expansion of the welfare state, at least throughout the industrial world.

It is the fear that rapid globalization is disrupting domestic distributive justice that has sparked an intensive research agenda in recent years on the relationship between such variables as greater openness on the one hand and changes in poverty and income inequality on the other.[11] In an important review of the literature, for example, William Cline has argued that greater openness to trade has contributed to an increase in wage inequality in the United States. While certainly not the sole determinant of rising inequality (technological change and immigration are also prominent factors), trade is responsible for perhaps 25 percent of the change in earnings. He argues that the "basic policy conclusion" stemming from his analysis "is that a commitment to open trade needs to go hand in hand with a commitment to a whole array of *domestic policies* that help ensure that society evolves in an equitable rather than an inequitable direction."[12] As noted above, those policies, at the limit, could exempt certain sectors of the economy from globalization altogether. Because countries will often not adopt these policies, greater openness may often undermine domestic distributive justice.

Communitarian critiques rest comfortably on mainstream economic theory in important respects. Economists commonly hold that "countries shape their own destiny," and endogenous growth theory emphasizes the role of domestic policy choices in promoting investment and creating human capital. From this standpoint, globalization offers states tremendous opportunities to increase their technological base through trade and foreign direct investment, and in turn improves their chances for sustained growth. Yet some of those opportunities might best be seized in the context of domestic measures that promote, say, "infant industries," such as the United States or Germany did in the nineteenth century and as China is doing today. One question that communitarians pose is whether today's "rules-based" international economic regime is making it much more difficult for states to pursue such growth-promoting domestic policies, and whether the advanced industrial states are using those rules to hinder the growth prospects of developing countries. Furthermore, mainstream economic theory recognizes that globalization can undermine domestic wage structures and income levels, and thus pose an obstacle to countries that wish to ensure distributive justice domestically. The most prominent theoretical framework for analyzing the distributive effects of free trade within a country is provided by the Heckscher-Ohlin-Samuelson (HOS) model, which elegantly explains trade patterns in terms of the relative abundance of the factors of production (land, labor, and capital) within countries. Simply stated, countries with a relative abundance of labor will produce and export labor-intensive goods, while countries that are relatively capital-abundant will export capital-intensive goods and import labor-intensive products (thus, Sweden sells machinery to China and, in return, buys textiles). While such trade will promote greater efficiency in all participating economies, it will have significant effects on the incomes of each of the factors of production as well. Because of that, the present rules-based international trade regime can limit the ability of states to respond to those effects in a manner consistent with domestic distributive justice.

It is worth emphasizing that, for labor-abundant developing countries, HOS offers a promising theoretical result: with greater openness, there will be an increase in the price of those products manufactured by relatively abundant, unskilled labor, and a consequent rise in the real wage for unskilled workers. To the extent that unskilled labor in developing countries comes from the lower income deciles, openness promises an increase in these workers' wages. Indeed, the data suggest that, across a panel of developing countries, greater openness (defined as trade as a share of Gross Domestic Product [GDP]) is associated with higher incomes for the poor in absolute (but not relative) terms.[13]

The flip side of this story from the communitarian perspective is that trade can reduce the incomes of the working poor in industrial countries, who become displaced by cheap imports of manufactured goods, textiles, and other commodities. Increased immigration from poor countries can also have this effect. Indeed, it is for this reason that many communitarians are comfortable with strict limits on immigration.

In short, communitarians have expressed justified concern with the effects of greater openness to trade on the capacities of domestic societies to provide adequate economic opportunities for unskilled workers and the poor. As we have seen, greater openness does hold the promise of higher incomes for unskilled workers in developing countries. But this is so only if we assume that industrial nations are open to their exports, and that domestic labor market regulations enable workers to profit from the fruit of their labor. For the poor and the unskilled in rich countries, in contrast, even the potential benefits of globalization are less obvious. For while they may benefit from lower consumer prices, they may also experience falling wages and the costs from the erosion of other labor market institutions such as unions and collective bargaining arrangements. Communitarian critics, then, have a sound basis for questioning whether the present international economic order is just according to their model.

A LIBERAL INTERNATIONALIST MODEL INTERNATIONAL TRADE AND THE PROMISE OF ECONOMIC CONVERGENCE

To simplify a complex tradition, liberal internationalists hold that something like a states system—nowadays popularly referred to as the "international community"—has evolved over time, with its members, the states, gradually assuming rights and obligations with respect to a set of generally agreed-upon principles, norms, and rules. The fundamental norm that regulates the international community is respect for state sovereignty and, consequently, there is a right to noninterference in domestic affairs. These principles imply that a primary concern of justice in this model is the equality in the status of states as members in the international system, and they provide the basis not only for international negotiations and agreements but for world order more generally. According to liberal internationalists, these principles are vital, even if adherence to them is often halfhearted and inconsistent. Indeed, they have shaped the normative domain of world politics in significant ways and provide the basis for the articulation of an increasing number of rules and ever-deeper interactions, including those associated with the global economy.[14]

The international trade regime, for instance, represents an agreement among states to trade with one another on the basis of most-favored nation status, and to negotiate trade deals on the basis of reciprocity. Liberal internationalists therefore tend to conceive of economic justice in terms of mutually advantageous and noncoercive agreements reached by the "society of states." The ethical problem that these states face is how to construct and maintain economic arrangements that contribute to public goods such as peace, prosperity, and stability that benefit every member of the international community. One might reasonably assert that the international community has adopted (rhetorically if not always in practice) a variant of the liberal internationalist approach to economic justice since the end of World War II: that is, a model of justice that has rested upon a combination of trade and aid. Liberal internationalists do not, of course, hold that today's economic arrangements among states actually reflect their ideal-type. As Dani Rodrik reminds us, "Global economic rules are not written by Platonic rulers . . . those who have power get more out of the system than those who do not."[15] Indeed, it is understanding and criticizing the exploitative use of international power that is the central normative concern of most liberal internationalist thinkers.

Charles Beitz has presented the deepest philosophical critique of our present international economic order from a liberal internationalist perspective.[16] Like other liberal internationalists, Beitz represents the international system as a society of states whose representatives are tasked to establish a set of just principles that are to serve as the basis for the political and economic arrangements that are to govern their interactions. By applying certain aspects of Rawls's conception of domestic justice to world politics, and to the international economy more specifically, however, he arrives at some fairly radical results.

Drawing on Rawls's characterization of the "original position," Beitz has us imagine a group of representatives from rich and poor countries who are bargaining over the terms of their interactions. Since they are negotiating from behind a "veil of ignorance," unaware of their particular resource endowments, Beitz assumes that each negotiator would be risk averse and thus fearful about

their particular condition. He posits that "not knowing the resource endowments of their own societies . . . they would agree on a resource redistribution
principle. . . ."[17] The resource redistribution principle is Beitz's rough analogue
to the Rawlsian difference principle, preserving the background justice of the
international economic order.

A state's initial economic condition qua resource endowment will significantly shape its future development. And since states have no prior moral claim
to the resources located on their territory, patterns of inequality and poverty
that result from an international system that fails to incorporate a resource
redistribution principle will be unjust.

It may be argued, however, that a resource redistribution mechanism is not
necessary for preserving the justice of the international economy because free
trade provides an alternative mechanism for overcoming initial resource inequalities. This claim is based on the thesis of economic convergence. Most
countries are abundant in certain factors of production relative to other countries. China, for example, is relatively abundant in labor compared to the United
States, but the United States is relatively abundant in capital or land as compared to China. The theory of economic convergence has been a staple of the
international trade and development literatures for most of the postwar era.
Because international trade makes it possible for developing countries to import
technologies that would allow them to have a higher rate of growth than developed countries, they are expected eventually to "catch up" and reach the
income level of richer countries. Liberal internationalists, it might therefore be
argued, should support a free trade regime because openness leads toward long-
run income convergence with regions that are initially wealthier. Indeed, from
this perspective, free trade may be viewed as the solution to international economic justice, for the very reason that it promises long-run convergence and
the provision of important global public goods.

Unfortunately, as Jeffrey Sachs and Andrew Warner report, the evidence to
date has dashed any theoretical expectations that conditional convergence
would take place. They write that 'in recent decades there has been no overall
tendency for the poorer countries to catch up, or converge, with the richer
countries."[18] According to them, at least part of the blame rests with rich industrial states that have failed to open their markets in a way that would promote
the development and growth of the poorest countries.

Might it be argued that developing countries as a group have failed to converge with their industrial counterparts, but that those among them with open
economies have done better than those with closed? What is the relationship
between openness and growth? While these questions remain hotly contested
among economists, the evidence that is now available only weakly supports the
contention that openness leads to sustained growth.[19] Indeed, the failure of
developing countries to converge more rapidly with industrial ones remains
among the chief puzzles now being addressed by development economists. For

these reasons, liberal internationalists are justified in remaining skeptical that the international economic order is just according to their model.

A COSMOPOLITAN MODEL BRINGING JUSTICE TO THE GLOBAL POOR

For cosmopolitan theorists, international economic justice must be assessed in terms of its effects on individual persons. Prioritarian cosmopolitans hold that we must give special consideration to the interests of persons who are very badly off. The question that prioritarian cosmopolitans pose of modern globalization concerns the effects of the rules structuring the world economy on the poor and least advantaged. Thomas Pogge, for example, has recently argued that "the affluent countries and their citizens . . . impose a global economic order under which millions avoidably die each year from poverty-related causes."[20] This global order and its associated rules influence poverty levels within nations as well as the domestic income distribution—for example, by rewarding domestic elites in developing countries who help multinational firms to gain market access.

It must be emphasized that cosmopolitans take seriously in a way that others do not the problem of state failure and also unjust states. While recognizing that states could serve the cosmopolitan end of a social arrangement in which each individual is treated equally or fairly, they also accept that many governments around the world lack the will or capability to provide for the basic needs of their citizens, especially those who, due to income, gender, race, religion, or other factors, are most vulnerable. Cosmopolitans simply reject the notion that the bad luck of certain persons to find themselves locked up in states that deny basic human rights is reason enough for those of us who are fortunate to turn our backs on their plight. As a consequence, "cosmopolitans . . . have argued that efforts to secure justice should focus on the reform of social arrangements beyond the nation state."[21]

What kinds of models and data are helpful in assessing the effects of global arrangements on the poor and least advantaged? Disentangling international and domestic effects is a difficult exercise. However, two ways of doing so were suggested in the earlier sections of this essay: the HOS framework that examines the distributive effects of free trade, and the convergence models that posit a relationship between openness and growth (with the underlying assumption being that growth benefits the poor). A third and more direct approach would be to follow Pogge's lead and examine the effects of a given set of international rules on the poor in developing countries, who by any plausible measure would qualify as the world's least-advantaged persons. One might start this assessment with focusing more narrowly on the rural poor, who are often among the very poorest in developing countries. Thus, we might ask with greater precision: What are the effects of global trade rules on the incomes of the rural poor?

To begin our assessment of multilateral trade rules from this perspective we might wish to examine the actual structure of international tariff and nontariff measures and see if we can detect some pattern with respect to their incidence. Recent studies of the international trade regime, for example, find that the "tariffs used by industrial nations bear more heavily on products of export interest to developing countries than on imports from other industrial nations."[22] Further, tariff protection on labor-intensive products in which developing countries have an advantage remains high—for example, "applied tariffs on textiles and clothing are three times the average in manufacturing." Overall, products subject to high tariffs in the industrial world represent more than 11 percent of developing country exports to those markets. In addition, according to a recent report prepared by the IMF and World Bank, "agricultural subsidies in industrial countries undermine developing countries' agricultural sectors and exports by depressing world prices and pre-empting markets."[23] Thus, it is unskilled labor and the rural poor in developing countries that face relatively high tariff barriers, which limit the incomes they can expect to receive from world trade.

Let us look more specifically at the case of tariff escalation against developing countries, where tariffs increase with value added. The average, post–Uruguay Round tariff on industrial raw materials is negligible, less than 1 percent. But tariffs on finished industrial products jump to 6.2 percent. With respect to natural resource–based products, the tariff on raw materials is 2 percent, jumping to 5.9 percent for finished products.[24] As the IMF and World Bank conclude, tariff escalation is frequently aimed at "products in which many developing countries have comparative advantage."[25]

It should be noted that one "source" of this unfairness in the international trade rules is structural. Trade policy is typically shaped by the mercantilist preferences of vote-maximizing political leaders, who seek the maximum amount of openness abroad in return for the minimum amount of openness at home so that both export-oriented and import-sensitive domestic sectors are satisfied. In practice trade opening tends to be negotiated on the basis of reciprocity, whereby the European Union opens itself to $1 billion of American exports if the United States agrees to do the same. Given the reciprocal nature of bargaining in the WTO, it is difficult for small, developing countries to have much voice in the proceedings, since neither the United States nor the European Union has much interest in accessing their markets. As a consequence, they have nothing to bargain in exchange for greater access to the American or European agricultural markets. These structural problems in the rules and procedures associated with the trade regime generate economic patterns that are widely held to be unjust to poor countries and especially poor persons residing within them.

The prioritarian cosmopolitan view of international economic justice poses a profound set of both theoretical and policy challenges. While not denying the roles and responsibilities of national elites in extracting rents from their societies and oppressing the poor, this position forces us to ask whether the international arrangements we have shaped actually help or hinder the life chances of the world's most vulnerable citizens.[26] As we have seen, there is good reason to believe that the current structure of the international trade regime, to provide just one prominent example, is tilted in important respects against the interests of the rural poor. A more detailed empirical examination would undoubtedly uncover other examples that show that international trade and financial agreements often favor certain groups over others. In these important senses, cosmopolitans should hold that the global economy is unjust according to their model.

FROM THEORY TO POLICY ECONOMIC JUSTICE AND THE INTERNATIONAL SYSTEM

The purpose of this section is to characterize and assess some of the ways in which the major international financial institutions, the World Bank and IMF, conceive of the problem of economic justice at the present time. This does not mean, of course, that either the Bank or Fund seek to defend their policies and programs explicitly on the basis of any particular theory of justice; instead, the point of this exercise is to explore the implicit theories of economic justice that seem to play some role in shaping their behavior, while recognizing that concepts of social or economic justice are not mentioned as explicit goals on the agendas of international trade and financial institutions (although, as a result of nongovernmental organizations' campaigns for economic justice, "justice" has been frequently invoked in policy discourse during the Doha Development Round of the WTO).

The World Bank and IMF seem to be adopting what might be called a "quasi-prioritarian" approach to international economic justice, prioritizing the eradication of global poverty as a direct policy objective.[27] As the World Bank puts it, "Poverty reduction is the most urgent task facing humanity today."[28] More laconically, the IMF has reported that "the September 1999 Annual Meetings [of the World Bank and IMF] resulted in a clear mandate for the IMF to integrate the objectives of poverty reduction and growth more fully into its operations . . . and to base these operations on national poverty reduction strategies."[29] In short, the IMF is now expected by its member states to be "more pro-poor."[30]

The underlying argument is that rich polities have a duty to assist the least-advantaged countries so that they may help their least-advantaged persons. What should we make of such an approach to international economic justice? The first question concerns the agents of the alleged injustice according to this view. It seems, at first glance, that there are two. First, there are national systems of welfare, which have failed to make adequate transfers to the poor or provide sufficient opportunities (educational and otherwise) to them. Second, there is the society of states, which has failed to meet its collective responsibility by failing to provide transfers that are adequate for meeting the basic needs of the poor. It is important to appreciate the institutional significance of this "new" approach to multilateral assistance. When poor countries come to the IMF for aid, they are now required to present "poverty reduction" strategies as a condition for fresh loans. Programs supported under the Poverty Reduction and Growth Facility (PRGF)—the IMF's low-interest lending facility for low-income countries—seek to increase the amount of public spending than would normally be the case under typical IMF conditionality clauses, so long as such higher spending results in an increase in expenditures that are deemed to be "pro-poor." Working with the World Bank and bilateral donors, the IMF's hope is that the increased public spending called for by the PRGF will be supported by foreign assistance, although the Fund now accepts "higher spending . . . when a shortfall in assistance materializes."[31]

The particular expenditures that are deemed pro-poor include those in education and health care. According to the Fund, "Countries with PRGF-supported programs are allocating more to education and health care, as a percent of GDP, as a share of total government spending, and in per capita terms."[32] It should be emphasized, however, that the Fund admits that its capacity to monitor whether these additional expenditures are really pro-poor must be improved, and this requires more sophisticated "poverty and social impact analysis." Additional spending for education, for example, could be diverted to privileged bureaucrats rather than to poor children.

But let us put that possibility aside and suppose that the PRGF is used efficiently and effectively. The underlying assumption of the quasi-prioritarian approach then must be that national welfare systems have failed only because they face a budget constraint that is inadequate to provide for the needs of their citizens.[33] Because government funds are inadequate, those with sufficient personal means are able to privatize certain services, such as health care and education, while those in the lowest income brackets receive little if any public benefit. Given the suffering thus produced as a result of inadequate government funding of the kinds of services that are now widely viewed as "rights," the society of states therefore has the duty to provide the additional funds needed to alleviate the human suffering entailed by the lack of domestic budget capacity.

Of the three models outlined in the previous section, cosmopolitans who hold the prioritarian view would likely have the greatest sympathy with the pro-poor approach being taken by the multilateral institutions at the present time.[34] Communitarian theorists would likely question the desirability and feasibility of allowing international financial institutions to play such an influential role in shaping the domestic order of different societies. Liberal internationalists, too, might be uncomfortable with the degree of intervention in domestic affairs implied by the pro-poor approach of the World Bank and IMF, with its endless reporting requirements and demands for particular budgetary allocations. Liberal internationalists tend to view economic justice in terms of relations among states, and while foreign aid might well play a critical role in international economic justice, the use of that aid should generally be left to the government in question.

But the quasi-prioritarian position of the Bank and Fund does raise the intriguing possibility that cosmopolitan theories are having greater influence than was true earlier in the postwar period, when "duties of assistance" were clearly to other states—especially those that were deemed important to the Cold War struggle—as opposed to particular groups within them. Perhaps this shift is due to the spread of liberal democratic values, with their emphasis on the individual's worth. Pursuing the normative sources of this new development framework would provide a useful exercise in analyzing how the international community builds, in practice, its approach to economic justice. At the same time, careful assessments of the lending programs of the World Bank and IMF are required in order to learn if they really are "pro-poor," as advertised, or whether this is simply rhetoric.

CONCLUSION

One of the major issues that must be faced in developing a sound conception of international economic justice is the conflicts and trade-offs among the various ideal-typical approaches that I have described in this essay. Imagine, for example, a world in which globalization makes it more difficult (for example, because of capital flight) for states to craft the kinds of compensatory policies that William Cline and others have argued are necessary if free trade is to be considered equitable or legitimate by domestic societies. In that case, governments may seek to maintain the social compact at home through policies—such as protectionism—that have adverse effects abroad. These conflicts and trade-offs between domestic and international economic justice cannot be easily resolved.

But despite the presence of such tensions in the global economy, we have also seen that scholars of international economic justice share a common concern regarding the effects of the current rules that govern world trade, finance, and investment. A promising starting point for a progressive research agenda, therefore, might be found in an analysis of the current normative structure of the leading international financial and economic institutions. And in recent years, that has become the focus of increasing attention from economists and political philosophers alike. If we are to promote a progressive research agenda, surely more analysis is needed of the multilateral institutions that play such a large role in shaping international economic transactions and, increasingly, domestic economic policies as well—the WTO, IMF, and World Bank, to name the most prominent. How should these organizations be assessed from the perspective of international economic justice? Is the system of weighted voting, as found within the IMF, consistent with justice? Can and should the structure of multi-lateral trade negotiations, which are based on the principle of reciprocity, be reformed in order to give more voice to developing countries? These questions indicate an intellectual and practical challenge of great urgency.

NOTES

This essay appeared in *Ethics & International Affairs* 18, no. 2 (2004): 79–92. It draws on Ethan B. Kapstein, *Economic Justice in an Unfair World: Toward a Level Playing Field* (Princeton, NJ: Princeton University Press, 2006). I thank Christian Barry, Charles Beitz, Thomas Pogge, and several anonymous reviewers for comments on earlier drafts, and seminar participants at the American Political Science Association, Cornell University, and Sciences Po for posing difficult questions that forced clarification of the points presented here.

1.   A notable exception where empirical evidence looms large is Thomas Pogge, *World Poverty and Human Rights*, second edition (Cambridge: Polity Press, 2008).

2.   A nice model is provided by Sanjay G. Reddy and Thomas Pogge, "How *Not* to Count the Poor," in *Debates in the Measurement of Global Poverty*, ed. Sudhir Anand, Paul Segal, and Joseph Stiglitz (New York: Oxford University Press, in press); also available at www.socialanalysis.org.

3.   For a useful review of approaches to international distributive justice that employs different typologies, see Charles R. Beitz, "International Liberalism and Distributive Justice: A Survey of Recent Thought," *World Politics* 51, no. 1 (1999): 269–96.

4.   Although I use the terms "economic justice" and "distributive justice" interchangeably, the term "distributive justice" has a broader meaning beyond economic resources, reflecting the distribution of, say, opportunity.

5.   Edmund S. Phelps, ed., *Economic Justice* (Baltimore: Penguin, 1973).

6.   John Rawls, *A Theory of Justice* (Cambridge, MA: Harvard University Press, 1971).

7.   I thank an anonymous reviewer for highlighting this point.

8.   For some relevant statistics, see UNDP, *Human Development Report 2004* (New York: Oxford University Press, 2004), ch. 2.

9.   I use the term "income distribution" as opposed to "income inequality" to suggest the concern that some theorists have with respect to the *particular* income shares of specific groups, such as the level of income of the poorest deciles. My use of the term "income distribution" would encompass, say, lump-sum payments to bring people out of poverty.

10.   John Gerard Ruggie, "International Regimes, Transactions, and Change: Embedded Liberalism in the Postwar Economic Order," in *International Regimes*, ed. Stephen D. Krasner (Ithaca, NY: Cornell University Press, 1983).

11.   See, e.g., William R. Cline, *Trade and Income Distribution* (Washington, DC: Institute for International Economics, 1997).

12.   Ibid., 275 (emphasis added).

13.   Geoffrey Bannister and Kamau Thugge, "International Trade and Poverty Alleviation," IMF Working Paper 01/54 (2001), 8.

14.   For a skeptical view regarding the spread of international law, see Eric A. Posner, "Do States Have a Moral Obligation to Obey International Law?" *Stanford Law Review* 55, no. 5 (2003): 1901–19.

15.   Dani Rodrik, "Feasible Globalizations," NBER Working Paper W9129 (2002), 24.

16.   See Charles R. Beitz, *Political Theory and International Relations*, revised edition (Princeton, NJ: Princeton University Press, [1979] 1999).

17.   Ibid., 142.

18.   Jeffrey D. Sachs and Andrew Warner, "Economic Reform and the Process of Global Integration," Brookings Paper on Economic Activity 1 (1995), 3.

19.   It should be emphasized that most economists believe strongly in a positive relationship between openness and sustained growth, even if modeling and testing that relationship has proved difficult. For a critique of methodology, see Francisco Rodriguez and Dani Rodrik, "Trade Policy and Economic Growth: A Skeptic's Guide to Cross-National Evidence," NBER Working Paper 7081 (1999).

20.   Thomas Pogge, "Moral Universalism and Global Economic Justice," *Politics, Philosophy & Economics* 1, no. 1 (2002): 43.

21.   Christian Barry, "Global Justice: Aims, Arrangements, and Responsibilities," in *Can Institutions Have Responsibilities? Collective Moral Agency and International Relations*, ed. Toni Erskine (London: Palgrave, 2003), 226.

22.   Don P. Clark, "Are Poorer Developing Countries the Targets of U.S. Protectionist Actions?" *Economic Development and Cultural Change* 47 (October 1998): 193.

23.   Staffs of the IMF and World Bank, "Market Access for Developing Countries' Exports," (April 27, 2001), 5, www.imf.org/external/np/madc/eng/042701.pdf.

24.   Ibid., 23.

25.   Ibid.

26.   Indeed, such views often emphasize the ways in which the present global economic order helps national elites to further entrench their advantages. See Pogge, "Moral Universalism and Global Economic Justice."

27.   I call it "quasi" because, in practice, the Bank still has distributive criteria that are regional; it does not focus solely on the poor, wherever they are found.

28.   World Bank, *World Development Report 1996: From Plan to Market* (New York: Oxford University Press, 1996).

29.   International Monetary Fund, *World Economic Outlook: Trade and Finance* (Washington, DC: IMF, 2002), 3.

30.   Ibid., 4. While it is not possible to provide an intellectual history of this "shift" toward a more "pro-poor" policy stance within the multilateral institutions (as against, say, a narrower emphasis on economic growth alone), civil society organizations appear to have played a seminal role. The Catholic Church and a highly energized group of civil society organizations made it impossible for international financial organizations to ignore the problem of developing world debt during the Jubilee 2000 campaign. And organizations such as Oxfam have intensified long-standing demands that the trade regime be reformed in a way that is more favorable to the poor.

31.   Ibid., 7.

32.   Ibid., 8.

33.   John Rawls, *The Law of Peoples* (Cambridge, MA: Harvard University Press, 1999).

34.   This is not to say that they would endorse these policies, but that the stated aim of these policies is consonant with their approach.

Chapter 3

The Invisible Hand of the American Empire

Robert Wade

BEFORE SEPTEMBER 11, 2001, only critics linked the United States with empire. Since then many neoconservative commentators have talked with pride and promise of the "new American empire," "the new Rome," referring to the unipolar structure of the interstate system and America's dominant position of military and political power. But this empire has another face: the framework of international economic rules and rule-making organizations. With whatever degree of intentionality, today's international economic architecture ensures that the ordinary operation of world market forces—the process we call globalization—tends to shore up American power by yielding disproportionate economic benefits to Americans and conferring autonomy on U.S. economic policymakers while curbing the autonomy of all others. It is legitimized by the widespread belief that markets are an expression of the deepest truths about human nature and that as a result they will ultimately be correct.[1] The economic benefits that accrue to the United States as the result of the normal working of market forces within this particular framework then provide the basis of American military supremacy, which helps to protect the framework.

To see this, try a thought experiment. Suppose you are an aspiring modern-day Roman emperor in a world of sovereign states, international markets, and capitalist economies. In order not to have to throw your military weight around more than occasionally, you need to act through hegemony rather than coercion and others must think that your predominance is the natural result of common-sensical institutional arrangements that are fair and just. If you—a unitary actor—could single-mindedly create an international framework of market rules to promote your interests, what kind of system would you create? After describing this imaginary system I will show how close it is to our current world system—surprisingly so, given that the United States is not at all a unitary actor.

ECONOMIC GOALS OF THE HEGEMON

As an aspiring hegemon, you need world economy arrangements that will yield you high economic growth, low inflation, low interest rates, high investment, high consumption, a high value of your currency (the dollar), and high prices of your equities. Out of this prosperity you can finance a military many times bigger than anyone else's. You want to be able to ignore the resulting high current-account deficits, and let the rest of the world's savers finance them at very low interest rates (that is, at a very low financial cost to your economy). In this way your citizens do not have to cut their consumption to free resources for the military sector—they can have more guns *and* butter than anyone else.

You also want to be able to set key global market parameters in response to your own domestic conditions, especially the value of your currency. To sustain these parameters at your desired level, you need to be able to thwart resistance to your decisions from other major states and decisions in other states that are not to your liking—as, for example, decisions to revalue a currency.

You want the rest of the world—beyond the major states—to depend heavily for its prosperity on exporting to your market, and not to have a strong endogenous growth mechanism. In this way you can harness the rest of the world to your rhythms.

INTERNATIONAL FINANCIAL ARCHITECTURE

An international financial architecture that is conducive to your interests will have several features. First, there must be no constraint, such as a gold standard, on your ability to create your currency at will, so that you can finance large current-account deficits with the rest of the world simply by selling your government's debt securities.

Second, your currency must be the main international currency for foreign exchange reserves, international trade, and foreign exchange speculation. This ensures robust demand from the rest of the world to hold your assets, especially from the regions that are accruing the current-account surpluses that are the other side of your deficits. As a result, you can run your economy at a high growth rate with less fear of exchange rate volatility and macroeconomic instability than could other sovereign debtors, because when your currency falls relative to other currencies your debt service also falls—since your debt repayments are denominated in your own currency. This gives you more policy flexibility, especially freedom to run big deficits, than other debtors have. Most debtor nations are vulnerable to falls in the value of their currency, because their foreign debt burden goes up when the value of the currency falls; and they are therefore vulnerable to the demands of the creditors, who can influence the state of confidence in the foreign exchange markets and therefore the prospects of a fall in the debtor's currency. However, you, the emperor, want to arrange things so that you can borrow heavily from abroad—and sustain a large stock of debt held by foreigners—while escaping the usual drawbacks of being a debtor economy.

Third, your financial markets must be dominant in international finance. With the biggest, deepest financial markets and with world liquidity (specifically, foreign exchange reserves) being constantly pumped up by your deficit financing, you become the world's savings entrepôt. Your financial firms arrange the inflows of foreign funds needed to finance your deficits; and they also repackage these funds and invest them back in the rest of the world. Hence your financial firms benefit in boom times, and they benefit in crisis times in the rest of the world (provided the crisis is not bigger than regional) because they do the transactions of flight capital from the crisis region into your safe assets.

Fourth, there must be a single integrated private capital market worldwide, with no barriers to capital flows and no barriers to your financial services firms to enter and exit other countries' markets. Thus the principle of exit, or liquidity, becomes the basic principle of the international economic order, so as to give your asset holders maximum freedom to move in and out of markets anywhere in the world according to short-run profit considerations. It minimizes the extent to which other states can run their political economies on the principle of commitment or long-term obligations and the extent to which they can create an egalitarian capitalism under strict social controls. It supports your central international location.

DERIVED POWER

These four features of the international financial architecture give you powerful tools of *economic* statecraft relative to everyone else. You have more autonomy to affect the value of your currency in the foreign currency markets, compared to that of other states. In general you want the dollar to be highly valued. The high dollar makes your imports relatively cheap, which keeps domestic inflation down and consumption and investment up. At the same time the inflow of foreign funds needed to finance your deficits exerts downward pressure on your domestic interest rates, despite the high dollar. The lower interest rates also keep consumption and investment up. High investment (financed from the rest of the world's savings, since yours are low) keeps parts of your economy on the world frontier of innovation and productivity. The high dollar also helps your foreign mergers and acquisitions and your foreign military expenditures.

On the other hand, you also want the autonomy to make the dollar fall in order to deal with domestic problems, perhaps in order to boost exports, revive domestic industry, and shift growth and employment to your citizens at the expense of other countries. When the main foreign exchange markets in the world are in your territory and your own nationals are playing the markets speculatively, a signal from your central bank that it is planning to change direction in exchange rate policy is instantly multiplied by your own nationals shorting the dollar. They are your policy multiplier. And when your currency accounts for the great majority of other countries' foreign exchange reserves the effect is amplified. You have the capacity to shift the dollar's value just by voicing an expectation.

Not only can you affect your own domestic conditions just by managing expectations, but you can also shift your parameters and the markets' expectations about conditions elsewhere so as to hurt the macroeconomic conditions of would-be rival states. Rival states may have to secure your cooperation in setting the value of some of their key parameters. For example, if they want to revive their economies from a downturn and lower their interest rates in order to depreciate their currency against yours, they need your cooperation not to lower your interest rates—more than you need their cooperation in the opposite case.

The main danger with this power is that it overperforms and the dollar crashes. But you can rely on help from other central banks and finance ministries, since the last thing they want is a crash in the value of the main international currency.

The system puts poor countries in your power. It encourages them to borrow internationally, with the debt denominated in your currency and at variable interest rates linked to your interest rates. Hence your decisions about your currency, your interest rates, and your protection against imports from poor countries profoundly affect economic conditions in poor states—but not vice versa. In conditions of open capital markets, floating exchange rates, and debt incurred at variable interest rates, poor economies are likely to have more volatile growth, more financial crises, and hence higher demand for foreign exchange reserves of your assets (such as your treasury securities).

In fact, in several ways currency crises in poor countries help your economic growth, your economic preeminence, and your hegemony. They generate large inflows of funds into your financial markets even at low rates of interest. They also make the rest of the world more responsive to your signals about your intentions toward your currency and your interest rates. And they reduce the likelihood that over the long haul challengers to your dominance will arise from among the poor countries.

This economic system depends on a political system of sovereign states, not colonies, that can be made responsible for handling the crises it generates in particular territories. It is a post-imperial empire. Only in cases of failing or rogue states that control vital resources do you intervene directly.

INTERNATIONAL ORGANIZATIONS

To supervise this international framework you need a flotilla of international organizations that look like cooperatives of member states and confer the legitimacy of multilateralism, but that you can control by setting the rules and blocking outcomes you do not like.

During crisis periods poor countries have to depend on bailouts from these organizations, and you can set the terms of the bailouts. You use the bailouts to "restructure" the crisis economies in such a way as to prioritize the repayment of your creditors and the advancement of your agenda of worldwide liberalization, privatization, and free capital mobility. The bailout conditionality may include cuts in the borrowing country's spending on health, education, and infrastructure in order to free up resources for debt servicing; a domestic recession for the same reason; a currency devaluation to generate more exports; elimination of capital controls; and cuts in tariff and nontariff barriers. Replicated across multiple crises these conditionalities generate intense competition among exporters from poor countries, which gives you an inflow of imports at constantly decreasing prices relative to the price of your exports, keeping your inflation down and your living standards up, while poor countries' terms of trade fall and perhaps their living standards too.

The bailout mechanism through international organizations has another useful function—it lets you shift the risks of debt default away from your private banks to the member states of the international organizations. In the face of a possible debt default to your banks you order one or more international organizations to lend heavily to the indebted countries, on the understanding that the countries will use the money to repay your banks. Your banks take the private profits, and you help them to spread the losses onto the rest of the world.

Likewise you use international organizations to confer the legitimacy of multilateralism—"the wish of the world community"—on your stringent rules of copyright and patent protection. Copyright and patents are one area where you would not preach the doctrine of liberalization but rather stress the imperative of protection—your artists and innovators being the predominant holders of copyright and patents. Therefore, you get the international organizations to embrace rules that set a long minimum period for patents and maximize the range of things over which private patent rights can be granted (for example, naturally occurring microorganisms, biological processes, and "community knowledge," including knowledge of traditional healers). Your firms must be able to patent *anything* they wish and then securely enjoy the rents for at least twenty years.

You also use international organizations to secure agreements that make it illegal for other countries to treat your firms operating in their territory differently from the way they treat their own firms. Measures to place your firms' foreign subsidiaries under various sorts of performance requirements—for local content, exports, joint venturing, technology transfer—are not allowed, because they might limit your firms' freedom of action. Your aim is to facilitate your firms' shifting of lower value-added operations to lower-wage countries while holding the higher value-added operations (innovation, marketing, and distribution) in your territory.

You also support agreements for reduced trade barriers, and you sponsor multilateral negotiations to do so in "development rounds." However, you craft the agreements so that you can maintain your barriers against other countries' exports in sectors important for your voters and financial backers—now described not as protection but as measures to protect your health, safety, the environment, and national security. Further, you maintain with any necessary rhetorical justification an escalation of obstacles to trade, such that the higher the value added the higher the obstacles—and therefore the higher the probability that profit-seeking firms will maintain the high value-added operations in your territory.

You combine pressures to expand the scope of the private sector in poor economies (partly via bailout requirements for cuts in public spending on social sectors) with international agreements on free trade in services, so that your private firms can take the world as their oyster for providing education, health, pension, and other services.

Finally, you advance your agenda by having multiple negotiating forums so that you can "forum shop." If you are forced by rules of multilateralism to give up more than you want to in one forum, you switch to another forum in which you have more power. Or you take agreements reached in a multilateral forum (on patents, for example) and then "turbo-charge" the agreements in bilateral or regional negotiations. You say to particular countries or blocs of countries, "You agreed to this and this in the multilateral agreement; but if you want to enjoy continued low tariff access to our market, without risk of us raising tariffs on your exports, you'd better agree to even more."

FOREIGN POLICY

Your foreign policy seeks to befriend the upper classes elsewhere and make sure they have good material reasons for supporting the framework. It seeks to render it unlikely that elites and masses should ever unite in nativistic reactions to your dominance or demand "nationalistic" development policies that nurture competitors to your industries. Your foreign policy needs to include a strategic immigration policy that attracts the best brains in the rest of the world to your universities, firms, and research institutes. You want to have media, business schools, universities, think tanks, and management consultants that are independent enough to provide feedback on how to keep the system and your dominant position in it from falling into crisis.

Your foreign policy also calls for a very large military, so as to be able to back your hegemony with coercion. The world financial architecture allows you to fund overwhelming military strength "on the cheap." You can then shape the geopolitical security of all other states more than they can shape yours. You can control the sources and supply routes of the world's vital energy resources. You can "cash in" your military dominance in return for support for the various policies and agreements that boost your economic power.

THE BOTTOM LINE

This international economic architecture allows your people to consume far more than they produce; it allows your firms and your capital to enter and exit other markets quickly, maximizing short-run returns; it locks in net flows of technology rents from the rest of the world for decades ahead and thereby boosts incentives for your firms to innovate; and through market forces seemingly free of political power it reinforces your geopolitical dominance over other states. All the better if your social scientists explain to the public that a structureless and agentless process of globalization—the relentless technological change that shrinks time and distance—is behind all this, causing all states, including your own, to lose power vis-à-vis markets. You do not want others to think that globalization within the framework you have constructed raises your ability to have both a large military and prosperous civilian sector while diminishing everyone else's.

REAL-WORLD QUALIFICATIONS

A Machiavellian account of the U.S. role in the world economy since the end of the Bretton Woods fixed exchange rate regime around 1970? Certainly. To bring it closer to the real world we need to bring in a number of qualifications.

In reality the United States is far from being a unitary actor in pursuit of a grand design. Its central bank, the Federal Reserve, is independent of its finance ministry, the U.S. Treasury. Its policies are much affected by private-sector pressures, organized by economic sector and geographical region. Its trade protection, for example, is partly about chasing votes. The system was not the creation of the United States alone, either: Europe and Japan have joined in, though quite often in the face of force majeure. In the real world high U.S. living standards—and the ability to have more guns and butter than anyone else—depend not only on the ability to sustain large current-account deficits and earn large profits in finance. They also depend on a high rate of innovation in goods and services, which is only partially explained by the financial and selective immigration factors considered here.

In the real world the United States's ability to run large current-account deficits and maintain a large stock of dollar financial assets in foreign hands is a double-edged sword. It does give the United States an almost free lunch by allowing it to attract the necessary financing even while paying low interest rates. However, this "hegemonic debtor's gain" can turn into a "normal debtor's curse" if—as at present—the U.S. domestic and external debt rises to the point where the United States has to plead with other countries to revalue their

currencies and to go on holding dollar assets in the face of higher returns elsewhere and opportunities to diversify into an alternative international currency,
such as the euro. A loss of foreign cooperation might lead to sudden falls in the
value of the dollar, and even though this would not carry the normal debtor's
curse of raising the burden of debt servicing it could still inflict costs on the
U.S. economy. These costs could be serious, given that foreign official holdings
of Treasury securities now amount to about one-third of the total Treasury-
issued debt.

To some extent this curbs U.S. autonomy, and specifically the country's
monetary power vis-à-vis creditor governments. But only to some extent, since
creditor governments barely attempt to coordinate their monetary decisions
among themselves in order to counter the influence from the large U.S. economy. And it is striking how the East Asian countries—by far the world's biggest
surplus countries—continue to hold mostly dollars, even though it is a certain
bet that the dollar will fall over the next several years. They do so for two main
reasons. First, they wish to maintain their currency at a relatively low value
against the dollar as a way to maintain export competitiveness and keep up
domestic employment. The by-product of this export-led growth strategy is the
holding of a large stock of dollar reserves. Second, because they still trade mostly
with the United States rather than the European Union, they do not want the
disruptions caused by diversifying out of dollars and making the value of the
dollar more volatile. They see the likely commercial losses as bigger than the
likely financial losses of holding mainly dollars.

My imaginary account also ignores the evolution of the system. The system
is less engineered "by design" than it implies. For example, the deep U.S. bond
markets were initiated by the heavy debt financing of the two world wars. Unin-
tendedly, the U.S. attempts in the 1960s to regulate interest rates led to the
development of an offshore and unregulated financial market for dollars, which
in turn generated pressures to liberalize capital markets worldwide. On the
other hand, the explosive growth in the world bond market since the 1980s has
clearly been by design. In order to fund massive budget deficits policymakers
sought to stimulate a bond market by tax cuts for the rich and the virtual
elimination of taxes on capital gains.

Prior to the 1970s the United States dominated through production, not
financial services, and therefore faced recurrent crises of excess capacity or over-
accumulation of capital. It responded with varying combinations of New Deal–
type investments in infrastructure, education, and social spending, Marshall
Plan–type investments abroad, privatization drives, and war—all ways to absorb
the excess domestic capacity, create new consumers abroad, or destroy capacity
abroad. Since the 1970s the American system has developed a complementary
line of response, domination through finance, as a way of expanding the play
of the liquidity principle on behalf of U.S. holders of financial assets—making

them mobile enough to save themselves from the periodic crises of excess capacity in the United States and elsewhere. My thought experiment emphasizes how a modern-day emperor would seek to cement this kind of domination through finance.

Again, one should distinguish between the faults of a very unequal, unipolar structure of wealth and power and the faults of the state that occupies the top position. One can be critical of the U.S. role while still recognizing that—if the unipolar structure is taken as given—the world is probably better off with the United States as the top dog than any of the likely alternatives. Certainly, when America has used its clout to "think for the world," the engineering of its dominance has at times been for the general good.

REAL-WORLD LIKENESSES

However, it is also true that the United States has often used its clout solely in the interests of its richest citizens and most powerful corporations, and this latter tendency has been dominant lately. In particular, the U.S. blockage on climate change; its protection of the agriculture, steel, apparel, and footwear sectors; its privileging of the interests of U.S. oil corporations; its willingness to invade Iraq partly to make sure that Russian, French, and Chinese companies do not get a lock on Iraq's enormous oil reserves (the second largest proven in the world); and its insistence that Iraqi oil reverts to being priced and paid for in U.S. dollars after Saddam Hussein's regime began to insist on euros and other oil exporters (Iran, Venezuela, Russia) began to show signs of making the same switch.[2]

My account of what the emperor wants with regard to patents and copyright corresponds closely to what the United States has obtained in the World Trade Organization's (WTO) Trade-Related Aspects of Intellectual Property Rights agreement—and when the subsequent Doha ministerial meeting clarified the interpretation in a way favorable to the developing countries, the United States and other rich countries shifted forums to bilateral and regional trade agreements and to the World Intellectual Property Organization to implement more demanding intellectual property standards. With regard to unrestricted foreign direct investment, my account corresponds closely to the WTO's Trade-Related Investment Measures. And the WTO's General Agreement on Trade in Services is facilitating a global market in private health care, welfare, pensions, education, and the like, in which U.S. firms tend to have an advantage. This may well undermine political support for universal access to social services in developing countries and facilitate upper-class citizens' "exit" from their nations as fate-sharing communities—making any kind of nationalistic or regional challenge to the current world rules less likely.[3]

The United States has steered the World Bank—through congressional conditions on the replenishment of the funds of the Bank's soft-loan facility, the

International Development Association—to launch its biggest refocusing in a decade: a "private sector-led development" agenda devoted to accelerating the private (and nongovernmental organization) provision of basic services on a commercial basis. Yet the Bank has made no evaluation of its earlier, highly controversial efforts to support private participation in social sectors. Its new emphasis on private sector–led development, especially in the social sectors, is largely due to intense pressure from the United States.

The United States has encouraged developing countries to promote "external integration" into the world economy but not to promote, via industrial policies, "internal integration" between industrial, rural and urban, consumption and investment sectors; yet the twin-track approach of export orientation and import replacement is vital for stable growth that is not a hostage to export markets. Indeed the United States has been leading the drive, via the WTO agreements and via bilateral or regional free trade agreements and investment treaties, to coerce or induce other countries to abandon industrial policies that promote upgrading and diversification of their industries and services. At the same time the United States itself has for decades mounted a large-scale industrial policy that nurtures high-tech industries (including computers, advanced sensor devices, stealth materials, aircraft) with massive amounts of public finance and public authority. Much of it is flatly inconsistent with WTO agreements but protected from sanction by the rhetorical shield of "defense policy."

The United States's single most important thrust since the 1970s has been for open capital accounts and freedom of entry and exit for financial service firms. The institution of these rules is causing a parametric shift in the whole world economy, resulting in the loss of ability of all states to resist other parts of the U.S. agenda. The removal of restrictions on capital mobility, far from being a neutral policy, makes the adoption of an egalitarian capitalism under social regulation much more difficult, by weakening the means by which a national government could implement such a collective choice. This understanding is implied in the statement by U.S. deputy treasury secretary Lawrence Summers: "At Treasury, our most crucial international priority remains the creation of a well funded, truly global capital market."[4] The International Monetary Fund (IMF), too, pushed by the U.K. Treasury with the support of the U.S. Treasury, got its board of governors to endorse a plan to amend the articles of agreement for only the fourth time in its history, in 1997, to add "the promotion of capital flows" to the goals of the organization and add "the capital account" to its jurisdiction.

The IMF, urged on by the U.S. Treasury, went so far as to twist the arm of Ethiopia, one of the poorest countries in the world, to open its capital account in 1996–97. When the government refused (advised by the World Bank's recently appointed chief economist, Joseph Stiglitz) the Fund made Ethiopia ineligible for the low-interest loans through the Extended Structural Adjustment Program, even though the government had already met virtually all other of the Fund's conditions. With that Ethiopia also lost its access to several other sources of cheap funds, including the World Bank, the European Union, and bilateral lenders—the eligibility for which is conditional on eligibility for the Fund's program.[5]

The drive to lock in a world commitment to open capital accounts stalled in the wake of the East Asian crisis of 1997–98. But by 1999 the IMF managing director, Michel Camdessus, was already saying, "I believe it is now time for momentum to be reestablished. . . . Full liberalization of capital movement should be promoted in a prudent and well-sequenced fashion."[6] In 2003 U.S. treasury undersecretary John Taylor testified that the U.S. government believes the ability to transfer capital "freely into and out of a country without delay and at a market rate of exchange" is a "fundamental right," and that no country should ever impose restrictions on capital flows in times of financial crisis. The U.S. government, he said, is insisting in its free trade agreements and bilateral investment treaties that its counterpart governments agree never to place restrictions on capital flows, with provision for U.S. investors to claim for compensation if they do.[7]

These statements reflect not so much a failure to learn as "unlearning." The present push for free capital mobility repeats the faults of the 1920s. Then the U.S. and the U.K. governments and bankers concerted their demands for a new financial architecture based on balanced budgets, independent central banks, restoration of the gold standard, and free capital movements. They pushed this agenda through bilateral dealings with the war-devastated countries of Europe and through the Financial Committee of the League of Nations. The policies helped to usher in a spectacular financial boom that ended in economic collapse. Nevertheless, four years into the Great Depression, the World Economic Conference of 1933, led by the United States and the United Kingdom, continued to make the same four demands, with special emphasis on independent central banks and abolition of capital controls. It was only with the 1944 Bretton Woods agreement, which left the option of capital controls to the discretion of individual states provided that the controls were not intended to restrict trade, that this lesson was learned. John Maynard Keynes considered this to be perhaps the most important part of the agreement. "What used to be heresy is now endorsed as orthodox," he wrote. "Our right to control the domestic capital market is secured on firmer foundations than ever before, and is formally accepted as a proper part of agreed international arrangements."[8] Keynes of course had in mind the United Kingdom's precarious position as a massive wartime borrower facing the prospect of postwar insolvency if capital could leave the country unrestricted. But he also considered that world economic stability required that capital controls be an acceptable weapon of national economic management.

FROM UNIPOLAR TO MULTIPOLAR GLOBALIZATION

The current talk about "globalization" presents it as a general shrinkage of time and distance and widening of opportunities for all, with a corresponding erosion of the power of states to oppress their populations. Joseph Nye suggests that, although the world is very much "unipolar" on the chessboard of classic interstate military issues, it is "multipolar," or one of "balance of power," on the chessboard of interstate economic issues and "chaotically organised among state and non-state actors" on the third chessboard of transnational economic issues. "It makes no sense at all to call this [the second and third chessboards] a unipolar world or an American empire," he says.[9]

It is true that Europe and East Asia are not as passive as my empire picture suggests. For example, of the three-quarters of total world foreign currency reserves that are held in U.S. dollars, well over half are held by East Asian governments.[10] As noted, this reflects not only their large current account surpluses but also a policy strategy to preserve export competitiveness by maintaining a relatively low value of their currencies vis-à-vis the dollar. Now the imbalances are so large that if the U.S. authorities want to make the dollar fall in value gradually rather than precipitously, they do need to secure the cooperation of East Asian governments—and others—to go on buying U.S. liabilities, and revalue, or in the case of China, further open its domestic market.

Nevertheless, the bigger story is that economic globalization is being channeled by rules of the international economic regime, in the making of which the United States has exercised by far the dominant voice. Rules such as those for patents and copyright—which far from shrinking time and distance actually slow the diffusion of technology to the rest of the world and boost technology rents flowing to, disproportionately, Americans. And rules such as those that result in the U.S. dollar being the main international currency, the United States having the biggest financial sector, and free capital mobility worldwide. Globalization so constructed frees the U.S. government of constraints in key areas of economic policy while putting other states under tighter constraints.

This is the paradox of economic globalization—it looks like "powerless" expansion of markets but it works to enhance the ability of the United States to harness the rest of the world and fortify its empire-like power.[11] And since it is occurring in a world of "sovereign" states its costs can be made the responsibility of each state to handle, not that of the prime beneficiary.

It is true and important that a lot of people in the world, especially in East Asia, are a lot better off than they were twenty years ago, and that this improvement would not have been possible had they not had access to rich country markets and rich country technology. To this extent the U.S.–directed globalization has worked. On the other hand, average living standards have risen hardly at all in Latin America, Africa, the non-oil-producing Middle East, and much of South Asia since 1980. World income inequality has almost certainly widened.[12] The surge of jobs in apparel in China and Mexico during the 1990s— thanks to exports to North America—went with a fall in real wages and a sharp deterioration in working conditions (measured by what one report describes as the "startlingly high" incidence of violence and severed limbs and fingers in factories owned by Taiwanese, Korean, and Hong Kong intermediaries).[13]

Slow economic growth and vast income disparities, when seen as blocked opportunities, breed cohorts of partly educated young people who grow up in anger and despair. Some try by legal or illegal means to migrate to the West; some join militant ethnic or religious movements directed at each other and their own rulers; but now the idea has spread among a few vengeful fundamentalists that Western countries should be attacked directly. The United States and its allies can stamp out specific groups by force and bribery. But in the longer run, the structural arrangements that replicate a grossly unequal world have to be redesigned, in way as significant as the redesign at the Bretton Woods conference was toward the end of World War II, so that globalization working within the new framework produces more equitable results.

The world would benefit from a less unipolar structure. A little competition between core states of the world economy for support from developing countries might lead to more commitment in the core states to creating dynamic capitalisms in developing countries, as was the case in geopolitically sensitive countries during the first decades of the Cold War.[14] To counterbalance American power, Europe, whether as a federation or as a "Europe of nations," has to create arrangements that permit a common foreign policy. This implies, among other things, that expansion to the East should be slowed down or two-tracked, because the entry of many new states seeing America as their protector against the overbearing leading states of the European Union will make it next to impossible for Europe to agree on any common foreign policy that runs counter to U.S. wishes.

In the longer term we should look to growing cooperation between Europe and an East Asian bloc led by China and Japan, the third major growth pole in the world economy. A Eurasian power bloc would bolster itself with links to energy sources in the Persian Gulf and to military might in Russia, and would exploit new energy resources and shipping routes in the Arctic Ocean as the ice melts.[15] Political leaders across Eurasia should set their sights on this project with the same steady prioritization as leaders of postwar Europe gave to the making of what became the European Union, regardless of America's approval or lack of it.

NOTES

Revised in 2008, this essay first appeared in *Ethics & International Affairs* 17, no. 2 (2003): 77–88 as part of "The Revival of Empire," a special section with further contributions from Jedediah Purdy, Pratap Bhanu Mehta, Jean Bethke Elshtain, and David Singh Grewal. The full set of essays can be reviewed at www.cceia.org/resources/journal/17_2/index.html.

1.   This is Joshua Cooper Ramo's statement of the core economic value of Alan Greenspan, former chairman of the U.S. Federal Reserve, in "The Three Marketeers," *Time*, February 15, 1999. For an astonishing illustration of this belief in action, see John Poindexter's scheme to create a futures market in political events such as terrorist attacks, assassinations, and coups. Carl Hulse, "Pentagon Prepares a Futures Market on Terror Attacks," *New York Times*, July 29, 2003.

2.   David Gisselquist, *Oil Prices and Trade Deficits: U.S. Conflicts with Japan and West Germany* (New York: Praeger, 1979), argues that the United States ensured the primary role for the dollar by getting OPEC to agree to accept payments for oil in dollars.

3.   Robert Wade, "What Strategies Are Viable for Developing Countries Today? The World Trade Organization and the Shrinking of 'Development Space'," *Review of International Political Economy* 10, no. 4 (2003): 621–644. For the crucial role of counterfeiting in East Asia's development, see Robert Wade, *Governing the Market: Economic Theory and the Role of Government in East Asian Industrialization* (Princeton, NJ: Princeton University Press, [1990] 2004), 268, 294.

4.   Lawrence Summers, "America's Role in Global Economic Integration" (speech, "Integrating National Economies" conference, Brookings Institution, Washington, DC, January 9, 1996); available at www.ustreas.gov/press/releases/pr9701091.htm.

5.   For the rest of the story, see Robert Wade, "Capital and Revenge: the IMF and Ethiopia," *Challenge* 44, no. 5 (2001): 67–75.

6.   Michel Camdessus, "Governments and Economic Development in a Globalized World" (speech, 32nd International General Meeting of the Pacific Basin Economic Council, Hong Kong, May 17, 1999); available at www.imf.org/external/np/speeches/1999/051799.htm. The IMF has softened its insistence on capital-account liberalization since Camdessus left in 2000. A recent paper coauthored by IMF chief economist Kenneth Rogoff admits, "it is difficult to establish a robust causal relationship between the degree of financial integration and output growth performance . . . there is evidence that some countries may have experienced greater consumption volatility [hence welfare volatility] as a result [of financial integration]." Eswar S. Prasad et al., "Effects of Financial Globalization on Developing Countries: Some Empirical Evidence" (March 17, 2003), 6, www.imf.org/external/np/res/docs/2003/031703.pdf.

7.   John B. Taylor, testimony before the Subcommittee on Domestic and International Monetary Policy, Trade, and Technology, Committee on Financial Services, U.S. House of Representatives (April 1, 2003), www.ustreas.gov/press/releases/js149.htm.

8.   Quoted in Louis W. Pauly, *Who Elected the Bankers? Surveillance and Control in the World Economy* (Ithaca, NY: Cornell University Press, 1997), 94.

9.   Joseph S. Nye Jr., "A Whole New Ball Game," *Financial Times*, December 28/29, 2002.

10.   Martin Wolf, "Asia Is Footing the Bill for American Guns and Butter," *Financial Times*, February 19, 2003.

11.   See Peter Gowan, "Explaining the American Boom: The Roles of 'Globalisation' and United States Global Power," *New Political Economy* 6, no. 3 (2001): 359–74; Peter Gowan, *The Global Gamble: Washington's Faustian Bid for World Dominance* (New York: Verso, 1999);

and Richard Duncan, *The Dollar Crisis: Causes, Consequences, Cures*, revised edition (Singapore: Wiley, 2005).

12.   Robert Wade, "Is Globalization Reducing Poverty and Inequality?" *World Development* 32, no. 4 (2004): 567–89; Robert Wade, "Globalization, Growth, Poverty, Inequality, Resentment, and Imperialism," in *Global Political Economy*, ed. John Ravenhill, second edition (New York: Oxford University Press, 2008).

13.   Robert J. S. Ross, and Anita Chan, "From North-South to South-South: The True Face of Global Competition," *Foreign Affairs* 81, no. 5 (2002): 8–13.

14.   Robert Wade, "Creating Capitalisms," introduction to *Governing the Market* (see note 3).

15.   Robert Wade, "Why a Warmer Arctic Needs New Laws," *Financial Times*, January 15, 2008.

Accountability in International Development Aid

Leif Wenar

CONTEMPORARY MOVEMENTS for the reform of global institutions advocate greater transparency, greater democracy, and greater accountability. Of these three, accountability is the master value. Transparency is valuable as means to accountability: more transparent institutions reveal whether officials have performed their duties. Democracy is valuable as a mechanism of accountability: elections enable the people peacefully to remove officials who have not done what it is their responsibility to do. "Accountability," it has been said, "is the central issue of our time."[1]

The focus of this essay is accountability in international development aid: that range of efforts sponsored by the world's rich aimed at permanently bettering the conditions of the world's poor.[2] We begin by surveying some of the difficulties in international development aid that have raised concerns that development agencies are not accountable enough for producing positive results in alleviating poverty. We then examine the concept of accountability, and survey the general state of accountability in development agencies. A high-altitude map of the main proposals for greater accountability in international development follows, and the essay concludes by exploring one specific proposal for increasing accountability in development aid.

THE CHALLENGES OF DEVELOPMENT AID

International development projects aim to improve the well-being of the poor in the medium to long term. According to the World Bank, there are currently more than 80,000 development projects underway.[3] Typical projects include constructing dams to improve irrigation in Laos, teaching basic reading skills to pastoralists in Kenya, staffing remote health care clinics in Bangladesh, organizing a farmer's cooperative in Nepal, and running a microlending program to help poor women start their own businesses in Mali.

All of these development projects attempt to transform resources drawn from rich individuals into permanent benefits for those living in poverty.

Deploying these resources so that they make a positive contribution to the lives of the poor is always challenging, with the challenges coming along three dimensions. First, any given development project will be technically quite complex. Second, project resources will tend to be diverted away from the intended beneficiaries. Third, the aggregate flow of aid resources into a country can itself generate negative effects. Following is a catalogue of the main factors along these three dimensions that can make poverty alleviation difficult.

First, any development project will face technical challenges in design and management.[4] Most development planners face the dilemma that projects must be sensitive to local skills and customs to ensure participation and so success; yet the success of a project also turns on effecting significant changes in the productive, or political, or reproductive practices of those who are meant to participate. Asia and Africa are speckled with decaying infrastructure projects from earlier eras of development aid whose operation did not fit with the skills and customs of the target populations. Projects intended to resettle communities, or to empower marginalized groups, or to democratize local politics typically disrupt settled practices in ways that some naturally resist. When a project's success will depend on a change in gender or sexual relations—such as in female literacy or AIDS-prevention projects—these kinds of difficulties are intensified. Moreover, the environment in which a project is being executed is likely to change during the period when the project is implemented. Project managers will expect to confront economic or environmental shocks, or new directives from local government, or new players who enter trying to capture project resources, or new attitudes toward the project and its staff among the project's intended beneficiaries.[5]

Second, project resources will typically be diverted away from the project's target population.[6] Most of the diversionary pressures on project resources can be traced to the poor state institutions within poor countries. In most poor countries state institutions are either quite weak, or are strong and self-serving. Indeed, most poor people in most poor countries remain poor at least in part because their political institutions are inefficient, or venal, or rapacious, or absent altogether.

If a development project is implemented through the ministries of the poor country, project funds and supplies may be diverted at the national, district, or local levels of governance. If the implementing agency is an international aid nongovernmental organization (NGO), there is also significant potential for resource diversion. Aid NGOs often have to fund the government of the poor country directly: either to get permission to carry out their projects, or through paying local taxes. These payments from NGOs can support the rule of authoritarian leaders and feed corruption in the bureaucracy. NGOs must sometimes pay corrupt officials or warlords in order to maintain their headquarters in the national capital, and must sometimes pay off or even employ criminals in order to carry out their projects in the field. Those who exercise illegitimate power in a country are often glad to welcome aid agencies in, as having agencies in the country will increase their opportunities for patronage.[7] And NGOs by definition have no official power of their own, which limits their ability to bargain with governments and criminals.

This potential for resource diversion illustrates what might be called "the iron law of political economy": in the absence of good institutions, resources tend to flow toward those who have more power. The less powerful people are, the harder it is to get resources to them. A well installed in a remote village will not help the poorest if after the aid agency leaves the well is taken over by a local gang, thus forcing the poorest villagers to travel even farther to get fresh water. The benefits to the poorest of paying doctors to staff rural health clinics will be limited if, as in Bangladesh, the doctors are absent from the clinic for 74 percent of the time for which they are paid.[8] Even an enormous poverty-relief program like Mexico's PRONASOL, which spent over one percent of the country's Gross Domestic Product (GDP) per year for five years, will not relieve poverty if the funds are primarily used by public officials to support the ruling party through electioneering and clientage.[9]

Without the checking mechanisms of good institutions in place, it is difficult to get resources for development to flow toward those who have the least power. The richer, stronger, healthier, better armed, better fed, better educated, and better located people are, the more likely they are to capture the benefits from any stream of resources.

The third dimension of complexity in development work runs through the other two, and emerges from the aggregation of aid resources flowing into a country at any one time. Poor governments that receive a significant percentage of their budgets from aid may become less capable of independent political action. They may also become more responsive to donors than to their own citizens, and they may generate a domestic culture of rent seeking.[10] Significant aid inflows may weaken a poor country's competitiveness and limit employment growth in labor-intensive and export industries.[11] When multiple donors and ministries fail to coordinate their programs, there is also considerable potential for waste, coverage gaps, and policy conflict.[12] As a recent United Nations Development Programme (UNDP) report notes, in Tanzania in the mid-1980s some 40 donors maintained 2,000 different aid projects.[13] The task of joining up these projects into a coherent overall pro-poor strategy would be monumental, even if there were some agency that could take it on.

In sum, the major challenges in development work arise from the complex nature of the projects, from the diversionary pressures on resources, and from the emergent effects of large aggregations of aid resources. All of these challenges decrease the odds that the resources put into aid will, ultimately, produce net benefits for the poor. The past twenty years have seen a greater awareness of these challenges to success in development. This period has also seen a series of discouraging studies on the overall effectiveness of development aid.[14] These two factors, along with the increasing public awareness of the moral imperative to reduce severe poverty, have combined to push the topic of accountability to the top of the development agenda.

THE CONCEPT OF ACCOUNTABILITY

A familiar legal maxim says: "Justice must be done, and justice must be seen to be done." A parallel maxim captures the concept of accountability: "Responsibility must be fulfilled, and responsibility must be seen to be fulfilled."

Accountability is second-order responsibility. When we say that someone is *responsible* for something, we mean that it is up to them to take care of it. When we say that someone is *accountable* for something, we mean that they have an extra responsibility on top of this—a responsibility to be able to show that they have fulfilled their original responsibility. It is up to an accountable agent to be able to show that they have done what it is up to them to do.[15]

Accountability always carries with it the possibility of negative evaluation and sanction.[16] Accountable agents who fail to show that they have fulfilled their responsibility may be blamed, and subject to warning, reprimand, dismissal, fines, criminal penalties, withholding of future donations, removal from office, and so on. Accountability also of course carries the possibility of positive evaluation, and so also the possibility of praise, promotion, re-election, and so on.[17]

An accountable agent is accountable *to* some person or agency. Accountability has a "direction"—it points to those to whom one must give account. For example, the board of a corporation has a duty to the shareholders to be able to show that it is running the company well, and the shareholders have a corresponding claim that the board be able to account for its decisions.

Any authority at whom accountability points will have distinguishable powers, even when these powers are all in the hands of a single actor. A finer analysis will separate out *standard-setting*, *performance-measuring*, and *sanctioning* powers. The power to set standards is the power to determine what norms the accountable agent must satisfy. The power to judge whether the agent has in fact satisfied the relevant norms is a second type of power. The third type of power is the power to penalize an agent found to have failed to live up to the norms it is bound by. In articulated systems of accountability such as advanced legal systems, these powers may be spread among different authorities. For example, within an advanced legal system, it may be that standard-setting powers are held by a legislature, performance-measuring powers are held by grand juries, and sanctioning powers are held by trial judges.

An agent can be responsible without being accountable. Adults are responsible for maintaining their own physical fitness, but they are not accountable to their fellow citizens for this. Similarly, an absolute monarch might be responsible for the good of his people without being accountable to anyone for the course of his rule.

Why is it important sometimes to make agents not only responsible but accountable? There are, after all, costs to imposing the extra responsibility of accountability.[18] It may be quite *expensive* to be made accountable. For instance, making an aid NGO accountable may mean that it has to divert funds away from running programs in order to show that its programs are effective. Accountability is also the opposite of trust: making an agent accountable can signal to that agent that outsiders *distrust* the agent to fulfill its responsibilities. Moreover, accountability brings with it a certain *formal or legal structuring* of relationships. The demands of accountability may focus the accountable agent's activities on satisfying certain bureaucratic requirements instead of pursuing its underlying mission. Increasing an agent's accountability can even be *dangerous*, as when greater transparency in an aid agency's efforts to empower the poor allows vested interests more easily to identify and threaten those working for political reform.

Accountability has costs; yet these costs can sometimes be outweighed. The following list sets out some of the categories of benefits of accountability:

- *Incentives to agents.* An agent who knows that its affairs must be capable of withstanding scrutiny will have incentives to respond to the values of those to whom it is accountable. So, commonly, an accountable agent can be expected to put *more effort* into fulfilling its responsibilities, to be *more efficient*, to maintain *higher ethical standards*, to take *extra care in planning and acting*, and so on. Accountable agents also tend to be more *consistent*, since their actions have set visible precedents and are open to challenge.[19]
- *Assurance to principals.* Typically accountable agents are representatives of others. Aid workers running a polio vaccination program represent those who donated money for that purpose. Making the aid workers accountable provides *assurance* to the donors that the workers have acted so as to discharge some of their responsibilities toward the children. Moreover, accountability can help to *solve coordination problems* by providing this assurance. An accountable actor can show that it is capable of discharging its responsibilities, and so may become the focal agent of many principals. An NGO with a reputation for accountability may be more effective, because many people converge on directing their resources to it.
- *Knowledge.* When agents are accountable, their actions are more open to scrutiny. This makes it easier to subject their actions to *systematic study*, and may assist the *spread of good practices*.
- *Transparency.* As just mentioned, the knowledge generated by procedures of accountability can be instrumentally valuable. Some may also think that a more transparent system is morally better in itself, or that transparency is constitutive of a system that has some other virtue like *justice*.

- *Desert*. When agents are held accountable, it is more likely that what they receive will track what they deserve. Mechanisms of accountability also allow those who are evaluating the accountable agent to have more *confidence* in their judgments about what that agent deserves, and it *protects* the accountable agent against undeserved damage to their reputation. Some may also think that certain principals (for example, democratic citizens) have a certain *status* or *standing* that can only be fittingly recognized by making their agents (government officials) accountable to them.

These are some of the values surrounding accountability. Yet making agents more accountable is not always beneficial overall. U.S. presidential elections are a mechanism of accountability; yet one could imagine how burdensome it would be were these elections held quarterly instead of quadrennially. Increasing accountability can increase efficiency, and assurance, and honesty, but it can also waste resources, divert attention toward irrelevant targets, and foster distrust. Only when the benefits of making an agent more accountable outweigh the costs of doing so will it be morally important to increase that agent's accountability in some specific way.

A SURVEY OF ACCOUNTABILITY IN INTERNATIONAL DEVELOPMENT

Accountability should only be increased when its benefits are worth its costs. That fact would not be worth special mention had accountability not become a sort of philosopher's stone in recent discussions of development. In the current political environment, it is advantageous for development agencies of all kinds to claim that they are highly accountable, even if they are not, and even if there is no good reason for them to be so. What follows is an overview of the state of accountability in development aid.

One can get an initial sense of the ethical and practical issues surrounding accountability in development aid by viewing development from the broadest moral perspective. Morally, the fundamental relationship in international development is between the rich individuals who provide resources through taxes or private donations on the one side, and the poor individuals who are the intended beneficiaries of these resources on the other. Within this fundamental relationship responsibility is not accompanied by accountability. Rich individuals are entirely unaccountable to the poor for discharging their responsibilities to aid. If rich individuals fail to provide enough resources to address severe poverty, or fail to direct their resources in ways that relieve poverty, they face no sanction whatsoever. The power of any collection of poor people to penalize any collection of rich people for generating insufficient or ineffective development aid is virtually zero. Moreover, there is no practical way of increasing accountability within this relationship. The enforcement of any norms of accountability on rich individuals would impose costs that rich individuals would never accept.

The more specific contemporary concerns about accountability in development have centered on the intermediate institutions that link the rich with the poor. Any development effort will involve a chain of intermediate institutions,. which will typically be made up of some combination of institutions of the following four types: governments of rich countries, governments of poor countries, international financial institutions (such as the World Bank), and aid NGOs.

The main ethical concern is that these institutions may fail to use the resources entrusted to them effectively to relieve poverty. In theory, if these intermediate institutions should be accountable to anyone, they should be accountable either to the poor individuals who are the intended beneficiaries of the development projects, or to the rich individuals who provide the money to fund the projects, or to both.

However, when we look at these chains of intermediate institutions, we find little power of accountability located at either end. Neither rich nor poor individuals presently have much ability to sanction these intermediate institutions for failing to turn the resources provided into demonstrably effective poverty-relief projects. In the most general terms, this is because the intended beneficiaries—who are often well placed to know whether the aid is working—are very poor and so have little power to sanction anyone. Meanwhile the rich individual taxpayers or donors who might sanction the failure of intermediate institutions face very high costs in determining which poverty-relief efforts have been successful.

Moreover, the institutions intermediate between the rich funders and the intended beneficiaries do not tend to face the pressures that keep other institutions accountable to their funders and their beneficiaries. Consider, for example, international aid NGOs. Aid NGOs are not run for profit, so are not accountable for providing good projects in the way that businesses are held accountable for providing good products and services through consumer choice. Nor of course are aid NGOs accountable to any democratic electorate. And the checks that can constrain government agencies, such as media scrutiny and academic study, in fact put quite weak pressure on aid NGOs to ensure effectiveness in aiding the poor. Since NGOs are bringing money into a poor country—typically by implementing smaller, local projects—the government and the media in the poor country generally do not give NGO effectiveness serious scrutiny. Moreover, the failure of a complex development project in a poor country is not something to which the international media ordinarily attends. While academics do publish studies of the effectiveness of NGO-implemented projects, there are presently few paths for translating these studies into sanctions for poor performance. And external audits on aid NGOs cover only the basics of financial probity, without touching on the effectiveness of the NGOs' projects.[20]

The intermediate institutions that are the most accountable to both rich and poor individuals are their respective national governments. Here again, however, the degree of accountability is quite limited. Rich individuals can in theory put pressure on their countries' aid bureaucracies through elections, lobbying, and public advocacy. Poor individuals can protest—and in some cases strike or vote—when international aid resources are not used in ways that they accept. Yet in general rich individuals find it very difficult to determine which of their governments' poverty relief efforts should be sanctioned for poor performance; and the poor mostly find themselves outmaneuvered or simply outgunned by the authorities within their states.[21] So we do not find much power in either rich or poor individuals to sanction intermediate institutions for the failure of development projects.

What we do find is some accountability between the connecting links within the chains of intermediate institutions. It is these internal relations of accountability that have been the subject of most recent attention and movements for reform. For example, there have been several proposals to restructure the voting system within the World Bank that aim to make the Bank more accountable to the governments of poor countries.[22] Or again, the Organization for Economic Cooperation and Development (OECD) countries have recently begun to make aid transfers more conditional on good governance in poor countries in an effort to make the governments of poor countries more accountable to the governments of rich ones.[23]

In evaluating such proposals for increasing accountability between linking institutions, attention to the costs and the benefits is particularly vital. There is nothing intrinsically valuable about making one institution more accountable to another. Increasing accountability between institutions always involves costs, and these costs should only be borne when they are outweighed by the benefits. Reducing severe poverty is by far the most urgent goal of development aid, so increasing accountability between institutions will be important primarily insofar as this leads to more effective poverty relief.

A corollary of this thesis is that the mere presence of accountability mechanisms between aid institutions is not sufficient to help reduce poverty. Indeed, mechanisms of accountability can impede poverty relief. The accountability mechanisms of the United States Agency for International Development (USAID), which is the main ministry that disburses official American aid, are an example of this.[24] USAID budgets operate on a yearly cycle; every year both houses of Congress and the State Department negotiate over which programs to fund.[25] The State Department typically attempts to deploy USAID money to reward or incentivize the governments of politically strategic allies. Congress, by contrast, responds to pressures of American interest groups, such as farmers and shippers who want to export excess U.S. grain on U.S. ships, or to ethnic groups who want funds channeled to foreign countries where their ethnicity predominates, or to manufacturers who want money given to foreign governments on the condition that the money be used to buy their manufactured goods.[26]

USAID accountability mechanisms work primarily to assist these domestic political and economic interests. Because of the competitive nature of the budgeting process, each interest group requires a detailed report from the agency who receives the funding—not primarily to assess whether a program has benefited the poor overseas, but rather to lay down a negotiating marker for the next budget cycle. The result of the USAID budgeting process is a system of heavy accountability that hinders poverty relief. The funds that USAID disburses are at best contingently related to long-term pro-poor goals, and the accounting requirements on recipient aid agencies take resources away from their efforts to help the poor. It should be noted that the lack of pro-poor accountability in USAID is not attributable to an idiosyncratic American meanness or ineptitude, but rather to the fact that funds are disbursed by a bureaucracy on which any pressures to help the foreign poor are almost entirely overwhelmed by pressures arising from domestic political and economic interests.[27] Accountability mechanisms are unlikely to further the cause of poverty reduction if they are not specifically designed to do this.

THE ACCOUNTABILITY OF AID NGOS

Of all the links of accountability within development aid, the most discussed recently have been those involving international aid NGOs such as Oxfam, Care, and Save the Children. NGO accountability is in many ways a more revealing topic than World Bank or International Monetary Fund (IMF) accountability, since these international financial institutions are clearly more accountable overall (although perhaps, as many have suggested, not to the right people or in the right ways).[28] NGO accountability is also an intriguing topic because it raises the question of whether NGOs—which often aim to hold others to account by, for example, publicizing public corruption or unfairness in trade— are themselves accountable.[29] The goal in examining NGO accountability in this section will not be to recommend any particular change in accountability mechanisms, but to survey the current state of NGO accountability and to compare two major approaches to NGO reform.

Financial probity is the aspect of NGO accountability that has received the most public attention. Most NGOs are legally accountable to their trustees, who ordinarily provide light oversight concerning fiscal management. NGOs must also typically account for their activities to the governments of the poor countries in which they operate, and sometimes also to the government of the country in which they are based; yet this usually amounts to little more than filing some perfunctory reports and being subject to an occasional audit.[30] These relatively relaxed standards regarding financial probity seem appropriate, since there is a general consensus that most aid NGOs handle their finances responsibly. The issue of most serious concern is not whether aid NGOs are engaging in defalcation, but whether they are using their resources effectively to benefit the poor—not their propriety, but their performance.

Regarding performance, no aid NGO is accountable in a significant way for benefiting the poor in the long term. If an aid NGO fails effectively to help the poor, there are virtually no mechanisms in place to sanction it. NGOs do not release (and, as we will see, often do not even collect) the information about project effectiveness that would enable private donors to hold them accountable for their successes and failures. The fund-raising materials that aid NGOs target at the public are not reliable sources of information for evaluating the agencies' effectiveness.[31] And the one financial figure that the public has tended to focus on—the ratio of fund-raising to administrative costs—has no standard meaning and little relevance to program success. Donor countries and multilaterals have recently been increasing their requirements on NGOs to report on project planning, finances, and progress.[32] Yet these funders generally do not sanction the NGOs they fund for lack of long-term benefit to their intended beneficiaries. Moreover, aid agencies tend to abide by a "code of silence" that bars them from criticizing each other for failing to mount effective projects.[33] And aid NGOs are accountable to the recipients of their aid for long-term impact virtually not at all.

Several theorists have observed that this lack of accountability in aid NGOs seems remarkable.[34] Organizations which have as their mission to improve the long-term conditions of the poor have virtually no responsibility to prove that they are accomplishing this mission. From the perspective developed here, the lack of accountability in aid NGOs is certainly a matter of concern. Yet the lack of NGO accountability should not generate hasty calls for reform.[35] Increasing NGO accountability will only be important when the reforms will be feasible, beneficial, and worth the costs that such mechanisms inevitably generate. Increasing NGO accountability will only be important insofar as this works to reduce poverty.

In contemporary discussions of NGO accountability, there are two main models for reform. One is that NGOs should increase their accountability upward—that is, their accountability to their trustees, to governments, or to the international financial institutions. The other major model for reform is that NGOs should increase their accountability downward—that is, their accountability to the poor individuals who are the intended beneficiaries of their programs. Each model for reform brings with it characteristic patterns of concerns.

Proposals for increased upward accountability for NGO are the most common.[36] Governments and the international financial institutions have underutilized capacity to sanction poor NGO performance by withholding future funding, and governments in particular have the ability to set legal requirements on NGOs for greater transparency and efficiency. Governments and the international institutions also have a great deal of technical expertise in development, as well as research departments with the capacity to collect and analyze a wide range of data on which kinds of projects are tending to be successful and which are not.

However, there are also clear risks in increasing NGO accountability upward. As we have seen in the USAID case, there is always the danger of state-NGO relations being driven by political and economic interests within the donor state that have little concern for helping the world's poor. Moreover, procedures for upward accountability tend to be time-consuming and bureaucratic. Standardized reports from the field may not reflect the realities in the field, and writing these reports takes resources away from implementing the projects. Moreover, upward accountability tends to be inflexible and only slowly responsive, thus limiting the ability of aid agencies to react quickly to the changes in circumstances that inevitably take place on the ground. There is also the risk that the threat of sanction will dissuade NGOs from attempting innovative strategies for development, or from undertaking more difficult projects.[37] Upward accountability is potentially useful for redirecting development aid based on past performance, but it risks hindering the effectiveness of the projects that are underway.

In recent years, there has been considerable enthusiasm for increasing NGO accountability downward, much of which has centered on a set of approaches called "participatory development."[38] Participatory development aims to engage the poor in the design, implementation, and evaluation of the development projects which target their poverty. The idea behind participatory development is to involve the poor in projects so that projects become more sensitive to local practices and aspirations, while also encouraging greater participation in the programs by giving the beneficiaries a sense of ownership in them. For example, Albanian villagers have been consulted as to what form a microlending program might take so as to be most useful to them, and residents of a Brazilian shantytown have been asked to help develop indicators for evaluating the success of a housing rights campaign. The obvious advantages of participation are that it draws on the greatest pool of knowledge about local circumstances, while also including the poor in projects in ways that can lead to lasting improvements in their conditions.

Involving the poor in the design and implementation of development projects can be an effective technique for improving project outcomes. Yet it is difficult to translate such involvement into mechanisms for accountability.[39] It is one thing to listen to the poor when designing a project, and another to give the poor the power to penalize what they judge to be bad performance.[40] In the terms of the conceptual analysis above, the poor may at best now have some limited standard-setting and performance-measuring powers. Yet they always lack the crucial power to sanction.[41] Even agencies like ActionAid and Save the Children U.K., which are in the vanguard of agencies promoting participation by the poor, do not allow the poor to penalize agency personnel or to redirect resources against staff wishes. In these agencies' projects, information flows to and from the poor, but the power over resources remains as always top-down.[42] As things stand, this seems almost inevitable. The poor have no way to force NGOs to cede power to them, and it is extremely rare for organizations (or, for that matter, for individuals) freely to grant to others the power to discipline them for not fulfilling their responsibilities.[43]

Despite the attractive sound of increased downward accountability, the most feasible proposals for reform are therefore those that make rich actors the agents of accountability. Only power balances power, and it is in general only the rich and their agents who will be able to hold the rich and their agents to account.

A PROPOSAL FOR INCREASING ACCOUNTABILITY IN DEVELOPMENT AID

There are many ways of construing the direction of mechanisms for accountability besides upward and downward. Recently there have been "hybrid" proposals for "mutual," "diagonal," and even "transversal" accountability.[44] Here I will explore the potential of one mechanism of "horizontal" accountability. In horizontal accountability, agents who are engaged in an activity regulate themselves. Examples of mechanisms of horizontal accountability are ombudsmen, ethics committees, and administrative courts.[45] The proposal that follows aims to set out a mechanism of horizontal accountability to oversee one of the most important parts of the development cycle: the evaluation of projects. This proposal to increase accountability in evaluation is put forward as a plan for a feasible mechanism of accountability whose benefits in terms of poverty relief seem likely to outweigh its costs.[46]

The evaluation of a development project is the primary mechanism by which the success of the project is judged. Evaluation is therefore the major mechanism through which it could be known which development agencies are being effective in alleviating poverty, and which types of projects work in different settings.

Development evaluation is its own professional specialization, with university-based training programs, departments within aid agencies and government ministries, a specialized literature, international conferences, and so on. Evaluation is professionalized because development projects are typically very difficult to assess. An evaluator must judge what effects a given intervention (like an AIDS education program or a clean water initiative) has had within an extraordinary complex causal environment, and can only make these judgments by contrasting the current situation with a counterfactual hypothesis concerning what would have happened had the intervention not been made. The difficulties in projecting accurate counterfactuals are significant, and the estimation of project effectiveness will depend greatly on which hypothesis is chosen.[47] More-over an evaluator must consider not only the effectiveness of the project in meeting its goals, but also its efficiency in terms of cost. An evaluator must in addition try to predict the long-term effects of the project, since these effects are typically the most vital for the project's success. Because of all of these complexities, there is a great deal of latitude in judging how successful any given project has been and will be.

It is likely that the latitude available to project evaluators, combined with the general lack of accountability in development agencies, has resulted in a serious positive bias in project evaluation. It is likely, that is, that evaluators tend to attribute more success to projects than is warranted.[48] We can see why this phenomenon is likely to occur before assessing the significance of its occurrence.

The reasons for the positive bias are simply that all parties (besides the poor) have an interest in projects being evaluated positively, and that there are few mechanisms of accountability in place to check this tendency. Aid agencies have an interest in positive evaluations, since these positive reviews will confirm their image of effectiveness and possibly help with fund raising. The governments of funding countries and recipient countries have interests in positive evaluations, since these validate their approval of the projects. And, most importantly, the evaluators themselves have strong reasons to submit positive evaluations. This is obvious for the "self-evaluations" that are done for most smaller development projects, where the group that has implemented the project also judges the success of the project. It is also true of evaluators who are hired as outside consultants for larger projects, since these consultants know that their future employment may turn on a favorable review of the project of the agency that employs them. Even in-house evaluators, like those who work in the institution-ally insulated evaluation department of the World Bank, know that the way to get ahead is not to file too many reports that their agency's projects have failed.[49]

Examples of falsely positive evaluations, and the pressures to file such evalua-tions, are well known to evaluation professionals.[50] One consequence of this apparently widespread positive bias is that it amplifies the difficulties in obtain-ing reliable information about what types of projects work in which settings. The latest report of the evaluation department of the World Bank has concluded that the capacity of the Bank to measure the impacts of its efforts on poverty remains weak.[51] And a major, independent study of NGO effectiveness states that

A repeated and consistent conclusion drawn across countries and in rela-tion to all clusters of studies is that the data are exceptionally poor. There is a paucity of data and information from which to draw firm conclusions about the impact of projects, about efficiency and effectiveness, about sustainability, the gender and environmental impact of projects, and their contribution to strengthening democratic forces . . . and institutional capacity.[52]

As one reviewer concluded, "Multi-country studies raise serious doubts as to whether many NGOs know what they are doing, in the sense of their overall impact on people's lives."[53]

The benefits of enhancing the quality of evaluations are straightforward. The effectiveness of development assistance depends on the capacity of its practitioners to allocate resources in such a way as to maximize project impacts. If project evaluations can routinely make sound estimates of likely project impacts and cost-effectiveness, this will increase both the capacity and the incentives for planners to make the judgments upon which the effectiveness of development assistance depends. Since managers will gain from evaluations a more nuanced understanding of the consequences of their resource-allocation choices, the quality of these choices will improve over time. Since managers will anticipate that the consequences of their choices will be clearly identified in an evaluation, they will be more likely to take corrective action when this is needed. Donors who receive credible assurance about the quality of development programs and projects will be more confident in increasing their aid budgets.

Evaluators are currently employed by those who fund the projects that they evaluate. These funding organizations have strong interests in receiving positive evaluations of their projects' effectiveness. The structural problem that evaluators face in this way parallels the situation of accountants and auditors in publicly traded corporations. The accountants who keep the books and the auditors who check the books are employed by the managers of the firms being assessed. Yet the interest of corporate managers in using corporate resources for private purposes conflicts with the shareholders' interest in managers promoting profits. Accountants and auditors are protected from being "captured" by the private interests of management by the rules of their professions, as codified, for example, in the Generally Accepted Accounting Principles (GAAP), which are interpreted by associations of their peers. The aim of the proposed evaluation association is to generate an analogous set of principles and institutional capacities for evaluation professionals in development aid. A professional association of project evaluators would provide a counterweight to the institutional incentives for positive bias, while also improving the techniques of project evaluation.

The evaluation association would have the following structure. It would have a guide book, criteria for membership, a stamp, a standards committee, and a repository database. The guidebook would lay out general principles for project evaluation, focusing on likely project impacts and cost-effectiveness. Any member conducting an evaluation under the association's stamp would be bound to follow the approach laid out in the guidebook or risk losing membership. This rule would be the source of the evaluator's independence from project management. The standards committee would be responsible for determining if evaluations comply with the association's standards. Each evaluation completed under the association's stamp would be indexed and included in a database in the repository. The repository would be made accessible to the association's members, to donor agency officials, and to project managers.

In addition to enhancing evaluator independence, the association would through its repository also support methodological advances in evaluation practice. The availability of independent evaluations would create incentives for decentralized improvements in evaluation practice, as evaluators use the repository to identify more effective approaches to impact assessment problems. These improvements will then in turn feed into improvements in project design. In this way the development community could through its own efforts generate a better understanding of what works to reduce poverty.

For the evaluation association to become viable, it would need a critical mass of members (evaluators), and these members would need a market for their services. This presents a "chicken and egg" challenge for the early stages of the association: evaluators may not invest in joining the association without a secure market, and donors may not hire evaluators (possibly at a premium) who limit their influence on the evaluation process. Both evaluators and donors may recognize that an evaluation association is in the interests of the development community; yet they face a collective action problem in getting it off the ground. The best way to address this problem is for prospective stakeholders to be involved in designing the association. The initial challenge for the evaluation association would be to give the stakeholders a sense of common cause without compromising the association's independence and so its rationale. It is particularly important that these stakeholders agree on the principles of evaluation to be used in the guidebook, and on the procedures for withdrawing the stamp from those judged not to have followed these principles.

Creating the evaluation association would involve moderate monetary start-up costs, as well as continuing costs associated with the operation of a new professional organization. These costs would be comparatively minor were the association to become effective in improving the evaluation of development projects. The association would also generate the transaction costs associated with adding any new layer of bureaucracy to a managerial system. These bureaucratic costs seem worth bearing. One general difficulty in development is that there are few cross-institutional mechanisms of accountability whose specific aim is to increase aid effectiveness. The institutional frameworks that link development agencies are weak and unstructured, just as the institutions of governance in many poor countries are weak and unstructured. And evaluation in particular is still in its early stages of evolution: there are many development specialists who have observed the genesis of the entire field within the span of their own careers.[54] Getting the institutional setting right for evaluation, so that incentives point in the right direction and information flows more freely among aid agencies, has the potential significantly to increase our understanding of what aid works.[55]

The proposed evaluation association would be a mechanism of horizontal accountability that makes evaluators more accountable to their peers. In providing this level of horizontal accountability, the association would also generate information about project effectiveness that would increase the vertical accountability of aid agencies to funding bodies, and eventually perhaps even to rich individuals. However, even if the evaluation association did come to be successful, its beneficial effects would be primarily at the level of improved design and implementation of projects. The association would leave many of the problems of diverted resources and project aggregation unaddressed. Given the generally low starting level of accountability in development aid, and the need for care because of the potential risks of reforms, such modest proposals for progress seem the best that can be hoped for.

THE CHALLENGE OF ACCOUNTABILITY

Development aid poses a series of complex challenges. Projects must both fit and revise local skills and customs; the institutional setting within which the projects are undertaken is typically dysfunctional or chaotic; more powerful actors at all levels are constantly attempting to capture the resources intended for the worst-off; and the conglomeration of development efforts can generate antidevelopment effects. It is these difficulties and the uncertain record of aid effectiveness that have spurred movements for greater accountability in development aid.

Morally, the greatest need for accountability would be for the rich to be accountable to the poor for effective and sufficient development aid. But significant accountability of that kind is nonexistent and probably impossible. The second most important connection of accountability would be for intermediate institutions to become more accountable for the effectiveness of projects either to the rich individuals who fund them or to the poor individuals who are meant to benefit from them. However, the complexities of development work and the poor's lack of power mean that there is currently little significant accountability to either rich or poor individuals.

Where there is some degree of accountability it is between the intermediate institutions. In some cases, as with USAID, the accountability mechanisms in place do not work to reduce poverty. In these cases, there is a strong argument for institutional reform. In other cases, as with aid NGOs, accountability for effective poverty relief is almost entirely absent. This is not in itself an indictment of aid NGOs. Greater accountability is not always good and when greater accountability in development agencies would be good, its value is only instrumental, not intrinsic. The overriding value when considering reform of aid institutions is what works to reduce poverty. There is a need to be more forth-right about the current state of accountability within international development aid. This would help to shift the focus onto those specific proposals for increasing accountability that will lead to long-term improvements in the lives of the world's poor.

NOTES

This essay appeared in *Ethics & International Affairs* 20, no. 1 (2006): 1–23. My thanks to the Carnegie Council for Ethics in International Affairs for supporting the research for this chapter through a fellowship in their Justice and the World Economy program, and the participants in the discussions of the chapter at Princeton University, University College London, and the Carnegie Council. I would especially like to thank Christian Barry, James Cairns, Paul Clements, Sakiko Fukuda-Parr, Lisa Fuller, Graham Harrison, Bruce Jones, Madeleine Lynn, Roger Maconick, Lydia Tomitova, and Jonathan Wolff for their criticisms and advice.

1. Coralie Bryant, quoted in Jon Christensen, "Asking the Do-Gooders to Prove They Do Good," *New York Times*, January 3, 2004.

2. This chapter does not discuss international humanitarian ("emergency") aid. Fiona Terry, *Condemned to Repeat? The Paradox of Humanitarian Action* (Ithaca, NY: Cornell University Press, 2002) is an excellent discussion of the issues that have raised concerns about accountability in humanitarian aid agencies. See also the Humanitarian Accountability Partnership International website at www.hapinternational.org. I bracket for the time being the point that a significant proportion of what is counted as international development aid is not given with the aim of bettering the conditions of the poor, but is given for political and strategic reasons.

3. Michael Fleshman, "Africa Pushes for Better Aid Quality," *Africa Recovery* 17, no. 4 (2004): 18. In this section, and in the two that follow, I draw on Leif Wenar, "What We Owe to Distant Others," *Politics, Philosophy & Economics* 2, no. 3 (2003): 283–304; and Leif Wenar, "The Basic Structure as Object: Institutions and Humanitarian Concern," in *Global Justice, Global Institutions*, ed. Daniel Weinstock (Calgary: University of Calgary Press, 2007).

4. Charles Handy, *Understanding Organizations*, 4th ed. (New York: Penguin, 2005); and Basil Edward Cracknell, *Evaluating Development Aid: Issues, Problems, and Solutions* (New Delhi: Sage, 2000).

5. It is not uncommon for projects to face internal as well as environmental challenges, for example, when a funder fails to follow through on its commitment to provide resources during the implementation of the project.

6. Norman Uphoff, "Why NGOs Are Not a Third Sector: A Sectoral Analysis with Some Thoughts on Accountability, Sustainability, and Evaluation," in *Non-Governmental Organizations—Performance and Accountability: Beyond the Magic Bullet*, ed. Michael Edwards and David Hulme (London: Earthscan, 1995); and Peter Oakley, *The Danish NGO Impact Study: A Review of Danish NGO Activities in Developing Countries* (Oxford: INTRAC, 1999), 81–83.

7. Susan Rose-Ackerman, "Governance and Corruption," in *Global Crises, Global Solutions*, ed. Bjørn Lomborg (Cambridge: Cambridge University Press, 2004).

8. Nazmul Chaudhury and Jeffrey Hammer, "Ghost Doctors: Absenteeism in Bangladeshi Health Facilities," World Bank Policy Research Working Paper 3065 (2003).

9.   See Denise Dresser, "Bringing the Poor Back In: National Solidarity as a Strategy of Regime Legitimation," in *Transforming State-Society Relations in Mexico: The National Solidarity Strategy*, ed. Wayne Cornelius, Ann Craig, and Jonathan Fox (La Jolla, CA: Center for U.S.-Mexican Studies, 1994). Alberto Diaz-Cayeros and Beatriz Magaloni estimate that the PRONASOL funds, if perfectly targeted as monetary transfers, would have alleviated one third of the severe poverty in Mexico (where 15 percent of the population was under the $1 per day international poverty line during the period when the program was implemented). See Diaz-Cayeros and Magaloni, "The Politics of Public Spending: Part II, The Programa Nacional de Solidaridad (PRONASOL) in Mexico," World Bank Background Paper 28013 (2003), 2–3.

10.   Jean-Paul Azam, Shantayan Devarajan, and Stephen O'Connell, "Aid Dependence Reconsidered," World Bank Policy Research Working Paper 2144 (1999); Christopher Adam and Stephen O'Connell, "Aid, Taxation, and Development in Sub-Saharan Africa," *Economics and Politics* 11, no. 3 (1999): 225–53.

11.   Raghuram G. Rajan and Arvind Subramanian, "Aid and Growth: What Does the Cross-Country Evidence Really Show?" National Bureau of Economic Research Working Paper 11513 (2005).

12.   Fleshman, "Africa Pushes for Better Aid Quality," 18; and Michael Edwards and David Hulme, "NGO Performance and Accountability," in *The Earthscan Reader on NGO Management*, ed. Michael Edwards and Alan Fowler (London: Earthscan, 2002), 190.

13.   The report reads, "Whatever the projects' individual qualities, the collective impact was chaotic, because of the huge administrative burden on the Tanzanian government and because the projects employed large numbers of the most qualified people in the country, many of whom had been lured away from the public sector." UNDP, *Development Effectiveness Report* (New York: United Nations, 2003), 41.

14.   See, for example, Paul Mosley, John Hudson, and Sara Horrell, "Aid, The Public Sector and the Market in Less Developed Countries," *Economic Journal* 97, no. 387 (1987): 616–641; Peter Boone, "Politics and the Effectiveness of Foreign Aid," *European Economic Review* 40, no. 2 (1996): 289–329; Craig Burnside and David Dollar, "Aid, Policies, and Growth: Revisiting the Evidence," World Bank Policy Research Working Paper 3251 (2004); David Roodman, "The Anarchy of Numbers: Aid, Development, and Cross-Country Empirics," Center for International Development Working Paper 32 (2004); Rajan and Subramanian, "Aid and Growth"; and Edwards and Fowler, eds., *Earthscan Reader*, 190.

15.   Ruth W. Grant and Robert O. Keohane, "Accountability and Abuses of Power in World Politics," *American Political Science Review* 99, no. 1 (2005): 29–43.

16.   Robert D. Behn, *Rethinking Democratic Accountability* (Washington, DC: Brookings Institution, 2001), 3; and Andreas Schedler, "Conceptualizing Accountability," in *The Self-Restraining State: Power and Accountability in New Democracies*, ed. Andreas Schedler, Larry Diamond, and Marc F. Plattner (Boulder, CO: Lynne Rienner, 1999); Ronald Oakerson, "Governance Structures for Enhancing Accountability and Responsiveness," in *Handbook of Public Administration*, ed. James L. Perry (San Francisco: Jossey-Bass, 1989), 114; Norman Daniels and James E. Sabin, *Setting Limits Fairly: Learning to Share Resources for Health* (New York: Oxford University Press, 2002), 45–63.

17.   Some authors writing on development use the term "accountability" in a looser sense, requiring only that an accountable agent show itself to be responding to the demands of what it is responsible for; or in an "agency" sense, requiring that one actor be acting on behalf of another. See Hugo Slim, "By What Authority? The Legitimacy and Accountability of Non-Governmental Organizations," *Journal of Humanitarian Assistance* (March 2002);

Bernard Manin, Adam Przeworski, and Susan C. Stokes, "Introduction," 8–10; Jon Elster, "Accountability in Athenian Politics"; James D. Fearon, "Electoral Accountability and the Control of Politicians: Selecting Good Types versus Sanctioning Poor Performance," in *Democracy, Accountability, and Representation*, ed. Manin, Przeworski, and Stokes (Cambridge: Cambridge University Press, 1999); Richard Mulgan, "Accountability: An Ever-Expanding Concept?" *Public Administration* 78, no. 3 (2002): 555–73; Simon Burall and Caroline Neligan, "The Accountability of International Organizations," GPPi Research Paper 2 (Geneva and Berlin: Global Public Policy Institute, 2005).

18.   See Elster, "Accountability in Athenian Politics"; Edwards and Hulme, "NGO Performance and Accountability," 196; Alnoor Ebrahim, "Accountability in Practice: Mechanisms for NGOs," *World Development* 31, no. 5 (2003): 813–29; Tina Wallace and Jennifer Chapman, "An Investigation into the Reality Behind NGO Rhetoric of Downward Accountability," in *Creativity and Constraint: Grassroots Monitoring and Evaluation and the International Aid Area*, ed. Lucy Earle (Oxford: INTRAC, 2004); and Lisa Jordan, "Mechanisms for NGO Accountability," GPPi Research Paper 3 (2005). For a sensitive and wide-ranging analysis of the costs of accountability, see Onora O'Neill, *A Question of Trust: The BBC Reith Lectures 2002* (Cambridge: Cambridge University Press, 2002).

19.   Titus Alexander, "In the Name of the People: Strengthening Global Accountability," One World Trust Discussion Paper (2002).

20.   Occasionally a nonspecialist book that describes the failings of NGO development efforts attracts some public attention; e.g., Alex de Waal, *Famine Crimes: Politics and the Disaster Relief Industry in Africa* (Bloomington: Indiana University Press, 1998); and Michael Maren, *The Road to Hell: The Ravaging Effects of Foreign Aid and International Charity* (New York: Free Press, 2002). The main effect of such books seems to be to reinforce generalized aid skepticism in some segments of the public instead of leading to sanctions on specific NGOs.

21.   John M. Ackerman, "Co-Governance for Accountability: Beyond 'Exit' and 'Voice'," *World Development* 32, no. 3 (2004): 447–63.

22.   Ngaire Woods, "Making the IMF and the World Bank More Accountable," *International Affairs* 77, no. 1 (2001): 83–100; Devesh Kapur, "The Changing Anatomy of Governance of the World Bank"; Bruce Rich, "The World Bank under James Wolfensohn," in *Reinventing the World Bank*, ed. Jonathan R. Pincus and Jeffrey A. Winters (Ithaca, NY: Cornell University Press, 2002).

23.   OECD, *Action for a Shared Development Agenda* (Paris: OECD, 2002).

24.   USAID controlled $5.7 billion of the $12.6 billion U.S. foreign aid budget in 2004. The Millennium Challenge Corporation is now growing rapidly, and its ascendancy will represent a major shift in how U.S. aid is administered. See Curt Tarnoff and Larry Nowels, "Foreign Aid: An Introductory Overview of U.S. Programs and Policy," (Washington, DC: Congressional Research Service Report for Congress, 2004).

25.   Here I draw on Paul Clements, "Development as if Impact Mattered" (Ph.D. dissertation, Woodrow Wilson School of Public & International Affairs, Princeton University, 1996).

26.   Peter J. Schraeder, Steven W. Hook, and Bruce Taylor, "Clarifying the Foreign Aid Puzzle: A Comparison of American, Japanese, French, and Swedish Aid Flows," *World Politics* 50, no. 2 (1998): 294–323. The Congressional Research Service reports: "Most U.S. foreign aid is used for procurement of U.S. goods and services, although amounts of aid coming back to the United States differ by program. No exact figure is available due to difficulties in tracking procurement item by item, but some general estimates are possible for individual programs,

though these may differ year to year . . . Food assistance commodities are purchased wholly in the United States, and most expenditures for shipping those commodities to recipient countries go entirely to U.S. freight companies. Under current legislation, three-fourths of all food aid must be shipped by U.S. carriers. On this basis, a rough estimate suggests that more than 90%—at least $1 billion in FY2004—of food aid expenditures will be spent in the United States . . . Most bilateral development assistance and the ESF, NIS and SEED components of economic, political and security assistance support programs in developing countries and the new European democracies, respectively. Although a small proportion of funding for these programs results in transfers of U.S. dollars, the services of experts and project management personnel, and much of the required equipment, is procured from the United States. According to USAID, 81% of total USAID procurement between October 2002 and September 2003 under these programs came from U.S. sources." Tarnoff and Nowels, "Foreign Aid," 18–19.

27.   See ibid., 294–323; and Alberto Alesina and David Dollar, "Who Gives Foreign Aid to Whom and Why?" *Journal of Economic Growth* 5, no. 1 (2000): 33–63.

28.   Jonathan A. Fox and L. David Brown, *The Struggle for Accountability: The World Bank, NGOs, and Grassroots Movements* (Cambridge, MA: MIT Press, 1998); Robert Dahl, "Can International Organizations Be Democratic?" in *Democracy's Edges*, ed. Ian Shapiro and Casiano Hacker-Cordon (Cambridge: Cambridge University Press, 1999); and Grant and Keohane, "Accountability and Abuses of Power in World Politics." For critical views on these institutions generally see the Bretton Woods Project website at www.brettonwoodsproject .org. The World Bank has an Inspection Panel, to which individuals and groups can protest that a Bank-funded project has harmed or will harm their interests. The effectiveness of the Inspection Panel as a mechanism of accountability has been controversial; see Dana Clark, Jonathan Fox, and Kay Treakle, eds., *Demanding Accountability: Civil Society Claims and the World Bank Inspection Panel* (Lanham, MD: Rowman & Littlefield, 2003).

29.   Grant and Keohane, "Accountability and Abuses of Power in World Politics"; Paul Wapner et al., symposium on "The Democratic Accountability of Non-Governmental Organizations," *Chicago Journal of International Law* 3, no. 1 (2002). For views critical of NGO accountability, see the papers from the American Enterprise Institute's June 11, 2003 conference in Washington, DC, "We're Not from the Government, But We're Here to Help You"; available at www.ngowatch.org/ngo.htm. The discussion of NGOs here focuses primarily on how NGOs fund and implement development projects. Several major NGOs are increasingly engaged in political advocacy campaigns, and accountability for such campaigns will remain limited by the great difficulties of measuring their impacts on poverty. It should also be noted that while the study of NGOs reveals much about the state of accountability in development aid, discussions of NGO effectiveness should be kept in context. NGOs account for a relatively small percentage of global aid expenditure, the most commonly cited figure being 15 percent of the total.

30.   Edwards and Hulme, "NGO Performance and Accountability."

31.   See ibid., 190: "Internal evaluations are rarely released and what *is* released comes closer to propaganda than rigorous assessment"; and Slim, "By What Authority?"

32.   John de Coninck, *Current Procedures and Policies Dominating Aid: Building Strong Relationships and Enabling NGOs to Meet their Stated Aims?* (Uganda: Community Development Resource Network, 2004); and Wallace and Chapman, "An Investigation into the Reality Behind NGO Rhetoric of Downward Accountability."

33.   Ian Smillie, "Changing Partners: Northern NGOs, Northern Governments," in *Non-Governmental Organizations and Governments: Stakeholders for Development*, ed. Ian Smillie and Henry Helmich (Paris: OECD, 1993).

34. See ibid.; Edwards and Hulme, "NGO Performance and Accountability"; and Peter Shiras, "The New Realities of Non-Profit Accountability," *Alliance* 8, no. 4 (2003).

35. See John Hailey and Mia Sorgenfrei, "Measuring Success: Issues in Performance Measurement," INTRAC Occasional Paper 44 (2004), which also contains a history of performance measuring standards in the private and public sectors.

36. Ebrahim, "Accountability in Practice."

37. See Edwards and Hulme, eds., *Non-Governmental Organizations*; Coninck, *Current Procedures and Policies Dominating Aid*; and Jordan, "Mechanisms for NGO Accountability."

38. Richard Chambers, *Whose Reality Counts? Putting the Last First* (London: ITDG Press, 1997); Somesh Kumar, *Methods of Community Participation* (London: ITDG Press, 2003); Chris Roche, *Impact Assessment for Development Agencies: Learning to Value Change* (Sterling, VA: Stylus, 1999); Frits Wils, "Scaling Up Mainstream Accountability: The Challenge for NGOs," in *Non-Governmental Organizations*, ed. Edwards and Hulme. For some doubts see Frances Cleaver, "Beyond Partnership: Getting Real about NGO Relationships in the Aid System," in *Earthscan Reader*, ed. Edwards and Fowler.

39. Wallace and Chapman, "An Investigation into the Reality Behind NGO Rhetoric of Downward Accountability."

40. Burall and Neligan, "Accountability of International Organizations."

41. Roche, *Impact Assessment*.

42. Yedla Padmavathi, "Whose Dreams? Whose Voices? Involving Children in Project Management," and Jennifer Chapman, Rosalind David, and Antonella Mancini, "Transforming Practice in ActionAid: Experiences and Challenges in Rethinking Learning, Monitoring and Accountability Systems," in *Creativity and Constraint*, ed. Earle.

43. Norman Uphoff, "Why NGOs Are Not a Third Sector: A Sectoral Analysis with Some Thoughts on Accountability, Sustainability, and Evaluation," in *Non-Governmental Organizations*, ed. Edwards and Hulme, 20. There is anecdotal evidence that in some sub-Saharan African states, the saturation of aid agencies on the ground is great enough that community leaders do have some power to choose among the various projects that different agencies offer. This may provide an accountability mechanism analogous to that of consumer choice among for-profit corporations, as community leaders have the power to choose the "service" that will serve them or their community best. One might speculate that this mechanism of accountability might become more important were significantly more aid funds channeled through NGOs.

However, as it stands the power of choice mostly goes in the other direction: NGOs can choose which communities to work in, and are less likely to choose to work in communities that have the capacity to sanction them. For instance, NGOs would be much less willing to work in jurisdictions where there is a World Bank–style Inspection Panel (see note 28), or still less where they could be sued for negligence (as Kunibert Raffer recommends with respect to the international financial institutions, in his "Reforming the Bretton Woods Institutions," *Zagreb International Review of Economics and Business* Special Issue [2002]: 97–109).

44. Organization for Economic Cooperation and Development, "Paris Declaration on Aid Effectiveness" (Paris: OECD, 2005); Ackerman, "Co-Governance for Accountability"; and Anne Marie Goetz and Rob Jenkins, "Hybrid Forms of Accountability and Human Development: Citizen Engagement of a New Agenda," Background Paper for *Human Development Report 2002* (New York: UNDP, 2002).

45. See Guillermo O'Donnell, "Horizontal Accountability in New Democracies," in *The Self-Restraining State*, ed. Schedler, Diamond, and Plattner; and Ackerman, "Co-Governance for Accountability."

46.   I draw here on a proposal for an evaluation association co-authored with Paul Clements. Clements came up with the idea for the association is the driving force behind the proposal.

47.   Roche, *Impact Assessment*; and Simon Starling, "Balancing Measurement, Management, and Accountability: Lessoned Learned from Save the Children U.K.'s Impact Assessment Framework" (paper presented at INTRAC Conference, Oxford, March 31–April 4, 2003). The use of randomized evaluation methods to address the problem of counterfactuals is a promising recent development. See Esther Duflo and Michael Kremer, "Use of Randomization in the Evaluation of Development Effectiveness," in *Evaluating Development Effectiveness*, ed. George Pitman, Osvaldo Feinstein, and Gregory Ingram (New Brunswick, NJ: Transaction Publishers, 2005).

48.   Jerker Carlsson, Gunnar Kohlin, and Anders Ekbom, *The Political Economy of Evaluation: International Aid Agencies and the Effectiveness of Aid* (London: Macmillan, 1994); Paul Clements, "Informational Standards in Development Agency Management," *World Development* 27 (1999): 1359–81.

49.   Carlsson et al. (see note 48) report on the related process of project appraisal that "Even an appraisal system as rigorous as the World Bank's is in practice continuously being manipulated, because it is subordinated to the individual interests of POs [project officers] (getting projects to the Board) as well as the organization's own objectives (meeting the disbursement targets). . . . Individuals are rational in the sense that they defend their, or their group's, interests." The authors of this book do not allege that evaluations are positively biased but rather that evaluations are based on such inconsistent assumptions and methodologies that they are practically useless.

50.   Clements, "Informational Standards."

51.   World Bank, *2004 Annual Review of Development Effectiveness* (Washington, DC: World Bank, 2005), 51–52.

52.   Roger C. Riddell et al., "Searching for Impact and Methods: NGO Evaluation Synthesis Study" (Helsinki: Institute of Development Studies, 2001), 99, also say, "If there is one consistent theme to come out of the majority of the country case studies it is that for the sheer numbers of evaluations that have been carried out, there are very few rigorous studies which examine impact: improvements in the lives and livelihoods of the beneficiaries" (24). Similar conclusions are reached in Oakley, *The Danish NGO Impact Study*, 29–51.

53.   Rick Davies, "Monitoring and Evaluating NGO Achievements," in *The Arnold Companion to Development Studies*, ed. Vandana Desai and Robert B. Potter (London: Hodder Arnold, 2002), 524; also see Stein-Erik Kruse, "Meta-Evaluations of NGO Experience: Results and Challenges," in *Evaluating Development Effectiveness*, ed. Pitman, Feinstein, and Ingram.

54.   Cracknell, *Evaluating Development Aid*, contains a good introduction to the history of evaluation. One sees in this book how evaluation professionals have within the short span of forty years invented, standardized, and refined the fundamental techniques of project analysis, as well as the basic norms of professionalism. See Roche, *Impact Assessment*, on the even more recent evolution of (long-term) impact assessment.

55.   One reviewer for *Ethics & International Affairs* raised the possibility that project evaluation faces too many technical and methodological difficulties to be rigorous and reliable except in very rare circumstances. Yet given that proposals like the current one seem feasible and their potential benefits appear to be significant, it seems too early to give in to skepticism concerning the possibilities for making progress on evaluation.

Chapter | 5

World Poverty and Human Rights

Thomas Pogge

DESPITE A HIGH AND GROWING global average income, billions of human beings are still condemned to lifelong severe poverty, with all its attendant evils of low life expectancy, social exclusion, ill health, illiteracy, dependency, and effective enslavement. The annual death toll from poverty-related causes is around 18 million, or one-third of all human deaths, which adds up to approximately 360 million deaths since the end of the Cold War.[1]

This problem is hardly unsolvable, in spite of its magnitude. In 2004, the 2.5 billion people counted as living below the World Bank's more generous $2 per day international poverty line—though constituting 39 percent of the world's population—accounted for only about 1 percent of the global product, and would have needed only 0.7 percent more to escape poverty so defined.[2] By contrast, the high-income countries, with one billion citizens, had about 80 percent of the global product.[3] With our average per capita income some 200 times greater than that of the poor (at market exchange rates), we could eradicate severe poverty worldwide if we chose to try—in fact, we could have eradicated it decades ago.

Citizens of the rich countries are, however, conditioned to downplay the severity and persistence of world poverty and to think of it as an occasion for minor charitable assistance. Thanks in part to the rationalizations dispensed by our economists, most of us believe that severe poverty and its persistence are due exclusively to local causes. Few realize that severe poverty is an ongoing harm we inflict upon the global poor. If more of us understood the true magnitude of the problem of poverty and our causal involvement in it, we might do what is necessary to eradicate it.

That world poverty is an ongoing harm *we* inflict seems completely incredible to most citizens of the affluent countries. We call it tragic that the basic human rights of so many remain unfulfilled, and are willing to admit that we should do more to help. But it is unthinkable to us that we are actively responsible for this catastrophe. If we were, then we, civilized and sophisticated denizens

of the developed countries, would be guilty of the largest crime against humanity ever committed, the death toll of which exceeds, *every week*, that of the 2004
tsunami and, every three years, that of World War II, the concentration camps
and gulags included. What could be more preposterous?

But think about the unthinkable for a moment. Are there steps the affluent
countries could take to reduce severe poverty abroad? It seems very likely that
there are, given the enormous income inequalities already mentioned. The common assumption, however, is that reducing severe poverty abroad at the
expense of our own affluence would be generous on our part, not something
we owe, and that our failure to do this is thus at most a lack of generosity that
does not make us morally responsible for the continued deprivation of the poor.

I deny this popular assumption. I deny that the one billion citizens of the
affluent countries are morally entitled to their 80 percent of the global product
in the face of much larger numbers of people mired in severe poverty. Is this
denial really so preposterous that one need not consider the arguments in its
support? Does not the radical inequality between our wealth and their dire need
at least put the burden on us to show why we should be morally entitled to so
much while they have so little? In *World Poverty and Human Rights*,[4] I dispute
the popular assumption by showing that the usual ways of justifying our great
advantage fail. My argument poses three mutually independent challenges.

ACTUAL HISTORY

Many believe that the radical inequality we face can be justified by reference to
how it evolved, for example through differences in diligence, culture, and social
institutions, soil, climate, or fortune. I challenge this sort of justification by
invoking the common and very violent history through which the present radical inequality accumulated. Much of it was built up in the colonial era, when
today's affluent countries ruled today's poor regions of the world: trading their
people like cattle, destroying their political institutions and cultures, taking their
lands and natural resources, and forcing products and customs upon them. I
recount these historical facts specifically for readers who believe that even the
most radical inequality is morally justifiable if it evolved in a benign way. Such
readers disagree about the conditions a historical process must meet for it to
justify such vast inequalities in life chances. But I can bypass these disagreements because the actual historical crimes were so horrendous, diverse, and
consequential that no historical entitlement conception could credibly support
the view that our common history was sufficiently benign to justify today's huge
inequality in starting places.

Challenges such as this are often dismissed with the lazy response that we
cannot be held responsible for what others did long ago. This response is true
but irrelevant. We indeed cannot inherit responsibility for our forefathers' sins.
But how then can we plausibly claim the *fruits* of their sins? How can we have

been entitled to the great head start our countries enjoyed going into the postcolonial period, which has allowed us to dominate and shape the world? And how
can we be entitled to the huge advantages over the global poor we consequently
enjoy from birth? The historical path from which our exceptional affluence
arose greatly weakens our moral claim to it—certainly in the face of those whom
the same historical process has delivered into conditions of acute deprivation.
They, the global poor, have a much stronger moral claim to that 1 percent of
the global product they may need to meet their basic needs than we affluent
have to take 80 rather than 79 percent for ourselves. Thus, I write, "A morally
deeply tarnished history should not be allowed to result in *radical* inequality."[5]

FICTIONAL HISTORIES

Since my first challenge addressed adherents of historical entitlement conceptions of justice, it may leave others unmoved. These others may believe that it
is permissible to uphold any economic distribution, no matter how skewed, if
merely it *could* have come about on a morally acceptable path. They insist that
we are entitled to keep and defend what we possess, even at the cost of millions
of deaths each year, unless there is conclusive proof that, without the horrors
of the European conquests, severe poverty worldwide would be substantially
less today.

Now, *any* distribution, however unequal, *could* be the outcome of a sequence
of voluntary bets or gambles. Appeal to such a fictional history would "justify"
anything and would thus be wholly implausible. John Locke does much better,
holding that a fictional history can justify the status quo only if the changes in
holdings and social rules it involves are ones that all participants could have
rationally agreed to. He also holds that in a state of nature persons would be
entitled to a proportional share of the world's natural resources. Whoever
deprives others of "enough and as good"—either through unilateral appropria-
tions or through institutional arrangements, such as a radically unequal property regime—harms them in violation of a *negative* duty. For Locke, the justice
of any institutional order thus depends on whether the worst-off under it are at
least as well off as people would be in a state of nature with a proportional
resource share.[6] This baseline is imprecise, to be sure, but it suffices for my
second challenge: however one may want to imagine a state of nature among
human beings on this planet, one could not realistically conceive it as involving
suffering and early deaths on the scale we are witnessing today. Only a thoroughly organized state of civilization can produce such horrendous misery and
sustain an enduring poverty death toll of 18 million annually. The existing distribution is then morally unacceptable on Lockean grounds insofar as, I point out,
"the better-off enjoy significant advantages in the use of a single natural
resource base from whose benefits the worse-off are largely, and without compensation, excluded."[7]

The attempt to justify today's coercively upheld radical inequality by appeal to some morally acceptable *fictional* historical process that *might* have led to it thus fails as well. On Locke's permissive account, a small elite may appropriate all of the huge cooperative surplus produced by modern social organization. But this elite must not enlarge its share even further by reducing the poor *below* the state-of-nature baseline in order to capture *more* than the entire cooperative surplus. The citizens and governments of the affluent states are violating this negative duty when we, in collaboration with the ruling cliques of many poor countries, coercively exclude the global poor from a proportional resource share and any equivalent substitute.

PRESENT GLOBAL INSTITUTIONAL ARRANGEMENTS

A third way of thinking about the justice of a radical inequality involves reflection on the institutional rules that sustain it. Using this approach, one can justify an economic order and the distribution it produces (irrespective of historical considerations) by comparing them to feasible alternative institutional schemes and the distributional profiles they would produce. Many broadly consequentialist and contractualist conceptions of justice exemplify this approach. They differ in how they characterize the relevant affected parties (groups, persons, time slices of persons, etc.), in the metric they employ for measuring how well off such parties are (in terms of social primary goods, capabilities, welfare, etc.), and in how they aggregate such information about well-being into one overall assessment (e.g., by averaging, or in some egalitarian, prioritarian, or sufficientarian way). These conceptions consequently disagree about how economic institutions should best be shaped under modern conditions. But I can bypass such disagreements insofar as these conceptions agree that an economic order is unjust when it—like the systems of serfdom and forced labor prevailing in feudal Russia or France—foreseeably and avoidably gives rise to massive and severe human rights deficits. My third challenge, addressed to adherents of broadly consequentialist and contractualist conceptions of justice, is that we are preserving our great economic advantages by imposing a global economic order that is unjust in view of the massive and avoidable deprivations it foreseeably reproduces: "There is a shared institutional order that is shaped by the better-off and imposed on the worse-off," I contend. "This institutional order is implicated in the reproduction of radical inequality in that there is a feasible institutional alternative under which such severe and extensive poverty would not persist. The radical inequality cannot be traced to extra-social factors (such as genetic handicaps or natural disasters) which, as such, affect different human beings differentially."[8]

THREE NOTIONS OF HARM

These three challenges converge on the conclusion that the global poor have a compelling moral claim to some of our affluence and that we, by denying them what they are morally entitled to and urgently need, are actively contributing to their deprivations. Still, these challenges are addressed to different audiences and thus appeal to diverse and mutually inconsistent moral conceptions.

They also deploy different notions of harm. In most ordinary contexts, the word "harm" is understood in a historical sense, either diachronically or subjunctively: someone is harmed when she is rendered worse off than she was at some earlier time, or than she would have been had some earlier arrangements continued undisturbed. My first two challenges conceive harm in this ordinary way, and then conceive justice, at least partly, in terms of harm: we are behaving unjustly toward the global poor by imposing on them the lasting effects of historical crimes, or by holding them below any credible state-of-nature baseline. But my third challenge does not conceive justice and injustice in terms of an independently specified notion of harm. Rather, it relates the concepts of *harm* and *justice* in the opposite way, conceiving harm in terms of an independently specified conception of social justice: we are *harming* the global poor if and insofar as we collaborate in imposing an *unjust* global institutional order upon them. And this institutional order is definitely unjust if and insofar as it foreseeably perpetuates large-scale human rights deficits that would be reasonably avoidable through feasible institutional modifications.[9]

The third challenge is empirically more demanding than the other two. It requires me to substantiate three claims: Global institutional arrangements are causally implicated in the reproduction of massive severe poverty. Governments of our affluent countries bear primary responsibility for these global institutional arrangements and can foresee their detrimental effects. And many citizens of these affluent countries bear responsibility for the global institutional arrangements their governments have negotiated in their names.

TWO MAIN INNOVATIONS

In defending the claims underlying my three challenges, my view on these more empirical matters is as oddly perpendicular to the usual empirical debates as my diagnosis of our moral relation to world poverty is to the usual moral debates.

The usual *moral* debates concern the stringency of our moral duties to help the poor abroad. Most of us believe that these duties are rather feeble, meaning that it isn't very wrong of us to give no help at all. Against this popular view, some (Peter Singer, Henry Shue, Peter Unger) have argued that our positive duties are quite stringent and quite demanding; and others (such as Liam Murphy) have defended an intermediate view according to which our positive duties, insofar as they are quite stringent, are not very demanding. Leaving this whole debate to one side, I focus on what it ignores: our moral duties not to harm. We do, of course, have positive duties to rescue people from life-threatening poverty. But it can be misleading to focus on them when more stringent negative duties are also in play: duties not to expose people to life-threatening poverty and duties to shield them from harms for which we would be actively responsible.

The usual *empirical* debates concern how developing countries should design their economic institutions and policies in order to reduce severe poverty within their borders. The received wisdom (often pointing to Hong Kong and, lately, China) is that they should opt for free and open markets with a minimum in taxes and regulations so as to attract investment and to stimulate growth. But some influential economists call for extensive government investment in education, health care, and infrastructure (as illustrated by the example of the Indian state of Kerala), or for some protectionist measures to "incubate" fledgling niche industries until they become internationally competitive (as illustrated by South Korea's growth spurt). Leaving these debates to one side, I focus once more on what is typically ignored: the role that the design of the *global* institutional order plays in the persistence of severe poverty.

Thanks to the inattention of our economists, many believe that the existing global institutional order plays no role in the persistence of severe poverty, but rather that national differences are the key factors. Such "explanatory nationalism"[10] appears justified by the dramatic performance differentials among developing countries, with poverty rapidly disappearing in some and increasing in others. Cases of the latter kind usually display plenty of incompetence, corruption, and oppression by ruling elites, which seem to give us all the explanation we need to understand why severe poverty persists there.

But consider this analogy. Suppose there are great performance differentials among the students in a class, with some improving greatly while many others learn little or nothing. And suppose the latter students do not do their readings and skip many classes. Such performance differentials surely show that local, student-specific factors play a role in explaining academic success. But they decidedly *fail* to show that global factors (the quality of teaching, textbooks, classroom, etc.) play no such role. For example, it remains possible that the teacher is uninspiring, and thereby dampens the performance of all students. And it remains possible that poor attendance and preparation arise from the teacher's efforts failing to engage the interests of many students or from his sexist comments demotivating half his class. Analogues to these three possibilities obtain with regard to global institutional arrangements. Its design may be—and actually is, I argue—highly unfavorable for the poor and very supportive of corrupt and dictatorial government especially in the resource-rich poor countries.

Once we break free from explanatory nationalism, global factors relevant to the persistence of severe poverty are easy to find. In the WTO negotiations, the affluent countries insisted on continued and asymmetrical protections of their markets through tariffs, quotas, antidumping duties, export credits, and huge subsidies to domestic producers. Such protectionism provides a compelling illustration of the hypocrisy of rich states that insist and command that their own exports be received with open markets.[11] And it greatly impairs export opportunities for the very poorest countries and regions. If the rich countries scrapped their protectionist barriers against imports from poor countries, the populations of the latter would benefit greatly: hundreds of millions would escape unemployment, wage levels would rise substantially, and incoming export revenues would be higher by hundreds of billions of dollars each year.

The same rich states also insist that their intellectual property rights—ever-expanding in scope and duration—must be vigorously enforced in the poor countries. Music and software, production processes, words, seeds, biological species, and medicines—for all these, and more, rents must be paid to the corporations of the rich countries as a condition for (still multiply restricted) access to their markets. Millions would be saved from diseases and death if generic producers could freely manufacture and market life-saving medicines in the poor countries.[12]

While charging billions for their intellectual property, the rich countries pay nothing for the externalities they impose through their vastly disproportionate contributions to global pollution and resource depletion. The global poor bene-fit least, if at all, from polluting activities, and also are least able to protect themselves from the impact such pollution has on their health and on their natural environment (such as flooding due to rising sea levels). It is true, of course, that we pay for the vast quantities of natural resources we import. But such payments cannot make up for the price effects of our inordinate consump-tion, which restrict the consumption possibilities of the global poor as well as the development possibilities of the poorer countries and regions (in compari-son to the opportunities our countries could take advantage of at a comparable stage of economic development).

More important, the payments we make for resource imports go to the rulers of the resource-rich countries, with no concern about whether they are demo-cratically elected or at least minimally attentive to the needs of the people whose resources they sell. It is on the basis of effective power alone that we recognize any such ruler as entitled to sell us the resources of "his" country and to borrow, to undertake treaty commitments, and to buy arms in its name. These interna-tional resource, borrowing, treaty, and arms privileges we extend to such rulers are highly advantageous to them, providing them with the money and arms they need to stay in power—often with great brutality and negligible popular support. These privileges are also quite convenient to us, securing our resource imports from poor countries irrespective of who may rule them and how badly. But these privileges have devastating effects on the global poor by enabling corrupt rulers to oppress them, to exclude them from the benefits of their coun-tries' natural resources, and to saddle them with huge debts and onerous treaty obligations. By substantially augmenting the perks of governmental power, these same privileges also greatly strengthen the incentives to attempt to take power by force, thereby fostering coups, civil wars, and interstate wars in the poor countries and regions—especially in Africa, which has many desperately poor but resource-rich countries, where the resource sector constitutes a large part of the gross domestic product.

Reflection on the popular view that severe poverty persists in many poor countries because they govern themselves so poorly shows, then, that it is evidence not for but against explanatory nationalism. The populations of most of the countries in which severe poverty persists or increases do not "govern themselves" poorly, but *are* very poorly governed, and much against their will. They are helplessly exposed to such "government" because the rich states recognize their rulers as entitled to rule on the basis of effective power alone. We pay these rulers for their people's resources, often advancing them large sums against the collateral of future exports, and we eagerly sell them the weapons on which their continued rule all too often depends. Yes, severe poverty is fueled by local misrule. But such local misrule is fueled, in turn, by global rules that we impose and from which we benefit greatly.

Once this causal nexus between our global institutional order and the persistence of severe poverty is better understood, the injustice of that order, and of our imposition of it, becomes visible: "What entitles a small global elite—the citizens of the rich countries *and* the holders of political and economic power in the resource-rich developing countries—to enforce a global property scheme under which we may claim the world's natural resources for ourselves and can distribute these among ourselves on mutually agreeable terms?" I ask. "How, for instance, can our ever so free and fair agreements with tyrants give us property rights in crude oil, thereby dispossessing the local population and the rest of humankind?"[13]

NOTES

Revised and updated in 2008, this essay first appeared as the subject of a symposium in *Ethics & International Affairs* 19, no. 1 (2005): 1–7, where it was followed by critical responses from Mathias Risse, Alan Patten, Rowan Cruft, Norbert Anwander, and Debra Satz, and my reply to the critics, "Severe Poverty as a Violation of Negative Duties." Risse's response and my reply to him are included as chapters 16 and 17 of this book. The remaining response pieces and the full text of the reply to the critics can be accessed online at www.cceia.org/resources/journal/19_1/index.html. I thank the editors of *Ethics & International Affairs* and my fellow symposiasts for making this exchange possible, and David Álvarez García, Nicole Hassoun, Keith Horton, Rekha Nath, and Ling Tong for their critical comments.

1.   World Health Organization, *World Health Report 2004* (Geneva: WHO, 2004), Annex Table 2; available at www.who.int/whr/2004.

2.   This estimate is based on the latest (2004) poverty statistics provided by the World Bank; available at iresearch.worldbank.org/PovcalNet/jsp/index.jsp. The $2 per day poverty line is defined in terms of a monthly consumption expenditure equivalent to the purchasing power that $65.48 had in the United States in 1993. To count as poor by this standard in the United States today, one would need to have to live on less than $98 per person per month

(www.bls.gov/cpi). The headcount figure provided, 46.75, gives the percentage of poor within the developing-country population which, in 2004, was 5,358.85 million. The poverty gap figure provided, 19.31, gives the average shortfall from the poverty line in percent. Because this shortfall is zero for the non-poor, the average shortfall among the poor is the ratio of poverty gap divided by headcount. So the average poor person lives 41.3 percent below the poverty line. For all poor people together, this works out to an annual shortfall (poverty gap) of about $300 billion (converted at market exchange rates). For an explanation of this rough estimate, see Thomas Pogge, *World Poverty and Human Rights*, 2–3 and 103, with notes. For a methodological critique of the World Bank's poverty statistics, see Thomas Pogge, "The First UN Millennium Development Goal: A Cause for Celebration?" *Journal of Human Development* 5, no. 3 (2004), as well as Sanjay Reddy and Thomas Pogge "How *Not* to Count the Poor," in *Debates in the Measurement of Global Poverty*, ed. Sudhir Anand, Paul Segal, and Joseph Stiglitz (New York: Oxford University Press, 2009); also available at www.socialanalysis.org.

3. World Bank, *World Development Report 2006: Equity and Development* (New York: Oxford University Press, in press), 293.

4. *World Poverty and Human Rights: Cosmopolitan Responsibilities and Reforms*, second edition (Cambridge: Poltly Press, 2008).

5. Pogge, *World Poverty and Human Rights*, 209.

6. For a fuller reading of Locke's argument, see ibid., ch. 5.

7. Ibid., 208.

8. Ibid., 205

9. One might say that the existing global order is not unjust if the only feasible institutional modifications that could substantially reduce the offensive deprivations would be extremely costly in terms of culture, say, or the natural environment. I preempt such objections by inserting the word "reasonably." Broadly consequentialist and contractualist conceptions of justice agree that an institutional order that foreseeably gives rise to massive severe deprivations is unjust if there are feasible institutional modifications that foreseeably would greatly reduce these deprivations without adding other harms of comparable magnitude.

10. Pogge, *World Poverty and Human Rights*, 145ff.

11. Ibid., 19–23.

12. Ibid., ch. 9.

13. Ibid., 148.

Chapter 16

Do We Owe the Global Poor Assistance or Rectification?
Response to Pogge

Mathias Risse

A CENTRAL THEME throughout Thomas Pogge's pathbreaking *World Poverty and Human Rights* is that the global political and economic order *harms* people in developing countries, and that our duty toward the global poor is therefore not to *assist* them but to *rectify injustice*.[1] But does the global order *harm* the poor? I argue elsewhere that there is a sense in which this is indeed so, at least if a certain empirical thesis is accepted.[2] In this essay, however, I seek to show that the global order not only does not harm the poor but can plausibly be credited with the considerable improvements in human well-being that have been achieved over the last two hundred years. Much of what Pogge says about our duties toward developing countries is therefore false.

Let me begin by clarifying what I mean by "the global political and economic order" ("the global order"). For the first time in history, there is one continuous global society based on territorial sovereignty. This system has emerged from the spread of European control since the fifteenth century and the formation of new states through wars of independence and decolonization. Even systems that escaped Western imperialism had to follow legal and diplomatic practices imposed by Europeans. This states system is governed by rules, the most important of which are embodied in the UN Charter. The Bretton Woods institutions (the World Bank, International Monetary Fund [IMF], and later the General Agreement on Tariffs and Trade [GATT]/World Trade Organization [WTO]) were founded as a framework for economic cooperation that would prevent disasters like the Great Depression of the 1930s. These institutions, together with economically powerful states acting alone or in concert, shape the economic order. Although this order is neither monolithic nor harmonious, it makes sense to talk about a global order that includes but is not reducible to the actions of states.

In what follows, then, I argue that this global order does not harm the poor according to the benchmarks of comparison used by Pogge, but that on the contrary, according to those benchmarks, this order has caused amazing improvements over the state of misery that has characterized human life throughout the ages. The global order is not fundamentally unjust; instead, it is *incompletely* just, and it should be credited with the great advances it has brought.

BENCHMARKS FOR HARM HISTORICAL REFERENCES

One might think the present extents of poverty and inequality by themselves reveal the injustice of the global order.[3] But they do not. While indeed 1.2 billion people in 1998 lived below the poverty line of $1.08 per day (in 1993 dollars, adjusted for differences in purchasing powers across countries), it is also true that there is now less misery than ever before, at least as measured in terms of any standard development indicator. The progress made over the last 200 years is miraculous. In 1820, 75 percent of the world population lived on less than $1 a day (appropriately adjusted). Today, in Europe, almost nobody does; in China, less than 20 percent do; in South Asia, around 40 percent do; and globally, slightly more than 20 percent do. The share of people living on less than $1 a day fell from 42 percent in 1950 to 17 percent in 1992. Historically *almost everybody* was poor, but that is no longer true.

It is true that the high-income economies include 15 percent of the population but receive 80 percent of the income. Around 1820, per capita incomes were similar worldwide, and low, ranging from around $500 in China and South Asia to $1,000–$1,500 in some European countries. So the gap between rich and poor was 3 to 1, whereas, according to UN Development Programme (UNDP) statistics, in 1960 it was 60 to 1, and in 1997, 74 to 1. But it is also true that, between 1960 and 2000, real per capita income in developing countries grew on average 2.3 percent (doubling living standards within thirty years). Britain's Gross Domestic Product (GDP) grew an average of 1.3 percent during its nineteenth-century economic supremacy. For developing countries, things have been better recently than they were for countries at the height of their power during any other period in history. In 1990 dollars, the average worldwide income per capita in 1950 was $2,114, while in 1999 it was $5,709; for developing countries income per capita increased from $1,093 to $3,100 during this period. Similar improvements were achieved in life expectancy, which rose from forty-nine years to sixty-six years worldwide, and from forty-four years to sixty-four years in developing countries, and thus has increased more in the last fifty years than in the preceding 5,000 years. Literacy rose from 54 percent in 1950 to 79 percent in 1999. Infant mortality fell from 156 to 54 per 1,000 live births worldwide. Furthermore, while the UNDP inequality statistics quoted above used international exchange rates, things look different if one uses the Purchasing Power Parity (PPP) standard. According to such calculations, which account for what money buys in different countries, inequality had risen by 1960 to 7 to

1 and has since fallen to about 6 to 1 because of higher growth in the developing world.

Development aid, which has often been given for strategic reasons, has declined since the end of the Cold War, and currently makes up a tiny percentage of donor countries' GDP.[4] Nevertheless, the resources transferred are substantial for those who receive them. In 1993, sub-Saharan countries received on average 11.5 percent of *their* Gross National Product (GNP) as aid (Zambia, 23.6 percent; Tanzania, 40 percent).[5] The Marshall Plan, hailed as the greatest aid program ever, has been estimated to have given its recipients on average 2.1 percent of GNP annually.[6]

WTO negotiations have not yet done as much for the poor as one might have hoped, and negotiators representing rich countries possess more bargaining power and often also more expertise than those of poor countries. Indeed, the WTO has so far opened markets too little. But it is also true that the WTO, by and large, represents a significant improvement over the GATT, and, for that matter, any previous system (e.g., ad hoc bilateral treaties or no clear rules at all) of regulating international trade. The GATT mostly aimed to reduce tariffs in Organization for Economic Cooperation and Development (OECD) countries and in sectors that mattered to them, while developing countries, through "special and preferential treatment," had a second-class status: in virtue of their "special and preferential" treatment they were free riders on GATT treaties, but their concerns were not on the agenda. That agriculture and textiles became part of WTO negotiations was a tremendous change for countries with a comparative advantage in such goods. Progress has been made in both areas. While the final results of the Doha Round of WTO negotiations with regard to agriculture are not settled (as of February 2005), the WTO is committed to eliminating export subsidies and to restricting other forms of export support in agriculture. Moreover, the quota system that has governed the textile sector since the 1960s is being phased out, and, as of January 1, 2005, all quotas have been eliminated. Things are changing slowly, but despite setbacks (such as the agreement on Trade-Related Aspects of Intellectual Property Rights [TRIPs], which will probably lead to a net redistribution to developed countries) great progress has arguably been made here too. Historically, negotiations exploring mutually acceptable solutions for worldwide problems are an anomaly. We are making progress.

What conclusion such statistics warrant depends on the time horizon considered (sub-Saharan Africa has made progress over a two-hundred-year horizon, but not for the last twenty years), whether one looks at absolute or relative quantities (the number of abysmally poor has remained unchanged for fifteen years, but their share of the world population decreased), and whether one looks at individuals or countries (the median developing country has experienced zero growth over the last twenty years; still, inequality between any two randomly chosen individuals has fallen, because of growth in India and China).

Still, what is remarkable is not that so many now live in poverty, but that so many do not; not that so many die young, but that so many do not; not that so many are illiterate, but that so many are not. By and large, if one looks at the last two hundred, one hundred, or fifty years, things have improved dramatically for the poor. The two-hundred-year and the fifty-year horizon (roughly speaking) are especially significant. The former captures the period in which the industrial revolution has perfected the system of the division of labor, which has in turn led to technological advancements (originating largely in what are nowadays industrialized countries) that have benefited everyone. The fifty-year horizon captures the period in which a network of international organizations characterizing the global order has come into its own—a network whose absence would harm its weakest members the most. Historically speaking, the global order seems to have greatly benefited the poor.[7]

OTHER BENCHMARKS FOR HARM COUNTERFACTUAL AND FAIRNESS

My argument so far may seem philosophically naive. For while these data may be useful to get some sense of the status quo and its historical background, it may be argued (in agreement with Pogge) that such data are useless *as a benchmark of whether harm has been done.* Surely, one may say, developing countries are better off now than two hundred years ago—but so were African Americans under Jim Crow vis-à-vis the antebellum days. Even two hundred years ago "we" and "they" belonged to a single global system, and "they" were already on a trajectory toward their current disadvantaged status. So it may seem cynical to say that developing countries are not being harmed because they are better off than at an earlier stage of an ongoing oppressive relationship. Should we not assess whether harm has been done by asking what things would have been like had European supremacists never invaded the rest of the globe?

The trouble with this benchmark is that it is impossible to say anything about it. It is conceivable, for example, that political structures would have emerged in Africa that would have allowed indigenous peoples to exploit the natural resource wealth of their continent, enabling them to build a culturally sophisticated and economically prosperous civilization. But it is equally conceivable that wars would have thwarted such efforts. The point is not that a certain threshold of reasonable certainty cannot be met, but that we must plead complete ignorance. The uncertainty of what people who, as it happened, were never born, would have done across centuries, how events would have turned out that, as it happened, never occurred, how lives would have been changed by innovations that, as it happened, were never made—such factors make it impossible to say what things would be like had the past been different. If we evaluate counterfactuals, we normally first assess what the world would be like were the antecedent true and then resort to cases where some claim similar to the antecedent in fact was true to evaluate whether the consequent of the counterfactual will be true in a world in which the antecedent is. Assessing the relevant count-erfactuals here is impossible, especially since much turns on exercises of the will of merely possible people.

Researchers in comparative politics do engage heavily in counterfactual rea-soning since causal claims depend on such speculation: they try to reduce the speculative part by *comparing*; that is, holding other factors constant, they com-pare countries in the WTO with similarly situated ones outside it; or they com-pare a country's period of not belonging to the WTO with its period of belonging. However, when assessing the global order as such, we cannot apply this technique of holding other factors constant and judge what the world would be like had the current global order not developed. We have only this one world to work with. So while we can make sense of claims about what the development of Poland would have been had it not joined the European Union, we cannot make sense of claims of what the world would now be like had the global order not developed.

Yet, *surely*, one may say, developing countries would be better off had they been left alone! While those counterfactuals may be difficult to assess conclu-sively, they are *plausible*, and worrying about their verifiability violates Aristot-le's advice to adjust accuracy standards to the subject matter. However, I suspect one may find this position obvious because one compares developing countries to industrialized countries, observes that the latter did not face similar interfer-ence, and concludes that without such interference Africa, for example, would have prospered. We must resist such reasoning, since the reasons why such regions fell to conquerors may be the same reasons why they would have been unable to prosper without external interference. The political scientist Jeffrey Herbst has emphasized, for example, that facts of physical geography in Africa made it difficult for powerful states to emerge, and this by itself makes for a big difference to Europe. And the historian Bernard Lewis has argued that the decline of Islamic societies was due to internal developments rather than inter-ference. While these are topics on which I cannot take a stance, we cannot simply assume that other parts of the world would have done better had they been left alone, and it is easy to see why we incline to do so.[8]

Maybe we get guidance to assessing the claim that "they" would be better off had "we" never invaded them by considering more empirically tractable claims, such as that developed countries are rich because they have oppressed develop-ing countries, and that colonialism has inflicted lasting harm. The first view was defended prominently by dependency theorists. Dependency theory comes in different versions, the strongest claiming that the development of "the North" entailed the underdevelopment of "the South" and a weaker version claiming that there is some other dependency of the South on the North—for instance, that the terms of trade weakened for "the South" as its natural resources became cheaper over time relative to manufactured goods from "the North." Yet depen-dency theory and related theories have become incredible to all but "a dwin-dling group of Marxist historians."[9] Such views have not withstood scrutiny, and even some of their strongest erstwhile defenders, like Brazil's former president Fernando Henrique Cardoso, have abandoned them. The exploitation, theft, and murder they brought upon other parts of the world notwithstanding, developed countries became rich because they industrialized, thereby benefiting from an ever more refined division of labor.

It is tempting to say that the global order must be unjust because colonialism has created disadvantaged countries. Yet this is not obvious. While it happened, colonialism disrupted people's lives, killing, mutilating, or enslaving many. But past injustice does not make the present order unjust, any more than past kindness makes it kind. We need arguments that there is persisting injustice rooted in colonialism. Historians tend to come to differentiated assessments of the colonial heritage. For instance, Fernand Braudel writes:

> Education and a certain level of technology, of hygiene, of medicine and of pubic administration: these were the greatest benefits left by the colonists, and some measure of compensation for the destruction which contact with Europe brought to old tribal, family, and social customs. . . . It will never be possible to gauge the full results of such novelties as employment for wages, a money economy, writing and individual ownership of land. Each was undoubtedly a blow to the former social regime. Yet these blows were surely a necessary part of the evolution taking place today. On the other hand, colonization had the real disadvantage of dividing Africa into a series of territories—French, English, German, Belgian, and Portuguese—whose fragmentation has been perpetuated today in too large a cluster of independent states, which are sometimes said to have "Balkanized" Africa.[10]

Most historians find colonial rule to have been inadequate while it lasted, but that does not mean that its legacy, all things considered, continues to impose harm that outweighs technological advances in infrastructure, medicine, and other areas that it brought. One does not need to be callous to think that, no matter how bad it was, one should not take for granted that colonialism created a world where the essence of the relationship between developed and developing countries is that the former *harm* the latter.

There is yet another way of articulating that developing countries are being harmed by the global order: a benchmark of fairness, where the reference point is a state of nature in which resources are distributed fairly. " 'Worldwide 34,000 children under age five die daily from hunger and preventable diseases.' Try to conceive a state of nature that can match this amazing feat of our globalized civilization!" writes Pogge.[11] However, no such state-of-nature references can help in this context. They cannot distinguish between the view that *the global order* harms developing societies (Pogge's view), and any other view explaining how the present magnitude of global poverty could have arisen. Such references can only show that things are not as they should be, which does not reveal who is to blame for it.

To conclude: the historical benchmark is the only benchmark among the three considered that we can make sense of, and in relation to that benchmark the global order has brought tremendous advances. Moreover, advances in medicine and food production are largely due to countries that have shaped that order. So, *as far as we can tell*, the global order has benefited the poor. Let me briefly return to the scenario of African Americans under Jim Crow: that, as some might argue, African Americans were better off under Jim Crow vis-à-vis the antebellum days. About this scenario we can say more than that things were better in 1950 than in 1850. We can say that some participants in a single society sharing economic and political institutions were relegated to an inferior status. This evil can also be attributed to a group of perpetrators. By contrast, we have not yet been able to identify an ongoing evil for which the global order is responsible that is comparable to the way in which Southern whites were responsible for the plight of African Americans long after the abolition of slavery. My reasoning does not therefore entail that Jim Crow should have inspired gratitude.

THE COSMOPOLITAN COMPLAINT AND EXPLANATORY NATIONALISM

I continue with a discussion of some of Pogge's arguments against the legitimacy of states as well as some alleged methodological biases that, according to Pogge, prevent us from seeing the harm states do (see chapter 7 of *World Poverty and Human Rights* for a statement of his conception of a political system characterized by vertical dispersal of sovereignty, which is meant to replace the states system).

The existence of states entails that life prospects differ vastly and are largely decided by birth. One may argue that since membership in political systems is as morally arbitrary as race, life chances should not be so determined. Cosmopolitans like Pogge insist that individuals are the unit of moral concern, should be so equally, and should be so equally *to* everybody. Cosmopolitans take the existence of states, and a global order composed of them, to be wronging individuals by failing to respect their moral equality. Moreover, the global order acknowledges as governments any regime in charge of an accredited territory. This order thus provides incentives for despots to seize power by granting them what Pogge calls the resource and borrowing privilege, which enables them to sell resources or borrow money on behalf of a country's people. Both points are expressed in what we may call the "Cosmopolitan Complaint": the global order harms individuals by sanctioning the sheer existence of states (which undermines the moral equality of individuals) as well as through an incentive system that instigates despotic regimes to seize power.

A methodological concern accompanies these moral worries, to wit, that many theories in the social sciences take states for granted and cannot assess the extent to which the states system, and international structures based on it, harms the poor by influencing who shapes policy, what their options are, and what the impacts of these policies are. Pogge calls this deficiency "explanatory nationalism"—the fallacy of tracing development outcomes exclusively to domestic factors. One view to which Pogge would presumably apply this criticism is a stance on an ongoing macroeconomic debate regarding the sources of wealth and poverty.[12] According to that view, the sources of wealth rest in institutional quality rather than in world market integration or geography. Institutions "are the rules of the game in a society or, more formally, are the humanly devised constraints that shape human interaction."[13] Yet those "humanly devised constraints" work to society's benefit only if most individuals support the "rules of the game." Moreover, while foreigners can destroy institutions, they can often do little to help build them.

The empirical support for this stance draws on data that do take states for granted.[14] Yet assessing whether the global order harms the poor while doing so, writes Pogge, is like explaining variance in student performances while ignoring teaching quality.[15] The Cosmopolitan Complaint and explanatory nationalism are related: the latter is one way of ignoring cosmopolitan concerns.

Let me begin my response with a brief comment on the resource and borrowing privilege. Pogge argues that by acknowledging those privileges, the global order is causally involved in perpetuating poverty. While a careful treatment of this subject goes beyond what I can do here (as well as beyond what Pogge himself provides), I would like to express some skepticism about these claims. Undoubtedly the global order sets incentives that may sometimes explain why at *that* time *these* people launched *that* coup. But there has been oppression, often motivated by the sheer desire to rule, much longer than a global order has created incentives for it. In light of this, one wonders whether the overall picture of oppression in the world would differ significantly if such privileges were only granted to regimes of impeccable moral standing. Authoritarian predators are *also* thieves, but they are mostly oppressors.

As far as the methodological worry concerning "explanatory nationalism," I agree that a society's economic and political status is shaped by a range of factors, some of which are domestic, some multilateral, and others global. For this reason, explanatory nationalism is as untenable as the view that a society's economic status is completely explained by global factors, a view Alan Patten calls "explanatory cosmopolitanism."[16] Yet although they organize data on a country-by-country basis, explanations of the causes of wealth (such as the institutional stance) can take note of nondomestic factors. The institutional view can do so by acknowledging circumstances under which, say, global factors are causally involved in the genesis of institutions. While the institutional stance explains growth in terms of institutions, it does not thereby commit itself to explaining institutions without reference to international factors. Overall, I think, explanatory nationalism in the social sciences is less of a problem than Pogge suggests.

Let us address the main point of the Cosmopolitan Complaint—the claim that the existence of states itself harms the poor. Consider the following prima facie case for states. First, individuals desire to live in peoples, groups tied together by what Rawls calls "common sympathies,"[17] that are, and for which individuals desire to be, the primary locus of social, economic, and political structures to which persons belong. Second, individuals desire that their people have the right to self-determination, and, barring unacceptable effects on others, this right should be granted. Third, citizenship in a self-determining people, though morally *arbitrary*, is morally *relevant*: moral equality across persons is consistent with governments giving special consideration to their citizens and citizens to each other. Fellow citizens are subject to the same body of laws that, in virtue of their impact on their autonomy, must be justifiable to each of them, but not to those not subject to them. While these views are consistent with a range of proposals about reforms of the existing states system, they are inconsistent with a principled rejection of states.[18]

This view should be developed by including an ideal of sovereignty not as complete absence of supervision but one in which countries are independent, in a sense in which colonies were dependent on their so-called mother countries. That qualified ideal of self-determination is, *as an ideal*, already embodied in the global order, as captured by UN documents. This prima facie case in support of states also sheds more light on Pogge's claims about the resource and borrowing privilege. The incentives that these privileges set for authoritarian predators cause harm in precisely those situations in which authoritarian predators are in charge and where self-determination of peoples is therefore *not* properly realized. To the Cosmopolitan Complaint that the global order should be denounced because it provides incentives for authoritarian predators to seize power, the response is that the circumstances under which that happens are precisely those under which one of its central ideals is not yet realized.

This prima facie case in support of states does not yet reject Pogge's claim that the sheer existence of states harms the poor. Undoubtedly, the existence of states *harms* individuals in the sense of thwarting many people's interests (e.g., the interests of those who would rather live elsewhere). Unclear, however, is whether this involves a *wrong*. To show that it does not, we need to add a justification of states *to those excluded from them*. The following ways of articulating the view that the existence of states constitutes a wrong strike me as most important, and it is these objections that must thus be refuted for it to be justified. First, one may say that such exclusion is wrongfully coercive, and second, that no group of people has the right to occupy land at the exclusion of others.

Elsewhere, I have offered responses to both of these objections, and will restrict myself here to a sketch of a response to the former.[19] States get much justification for prohibiting uncontrolled immigration if they do something morally defensible or praiseworthy, which they cannot do without having such power. What states do that justifies such protection is to provide for their members by maintaining a morally defensible legal framework and social system. Many states do not do so, and this justification fails to apply to those that do not. But there are states that pass the relevant moral tests, and hence acquire the right to maintain their existence by prohibiting uncontrolled access. It is consistent with this view that states have obligations toward people in need (refugees, asylum seekers), or must offer support in institution building. Regulating access to states is coercive, but only in the Hobbesian sense in which any impediment is a deprivation of liberty. Such coercion, justified along the lines just sketched, is similar to coercion in domestic contexts that keeps people from seizing each other's property. As individuals within states should be allowed to have property to pursue meaningful projects, states should be as well. Such coercion does not undermine the *moral equality* of persons and is not *wrongfully* coercive.

Much more needs to be said, but I think that states can indeed be justified in this way to those who are excluded from them. The Cosmopolitan Complaint therefore fails to show that the existence of states wrongs the poor. Moreover, the ideal of moral equality captured by Pogge's cosmopolitanism introduced above is consistent with this defense (which separates political equality from moral equality). On balance, I submit, we should not say the global order per se is *unjust*, but that it is *imperfectly developed*: it needs reform rather than a revolutionary overthrow (in the form of a replacement by a system of political units characterized by vertically dispersed sovereignty, as suggested by Pogge).

Pogge suggests that one goal of macroexplanations transcending national factors is to explain why so many countries are poor and so few are rich (as opposed to explaining the economic status of this or that country). Yet we must be careful in looking for this explanation. If one considers suicide rates in specific countries, microexplanations at the level of individual suicides will not capture the full story: societal factors have to be considered. There are two senses in which we can inquire about such factors. First, we may ask a noncomparative question about which societal factors matter; and second, we may ask a comparative question about why some particular country has a different suicide rate than similar countries. These two approaches are related (assessing the comparative claim is a way of ensuring that the noncomparative explanation is complete; assessing the noncomparative claim identifies those countries to which one should draw comparisons), but they respond to different inquiries.

Now consider the question "Why are so many countries poor and so few rich?" This question can only be asked noncomparatively: we have no sense of "what is to be expected" in the same way we do when other countries with certain characteristics have a lower suicide rate than the country we are considering. It is plausible to say that the country with a higher suicide rate "than expected" has good reason to identify and try to change the relevant factors because something is obviously going wrong in that society that does not go wrong in similarly situated societies. But this sort of reasoning does not apply if we have no clear sense of "what is to be expected," as is the case with the question "Why are so many countries poor and so few rich?" Whatever is wrong with the fact that "so many countries are poor and so few are rich," it is not that there is an obvious gap between "what is to be expected" and what is the case. The perception that there is such a gap may contribute to the intuition that evils like poverty and starvation must be attributable to some entity that can be regarded as "doing the harming." This perception rests on a mistake.

NOTES

This essay appeared in *Ethics & International Affairs* 19, no. 1 (2005): 9–18. It was originally presented at an author-meets-critic session held during the American Philosophical Association Eastern Division Meeting, Washington, DC, December 30, 2003. I am grateful to the audience for helpful discussion, as well as to Christian Barry for helpful comments.

1.   Thomas Pogge, *World Poverty and Human Rights: Cosmopolitan Responsibilities and Reforms*, second edition (Cambridge: Polity Press, 2008).

2.   I argue this in "How Does the Global Order Harm the Poor?" *Philosophy & Public Affairs* 33, no. 4 (2005): 349–376. The empirical thesis mentioned is the view that economic progress turns primarily on the quality of institutions. The view that the global order harms the poor in ways delineated by the institutional thesis is consistent with the view that that order must *also* plausibly be credited with massive improvements, which is the view defended here.

3.   Unless otherwise noted, data are from World Bank, *World Development Report 2000/2001: Attacking Poverty* (Washington, DC: World Bank, 2000); United Nations, "Report of the High-Level Panel on Financing for Development" ("Zedillo Report"); World Bank, "World Development Indicators 2002"; and Angus Maddison, *The World Economy: A Millennial Perspective* (Paris: OECD Development Center, 2001), table B 22, 265. See also Bjørn Lomborg, *The Skeptical Environmentalist: Measuring the Real State of the World* (Cambridge: Cambridge University Press, 2001), esp. Part II for the different approaches to measuring inequality.

4.   Alberto Alesina and David Dollar, "Who Gives Foreign Aid to Whom and Why?" *Journal of Economic Growth* 5 (2000): 33–64. According to the Zedillo Report, official development aid in 2000 was $53.1 billion, down from $60.9 billion in 1992; in 1998, $12.1 billion went to the least developed countries; official development aid in 1992 averaged 0.33% of *donors'* GNP, down to 0.22% in 2000, contrasted with the 0.7% of GNP that is widely agreed upon.

5.   Nicolas Van de Walle and Timothy A. Johnston, *Improving Aid to Africa* (Washington, DC: Overseas Development Council, 1996), 20.

6.   Herbert Giersch, Karl-Heinz Paqué, and Holger Schmieding, *The Fading Miracle: Four Decades of Market Economy in Germany* (Cambridge: Cambridge University Press, 1992), 98.

7.   This, I think, is true even though the absolute (as opposed to the relative) number of people living in poverty is now higher than it was 200 years ago; while I find it hard to muster a conclusive argument for that claim, I find it intuitive that what matters here are relative, rather than absolute, numbers.

8.   Jeffrey Herbst, *States and Power in Africa: Comparative Lessons in Authority and Control* (Princeton, NJ: Princeton University Press, 2000); and Bernard Lewis, *What Went Wrong? The Clash between Islam and Modernity in the Middle East* (New York: Oxford University Press, 2002).

9.   David S. Landes, *The Wealth and Poverty of Nations: Why Some Are So Rich and Some So Poor* (New York: W.W. Norton, 1998), 381, see also 429; Paul Bairoch, in *Economics and World History: Myths and Paradoxes* (New York: Harvester Wheatsheaf, 1993), argues that it was not because of exploitation of developing countries that developed countries did well. The classic of dependency theory is Fernando Henrique Cardoso and Enzo Faletto, *Dependency and Development in Latin America* (Berkeley and Los Angeles: University of California Press, 1979). See Landes, *Wealth and Poverty of Nations*, 510ff., for some comments on Cardoso's rise from leftist scholar to president of Brazil.

10.   Fernand Braudel, *A History of Civilizations* (New York: Penguin, 1987), 134.

11.   Thomas Pogge, "'Assisting' the Global Poor," in *The Ethics of Assistance: Morality and the Distant Needy*, ed. Deen K. Chatterjee (Cambridge: Cambridge University Press, 2004).

12.   I have adopted this view in Mathias Risse, "What We Owe to the Global Poor," *Journal of Ethics* 9, nos. 1–2 (2005): 81–117, as well as in "How Does the Global Order Harm the Poor?"

13.   Douglass C. North, *Institutions, Institutional Change, and Economic Performance* (Cambridge: Cambridge University Press, 1990), 3.

14.   Daron Acemoglu, Simon Johnson, and James Robinson, "The Colonial Origins of Comparative Development: An Empirical Investigation," *American Economic Review* 91, no. 5 (2001): 1369–1401; and Dani Rodrik, Arvind Subramanian, and Francesco Trebbi, "Institutions Rule: The Primacy of Institutions over Geography and Integration in Economic Development," *Journal of Economic Growth* 9, no. 2 (2004): 131–65.

15.   Pogge, "'Assisting' the Global Poor," 263.

16.   Alan Patten, "Should We Stop Thinking about Poverty in Terms of Helping the Poor?" *Ethics & International Affairs* 19, no. 1 (2005): 23.

17.   John Rawls, *The Law of Peoples* (Cambridge, MA: Harvard University Press, 1999), 24.

18.   This sketch must be extended to a full-fledged argument in support of the existence of states; I do some work toward that end in "What We Owe to the Global Poor." The distinction between "morally arbitrary" and "morally relevant," which I think is very important in this context, is due to Michael Blake, "Distributive Justice, State Coercion, and Autonomy," *Philosophy & Public Affairs* 30, no. 3 (2001): 257–97.

19.   Both points are addressed in "What We Owe to the Global Poor," but the concern about the original ownership of the earth is discussed most carefully in "How Does the Global Order Harm the Poor?" where, however, the concern is not with the legitimacy of states.

Chapter | 7

Baselines for Determining Harm
Reply to Risse

Thomas Pogge

MATHIAS RISSE DISCUSSES whether the global system of territorial sovereignty that emerged in the fifteenth century can be said to harm the poorer societies. This question is distinct from the question I raise in my book—namely, whether present citizens of the affluent countries, in collusion with the ruling elites of most poor countries, are harming the global poor. These questions are different, because present citizens of the affluent countries bear responsibility only for the *recent* design of the global institutional order. The effects of the states system as it was shaped before 1980, say, is thus of little relevance to the question I have raised. A further difference is that whereas Risse's discussion focuses on the well-being of societies, typically assessed by their GNP per capita, my discussion focuses on the well-being of individual human beings. This difference is significant because what enriches a poor country (in terms of GNP per capita) all too often impoverishes the vast majority of its inhabitants, as I discuss with the example of Nigeria's oil revenues.[1]

My focus is then on the *present* situation, on the radical inequality between the 2.5 billion suffering severe poverty and the 1 billion in the affluent countries, whose per capita share of the global product is some 200 times greater (at market exchange rates). This radical inequality and the continuous misery and death toll it engenders are foreseeably reproduced under the present global institutional order as we have shaped it. And most of it could be avoided, I hold, if this global order had been, or were to be, designed differently. The feasibility of a more poverty-avoiding alternative design of the global institutional order shows, I argue, that the present design is unjust and that, by imposing it, we are harming the global poor by foreseeably subjecting them to avoidable severe poverty.

The argument just summarized defines harm relative to a baseline that is different from the three baselines Risse considers: on my account, the global poor are being harmed by us insofar as they are worse off than anyone would be if the design of the global order were just. Now, standards of social justice are controversial to some extent. To make my argument widely acceptable, I invoke a minimal standard that merely requires that any institutional order imposed on human beings must be designed so that human rights are fulfilled under it insofar as this is reasonably possible. Nearly everyone believes that justice requires more, that an institutional order can be unjust even if it meets this minimal standard; and there is disagreement about what else justice requires. But I can bypass these issues so long as we can agree that an institutional order *cannot* be just if it *fails* to meet the minimal human rights standard. Because the present global institutional order falls short of even this minimal standard, and dramatically so, it can be shown to be unjust without invoking any more demanding and less widely acceptable standard.

Imagine for a moment a human world whose economic distribution resembles ours, but whose inhabitants have just sprung into existence. In this fictional world, the more powerful impose on the rest an institutional order that reserves for themselves the vast majority of income and wealth, thereby leaving the nonconsenting poor with insecure access to the most basic necessities. In regard to such a world, my argument and conclusion would be obvious and all but irresistible. In such a world, clearly, the global poor have a much stronger moral claim to the extra 1 percent of the global product they need for secure access to basic necessities than the powerful have to take 80 rather than 79 percent for themselves.

This thought experiment shows that if you, like most of this world's affluent, do not find my argument and conclusion obvious and irresistible, this is because the radical inequality of our world does have a history. You must be assuming that this history renders the moral claim the powerful have on the disputed 1 percent of the global product stronger, or renders the moral claim the global poor have on this disputed 1 percent weaker, than it would be without this history. However widespread among the affluent, this assumption is wrong. To show this, I discuss actual and fictional histories, including the three additional (historical and counterfactual) baselines Risse considers. I can do this in a purely defensive way. To protect my argument, all I need to show is that considerations invoking such baselines cannot upset my argument.

Risse rejects as excessively speculative counterfactual statements to the effect that there is more severe poverty in the world today than there would be if either humankind had settled into some Lockean state of nature or if the continents had not been unified through European conquest and colonization. There are no knowable facts, he thinks, on the basis of which we could make such comparisons. This skepticism suits me well. If such comparisons are unsound, then they cannot be invoked to damage my argument. Then the moral claim the global poor have to the disputed 1 percent cannot be undermined by showing that severe poverty would have been at least equally bad without the European conquest or in a Lockean state of nature. And our moral claim to the disputed 1 percent cannot be bolstered by showing that we would have been no worse off without the European conquest or in a Lockean state of nature.

Putting these two counterfactual baselines aside, "the historical benchmark is the only benchmark among the three considered that we can make sense of" (page 323, this book), Risse writes, and judges that the last few centuries have brought fabulous improvements in human well-being. This is quite true—at least so long as we look at aggregates and averages. But if we look at individual lives lived near the bottom, the statistics are less rosy. According to the World Bank, the number of people living below its $2 per day international poverty line has increased from 2,497 million in 1987 to 2,505 million in 2004.[2] The number of chronically undernourished human beings continues to hover around 800 million.[3] And the number of children under the age of five dying each year from poverty-related causes is still nearly 10 million, or 17 percent of all human deaths.[4] How do Risse's statistics help him answer these individual human beings living in extreme poverty when they ask us how we can justify imposing a global order designed so that it foreseeably produces a huge avoidable excess in misery such as theirs year after year?

Risse's glorious aggregate statistics—the increase in the global average income or in longevity—cannot silence these complaints. To the contrary, they show that the affluence of the nonpoor is increasing by leaps and bounds and that severe poverty is thus ever more easily avoidable. Such statistics can only exacerbate the scandal of severe poverty persisting on a massive scale.

Risse can say that, thanks to global population growth, the global poor constitute a shrinking percentage of humankind.[5] Or perhaps he can even say that, according to some statistical indicators, the world poverty problem is shrinking even in absolute terms. Such progress is better than no progress, to be sure. It means that severe poverty may one day be eradicated from this planet and that, over all of human history, fewer human beings will have suffered and died from severe poverty than would otherwise be the case. But all this cannot lessen the complaint of those who avoidably suffer and die against those who confine them to a life in grinding poverty.

To see this, consider a parallel case involving slavery.[6] Imagine once more a human world whose inhabitants have just sprung into existence. In this world, the more powerful whites impose an institutional order that facilitates and enforces the enslavement of blacks. This order and its imposition are unjust. Clearly, blacks have a strong moral claim to control their own bodies and labor power, and whites have no moral claim at all to treat black people as tradable commodities.

At this point, Risse's doppelgänger enters the scene, arguing that this conclusion about the imaginary world without history cannot be simply transferred into the actual world of 1845, where the citizenry of the United States was imposing an institutional order that facilitated and enforced the enslavement of blacks. The actual world of 1845 was different, says the doppelgänger, because it had a history, and a benign one at that: The proportion of slaves within the U.S.

population (or even the absolute number of slaves) had been shrinking, the nutritional situation of slaves had steadily improved, and brutal treatment, such as rape, whipping, and splitting of families, had also been in decline. Let us stipulate, for the sake of the argument, that the doppelgänger's historical assertions are entirely accurate. Do they weaken, *in any way*, the slaves' moral claim to legal freedom? Or do they support, *in any way*, a moral claim by the citizenry of the United States to perpetuate the institutional order that facilitated and enforced the enslavement of blacks?

Faced with this challenge, Risse has opted to answer these questions in the negative, thus dissociating himself from his doppelgänger's argument. He recognizes that this saddles him with a new task. He must now explain why his invocation of an upward historical trajectory should have moral relevance against the complaint by the global poor when it has no moral relevance against the complaint by slaves in the United States of 1845. Risse begins to do this by highlighting three purported differences between the two scenarios: Blacks "were relegated to an inferior status. This evil can also be attributed to a group of perpetrators," and both groups were "participants in a single society sharing economic and political institutions" (page 323, this book). Risse does not say which of these points render historical improvements relevant to present injustice, so let us consider all three.

The last two purported differences are easily denied: There is a group of perpetrators in both cases—namely, the citizens of the United States in 1845, and the politically influential global elite of the affluent today. And just as there was a single society with shared social institutions in the United States of 1845, so there is now "one continuous global society based on territorial sovereignty" worldwide (page 317, this book).

The first difference is real: blacks were a rigidly designated group of persons with inferior legal status, while the global poor are not as such rigidly singled out and relegated to an inferior status by current legal instruments. But why should this difference *make* a decisive moral difference?

To see that it makes little moral difference, we need only imagine the U.S. system of slavery modified so that anyone can fall into hereditary slavery under universalistic rules, perhaps through failure to repay a debt on schedule. Let us couple this modified system with the previous stipulation that the proportion of slaves within the population (or even the absolute number of slaves) has been shrinking, that the nutritional situation of slaves has steadily improved, and that brutal treatment has also been in decline. Do the stipulated historical improvements, in this modified case, render justifiable the citizens' imposition of an institutional order that facilitates and enforces the enslavement of defaulting debtors and their progeny? If Risse answers in the negative, then he still owes us an explanation of why he thinks that a decline in the plight caused by severe poverty over the last few centuries renders justifiable our continued imposition of a global order that is designed so that it foreseeably reproduces avoidable severe poverty on a massive scale.

THE CONTENT OF COSMOPOLITANISM

I respond only briefly to the second half of Risse's critique because I fully agree with him that we should reject what he calls "Pogge's claim that the sheer existence of states harms the poor" (page 325, this book). It is true that I consider myself a cosmopolitan. But if it is posited that "cosmopolitans take the existence of states, and a global order composed of them, to be wronging individuals by failing to respect their moral equality" (page 323, this book), then I must decline the label. I am not a cosmopolitan in this sense, because I do not believe Risse's empirical assertion that "the existence of states entails that life prospects differ vastly and are largely decided by birth" (page 323, this book). As my proposal for a Global Resources Dividend makes clear,[7] I think that radical inequality can be avoided and economic human rights securely maintained within a global system of states.

To be sure, I have advocated a vertical dispersal of political authority, which would expand the role and impact of supranational rules and organizations.[8] But this view has become rather commonplace in the eighteen years since I wrote the essay on which that chapter is based. In fact, precisely such an expansion has been occurring and accelerating, paradigmatically in the ever more consequential rules and agencies of the WTO and the European Union. If I am to be characterized as a radical, then it should not be because I, too, advocate such an expansion, but because the design of supranational rules and organizations I envision differs substantially from the design that is being implemented by the world's affluent and politically influential.

Here I agree with Risse that our present "global order is . . . *imperfectly developed*: it needs reform rather than a revolutionary overthrow" (page 326, this book). Minor redesigns of a few critical features would suffice to avoid most of the severe poverty we are witnessing today. In this sense, we are not far from a global institutional order that would satisfy the minimal human rights standard of justice. But I cannot agree with Risse that we should therefore refrain from calling the present global order unjust (page 326, this book). While the reforms needed for the sake of severe poverty avoidance are indeed small, the effects of our continued imposition of an unreformed global order are immense. It foreseeably causes millions of avoidable deaths from poverty-related causes each year. This is an imperfection. But it is also a massive crime against humanity.

NOTES

This is a revised excerpt from the essay that first appeared as "Severe Poverty as a Violation of Negative Duties" in *Ethics & International Affairs* 19, no. 1 (2005): 55–83.

1. Thomas Pogge, *World Poverty and Human Rights: Cosmopolitan Responsibilities and Reforms*, second edition (Cambridge: Polity Press, 2008), 119–20.

2.   See iresearch.worldbank.org/PovcalNet/jsp/index.jsp. I converted the percentages there given into absolute numbers with additional data kindly provided by Shaohua Chen of the World Bank.

3.   This figure is reported each year by the UNDP. The latest figure is 800 million. See United Nations Development Programme, *Human Development Report 2007/2008* (Basingstoke, UK: Palgrave Macmillan, 2007), 90; available at hdr.undp.org/en/reports/global/hdr2007–2008.

4.   UNICEF, *The State of the World's Children 2008* (New York: UNICEF, 2007), iii; available at www.unicef.org/sowc08.

5.   For example, those living below $2 a day in 1987 constituted 50 percent of the global population then, whereas those living below $2 a day in 2004 constituted only 39 percent; see www.census.gov/ipc/www/idb/.

6.   See Thomas Pogge, "Real World Justice," *Journal of Ethics* 9, nos. 1–2 (2005): 38–39.

7.   Pogge, *World Poverty and Human Rights*, 202–21.

8.   Ibid., 174–201.

Contributors

Christian Barry is lecturer in philosophy in the School of Humanities and senior research fellow at the Centre for Applied Philosophy and Public Ethics at the Australian National University. He is coauthor, with Sanjay G. Reddy, of *International Trade and Labor Standards: A Proposal for Linkage* (2008), and coeditor, with Thomas Pogge, of *Global Institutions and Responsibilities: Achieving Global Justice* (2005) and, with Barry Herman and Lydia Tomitova, of *Dealing Fairly with Developing Country Debt* (2007). He produces the online audio broadcast Public Ethics Radio and, between 2003 and 2007, was editor of *Ethics & International Affairs*.

Alex J. Bellamy is professor of peace and conflict studies at the University of Queensland. His books include *Kosovo and International Society* (2002), *Security Communities and Their Neighbours: Regional Fortresses or Global Integrators?* (2004), *Understanding Peacekeeping* (edited with Paul D. Williams and Stuart Griffin, 2004), *International Society and Its Critics* (editor, 2004), *Just Wars: From Cicero to Iraq* (2006), *Fighting Terror: Ethical Dilemmas* (2008), and *Responsibility to Protect* (2009). He serves on the editorial board of *Ethics & International Affairs*.

Seyla Benhabib is the Eugene Meyer Professor of Political Science and director of the Program on Ethics, Politics, and Economics at Yale University. Her publications include *The Claims of Culture* (2002) and *The Rights of Others* (2004), which in 2005 won the Ralph Bunche Award of the American Political Science Association and the Best Book Award of the North American Society for Social Philosophy. She is the author, most recently, of *Another Cosmopolitanism* (2006), and coeditor, with Ian Shapiro and Danilo Petranovich, of *Identities, Affiliations, and Allegiances* (2007).

Allen Buchanan is the James B. Duke Professor of Philosophy and Public Policy at Duke University, where he specializes in the philosophy of international law, political philosophy, and bioethics. His most recent books are *Justice, Legitimacy, and Self-Determination: Moral Foundations for International Law* (2003) and (with Dan W. Brock, Norman Daniels, and Daniel Wikler) *From Chance to Choice: Genetics & Justice* (2000). Professor Buchanan will give the 2009 Uehiro Lectures at Oxford University on the subject of the ethics of using biotechnology to enhance human capabilities. He serves on the editorial board of *Ethics & International Affairs*.

Joseph H. Carens is professor of political science at the University of Toronto. He is the author of *Culture, Citizenship, and Community: A Contextual Exploration of Justice as Evenhandedness* (2000), which won the 2002 C. B. Macpherson Prize of the Canadian Political Science Association. He is also the author or editor of three other books, and he has published more than sixty papers in journals and edited volumes. He is writing a book on the ethics of immigration. His paper "The Rights of Irregular Migrants" is the subject of a symposium in *Ethics & International Affairs* 22, no. 2 (2008).

Neta C. Crawford is professor of political science and African American studies at Boston University. Her recent work on intervention, prevention, and U.S. military strategy appears in *International Relations*, *Journal of Political Philosophy*, and in *Preemption: Military Action and Moral Justification*, edited by Henry Shue and David Rodin (2007). She is the author of *Argument and Change in World Politics: Ethics, Decolonization, Humanitarian Intervention* (2002), which was co-winner of the 2003 Jervis-Schroeder Award of the American Political Science Association for the best book on international history and politics.

David A. Crocker is senior research scholar at the Institute for Philosophy and Public Policy and the School of Public Policy at the University of Maryland. He specializes in social theory, development ethics, transitional justice, democratization, and the ethics of consumption. His books include *Praxis and Democratic Socialism: The Critical Social Theory of Markovic and Stojanovic* (1983), *Ethics of Consumption: The Good Life, Justice, and Global Stewardship* (edited with Toby Linden, 1998), and *Ethics of Global Development: Agency, Capability, and Deliberative Democracy* (2008).

Robyn Eckersley is professor in the School of Political Science, Sociology, and Criminology at the University of Melbourne, where she researches and teaches environmental politics, political theory, and global politics. Her books include *Environmentalism and Political Theory: Toward an Ecocentric Approach* (1992), *The Green State: Rethinking Democracy and Sovereignty* (2004), *The State and the Global Ecological Crisis* (edited with John Barry, 2005), and *Political Theory and the Ecological Challenge* (edited with Andrew Dobson, 2006). She serves on the editorial board of *Ethics & International Affairs*.

David C. Hendrickson is the Robert J. Fox Distinguished Service Professor of Political Science at Colorado College, where he teaches international politics and American foreign policy. He is the author or coauthor of seven books, including *Peace Pact: The Lost World of the American Founding* (2003) and *Union, Nation, or Empire? The American Approach to International Relations* (2009). His essays on American power have appeared in *The National Interest*, *World Policy Journal*, *Orbis*, and *Foreign Affairs*.

Alison M. Jaggar is College Professor of Distinction in Philosophy and Women and Gender Studies at the University of Colorado, Boulder. She has written a number of books, including *Feminist Politics and Human Nature* (1983) and *Abortion: Three Perspectives* (with Philip Devine, Michael Tooley, and Celia Wolf-Devine, 2008). She is editor of *Just Methods: An Interdisciplinary Feminist Reader* (2007) and *Pogge and His Critics* (2009). Her current book projects concern international ethics and global gender justice.

Ethan B. Kapstein is the Paul Dubrule Professor of Sustainable Development at INSEAD, and a visiting fellow at the Center for Global Development, Washington, D.C. He is the author of *Economic Justice in an Unfair World* (2006) and coauthor, with Nathan Converse, of *The Fate of Young Democracies* (2008).

Robert O. Keohane is professor of international affairs at the Woodrow Wilson School of Public and International Affairs, Princeton University. He is the author of *After Hegemony: Cooperation and Discord in the World Economy* (2005 [1984]) and *Power and Governance in a Partially Globalized World* (2002). He is the coauthor, with Joseph S. Nye Jr., of *Power and Interdependence* (third edition, 2001) and, with Gary King and Sidney Verba, *Designing Social Inquiry* (1994). He recently published *Anti-Americanisms in World Politics* (edited with Peter J. Katzenstein, 2007). Professor Keohane is a past president of the American Political Science Association and the International Studies Association.

Terry Nardin is professor and head of political science at the National University of Singapore. His books include *Law, Morality, and the Relations of States* (1983), *Traditions of International Ethics* (edited with David R. Mapel, 1992), *The Ethics of War and Peace: Religious and Secular Perspectives* (editor, 1996), *The Political Philosophy of Michael Oakeshott* (2001), *International Relations in Political Thought: Texts from the Ancient Greeks to the First World War* (edited with Chris Brown and Nicholas J. Rengger, 2002), and Michael Oakeshott's *Lectures in the History of Political Thought* (edited with Luke O'Sullivan, 2007). He serves on the editorial board of *Ethics & International Affairs*.

Thomas Pogge is professor of philosophy and international affairs at Yale University, research director in the Center for the Study of Mind in Nature at the University of Oslo, and adjunct professor in the Centre for Professional Ethics at the University of Central Lancashire. His books include *Realizing Rawls* (1989), *John Rawls: His Life and Theory of Justice* (2007), and *World Poverty and Human Rights: Cosmopolitan Responsibilities and Reforms* (second edition, 2008). He recently edited *Freedom from Poverty as a Human Right: Who Owes What to the Very Poor?* (2007).

Mathias Risse is associate professor of public policy and philosophy at the Harvard Kennedy School. His recent work on trade and migration appears in journals including *Politics, Philosophy & Economics*, and *European Journal of Philosophy*. He is writing a book titled *The Grounds of Justice: An Essay on Global Political Philosophy*. His essay "On the Morality of Immigration" is the subject of an exchange in *Ethics & International Affairs* 22, no. 3 (2008).

Joel H. Rosenthal is president of the Carnegie Council for Ethics in International Affairs, adjunct professor in the Department of Politics at New York University, chairman of the Bard College Globalization and International Affairs program, and senior fellow at the Stockdale Center for Ethical Leadership, United States Naval Academy. He is author of *Righteous Realists: Political Realism, Responsible Power, and American Culture in the Nuclear Age* (1991) and coeditor, with Albert C. Pierce and Anthony F. Lang Jr., of *Ethics and the Future of Conflict: Lessons from the 1990s* (2004). He is editor-in-chief of *Ethics & International Affairs*.

Michael J. Smith is Thomas C. Sorensen Professor of Political and Social Thought, director of the Interdisciplinary Program in Political and Social Thought, and associate professor of politics at the University of Virginia. His books include *Realist Thought from Weber to Kissinger* (1987) and *Ideas and Ideals: Essays on Politics in Honor of Stanley*

Hoffmann (edited with Linda B. Miller, 1993). Professor Smith has been on the board of trustees of the Carnegie Council for Ethics in International Affairs since 1994.

Robert Wade is professor of political economy at the London School of Economics and Political Science, and winner of the 2008 Leontief Prize for Advancing the Frontiers of Economic Thought. His interests include economic growth, financialization and financial crises, trends in global wealth distribution, and the functioning of multilateral economic organizations. He is the author of *Governing the Market: Economic Theory and the Role of Government in East Asian Industrialization* (2004 [1990]).

Leif Wenar holds the Chair of Ethics in the King's College London School of Law. His recent work on global justice appears in *Philosophy & Public Affairs*, *Journal of Political Philosophy*, *Freedom from Poverty as a Human Right* (edited by Thomas Pogge, 2007), *Pogge and His Critics* (edited by Alison M. Jaggar, forthcoming), and at www.policyinnovations.org and www.cato-unbound.org. He serves on the editorial board of *Ethics & International Affairs*.

Index

Abu Eissa, Farouk, 119
accountability in international development aid, 285–306; the accountability of aid NGOs, 291–92, 293–96, 300–301, 304n29, 305n43; categories of benefits, 289–90; and chains of intermediate institutions, 291–93, 300; and challenges of development aid, 285–88, 300, 301n5, 302n13; the concept of accountability, 288–90, 302n17; and diversion of project resources, 286–87, 302n9; downward (to beneficiaries), 295–96, 305n43; financial accountability, 293–94; horizontal (overseeing project evaluation), 296–300, 306n46; local effects of aggregate flow of resources, 287, 302n13; performance accountability, 294; and positive bias in project evaluations, 297–98, 306nn49–50; and powers (standard-setting, performance-measuring, sanctioning), 288; and professional association of project evaluators, 298–300, 306n55; and resource diversion, 286–87, 302n9; and responsibility, 288–89; upward accountability, 294–95; USAID poverty relief efforts, 292–93, 300, 303n24, 303n26
ActionAid, 296
adaptive preferences and "false consciousness," 210, 219, 226n13
Afghanistan, 108, 216, 223–24
African Union Mission in Sudan (AMIS), 103, 114–15, 121, 124n9. *See also* Darfur crisis and humanitarian intervention
African Union's Constitutive Act, article 4(h), 106
Ahmed, Leila, 218
aid. *See* accountability in international development aid; development aid
Algeria, 117, 120
Amnesty International, 55, 111, 205
Amos, Valerie, 223

The Anarchical Society (Bull), 73, 75
Annan, Kofi: and African Union Mission in Sudan, 115; Annual Report (1999) to the General Assembly on humanitarian intervention, 85; and humanitarian intervention in Darfur, 111, 115, 118; Nobel lecture and intervention/state sovereignty, 106; and world's failure to act in Rwanda, 96, 103
Aquinas, Thomas, 86–87
Arab League, 115, 118, 119, 121–22
Arendt, Hannah, 185–86, 198–200
Aristotle, 89
Armenian genocide, 23
Aron, Raymond, 32n5
Augustine, 87
Australia, 137, 241

Bairoch, Paul, 328n9
BAOBAB for Women's Human Rights, 222
Barry, Christian, 335
Beitz, Charles, 144, 260–61
Bellamy, Alex J., 335. *See also* Darfur crisis and humanitarian intervention; humanitarian intervention and international relations milieu
Benhabib, Seyla, 212, 335. *See also* cosmopolitan norms of justice; democracy and international law (alleged conflict between)
Berkeley, Bill, 52
Betts, Richard, 39
biodiversity: definition, 151n46; ecological intervention to prevent assaults on, 143–45; and international (environmental) customary law, 145; legal recognition of, 143, 151nn46–47; and states' territorial rights to control natural resources, 143–45, 151n53. *See also* ecological intervention
Bismarck, Otto von, 42

339

against humanity, 140–41. *See also* communitarian model of international economic justice

Convention on the Prevention and Punishment of the Crime of Genocide (1948), 188

cosmopolitanism: and explanatory nationalism, 324–27; and intervention for crimes against humanity, 140–41; Pogge and the "Cosmopolitan Complaint" regarding states and the global order, 323–27, 333; resource and borrowing privilege, 313–14, 324–25; and states' territorial rights to control natural resources, 144. *See also* cosmopolitan norms of justice; cosmopolitan (prioritarian) model of international economic justice

cosmopolitan norms of justice, 186–90; crimes against humanity, genocide, and war crimes, 187–88, 199–200; and democratic power of global civil society, 199; hospitality and sovereignty, 189, 192–93; and humanitarian intervention, 188; and international human rights regime, 187, 201n10; ontological status of, 199; philosophical questions raised by, 198–200; and "principle of rights"/"schedule of rights," 201n13; reconciling with unique traditions, 198–99; and state sovereignty, 188, 189–90, 192; transition to, 186–87, 201n9; and transnational migration, 189

cosmopolitan (prioritarian) model of international economic justice, 256–57, 262–64; attention to problem of state failure and unjust states, 262; data considered (changes in poverty rates among people), 256; and effects of global trade rules on the rural poor, 262–63; HOS framework and convergence models, 262; level of analysis (individuals), 256, 262; policy goal, 256; and quasi-prioritarian approach, 265–66, 268n34; questions relevant to prioritarian cosmopolitans, 256–57; and tariffs, 263; theoretical and policy challenges posed by, 263–64

Crawford, Neta C., 336. *See also* preventive war

crimes against humanity: adjudication of, 186, 199–200; Arendt on, 185–86, 199–200; and cosmopolitan norms of justice, 187–88, 199–200; definition, 152n61; evolution of concept, 187–88, 199–200; and "genocide," 185–86, 188; and "war crimes," 188

crimes against nature: and ecocide, 145–46; and eco-humanitarian interventions, 137–40; emerging norm of, 131. *See also* ecological intervention

Croat Nazis (Ustashi), 48–49

Crocker, David A., 336. *See also* reckoning with past wrongs (a normative framework for transitional justice)

customary law principle and ecological intervention, 137, 145, 149n21, 149n23

Danforth, John, 128n93

Darfur crisis and humanitarian intervention, 103–5, 110, 111–21; AMIS peacekeepers, 103, 114–15, 121, 124n9; case referred to ICC (2005), 104, 119–20; cease-fire breaches, 118; deaths, 103; initial international response (2003–2004), 111–14; Resolution 1556, 112–13, 115–16, 117, 121; Resolution 1564 and failure of robust approach, 116–18; "responsibility to protect" language, 112–13, 116, 122–23; the sanctions debate, 115–16, 117, 118, 119, 120–21; Security Council authorization for peace operation, 112, 120; Security Council debates about intervention, 103–4, 115–21; Sudanese government and Janjaweed militia, 103, 124n4; Sudanese government's compliance, 116, 117, 121, 128n93; and Sudanese sovereignty, 112, 122; travel ban, 120–21; UN draft resolution (2004), 111–12; UNMIS (UN Mission to Sudan), 104, 119, 120; violence in the camps, 119; the world's muted response, 103–4

democracy and international law (alleged conflict between), 185–203; cosmopolitan norms of justice, 186–90; and crimes against humanity, 185–88, 198–200; democratic rule and popular sovereignty/territorial sovereignty, 192; and Europe today, 195–98; and "genocide," 185–86, 188; Germany and citizenship rights, 193–98, 202n24; and guest-workers/third-country nationals, 192–93, 197–98; liberalism and democracy, 191; the paradox of democratic legitimacy, 190–98; and the "political community of fate," 195; and

Ehrenfeld, David, 141
Eichmann in Jerusalem (Arendt), 185–86
Elshtain, Jean Bethke, 140
environmental destruction: and affluent
    countries' disproportionate role, 313;
    compensation for, 222; and poor women
    in poor countries, 222. *See also* ecological
    intervention
essentialism, 208–10, 217, 218, 226n17
Ethiopia, 278–79
European Convention on Fundamental
    Rights and Freedoms, 193, 198, 201n10
European guest worker programs, 197–98,
    232, 245–46
European Union: Germany's membership
    and disaggregation of citizenship rights,
    196–97; and humanitarian intervention
    in Darfur, 111, 119; immigration admis-
    sions and family reunification, 235–36;
    and international human rights regime,
    201n10; Maastricht Treaty and reciprocal
    voting rights, 195–96; norms of hospi-
    tality with regard to third-country
    nationals, 193; and paradox of democratic
    legitimacy, 195–98; Turkey's entry into,
    197–98, 202n30
Evans, Gareth, 109
"explanatory cosmopolitanism," 324
"explanatory nationalism," 314, 324–27

Falk, Richard, 109
Farer, Tom, 70, 107, 108
feminism, 207–10. *See also* global justice for
    women (and perceived victimization by
    non-Western cultural practices)
"A Few Words on Non-intervention" (Mill),
    91
Fieschi, Sinibaldo, 87–88
Finnemore, Martha, 104
Formosa, Manuel, 60
France: and ICISS recommendations on
    intervention and "responsibility to pro-
    tect," 108; immigration admissions, 234;
    and intervention in Darfur, 112; and
    intervention in Rwanda, 125n19; nuclear
    testing case before ICJ, 137, 149n24
Franck, Thomas, 69, 76, 140, 150n37
Fraser, Nancy, 212
Fuller, Lon, 54
fundamentalism, 216, 218
The Fund for Peace, 109

General Agreement on Tariffs and Trade
    (GATT), 317, 319
Generally Accepted Accounting Principles
    (GAAP), 298
Geneva Convention Relating to the Status of
    Refugees (1951) and 1967 Protocol, 189,
    237, 239–40
genocide: Arendt on, 185–86, 200; and col-
    lective (multilateral) intervention, 80;
    and cosmopolitan norms of justice,
    187–88, 199–200; defining, 152n61; and
    ecocide, 137–38; as *jus cogens* norm, 137,
    149n25
Germany: compensation fund for Holocaust
    victims, 56, 63n36; EU membership and
    disaggregation of citizenship rights,
    196–97; guest-workers/third-country
    nationals in, 197–98; and humanitarian
    intervention in Darfur, 111, 112, 113, 119;
    and ICISS agenda on humanitarian inter-
    vention, 110; immigration admission cri-
    teria and postwar *Aussiedler* policy,
    247–48; nationalist ideologies and senti-
    ments since 1990s, 202n30; Supreme
    Court decision on election laws and alien
    suffrage rights, 193–98, 202n24
Gilpin, Robert, 11
Gisselquist, David, 282n2
global governance institutions. *See* legiti-
    macy of global governance institutions;
    legitimacy of global governance institu-
    tions (articulating a complex standard
    of)
globalization. *See* economic globalization
    and the American empire
global justice for women (and perceived vic-
    timization by non-Western cultural prac-
    tices), 205–30; adaptive preferences and
    "false consciousness," 209, 210, 219,
    226n13; the "autonomy by culture" thesis,
    211, 215–17; and colonialism, 215–16, 218,
    220; and contemporary fundamentalism,
    216, 218; and cultural relativism, 209, 210,
    226n23; culture-blaming that deflects
    attention from structural violence, 224,
    230n89; the debate in philosophy about
    non-Western cultural practices, 207–11,
    218–19; the debate in women's studies,
    207–8; definitions of "culture," 212,
    226n23; and essentialism, 207–8, 209, 210,
    217, 218, 226n17; and ethics of care, 210–11;